OFFICIAL REPORT

OF THE

ELEVENTH INTERNATIONAL

CHRISTIAN ENDEAVOR CONVENTION

HELD IN

Madison Square Garden, New York City,

JULY 7 TO 10, 1892.

With Report of

SIMULTANEOUS AND OVERFLOW MEETINGS.

First Fruits Press
Wilmore, Kentucky
c2015

First Fruits Press
The Academic Open Press of Asbury Theological Seminary
204 N. Lexington Ave., Wilmore, KY 40390
859-858-2236
first.fruits@asburyseminary.edu
asbury.to/firstfruits

TRUSTEES OF THE UNITED SOCIETY.

Rev. John Henry Barrows, D.D.
Rev. David James Burrell, D.D.
Rev. Teunis S. Hamlin, D.D.
Bishop Samuel Fallows, D.D.
Rev. Chas. A. Dickinson.
Rev. W. J. Darby, D.D.
Hon. John Wanamaker.
Rev. S. V. Leech, D.D.
10. Rev. Wayland Hoyt, D.D.
11. Rev. H. C. Farrar, D.D.
12. Mr. W. H. Pennell.
13. Rev. James L. Hill, D.D.
14. Rev. M. Rhodes, D.D.
15. Rev. Ralph W. Brokaw.
16. Rev. W. W. Andrews.
17. Rev. R. L. Swain, Ph.D.
18. Rev. John T. Beckley, D.D.
19. Pres. Wm. R. Harper, LL.D.
20. Mr. Choate Burnham.
21. Mr. W. J. Van Patten.
22. Rev. N. Boynton.
23. Pres. Merrill E. Gates, LL.D.
24. Rev. Gilby C. Kelly, D.D.
25. Rev. W. H. McMillan, D.D.

OFFICIAL REPORT

OF THE

ELEVENTH INTERNATIONAL

CHRISTIAN ENDEAVOR CONVENTION

HELD IN

Madison Square Garden, New York City,

JULY 7 TO 10, 1892.

With Report of

SIMULTANEOUS AND OVERFLOW MEETINGS.

COPYRIGHTED AND PUBLISHED BY
UNITED SOCIETY OF CHRISTIAN ENDEAVOR,
50 BROMFIELD STREET, BOSTON, MASS.
1892.

ELEVENTH INTERNATIONAL CONVENTION

OF THE

YOUNG PEOPLE'S SOCIETIES OF

CHRISTIAN ENDEAVOR.

NEW YORK, JULY 7-10, 1892.

THE largest Christian Endeavor convention which has yet been held, and in certain respects the most enthusiastic and inspiring, was that which convened in the Madison Square Garden, New York city, on the afternoon of Thursday, July 7, 1892. During all that day and the previous night, by railroad and steamboat lines, there poured into New York city a host of young people such as that city had never seen before. A conservative estimate placed the number of delegates at 32,000, to say nothing of the great multitude of those who took advantage of the reduced railroad rates to visit the city and were not registered as delegates.

The Committee of '92 had made preparations for a large convention, but events proved that their most generous calculations were too small. The immense stock of souvenir programs, badges, and maps of the city which they had provided was exhausted almost before the first session opened, and even the additional supply which the committee furnished was insufficient to meet the demand. The great auditorium of Madison Square Garden, although the largest audience room on the continent, seating 14,000 people, came far short of accommodating all who desired to attend the convention, and thousands of delegates were turned away at every session, unable to gain admittance. It was also found necessary to increase the provisions which had been made for simultaneous meetings in adjacent churches; and this was done to such an extent that on Sunday evening mass meetings were held in no less than eleven different places, including the Carnegie Music Hall and the Metropolitan Opera House. The presence of such a multitude of young people, actuated by a common religious impulse, made a most profound impression upon the the city's life, as was manifest on every hand, and perhaps in this fact were found the most important results of the convention.

The amphitheatre of the Garden, in which the principal sessions were held, proved to be a magnificent audience room, though it was not always easy for those who sat farthest away from the platform to hear distinctly. The decorations of the hall were abundant and tasteful; and especially at the evening sessions, with the 4,000 incandescent electric lights lining the great steel arches of the roof, collected in rosettes along the walls and culminating in a sp'endid monogram "C. E." over the platform, the effect was very beautiful. The amphitheatre being elliptical in form, the speaker's platform was placed at one end of the ellipse, with the choir seats (800) rising immediately behind and the reporters' tables on either side — "the sheep of the religious press on the right hand and the goats of the secular press on the left," as one paper expressed it. The delegates were seated according to States, the larger delegations occupying the main floor and the others filling the side tiers of seats and the balconies which extended entirely around the hall.

The weather during the convention was of the most delightful sort. Only on Friday evening a little rain fell, and the temperature on Sunday was uncomfortably warm within the Garden.

THURSDAY AFTERNOON.

The usual enthusiasm prevailed for an hour or more previous to the opening of the convention. As the various delegations marched into the hall, bearing their State banners and uniting their voices in song, they were roundly cheered, especially when something particularly unique was presented, such as the "yell" of the Ohio delegation: —

> O-hi-o!
> We wont go
> To the World's Fair
> If open on Sunday
> Or liquor sold there.
> O-hi-o!
> Ohio!!

The Ohio delegation also sang with great vigor a song composed by one of their number, to the tune of "Bringing in the Sheaves," as follows : —

> Hear the tramp of armies, see the host advancing!
> Lift aloft the banner, tell its legend o'er!
> See the flashing colors, sunlight on them dancing,
> Hear the watchword echoed, "Cleveland, '94!"
>
> REFRAIN. — "Cleveland, '94.! Cleveland, '94!"
> Pass along the watchward, "Cleveland, '94!"
>
> Armies from the eastward, from the lands of story,
> Turn with songs of praises towards a virgin shore;
> Armies from the westward sunset gates of glory
> Pass along the watchword, "Cleveland, '94!"

Higher lift the banner, speed the exultations,
 O'er and o'er again the shout in strength outpour
Till it be a welcome, given to the nations,
And the world be praising "Cleveland, '94!"

The Maryland delegation also sang, more quietly but with fine effect, a song to the well-known tune of "Maryland, my Maryland."

The delegation from Indiana joined in the following variation on "Marching through Georgia:"—

"Hurrah! hurrah! for Indiana's band,
Hurrah! hurrah! for Indiana's band,
We've come to give you greeting, and our offering to bring
Of love and devotion to Endeavor."

Kentucky's delegation sang, "I'll sing you a song of my old Kentucky home"; Canada responded with "Blest be the tie that binds"; another delegation started "Onward, Christian soldiers," and the whole hall was filled with exuberant enthusiasm.

Promptly at half past two, Pres. F. E. Clark, whose appearance on the platform was greeted with hearty applause, called the convention to order and announced that previous to the completion of the organization the audience would be led in a service of prayer and praise, conducted by Mr. Edwin F. See, general secretary of the Brooklyn Y. M. C. A. Mr. See came forward and gave out the hymn, "Onward, Christian Soldiers." Under the lead of Mr. Geo. C. Stebbins, with an instrumental accompaniment of two cornets, a piano, and an organ, the choir of 800 voices gave out the hymn,  which was immediately taken up by the vast audience and sung with much spirit. This was followed by that favorite hymn among all Christian Endeavorers, "At the Cross," which was sung even yet more impressively. Mr. See then read the first fourteen verses of the first chapter of Acts, after which prayer was offered by Mr. W. H. Pennell, the first signer of the C. E. constitution, and Rev. Nehemiah Boynton of Boston, the latter remembering especially Secretary John Willis Baer, who was prevented from being at the convention on account of ill health. The old hymn, "Jesus, lover of my soul," was then sung, after which Mr. See spoke as follows:—

ADDRESS OF MR. EDWIN F. SEE.

The Eleventh International Christian Endeavor Convention has been called to order; the delegates are assembled; the program is prepared; the speakers are ready. Are we to have the presence and power of the Spirit of God? The answer to that question, my friends, will depend entirely upon us. The Spirit of God is as real a power to-day as he was at Pentecost, and although circumstances may have changed, his reservoirs of blessing are just as full, and the spiritual laws in obedience to which we shall receive the blessings are not changed.

It seems to me that there are three words which ought to indicate the attitude of those in this audience to-day with regard to the Spirit of God. The first word is "desire," the second is "surrender," and the third is "expectation." Now we can have just as much of the Spirit of God in his power here to-day as we want to have. The Spirit of God is sensitive, and will not go

where he is not wanted. "I will pour water on him that is thirsty, and floods upon the dry ground." It is only the thirsty who receive the water of life. It is only the hungry who are fed with the bread of life. How much do we want the Spirit of God here to-day? How much do we want him in this convention? Do we want him as much as to enjoy any feature of the program? Do we want him as much as we want to hear this or that speaker? Do we want him more than any feature or all features combined of this great program? These may seem to be poor standards of comparison, but it is well for each of us to inquire, "How much do I want the Spirit of God to be present in this convention?" And as prayer is the expression of desire, so we need be much in prayer this afternoon. This is not the time for men to speak to us, but it is the time for us to speak to God.

And then a second condition of God's presence by his Holy Spirit is surrender — surrender of self and surrender of sin. Many people fear to follow the guidance of the Holy Spirit because they are afraid to follow where he may lead. How many people are afraid to receive the blessing of the Holy Spirit because they fear that they may have to give up some cherished sin. My friends, we must let go of sin, if we are to get hold of the Spirit of God.

And then, if we really desire the Spirit's presence and have surrendered ourselves to his guidance, we may be full of expectation for the result. The disciples doubted not for a moment, in that upper room where they were all gathered together with one accord, that the Spirit would come in his power according to the promise of Christ. The newspapers tell us that Mr. Gladstone has already selected his cabinet, so confident is he of the victory which he thinks he has won in the pending election. I think that while his confidence may be misplaced, ours never will be. The result is as sure as the promises of God. We may discount the future reverently to this extent: we may step out boldly, and if we have surrendered ourselves to the Spirit of God with a confidence that he will give us the blessing, we may thank him in advance for what he is going to give.

But we must all be of one accord in this matter, concentrated in thought and desire. It is a solemn thought that some of us may keep the Holy Spirit from coming in greatest power to this convention. Some of us may be non-conductors. Some of us, by attitude and action, may break the circuit and keep the Spirit of God from working to the fullest extent in this convention and on the hearts of its delegates. We need to be much in prayer this afternoon,— praise him as we supplicate and pray to him, for the apostle enjoins that we should combine thanksgiving with prayer and supplication. We have reason to praise him; and there are reasons which are apparent to every one, and every one of those reasons constitutes a guarantee from God of his continued goodness in time to come. Let us pray boldly, and as we come to the throne of grace doubt not that we shall receive a blessing.

Prayer was then offered by Rev. R. W. Brokaw, of Springfield, Mass., and Mr. W. J. Van Patten, of Burlington, Vt., followed by the hymn, "Blessed assurance Jesus has given."

President CLARK: Shall we now complete the organization of the convention?

Treasurer WM. SHAW: I must apologize for interrupting our president at this time, but I think I have a very reasonable excuse. Eleven years ago last

February the first society of Christian Endeavor was organized in the Williston Church, Portland, by Dr. Clark. That society still lives, and the pastor of that church is here this afternoon and has a word to say to this convention. As Dr. Clark has always preached loyalty to our pastors, he must make way for the pastor of Williston church, Rev. Dwight M. Pratt, of Portland, Me. [*Applause.*]

Mr. PRATT: My dear Dr. Clark, president of the United Society of Christian Endeavor: The Williston church of Portland, Me., is now known the world over as the birthplace of Christian Endeavor. It is my happy privilege as pastor of that church to bring to you and to this great convention the greetings of the mother society. The mother is proud of her children, and we trust also the children are equally happy in their mother. Portland, the homestead of Christian Endeavor, stands pre-eminently for three things: for poetry, for prohibition, [*applause.*] and for practical piety. [*Applause.*] It stands for poetry in the person of Longfellow, her beloved son, who has so lovingly sung the praises of the beautiful city by the sea; for prohibition, in the person of the venerable Neal Dow, [*applause*] whose hoary head is one of the city's chief crowns of glory and whose principles are per-  manently embodied in the Maine Law; and for practical piety, in the person of you, sir, [*prolonged applause*] the founder of the society of Christian Endeavor, whom Portland still claims as her own and whom she gave up only that you might ultimately become the pastor of the largest parish in the world. [*Applause.*] In fact, sir, you are the only minister of the gospel who can claim the entire earth as his parish, [*applause*] the only one who must take the railway and the steamship to visit the members of his flock, — for Australia is as much a part of the Christian Endeavor field as is America, and the city of Pekin as the city of Portland.

The present edifice of the Williston church was built under your earnest leadership. Its corner stone of granite indicates by its stability and permanence the kind of material that went into the spiritual edifice of which the material structure is only the symbol. The black walnut of its pulpit symbolizes by its durability and beauty of finish the kind of ministry under which Christian Endeavor was born. I hold in my hand, sir, a gavel, made of the granite of that corner stone and of the black walnut of that original pulpit. The Williston church presents this to you for permanent use in these annual Christian Endeavor gatherings. [*Enthusiastic applause.*] Every time you command, by its vigorous use, the respectful attention and silence of these vast assemblies, Williston Church may also be heard summoning her children to worship, devotion, and service. By its use you will still be associated with the church of your early love, and from the same pulpit — even though it be but from a small section of it — you will still preach and proclaim the same loving gospel that fell from your lips when Christian Endeavor was but a babe in the arms of its young mother. With great affection the members of the Williston society present to you this token of their love and this pledge of their growing and permanent interest in the grand enterprise so providentially entrusted to your wise and devoted leadership. [*Loud and prolonged applause.*]

Dr. CLARK: Mr. Pratt and my dear friends, I hold in my hand, as you have been told, a gavel for use at these conventions made of the pulpit and of the corner stone of Williston Church. As I understand it, the gavel is more than a personal gift to myself. It is for this convention and for all future conventions. In your name, and in the name of the conventions that are to follow, I accept this beautiful gift. It is most appropriate in this respect: that, as in every Christian Endeavor society to-day, in all those represented here, are the same principles of fidelity, of pledged faithfulness, of loyalty and of fellowship, which were in that first society, so in this gavel are the original elements that entered into that first pulpit and that first corner stone. It is typical of the fact that the underlying principles of Christian Endeavor are the same to-day that they were eleven years ago. Typifying this fact, and in the name of this convention, and with our heartiest thanks to Williston Church and her pastor, I most gratefully accept this gavel and now use it for the first time [striking the desk] in a Christian Endeavor convention. [*Great applause.*]

The organization of the convention was then completed by the election of Rev. H. W. Gleason, of Minneapolis, Minn., as scribe, and the appointment of the usual committees by the president, the names to be announced later.

Before proceeding with the program, Dr. Clark requested the delegates that they should all co-operate with him, and with subsequent chairmen, in making the convention as helpful as possible, especially by observing the strictest silence and refraining from sending unnecessary requests to the platform.

Dr. CLARK: And now, my friends, we have come to a most delightful part of this convention when we shall listen to the words of greeting from those who welcome us so kindly as our hosts. And from whom can we hear more appropriately than from that grand minister of the gospel, who is so beloved in New York city and throughout the country, — one who now extends, not for the first time, a word of welcome to the Christian Endeavor Society, but who, years ago, when it was small and comparatively weak, when it had few friends and some detractors, came and stood for Christian Endeavor at Saratoga and has stood for it ever since? Rev. Charles F. Deems, D.D., LL.D., pastor of the Church of the Strangers of New York city, will give us the word of welcome from New York. [*Enthusiastic applause.*]

ADDRESS OF DR. DEEMS.

Fellow Endeavorers : — To me has fallen the honor and the pleasure of welcoming, on behalf of the pastors of New York, to the greatest city in the youngest nationality, the largest body of organized Christian workers in the world. Without affectation or pretence I can understand why this honorable and pleasing duty should have been assigned to me. I am almost the patriarch of the pastorate in New York, a very few of my brethren having been pastors of the same church so long as I have. I am presumed, therefore, to know my colleagues. On the other hand, in the very beginning I heard the chirp of this young eaglet in its "down-east" nest, and have watched, and nursed, and cheered it until I have lived to see its wings spread wide, and its pinions in perpetual flutter as it soars high in mid ether and turns its unblinking eyes at the Sun of Righteousness. Then, perhaps I am the very person who should present the welcome of one of these parties to the other.

Of my brethren of the pastorate of New York I can speak the best things. I believe that there is not one of them faithless to the trusts confided in his hands by the great Head of the church. As a body, the clergy of New York are learned, faithful, courageous, devoted men of the gospel of the blessed God. Amongst them there is great independence of thinking, and they have repeated divergence of opinion, but they feel that they are set for the protection and propagation of our most holy faith; and I do not know a man amongst us who would deliberately hurt any human being, or maliciously oppose anything which he could be made to see had power in it to increase the sway of Jesus over the hearts of men. In the name of my beloved colleagues I extend to all representatives of the Y. P. S. C. E. a welcome to New York—our New York and yours; a welcome to our churches—our churches and yours; a welcome to our homes—our homes and yours. As we have prayed for you while you were coming, so now we pray that your sojourn in this city may be comfortable and edifying to you and prove an immense benediction to us and to our congregations.

As I have spoken my deliberate opinion of the pastors of New York, so I may express my opinion of the institution represented by this magnificent assemblage. From the beginning of its existence it has engaged my attention very closely. I have watched its growth not with the fear of suspicion, but with the trepidation of tender love. I have been afraid that grievous mistakes might be made by even the good men who have been engaged in its upbuilding. The very rapidity of its growth has sometimes made me afraid, but to-day I am permitted to give you a welcome with the most unqualified heartiness, because I can truly say that there is no management in America which seems to me to be less open to adverse criticism than the management of the Y. P. S. C. E. I know how much this is for me to say, but before you and the Great Captain of our salvation, I do say it most deliberately and most cordially.

That the Institution was needed seems to be indicated by the concurrence in its support of so many representative Christian men divergent in theology and in ecclesiastical views. That it has had the blessing of God and the good-will of men, and that it has supplied what has been called a "felt want," has been demonstrated by the rapidity of the extension of its operations, the very recital of which almost takes away one's breath. Eleven years ago there was 1 society. ten years ago there were 2, nine years ago there were 56, five years ago there were 2,314, to-day 21,080 societies are represented in the city of New York at the Eleventh Annual Convention. Nine years ago, I remember that there were 2,870 members in the 56 societies; five years ago there were 140,000 members in the 2,314 societies; one year ago it was announced in Minneapolis, that that there were 1,000,000 of members and to that number during the past year over 350,000 have been added; and there are now 21,080 societies with a membership of 1,370,200. Has there ever been a growth like that since the day the Lord Jesus Christ ascended up on high, and led captivity captive and gave gifts to men?

In welcoming you, would it be amiss to invite you to a brief study of the causes of this phenomenal growth?

First of all, I do not trace it to the form of the organization but to the spirit of this Society, which, more than any other found on earth in this nineteenth century, reminds one of Christ's Christianity. The Society does not depend for its existence and growth, as many ecclesiastical systems do, upon the strength and compactness of its organization, but, as most growing things do, upon the internal life of its individual members. No one can continue a member of the Y. P. S. C. E. who is not seeking to have the spirit of Christ. He may belong to a lodge, or even a church, and have no more the spirit of the Master than an outsider. He may belong for years to any one of those organizations, and never lift a finger nor wink an eye to bring himself or others to a higher life; but the very motive for joining one of our societies is to do that very thing. Its very operation continually keeps a man up to the activities of real Christian living, or grinds him out of the Society.

The binding and stimulating element in the Y. P. S. C. E. is the pledge taken by each active member. That pledge is worth your closest study. If it was not inspired by the Holy Ghost, it is one of the most remarkable of the inspired productions of the human intellect. It is thoroughly spiritual. It is thoroughly loyal to the local church to which the member of the society belongs, and thoroughly loyal to God's Christ. It combines faith and works just as the Holy Scriptures do. It is after the model of the Psalmist: "*Trust in the Lord and do good.*" It is after the model of the Apostle: "Show me thy *faith* by thy *works.*" It teaches that a Christian life is one that works from the inner man to the outer; and this is what distinguishes Christianity from all the other ethical cults in the world. It furnishes a constant spring of motion, not from a man's regard for the good opinion of his fellow men, but from his loyalty to his Divine Master. It is a manly pledge, because first given to God, and secondly, avoiding all puerile and impracticable details.

To show that these things are so, read its opening: " Trusting in the Lord Jesus Christ for strength, I promise Him that I will strive to do whatever He would like to have me do; that I will make it the rule of my life to pray and to read the Bible every day, and to support my own church in every way, especially by attending all her regular Sunday and midweek services, unless prevented by some reason which I can conscientiously give to my Saviour; and that, just so far as I know how, throughout my whole life, I will endeavor to lead a Christian life." It will be perceived that there is nothing in this pledge for which a member can be called to account except to the Judge of all earth. It will be seen that there is the promise only of *an endeavor* which can always be kept by the weakest member, whatever failure may occur in his practical life. The member does not promise to pray and read the Bible every day; he simply promises to make it *the rule of his life* to do this. For all failures he holds himself accountable only unto God, not to any human society. Now it is manifest that the manliest man in all America can sign that part of the pledge, and become better by the signing.

The second part of the pledge is that which has made the Endeavor Society a gymnasium of Christian activity. The active member promises to be at every prayer meeting of his society, and by speech, or prayer, or reading, there, amongst his brethren, of about the same age, all belonging to his own local church, to add something to the interest of the meeting. It is because of the general fidelity with which this pledge has been kept that the evangelical churches in America have, during the past ten years, become more interesting, more instructive, more profitable to the community, than during the fifty years which immediately preceded. To-day more than ever before Jesus Christ can look down upon the American churches and say, " Ye are my witnesses."

My dear brethren, it is to our loyalty to our local church, not merely to our denomination, that the Christian Endeavor movement largely owes its success. There have been other young people's societies inside the church and outside the church, but those inside have ordinarily distracted the congregation, and those outside have drawn away the members and weakened the church. I am an old pastor, and I declare to you on my honor that if I were this day pastor of any church in which the authorities would persist in allowing any other young people's society than the Y. P. S. C. E., I should instantaneously resign, if I could not break up such a society. It is because its members recognize the Christian Endeavor Society to be only a means and not at all an end — not existing to build up itself, but existing simply to build up the particular church of which it is a part — that this youngest Christian movement has had such wonderful growth.

Associate members are admitted to this society, but that is simply another name for inviting candidates for church membership. Let any student of ecclesiastical history see if he can discover any organization which has ever added to the churches of America 82,500 members in one year. He will find that the Y. P. S. C. E. did that in 1890, and did it from its members, in addition to its influence in bringing in others who were outside both church and society

If the Y. P. S. C. E. grows proportionately as it has since 1881, the close of this century will find 8,000,000 of names upon its roll. Now there might be 8,000,000 of names on any roll which might stand for only the figure 8 and six ciphers, but let us remember that on the rolls of the Y. P. S. C. E. it stands for 8,000,000 of real things; and that each one of those real things is human: and that each of those human beings is young; and that each one of those young persons loves the Lord Jesus Christ, the Captain of his salvation, with a passion; and that those Christian young persons are at work; and that they are engaged in constant, conservative, and aggressive work for real vital Christ-like Christianity, regardless of all scientific theology and all mere human ecclesiasticism.

What a prospect that spreads out for the future! If there be no faithlessness and no faltering, the man who in any city in America shall stand to welcome the convention of 1900 — may I be that man! — [*applause*] will have behind him a retrospect of magnificent achievement, and before him a vision as splendid as ever fell on John's anointed eyes on Patmos. The hope and the assurance of such a thing lie in the strenuous preservation and faithful observance of the active member's pledge. Drop that out and the Y. P. S. C. E. would soon be relegated to that church-closet in which are now lying the malodorous rags and remnants of all the young people's societies that fumed and fussed and fizzled and expired in all the past of our American church history. Let it be distinctly understood, let it be proclaimed, let it be maintained, that any association which claims to be a Y. P. S. C. E. and does not have this identical pledge, and does not insist upon the exact and constant observance of this pledge, is a delusion and a snare, to say the least, and that it lays itself open to the violent suspicion of being also a fraud.

The temptation will perpetually recur to lessen the rigor of the original pledge, in order to increase the number of the membership; but believe me that such a course will always be fatal; I hold my convictions on this subject from extensive, careful observation and from some bitter personal experience. Let me say that I believe that to any pastor a Y. P. S. C. E. of ten members living up to this pledge will be of more use than any kind of young people's society, of whatever numbers, without that pledge. It has been urged that young people in the church who are frivolous and worldly may be won into the Society by the loosening of the pledge. Suppose that were true: a Christian young man or woman who will not take that pledge is as worthless to Christ inside the society as outside; inside the church as outside. It is this blessed pledge which has won to our standard the really truly devout young servants of Jesus Christ. Lower or relax the pledge and you may lose them, for what is the use to a church member of any society of young people that does not have this pledge? I venture to call upon our whole body throughout the United States to furnish one single instance where the relaxing of the pledge has not been a deterioration to the society. I am on the search for one instance of the kind.

The injuriousness of relaxation I endeavored to illustrate to a body of representative Endeavorers one night in the parlor of my own church. I said something like the following: —

I have had a vision. In my vision I saw a man who had collected and tamed some cattle which he had corralled where many wild cattle were running loose. From motives of safety, he built his fence very high and very strong. One day he said to himself, " I am a fool. I have only this small herd and I have built a fence so high that everything that hath a hoof is excluded. Go to, now! This will I do: I will totally remove one panel of my fence and let down a little those next adjoining, and I will go away and get my dinner at my ranch. When the cattle outside see what a nice pen this is, and how open it is, they will come in." Saying which, he hastened off to dinner, smoked his pipe, and took a nap, and then rode back to his corral. His dismay was ludicrous. Not a single head of all the wild cattle had come in and those which he had possessed and made valuable had quietly sauntered out. And that was the result of *his* " liberal " policy.

To-morrow expunge the pledge from every Y. P. S. C. E. in America and we shall have found the eleventh convention to be the last of any notable size and any historical interest.

During the lifetime of our young Society the question of Christian union has attracted more interest than ever before since the Reformation. I do not attribute this interest altogether to the existence of our Society, although no violence would be done to probabilities, if such a statement were made, but I do wish to call attention to the immense promotion of Christian unity by the increase of interdenominational intercourse which has been brought about by our societies. The ecclesiastical projects have all been cold, faulty, pragmatical, and impracticable schemes, working from without, and binding people together with external cords. The work in this direction of the Y. P. S. C. E. has been more effective than all other things combined, because it has been spontaneous, without plan or purpose of unity, unworldly, spiritual, and Christly. Ecclesiastical uniters would bind unwilling people together by their thongs, but Christ would draw people together by the bonds of a man and the cords of love. Ecclesiastical reasoning endeavors to show that the way to bring about Christian unity would be for the members of each church to make some concessions, thus hurting their consciences, and to come together upon some common ground which not one of them would naturally or graciously wish to occupy. Now the Christian Endeavor movement is the very reverse of this; it binds each one of its members to devote his force to building up his own local church, believing that that course of conduct will be most pleasing to the Lord Jesus Christ. When this work is fully started in several churches, and the workmen begin to perceive that their fellow Christians in other churches are animated by the same spirit, conferences naturally occur, and these conferences grow, and because all are animated by the same spirit, and subordinate all society as well as all ecclesiastical operations to the promotion of the glory of Jesus Christ, they come to love one another for his dear sake. Now, love is the natural predecessor of courtship, as courtship is the natural forerunner of wedlock; and thus it has come to pass that, more than anything else, a movement designed to promote the glory of Christ through increased interest in each Christian's special church has done more than anything else to advance that only unity which is dear to the heart of Christ; not the putting of his people into one ecclesiastical field, but binding together his people, while they are preserving the individuality of their churches, their denominational personalities, so to speak; just as the Father and the Son are one without sacrifice of either's personality. In no other sense probably did Jesus Christ pray for Christian unity. His prayer was that the disciples which he left behind him, together with all those which should believe on Jesus through their word, "may be one"; He adds, "as Thou, Father, art in me and I in thee, that they also be one in us." There is no more indication of the desire of Jesus that we should lose our individuality by being united to all other Christian people than that the Father should lose his personality in that of the Son, or the Son his personality in that of the Father. To the fulfilment of his prayer, that all Christians might be one in the Father and in the Son, the Y. P. S. C. E. has contributed more than all the other movements of Christian people in the last five hundred years.

In grateful memory of all the Young People's Society of Christian Endeavor has already done for our Lord Christ, and in loving anticipation of what it is to be doing when all of us shall have ascended to the Great Convention on high, in behalf of the pastors of the Christian churches in the city of New York, I extend to you as a body and as individuals, dear sisters and brothers of the Y. P. S. C. E., in our eleventh convention assembled, a tender, warm, heartfelt welcome to our great, our growing, our beloved city of New York. O leave blessings for our churches and homes, and take blessings to all your homes and churches in the name of the Father and of the Son and of the Holy Ghost. Amen.

Many of Dr. Deems's utterances were received with emphatic approval by the audience, and at the close of his address he was accorded an ovation. The assembly then joined in singing the following hymn, to the tune of "The Star-spangled Banner," written by Dr. Deems for the convention of '92.

THE BANNER OF JESUS.

See, see, comrades! see, floating high in the air,
The love woven, blood sprinkled banner of Jesus!
The symbol of hope, beating down all despair,
From sin and its thraldom triumphantly frees us.
By the hand that was pierced it was lifted at first,
When the bars of the grave by our Captain were burst;

CHORUS. — That blood sprinkled banner must yet be unfurled
O'er the homes of all men and the thrones of the world.

Shout, shout, comrades; shout that our Captain and Lord,
That standard of hope first intrusted to woman;
And Mary, dear saint, in obeying His word,
Flung out its wide folds over all that is human;
So there came to embrace that sweet ensign of grace,
All the true and the great, all the best of our race.

CHORUS. — That blood-sprinkled banner, etc.

March, march, comrades! march, all the young, all the old,
The army of Christ and of Christian Endeavor;
With heroes our souls having now been enrolled,
Our banner we'll follow forever and ever.
For our march shall not cease, till the gospel of peace
Shall our race in all lands from its tyrant release.

CHORUS. — That blood-sprinkled banner, etc.

DR. CLARK: We will not forget that Brooklyn has an equally large place in our hearts with New York — that she also is one of our hostesses on this occasion. We are glad to have speak for Brooklyn one whom young people love for his courage and for the enemies he has made — Rev. Amzi Clarence Dixon, pastor of the Hanson Place Baptist church. (*Great enthusiasm and cheers, as Mr. Dixon rose to speak.*)

ADDRESS OF REV. A. C. DIXON.

While New York and Brooklyn are separated by a river of water, they are united by a bridge of iron. The river that separates us is mobile and fluctuating: the bridge that unites us is stable and permanent. The river, with its currents and commerce, is the symbol of unrest. The bridge poised above it, regardless of currents and noises, is the symbol of peace. So with all evangelical Christendom. Above the fluctuating issues that separate us and the noisy questions that distract us is the iron link of love for Christ and the church, that binds us together in peaceful union.

This Brooklyn bridge is also a link between the store and the home, the office and the church — in a word, between business and religion. After you have all had a taste of business in New York, you are invited to come across and get a taste of religion in Brooklyn. [*Laughter and applause.*] The kind of religion that we have I will not take time to describe. Be assured they are as multifarious as the business interests of New York. Compared with it Joseph's coat of many colors was a simple garment. We have all temperatures there, ranging from the steam in the boiler which runs the ministerial and ecclesiastical engine at the rate of seventy miles an hour, to the iceberg in the cold moonlight of an arctic winter of ritualism an intellectuality. In the name of both iceberg and engine I welcome you to Brooklyn. May the warmth of your presence melt the iceberg, and the wisdom of your counsels help us run the engine.

I delight to welcome you for what you are, an army of enthusiastic young soldiers under a common commander, a great band of active workers in a common vineyard, a large loving family with a common Father. I delight to welcome you for what you represent; and if I understand the motive and the spirit of Christian Endeavor, it represents, first of all, faith in the living God. The dying Christ is not forgotten; the blood that cleanses and runs through your thought works as the scarlet thread through the cordage of the British navy. There is no thought of covering the sacrifice of Abel with the fruits and flowers of Cain. Your first cry is, "Behold the Lamb of God," and your highest hope is at last to worship with the angels and before "the Lamb as it had been slain in the midst of the throne."

> "In the Cross of Christ you glory,
> Towering o'er the wrecks of time."

But the crucified Saviour is not all. I welcome you as in the line of apostolic succession, in witnessing for the risen Christ. Christ to you is not a mere historic fact, but a living and loving friend; to you "he ever liveth;" he leads, he guides, he blesses. And herein is the secret of success. The promised power at Pentecost was none other than God himself, and the Holy Spirit is still Immanuel, God with us; and if he blesses us not, it is because of our unbelief. To speak of the Spirit as a mere influence or emanation is a dishonor to God akin to blasphemy. Influences are mentioned by the Bible only once, and that by Job when in a sentimental mood he spoke of the " influences of the Pleiades." An influence is to the church to-day what the Pleiades are to the earth; power is the sun. God with us in his own person is the power with which he promises to endow us. The Lord Jesus was not a man of influence. He seems to have put a low estimate upon it when he made himself of no reputation, but he worked and taught under the power of the Spirit. The apostles were not men of influence, with the one exception of the apostle Paul, and he lost all he had after it was known he was converted. And he and Silas on one occasion did not have enough " influence " to keep out of jail: but they were in touch with a power that shook the jail doors open and let them out. [*Applause.*] Power with God is the need of the church. When the Spirit came as a rushing, mighty wind, filling the whole building where they were sitting, he meant to teach us the nearness of God to his assembled church. He would be the very atmosphere that we breathe. And when he came as tongues of fire he taught us that for the individual there must be special enduement for testimony. God anoints not the crowd, but the individual. I welcome you because you believe in God, the Spirit, loving, and leading, and working, and saving in our midst. Put the Spirit in the place of power. Isaiah said, " I saw the Lord sitting upon a throne, high and lifted up." That was the prophet's preparation for work. To-day the Spirit is on the throne. He holds the sceptre; he reigns in this dispensation; and the men are mighty who take their position beneath the throne, and crown the Spirit as well as Christ Lord of all. [*Applause.*] David said, " Because he is at my right hand, I shall not be moved." The right hand is the place of honor and authority. David put God in the place of honor. We expect God to put us by and by on the right hand; let us treat him as well as we expect him to treat us. Just in proportion as we put God on the throne, the powers of evil shall fall at his feet.

I welcome you in the next place, because you represent the living Word. " The word of God is sharper than any two-edged sword." It has been duly tested. You do not need to smear it with any acid of criticism. It has been in the soldier's hands and it has been proven to have in it good metal, with a keen edge and sharp point. The word of God, the sword of the spirit, is magnified by the Christian Endeavor movement. Some good English people have formed a Bible Defence Society. One has suggested that we now form a Sun Defence Society to protect the king of day against smoke and fogs. The Christian Endeavor movement is not for the defence of the Bible, the Bible is its defence. [*Loud applause.*] We are not seeking to establish the Bible: the Bible establishes us, and every other institution that is worth establishing. [*Applause.*]

"Take care of your mamma while papa is gone," said a father to his three-year-old child one summer morning as he started to the Adirondacks. That night the little fellow prayed, "Lord, bless papa and take care of him; bless Mary and take care of her; bless grandpa and take care of him; I will take care of mamma myself. Amen." The mother was amused to hear him so intent on taking care of her, while she was really taking care of him. I wonder if the angels never laugh as they look down at some of God's silly, earnest children, trying to take care of the Bible when really the Bible is taking care of them. [*Loud Applause.*] There is no need, allow me to say, for any Sun-Spot Society. I believe in gas and electricity, provided the gas is lighted. Let all the new discoveries that can be found be brought forth, but they need not try to take the place of the sun. The Christian Endeavor movement is not a gas company or an electric company. This organization is striving to induce men to come into the sunlight. It is a dispenser of food and medicine for which the world is dying, and not a laboratory for the analysis of new prescriptions. [*Applause.*] When the new light comes, if it comes from the sun, it is welcome; but if it be but the phosphorescent glow of the putrefying carcass of unbelief, it can be dispensed with. No, we believe in the Scripture, "In thy light shall we see light"; and when light comes we bring it into the light to see whether or not it is of kinship with the light from God. I welcome you in the next place, because you represent faith in a living church. The living God and a living Word will make a living church. "Ye must be born again" lies at the threshold of Christian Endeavor. First life, and then growth. There is no attempt to teach blind men colors, or deaf men music. First, the new birth and then the development in the divine nature to the largest possible extent. The living church must also be a live church. "Living at this poor dying rate" is out of date; and unless the life that is in us moves to activity, the world thinks of a dissecting table or of a cemetery. The fact is, dead things ought to be cut up or buried, and the world is not slow to bury a dead church or to dissect a dead Christian. The world respects Christian Endeavor because it is full of life and manifests that life upon every proper occasion. Let me give you an illustration. A man in New York stopped one day on Broadway in front of the window of a taxidermist, a man who makes his living by stuffing birds and animals. This man stood there and looked at an owl on a pedestal, and he said, "The man who stuffed that owl does not know anything about his business. The feathers are not right; the head is not right; the pose is not right," — just then the owl turned his head and winked his eye! That man walked off feeling that he was the biggest fool in New York. Now I submit the proposition: the moment that owl winked he was beyond that fellow's criticism. [*Laughter and applause.*] Men of God, young soldiers of Jesus Christ, if you wish to command the respect due to the name, you have got to show life. You have heard of that fellow — I think it was in Baltimore — brought in by the students of a medical college for dissection. They just flung him into a cart as if he was a pig, and rattled down the roughest pavements there were in the city. They brought him to the dissecting room and put him on a marble slab, and they straightened him out and put him in position, and got ready for business. They had no regard for him, no respect for him at all. By and by one of the seniors took off his coat, and, having arranged everything just right, took a scalpel and began operations on the man; and the moment the knife entered the flesh a finger moved, and then the man threw up an arm, and turned around and looked at him, and got up on the table. Now I tell you the respect of those few students began to rise, as they rose in a body, three steps at a time, to tell the professor that there was a living corpse in the dissecting room! When the professor came, at once he took off his hat to the fellow and said, "My friend, what hotel would you like to go to?" "Get him a good suit of clothes and give him just what he wants." It was the difference, you see, between a corpse and a man. When I hear a dead sermon I feel like dissecting it, and I usually cut the preacher half in two. A dead church calls for the graveyard or the dissecting table. You believe in a living church along the lines of Christ's thought.

Different kinds of life make different organizations. The life in one egg organizes a hen that takes to the barnyard; the life in another egg organizes a dove that takes to the field; the life in another egg organizes an eagle that takes to the sun. Some churches have life that produces organization which takes to everything else except the great work of saving souls — except the great commission of Jesus Christ when he said, " Go and disciple all nations, and I am with you as the omnipotent power." Christian Endeavor means organization produced by life along the Christly lines — along the thought of God for the sanctification of the saved and the salvation of the lost.

Here lies the secret of its marvellous growth. Believing in the living God, and the living Word, and the living church, alive with the life of God, it could not but be powerful. How can we get that power this afternoon? The burden of my prayer has been, not so much to make a speech, if you please, as to say something to indicate the source of the anointing of power of which I have spoken. Can we not here and now have a consecration service? Why not begin as we expect to end? We say to sinners, "Come to Jesus just as you are." They come, and are saved. Let us say to ourselves, "Come to the Spirit just as you are, and you shall be endued with power." Faith in Christ saves; faith in the Spirit empowers. Salvation is a backward look; power is an upward look. Many a man saved by faith is weak for lack of faith in the Spirit that gives power. The Bible says, "With thee is the fountain of life." Do we have to move God to endue us? A fountain does not need to be moved; it is already living. The well needs to be moved; the pump needs to be moved; but with God is the fountain of life, and all we need to do is to bring the empty vessels of our weakness and get beneath the overflowing fountain of God's fulness of life. And now at the inception of this meeting we may be filled with Christly life, if we are just willing to be filled, and then this life in us will make us a fountain in New York,— cleansing hearts, cleansing homes, cleansing Tammany itself; [*applause*] the power of God helping the city as never before may be the result of this magnificent meeting. Have we in us that fountain? Some of us have the pump life. Well, I would rather drink water drawn out of a pump than to perish with thirst. Some churches work on the pump principle. How we pastors have to pump sometimes to get a little money or to get a few workers, and we have to put on the handle a plate of oysters, and in the pump a dish of ice cream, and just pump away; and still the pump is better than nothing. Praise God for the pump! But the fountain is so much better; and if we are filled with God, we will have the fountain life, we will go out to every one that touches our personality.

Now may I close with the prayer of the Apostle Paul to the Ephesians. Is it not appropriate to this occasion? "I bow my knees unto the Father of our Lord Jesus Christ, of whom the whole family in heaven and on earth is named, that he may grant you, according to the riches of his glory, to be strengthened with might by his Spirit in the inner man; that he may dwell in your hearts by faith; that ye, being rooted and grounded in love, may be able to comprehend with all saints what is the breadth, and length, and depth, and height; and to know the love of Christ which passeth knowledge, that ye may be filled with all the fulness of God."

In the Atlantic Ocean, in the mountain lake, in the wayside spring, in the morning dew, we may see reflected the image of the same great sun. The sun has a way of adapting himself to the ocean, lake, spring, and dewdrop; and whether your capacity be vast like the ocean, or tiny like the dewdrop, God can fill you with his fulness. [*Loud applause.*]

Dr. Clark then announced that Mr. Ira D. Sankey, the eminent evangelist, would sing a hymn — an announcement that was received with great favor.

Mr. SANKEY: Before I try to sing a hymn for you to-day, I would like to give expression to my great joy in seeing this large congregation gathered to-day in the name of Jesus Christ. A little while ago it was said that the old Bible was to pass away; this meeting does not look as though it was passing away. They said, "Science is going to remove the Bible." My friend Dixon, as he spoke this afternoon, put me in mind of an incident I heard not long since in regard to the question of upsetting the Bible. An Irishman was building a stone wall down by a piece of meadow ground, and one of these wise philosophers came and said: "Patrick, that wall will fall down. I would not build any more. The wall is sure to fall. And Patrick said, "My dear sir, I call your attention to this fact, that I am building this wall four feet thick and three feet high, and when it tumbles over it will be taller than it was before." So I say about the Bible: when they have upset the Bible it will be larger than before. God bless this great assemblage that is gathered in the name of Jesus Christ.

A few years ago, as a vessel was crossing the Atlantic one stormy night, a great wave swept across the bow of the vessel, and one of the men on board was washed into the sea. The captain saw this man go overboard, and springing from the bridge he ran and seized a line and threw it out to the sinking man; but the vessel was passing on quickly in the darkness, and there was great fear that the man would not be able to lay hold of the line. By and by the line had gone out its full length, and they were afraid to draw it in for fear they might be drawing it away from the hand of the dying man. They waited and called out to him, "Have you got hold of the line?" and in the darkness there came a voice from the sea, "Aye, pull away, pull away. The line has hold of me." The man had slipped the line over his body and under his arms, and all they had to do was to pull him on board. So if the Gospel gets hold of us we will not lose our hold, but it will bring us safely into the harbor. May the Lord bless our little song this afternoon, "Throw out the Life Line." I want the whole congregation to join in the chorus of this hymn.

The audience did join very effectively in the chorus of the hymn, Mr. Sankey singing the verses as a solo. Dr. Clark then introduced President Merrill E. Gates, of Amherst College, to respond to the words of welcome on behalf of the trustees and delegates. Pres. Gates was received by the audience with much applause.

ADDRESS OF PRESIDENT GATES.

Your words of welcome have been eloquent and kind. We thank you for them. We might well be at a loss, in seeking to reply to them, were it not that our Master has left us instructions. We have come to you on his business. We are confident that he is with us, as we represent societies of Christian Endeavor in all parts of our land, — yes, in all parts of that whole earth for which Christ died and over which our Christ shall reign! And we remember that when Christ's church was wholly *young* and when *endeavor* in his name was its distinctive characteristic, the chief work of the church then, as now, was "to go before his face into every city and place where he himself was about to come." He gave to his earliest disciples as they went abroad on his service a command which is also for us in these latest times: "Into whatsoever city ye shall enter and they receive you, — say unto them, The kingdom of God is come nigh unto you;" and "into whatsoever house ye shall enter, first say, Peace be to this house."

We accept your welcome most cordially. We confidently expect God's blessing to attend this great gathering. And the blessing will be both yours and ours. For we are Christ's. Christ dwells in his people; and where his people are gathered in his name and for his glory, there he appears, to confirm the blessed gospel of glad tidings; and his peace shall fall upon you who receive us and upon us who come, to strengthen us all for new and high endeavor.

For the key-note of this convention is, and should be, "Endeavor." We *believe* in the future of these societies. We have confidence in the movement which these thousands of delegates represent.

This meeting commands the attention of the nation to-day. In what lies the true significance of the Endeavor movement? "The Young People's Society of Christian Endeavor." In this name every word is full of promise and potency!

We believe in the future of this work, first, because it is the work of *young* people. 'T is a great thing to be young! If only you learn in time how great are the possibilities of youth, to be young is a blessing. The thrill of super-abundant life in every nerve and artery, the zest of mere living, renders it a joy. The future is full of promise. Hope is still unslain. The eye is full of the eager expectancy that to-morrow, or perhaps to-day, will bring into one's life something finer, richer, fuller than has yet been seen or known. Young people are rich because the future is still theirs. To be young, is a good thing. But it is good, chiefly, because youth rightly used means the possibility of a noble and useful maturity, of a ripe old age; and these are far richer and better than is youth. To be young is to have the future still open, with all its possibilities. To be young, and in one's youth to walk with Christ, to believe on him, is to be assured of a successful life. We believe in this movement because it lays hold of the young, and thus lays hold of the future. And the past is of value only as out of it we learn so to think and act in the present as to make better the future.

The young are the future personified and embodied. With the young is the message for those who are still young. God has bound us together, as nations and neighborhoods, by relations of space. He has made close and dear the ties that bind us to those who dwell nearest us in space. True patriotism begins in the family and the neighborhood. The man who does not feel the tie that binds him to his neighbor, his town, his own city, is not likely to know the true power of patriotism. God has "set the solitary in families like a flock," and has given to us dear ties that bind families together in communities, and bind communities in a common national life, making the welfare of one's country an object, if needs be, to die for. [*Applause.*]

Just so, God has set us in especial relations to those of our own time of life, of our own generation. There is a voice which speaks to the men of a given decade in a language which is not fully understood by those who preceded them. The young can speak to each other as the old cannot speak to them. This does not mean that there is not a message of the greatest importance from the old to the young. But to get that message fairly into the life of the young, those among the young who see it and feel it must themselves utter it in their own way to the young! So God renews his message to men, sending the old truth by new voices to each new generation. Shall we doubt that he will have even richer and more gracious messages for our children than he has had for us? For one, I have only pity for the Christian who believes that God was with the early church, was with our ancestors and the Pilgrim Fathers, but is departing from us, and will not be with our children. How our Divine Teacher rebuked that spirit when he declared, "Now he is not the God of the dead but of the living." "I believe in the Holy Ghost, the Holy Catholic Church," and I believe in that blessed Holy Spirit as dwelling in the Holy Catholic Church, guiding us as he guided our fathers, and guiding our children and dwelling in them in even larger measure. Because to the young, as they go on in life, the voice of the living God will come with new power from those who are *young* with them because thus youth is consecrated in these *young* people's societies, we believe in them. [*Applause.*]

We have confidence in them, too, because they are *the people's* societies. This is a great *popular* movement, in the best sense of that word. And we believe in the people, in this dear land of ours. I do not say this loosely, as the demagogue says it. I do not mean that the majority is always right. I do not say it as if we believed, with Gambetta, that "the people must be considered as the exclusive, the perennial source of all rights; the will of the people must have the last word; all must bow before that will of the people." On the contrary, we believe, you and I, do we not, that *the majority never has a right to do what it pleases, except when it pleases to do what is right.* If any of you, young man or woman, have not yet seen clearly this great truth, as underlying our system of popular government, then the supreme question for you as a Christian and a citizen of the world's foremost republic is, "Do I firmly believe in an absolute standard of right and wrong, above all majorities, fixing the basis of the sovereignty of the people?" And God give you a clear answer! For in the clear answer to this question by the citizens of our land lies the hope of our beloved country and of the world.

But we believe that the great majority of the people *do* answer this question aright. Our people in their sober second thought are, on the whole, for righteousness. We believe that the common people of America are sound at heart and in life. We believe in commonplace people. Said Abraham Lincoln: "God Almighty must have thought a great deal of commonplace people or he never would have made so many of them." The glory of America is in its average people, its average homes. We believe in the average people who mean to "raise the average" of intelligence and goodness. And these societies are emphatically the people's societies. Since the people under God are sovereign, a movement in which all the good people of our land are interested is a movement which deserves attention and promises results.

But still farther we have faith in the movement, because it represents associated effort. It is a young people's *society*. The *Zeit-Geist*, the spirit of the times, is organized effort for associated endeavor. The life of this last quarter of the nineteenth century is marked by strong *associating* impulses. Organization is the watchword of the time. Labor organizes. Trades organize. Capital organizes. Selfish interests organize. Unselfish interests, too, must organize. Never before in the history of the world has man seen so truly the meaning of the solidarity of the race. The longing for associated effort, for affiliated life, is felt around the whole globe, like a vast force of gravitation moving all men toward their fellow-men. The Spirit of the Living God lays hold on this tendency of the time, lifts it up, sanctifies it, and we have the Young Men's Christian Associations, the intercollegiate and interseminary missionary conventions, the student volunteer missionary movement, which brings the church face to face with its own answered prayers, and forces every denomination of Christ's people to meet the decisive question, "Are you in earnest in praying for the conversion of the world, and will you *give* as you pray, that these young men and women, who are eager to go, may at once be sent as missionaries of the cross?" From this outreaching of the hearts of man toward his fellow-men has arisen this latest instrumentality of the church, the allied societies here represented. It is not a strange movement, although it is a new one. It follows the line of God's dealing with the church in history. The Holy Spirit, taking and applying the truth revealed in the Holy Scripture, works in the church by new means to secure the same ends,— the salvation of sinners, the sanctification and upbuilding of believers. And in the associated prayer and effort of these societies, we see a blessed fulfilment of Christ's prayer — the prayer in which, looking down the ages to us who have believed on him through the words his immediate followers were inspired to write for us, our Redeemer seems to hold you and me in his thought, and to pray for each one of us by name, as he says in that blessed seventeenth of John, "Neither pray I for these alone, but for them also which shall believe on me through their word; that they may all *be one*,— that the world may believe that thou didst send me." Because it advances this Christ-enjoined, God-given unity in associated effort for the cause of Christ, we rejoice in this movement.

But there remains in the name of these societies two significant words.

Endeavor is the secret of advance. Endeavor is the evidence of life. When an organism makes no endeavor as against its environment, it is dead. When a conscious person ceases to make endeavor, that person ceases to be. Endeavor makes all the difference between failure and success. While to "abide in Christ" is the secret of power for the Christian, unless there be the steadfast purpose and the strong endeavor to abide in him, the Christian will instead abide too much in self and in the world, and failing to abide in Christ will not "bring forth much fruit." Yet, if the highest results of all endeavor be simply to *abide* in Christ and to have the life of Christ abide in us, surely there must be a divine secret in this high endeavor. To abide in Christ is not to be passive in the ceaseless, world-wide struggle between right and wrong. It is to be gloriously active and victorious in that struggle. To abide in Christ is not to withdraw from active life. It is to live to the full, strenuously, effectively, most actively, but in life of which self is no longer the centre.

The true meaning of this word "endeavor," which gives substantive value to the name of these societies, can be understood only when you take with it the all-important adjective which precedes it. It is not the endeavor of mere restlessness seeking a change; it is not the unsanctified endeavor of wilfulness, determined merely to make things different in order to make itself felt. It is *Christian* endeavor that is the reason for the being of these societies. The "hiding of their power," the "secret of their strength" lies in that word *Christian*. Any failure to understand this is fatal to the life of a society, fatal to the usefulness of a member. The movement is to succeed, not because it is a popular movement of great numbers of young people associated in endeavor, however fiery-hearted and strong; but it is to succeed because it is *Christian*, and just in so far as it is Christian, and by no other power than the power of Christ, and through you only in proportion as the power of Christ is in you and works through you. In that text so often quoted to make young men rejoice in their youth, "I have written unto you, young men, because ye are strong," the true and only source of strength of young manhood, the only power that can redeem it from the awful moral weakness that always attends the vain overestimate of one's own strength, is given in the context as the reason why those young men to whom John wrote were "strong," because, he says, "the word of God abideth in you." No young people, singly or in associated efforts, are *strong*, unless "the Word of God abideth in them." And just in so far as that Word of the Living God abides in you and makes you truly *Christian*, just so far and no farther will you, my dear young friends and the societies you represent, succeed in the work we have at heart. As *Christian* Endeavor societies you will succeed and will bless the world. If the relative importance of these factors is changed, if the *youthful* characteristics, or the *society*, or the *endeavor* becomes more prominent, you will fail! [*Applause.*]

But you will *not* fail! "We know whom we have believed, and are persuaded that he is able to keep that which we have committed unto him against that day." That there may be no failure, what is the spring of endeavor, what is the secret of power? The great need of our young people to-day, and always, is a deeper, fuller, more abounding life.

> "'T is life whereof our nerves are scant,
> More life and fuller that we want."

We want more light! We want more power! We want more life! [*Applause.*]

To you in the morning-land of life has come the gracious, sweet, compelling invitation. You are called "into his marvellous light" to walk in the light, to be the "children of light." He invites you to be filled with his power. He offers you the full-flowing tide of his life, with its tireless energy to strengthen you for higher endeavor. You have felt the power of his voice calling you to this larger life. He has "drawn you with the cords of man." The desire of your hearts is for him. You have felt the divine passion of service to your fellow-men falling on you as you have come to understand that our fellow-men are perishing for the lack of what Christians must bring to them. In the restless movements of our time among all peoples, you have seen that Christ is the "Desire of the Nations," though they know it not.

How are we to lay hold of the power we ought to wield for Christ? How may we receive the full flow of his life in our lives? How may we move the world toward Christ? — for this and nothing less than this is our high endeavor.

Clearly, we need some strong elemental force that shall draw us by its powerful attraction toward goodness and duty when duty is plainly seen. We need some mighty, energizing force which, like heat or light or life-power, shall transmute knowledge into wise living, moral convictions into goodness of life, and noble thoughts and purposes into a will-power used in noble living, into character achieved. [*Applause.*]

Life is from Christ, our Sun of Righteousness. Given that subtle architectonic principle which builds up each organism after its kind, given that life principle which no analysis can quite reach, and which refuses to resolve itself into other forces, and biology shows us that we are still dependent on light and heat for the development of life. Not only must we go to Christ for the teaching from above which originates life, which gives new life when the soul is born again : but for heat and light, without which life must perish, we depend still on the Sun of our soul. No sun, no life or growth!

But once possessed of Christian life, how shall we get work done — work by the intellect, by the will lighted by the intellect and impelled by the emotions? We want not merely potential energy of soul, but *kinetic* energy, force expended in good work done. How move the dead weights of social statics, and carry the burdens of social reform? From what source shall we draw power? Is there a source of power to which we may safely send young people that they may draw unfailing supplies, that their lives may *go on* in achievement and development?

Here, too, we turn to the sun. All forms of power which we use in the physical world, the sun has stored up for us. We simply draw upon the limitless reserve of sun-power. Do you use steam, it matters not whether we draw our heat from wood or coal, or from the mineral oils, we are drawing in the last anaylsis from the sun.

But steam gives way to electricity, you say. Already this subtle power does service in a thousand ways. For the supply of electricity, already thoughtful inventors are turning toward the sun! Already they store up power from the restless tossing of the waves, which the sun-moved air-currents have set playing! Already they store up energy in heat and electricity, by using the changes in tide-levels, and thus for our daily tasks harness to our yoke the vast bulk of that huge, plunging ox, the moon, with crater-callous shoulder, and thus through moon-moved tides make fresh use of the sun's motor power.

But subtler still is the potent, silent power of the sun. The sun, shining calmly on the sensitive thermo-electric piles that simply absorb its rays, starts currents of power which, stored up for us, shall do our work through all dark days, and shall banish with brilliant light the darkness of our nights.

Does not all this wonderfully answer to the work on men's hearts of the Sun of Righteousness? From Christ, our Sun of Righteousness, stream light, and life, and power. That we may be filled with energy and light and power from him, we need only turn our faces fully toward him and draw life and strength from vision.

The secret of power for each of these societies lies in the heart-life of the individual Christians who are enrolled upon its list of members. If one by one the members live close to Christ, the society will be strong. The kingdom of God comes to human hearts, one by one. That kingdom prevails, as one by one loving hearts are made wholly loyal to Christ, our King.

Do you want light? Turn your face toward Christ, the Sun of Righteousness, and his light shall bathe you in a new life. Do you want a stronger life? Dwell in the thought of him who is the Fountain of Life; and " whosoever *will*, let him take the water of life freely." Do you want more love of your fellow-men, that service of God in serving well your fellow-men may be to you a constant, heartening joy? Keep close to the Great Heart of God in Christ, whose divine-human heart was moved with compassion and with world-swaying love, when he " saw the people scattered abroad as sheep having no shepherd."

Enter into the mighty power of his love for you,—not your love for Christ. That will not sustain you, but Christ's love for you, just as you are, drawing you out of your sins into his holiness. A personal loyalty to Christ, that is ready for any service, comes when we see clearly and say lovingly,

> "*Thine* was the life that was given,
> And *mine* was the life that was won."

Then there falls upon us power for service, as we realize that we are "loved with an everlasting love." When this personal message comes into the soul from him whom our souls love, we are girded afresh for service. "And behold a hand touched me,—and he said unto me, O Daniel, *man greatly beloved*, understand the words that I speak unto thee, and stand upright, for unto thee am I sent." In the sweet consciousness of a redeeming love, unmerited, unlimited, measured only by the Father's boundless love of Christ,—who says, "as the Father hath loved me,"—may each one of you find anointing for larger service.

> "So near, so very near to God,
> I cannot nearer be;
> For in the person of His Son
> I am as near as He.

> "So dear, so very dear to God,
> More dear I cannot be;
> The love wherewith He loves the Son,
> Such is His love to me!"

May this love of Christ crown you with its abiding joy, and thus may "the joy of the Lord be your strength" for fruitful endeavor!

After the applause following Pres. Gates's address had died away, a hymn was sung, and Chairman McEwen of the committee of '92 made several announcements. Dr. Clark then announced the following committees:—

Committee on Business. Rev. H. T. McEwen, New York; V. Richard Foss, Maine; C. B. Wilkins, Illinois; Edwin B. Hayes, California; J. Howard Breed, Pennsylvania.

Committee on Resolutions. Rev. J. T. Beckley, Pennsylvania; Rev. N. Boynton. Mass.; Miss Elizabeth N. Wishard, Indiana; E. A. Hardy, Ontario; Rev. S. V. Karmarkar, India.

Committee on Telegrams and Greetings. Rev. R. W. Brokaw, Mass.; Rev. George B. Stewart, Pennsylvania; Rev. Howard B. Grose, Ill.; Mrs. H. W. Linson.

Committee on Nominations. Rev. H. W. Sherwood, N.Y.; Mr. G. R. Lighthall, Quebec; William Blincoe, Oklahoma; Rev. H. N. Kinney, Connecticut; Miss Esther Clark, South Dakota.

Rev. R. V. Hunter, of Terre Haute, Ind., chairman of the committee appointed last year on Sunday closing of the World's Fair, was then introduced to present the report of the committee, as follows:—

REPORT OF THE NATIONAL COMMITTEE OF CHRISTIAN ENDEAVOR ON THE CLOSING OF THE COLUMBIAN EXPOSITION ON SUNDAYS.

Mr. Chairman:—There are some people who would like to have the World's Fair open on Sunday. Do we want the fair open on Sunday? [*Cries of* "*No, No!*"] I am glad to hear that expression of your opinion. There are a great many reasons offered by these people why the World's Fair should be open on Sunday; but it is a little like the Irish jury. The judge called the jury together, and found that one of the jurymen was absent.

"Is there anyone here," said he, "who can tell why that juryman is absent?" One man rose and said, "If it please your honor, I am his neighbor, and I can tell you all about it."

"What is the reason?" said the judge.

"Well, sir, if it please your honor, there are twenty-four good reasons why he should be absent to-day."

"Well, give the reasons, and do it in a hurry."

"Well, sir, if it please your honor, the man is dead, and could not come."

"That is sufficient," said the judge, "we will hear the twenty-three reasons some other time. [*Laughter*.]

Now I want to give but one reason why the World's Fair should be open on Sunday, and I will defer the other twenty-three reasons until some other time. They want the fair open on Sunday because there is revenue in it, they think. That is the reason of all reasons.

A mighty struggle is waging in our nation over our historic Sabbath. Shall we allow this restful day to be displaced by a Continental Sunday? More than a million Endeavorers join with other millions of good and patriotic people in protest.

This historic day means everything to labor, liberty, and the church. The good citizen, as well as the good Christian, must stand for that day which is the "corner-stone in the foundation, and the citadel in the defences of our free institutions; yea, the key-stone in the perfect arch of our national mission."

"From Maine to Georgia, from ocean to ocean, on one day of the week, by the laws of God and by the law of the land, the people rest." We should not repudiate this law in the year of grace, 1893.

A day which is a "city of refuge" to those whom soulless corporations and ungodly employers would oppress should not be surrendered without a struggle. If the Columbian Exposition is to be our Thermopylæ, like Leonidas and his heroic band, we should stand immovable against the heathen hordes. It should be understood that this question is one of theism and anti-theism. Whether or not the World's Fair, with all its accessories of evil, shall be opened on Sunday, is a contest, virtually, between the true religion and atheism. In the name of liberty, those who advocate Sunday opening, would destroy our institutions and bring perpetual ruin and blight upon the land that has nurtured them and that has furnished them with refuge from oppression.

This nation owes what it is largely to the Christian religion. To desecrate it would be to smite the breast that has nurtured us. As patriots, as intelligent beings and Christians can we do this irrational thing? "Forbid it, Almighty God!" Even the nations of Europe are repudiating the "Continental Sunday," which is now being forced upon us. Germany and France are crying out for a better observance of the day. Their Sunday has proven itself the foe of both man and God. This day must be preserved for reasons humane, patriotic, historic, moral and religious. The dial of civilization must not divert its course, as certain potent influences are now demanding.

Shall the Columbian Exposition, unmatched in history for its scope, munificence, and splendor, be prostituted to the furtherance of Sunday desecration? It is not a question as to whether the gates of this fair shall be opened on Sunday; but shall they *continue* to be opened? In the language of one of the commissioners: "The gates are now open." I understand that already thousands are visiting the grounds every Sunday.

There is great danger, also, that alcoholic drinks will be retailed upon the grounds, with the consent of the Local Directory and United States Commission. This makes us think of a bookman from Chicago. Somebody wrote to him ordering a list of books, among others one entitled "Candidates for Heaven." The bookman replied, "We have filled your order, sir, all except one; there are no candidates for heaven in Chicago." [*Laughter and applause.*] Now, that was a slander on Chicago. There are as good and heroic people in Chicago as in any place in the land. They are standing up manfully for the Sabbath. But these people who have the World's Fair in charge are not properly representing the Christian and moral sentiment of that great city.

This would be " adding insult to injury." This fair being organized under a special act of Congress would make the nation — our nation, mark you — responsible for these crimes. We, the people, compose the nation. We, then, are *particeps criminis* of broken law. As followers of the Nazarene we do not enjoy the situation. We do not care to have part in the sale of principle, and in the destruction of this Christian institution for a few " pieces of silver."

Who are these that demand that the gates of the Columbian Exposition shall be opened on Sunday?

1. Some who are financially interested in this monster project.
2. Some foreigners who are not accustomed to our American Christian Sabbath.
3. Americans, by birth, of the Ingersoll type.
4. A small proportion of ill-informed and misguided laboring people, who do not see that their advocacy of a Sunday Exposition is the forging of chains which will in time bind their class in a slavery more relentless than that of the black man prior to 1863.
5. A few people of respectability who care nothing for religion, and who have never weighed this question in its patriotic, humane, and historic bearings.

We believe these classes are largely in the minority. Yet there is great danger that because of their loud demands, *greatly assisted by monetary considerations*, they will carry the day. The mask was thrown aside recently when representatives of those who have the fair in charge appeared before a committee of congressmen soliciting additional financial help. It was freely admitted, according to press reports, that unless Congress granted the financial help asked for, the managers of the fair would disregard Sunday, and run the fair with a view to securing themselves. Thus a great exposition, claiming to be a " World's Fair," is to be run in the interests of a few persons. Sentiment, law, custom, morals, and religion are to be disregarded because, forsooth, certain men have invested largely and are now determined to make good their investments. The Columbian Exposition, it would seem, is more of a private enterprise, in the hands ot some godless and avaricious people, than national or international in its character.

Did Congress rebuke this spirit? Nay, nay! the House of Representatives proceeded to vote an appropriation to the fair, directing that the *Government exhibits* should be closed on Sunday. We have not yet seen where the Senate has taken similar action. It is our understanding that the matter is not settled until the Senate concurs. Should the Senate agree to the House resolution, then the authorities of the World's Fair are free to open the gates. All exhibitors are free to exercise their pleasure as to whether or not they will exhibit their wares, with the exception of the " Government Exhibit." We understand the machinery is not to run on that day. But that is of comparatively little consequence. The *gates will be open* and the attractions will be sufficient to draw immense crowds to Chicago. Innumerable excursions will run into the city; tens of thousands of people must labor in consequence; Sunday will be disregarded; good morals will be outraged; law will be broken; our nation will be disgraced in the eyes of the world, and Almighty God will be dishonored.

You ask: What can Christian Endeavorers do to avert this national disaster? We will first recite what your committee, appointed one year ago at Minneapolis, has tried to do through more than a million Endeavorers; then we will make some recommendations for action between this and the time for opening of the fair on May 1, 1893.

The National Christian Endeavor convention of last year passed some ringing resolutions on the subject of " Sunday Closing." A committee was appointed to carry out the work suggested by the resolutions. That committee was as follows: Rev. S. J. McPherson, D. D., Bishop Fallows, Col. G. R.

Clark, Hon. B. F. Jacobs, of Chicago; Rev. Dr. Tiffany, Minneapolis; Rev. Chas. F. Deems, D. D., New York; Hon. E. P. Searle, of Chattanooga; Hon. T. J. Kirkpatrick, of Springfield, Ohio; and Rev. R. V. Hunter, of Terre Haute.

Colonel Clark did not respond. During the autumn Dr. Tiffany, who had already shown a deep interest in the work and whose counsel gave promise of great value, passed to his reward. In the places of these two brethren Hon. W. H. McClain, of St. Louis, and Hon. W. B. Bently, of Des Moines, were appointed members of the committee. The committee has been so scattered that consultation has been had largely by means of correspondence. Two meetings, however, were called, one in Chicago early in December, and another in Indianapolis, April the 10th. The committee worked largely through the State organizations, the *Golden Rule*, and the religious newspapers of the various evangelical denominations, suggesting methods to be pursued, issuing various circulars, forms of resolutions, protests, memorials, etc., etc. Some of these were sent to State officers to be distributed among the societies and churches of their States. Thousands of circulars were distributed to those who wrote for them, attention having been called through the newspapers to the fact that the committee would forward literature to those who desired it. Circulars were not sent out in a wholesale fashion for the reason that the committee did not have sufficient funds with which to do so. The committee sent out a little less than a hundred newspaper articles, eight thousand pamphlets containing "Resolutions," "Forms of Protests," "List of Columbian Fair Commissioners," directions as to methods, and an argument in favor of closing the World's Fair on Sunday. Ten thousand circular letters of various kinds were sent to conventions, unions, and societies in the various States and Territories of the Union, to Canada, and to England. Many churches and pastors, and organizations of various kinds from different parts of the Union, were furnished with our literature upon request. Thousands of letters were written in reply to interrogatories concerning this burning question. The funds were furnished by a few individuals and societies, and by the *United Society, of Boston*. May God bless all those friends of the American Sabbath who helped so generously with their means. There are no outstanding bills against the committee. As a result of this work tens of thousands of letters have been written to United States senators, representatives, legislators, commissioners — State and National — begging that our nation may be spared the disgrace and humiliation of a violated Sunday and of a national saloon.

Resolutions and protests without number have been filed with the proper authorities, with what success the future alone will reveal. Your committee is of the opinion that *personal letters* written to those who are in authority, and *personal appeals* are more effective than resolutions and protests. As an evidence that our congressmen care but little for these protests, so long as they have no fear that their action will not be remembered against them at the polls, the following incident may illustrate: —

A member of your committee writes under date of June 23 as follows: "I am told by an eyewitness that a two-bushel basket of petitions against Sunday opening of the World's Fair were laughed over and drunk over by the congressional committee into whose hands they had fallen, and were never even read or examined, tabulated or counted."

Our congressmen must learn that there are questions which lie very near to the hearts of several million Americans other than the "Coinage of Silver" and "Tariff." We shall hope, however, that the better sentiment will yet prevail. Whether the exposition gates are closed or not, we must remember that the agitation of this question in the papers, in conventions, and in our societies has been a great educational institution to this generation of Christian Endeavorers in this country. Their attention has been directed to the character of the day, and to the necessity of its observance for sanitary, historic, moral, and religious reasons. They are now apprised of the dangers that threaten it, and they are becoming more and more familiar with the sources of this vicious and debasing attack. These considerations have led many Christian people to decide they cannot conscientiously attend the fair at all, if it be made a Sabbath-breaking institution.

In conclusion your committee would recommend: —

1. That this convention does reiterate and emphasize its action of one year ago in opposition to the opening on the Sabbath Day of any part of the World's Fair to be held in Chicago in 1893 It does not believe in any compromise.

2. That we call upon the authorities to forbid the sale of intoxicants on the Exposition grounds.

3. That we urge Congress to exercise its prerogative by passing a joint resolution instructing the United States commissioners to close the gates of the fair on Sunday.

4. That the Christian Endeavorers continue to protest, and to use every legitimate and honorable means within their power to preserve the good name of our Christian country and to prevent a violation of the Sunday statutes of Illinois, and of nearly all the other States of our Union; that we continue to protest, if necessary, up to the very day of the opening of the Exposition, May 1, 1893.

5. That the chairman and secretary of this convention be requested to telegraph the following to the speaker of the House of Representatives and to the president of the United States Senate: —

The Eleventh Annual Convention of Christian Endeavorers assembled in New York City, thirty thousand strong, and representing thirteen hundred thousand people, respectfully request the Senate of the United States in connection with the House of Representatives, to take such action as will *compel* the commissioners of the Columbian Exposition to close the gates of that great institution upon the first day of the week, commonly called Sunday, and to prohibit the sale of intoxicating liquors upon the grounds of the aforesaid fair.

All of which is respectfully submitted.

R. V. HUNTER,
Chairman of the Committee.

The reading of the committee's report was attended with marked demonstrations of approval. On motion it was referred to the committee on business. The hymn, "How firm a foundation," was then sung.

Dr. CLARK: The only shadow that I am aware of which has come upon this glorious convention is the shadow that we are deprived of the presence at this meeting of our beloved and honored general secretary, Mr. Baer. I cannot tell you how close to my heart it comes to tell you this news; but even this cloud has its silver lining in the fact that we believe that after a season of rest Mr. Baer's health will be renewed and restored, and that he will be able to carry on his work as before — at least, his office work. He will still continue to be the general secretary, and will receive your letters and do all he can to help forward the movement from the office, though he cannot, according to the advice of his physician, attend such a great meeting as this or our annual State conventions. But he is still our secretary and he will keep his chair. [*Applause.*] I am sure that it is the wish of this convention to send to him a telegram of sympathy and heartfelt love. [*Applause.*] Your applause sufficiently indicates this, and the committee on telegrams will, in behalf of this convention, prepare such a message.

The secretary's report will be read by the Rev. James L. Hill, D.D., of Medford, Mass.

Dr. HILL: My good friends, like the twelve tribes of Israel and like the clans of the valley we are all gathered here, each under his banner; but we are thinking for the moment of our secretary who is in comparative ill health, and I am sure that our emotion can be expressed in the lines: —

"Danes and Normans and Saxons are we,
But all of us Danes in our affection for thee." [*Applause.*]

Since the morning stars sang together there has never been, in point of vastitude, such a convention as this; but we are thinking of this secretary who has lived for this convention — who very nearly died for it, — and as we think of him I am sure that our sentiments are expressed as well in the lines: —

> " Our hearts, our hopes, our prayers, our tears,
> Our faith, triumphant o'er our fears,
> Are all with thee — are all with thee."

For us he has done a yeoman's service. He always moves in the lines of the least resistance. He is clear in his intellectual sight; he always has full grasp of his subject; he always strikes the very centre of the mark. It ought to be very easy for us in this convention to plant the banner on the heights up which he himself and his coadjutors have so gallantly carried it. It gives me great pleasure, — it is a decided honor to read his carefully prepared report.

ANNUAL REPORT OF JOHN WILLIS BAER, GENERAL SECRETARY.

Christian Endeavor has gained an irresistible momentum, for God directs its continuous and successful progress. How easily and certainly this could be proved in so many ways other than by delivering to you the statistics that have been gathered! Statistics? Figures? The best of Christian Endeavor cannot be reported in any such terms. Like many other of God's agencies for widening Christ's kingdom, its height and depth cannot be bounded by any expression within man's possibilities.

It is my privilege this afternoon to give you something of the area of Christian Endeavor as it spreads over this wide, wide world. Hence this statistical report, which at best is but a frame for the picture that you can bring before your mind's eye quite as well as can any one else, if you will take a stong grasp upon the evangelical, evangelistic gospel truth, which is emphasized by thousands of soldiers of the Lord Jesus Christ who are proud to fight for him under a common banner, with common methods of work, against a common enemy.

In 1881, there were 2 societies; in 1882, 7; 1883, 56; 1884, 156; 1885, 253; 1886, 850; 1887, 2,314; 1888, 4,879; 1889, 7,672; 1890, 11,013; last year at Minneapolis, 16,274; and to-day, after eleven years, in the morning light of the second decade, there are *regularly reported* societies to the number of 21,080, while we have reason to believe that societies of whose existence we know, but that have not been recorded, would bring the total up to 22,000. This recorded list is absolutely correct, so far as we know; it does not include a single Methodist society that has changed to an Epworth League, of which societies we regret to say there have been several hundreds.

Last year at Minneapolis many seemed greatly amused when I rang the changes on the word inter-*inter*-INTER-denominational. I would do it again this year, but will make a heroic resistance. Our good friend, Mr. Dickinson, has said, "Christian Endeavor is interdenominational, interurban, interstate, international, interracial; and, if it be true that there are other worlds than this, we shall find that it is *interplanetary*, simply because [and now note his reasoning], simply because it is based upon God's universal law of progress through self-denying endeavor and ministration." Let me prove it by the following statement: —

Thirty evangelical denominations are represented in this grand army battling for the right. We — and with pardonable pride let me emphasize that pronoun "we"; it is not the editorial "we," but *we Presbyterians* — lead, and marshal 4,806 societies in the van. Crowding fast upon us are 4,495 Congregational societies. Then come the Baptists with 2,736. The Methodists still hold the fourth place, notwithstanding the fact that we have lost a large number of societies that have become Epworth Leagues; however, counting the 240 Epworth

Leagues of Christian Endeavor, we have still 2,335 societies in the Methodist Episcopal Church North and South, the Methodist Church of Canada, and the African Methodist Episcopal Church. This figure does not include the Methodist Protestants, of which there are 422 that we have recorded. The Disciples of Christ are fifth, and have made great advances during the last year, as they now have 1,557 societies enrolled, and so on by denominations to the number of thirty different divisions of the church universal, each one emphasizing faith in the divine-human person and atoning work of our Lord and Saviour, Jesus Christ, as the only and sufficient source of salvation.

The spirit of federation and Christian fellowship increases. It is a legacy too precious to be held lightly, a possession too valuable to lose. Some who have

JOHN WILLIS BAER.

heretofore called the society undenominational, and have consequently held aloof from it, have become its ardent advocates and promoters, as they have become familiar with the principles and aims of our society.

It is a matter for congratulation that during the past year the attitude of almost every evangelical denomination has become increasingly friendly to the society. The Reformed (Dutch) Church was perhaps the earliest to indorse the movement; the Disciples of Christ, the Friends, and the Congregationalists have adopted resolutions in their highest ecclesiastical gatherings favoring the society. Many presbyteries and synods have cordially indorsed the society and its methods, while the Baptists, on the broad plane of fraternity, take Christian Endeavor societies into their Young People's Union without change of name or principles or interdenominational fellowship. Within the last few weeks the Cumberland Presbyterian Church emphatically and unanimously frowned upon any effort that might even seem to withdraw their young people from the Christian Endeavor movement. "In no one of the societies voting was there a single ballot favoring a denominational society," says the *Cumberland Presbyterian*. The Methodist Protestant denomination has emphatically declared for Christian Endeavor pure and simple; the Free Baptists have advocated "Advocates of Fidelity in Christian Endeavor"; the Evangelical Association declare themselves in favor of the "Keystone League of Christian Endeavor"; the United Brethren in Christ have, in a spirit of Christian fairness, declared that where a society takes the prayer-meeting pledge, it should take the name "Christian Endeavor"; while the Methodists of Canada are thoroughly committed to the "Epworth League of Christian Endeavor," a happy combination of the denominational and interdenominational names if such a combination is desired. Surely never so fully as to-day could Christian Endeavorers rejoice in the attitude of the denominations toward their society, with possibly one or, at the most, two exceptions.

New York still leads all the States, Territories, and Provinces in the number of societies, having 2,532; Pennsylvania is next, with 1,829, Illinois third, with 1,477; Ohio fourth, having 1,363 societies; Massachusetts, with 1,055, is fifth, and Iowa close behind, with 1,024. At St. Louis two years ago a badge-banner made up of badges from hundreds of societies was displayed amidst much enthusiasm. Acting upon the suggestion made by a delegate, it was decided to place that banner for one year in the custody of the State, Territory, or Province that should show the greatest proportionate increase in its number of local societies during the coming year. Oklahoma carried that banner away from Minneapolis, having made a wonderful record, increasing her list in one year *thirteen* times. Oklahoma is here to-day, and brings her banner; and, notwithstanding she has more than thrice as many societies as she had at Minneapolis, she cannot take the banner back this year, for another has outstripped her. The banner for the greatest *proportionate* increase of societies made this last year goes across the imaginary line to Manitoba, where Christian Endeavor, like their wheat, is graded No. 1 hard. Oklahoma makes the next best showing, then North Carolina, Idaho, and Prince Edward Island, in the order named.

You will remember that at St. Louis it was also decided that another badge-banner should be made and given at Minneapolis to the State, Territory, or Province that should show the greatest *absolute* gain in one year. Pennsylvania captured that banner, and it has been displayed at many a convention within the Keystone State during the last year. She, too, notwithstanding a great record again this year, will have to relinquish its possession, and turn the banner over, not to another State, but to a Province, Ontario! Ontario has made a net gain of 372 societies. That is the progress made in one year. Pennsylvania is next, and very close, with 366; Ohio, with 302, is third; Iowa, with 238, fourth: and Indiana fifth, with 235; and so on down the long list.

The growth in the South-land is particularly gratifying. President Clark visited their conventions this year, as I did last season; and we can say, from having been on the ground, that Christian Endeavor is to bind the hearts of the young people of the sunny South, not only to their own churches, but to the hearts of their brothers and sisters in the Northern States. If time permitted, I should like to give you a detailed account of "what God hath wrought," particularly in Tennessee, Georgia, Alabama, Texas, Louisiana, Arkansas, and Kentucky.

But there is still another banner to be given at this convention with the others to-morrow afternoon.

In March, 1884, the first Junior Society of Christian Endeavor was organized in Tabor, Iowa, by Rev. J. W. Cowan. And to-day there are hundreds of local unions of Junior societies. No branch of Christian Endeavor has a larger promise of usefulness. In every way are the Juniors being heard from. No convention program, be it local, State, or international, is complete unless generous provisions are made for the Juniors and their work.

Last year 855 societies had reported. There were many more, but we could not get any word from them. This year the Junior work has stepped forward indeed. Junior superintendents of State, Territorial, and Provincial unions, and of local societies, your work has been wonderfully blessed of God.

Notwithstanding it is particularly difficult to gather statistics from Junior societies, we have actually enrolled 1,719 this year, making a total to-day of 2,574 Junior societies of which we know. Illinois stood first last year, with 122 societies. She still stands first, and will carry away the new Junior banner, as she has regularly reported Junior societies to the number of 266; Pennsylvania is not very far behind, and is second, with 257; New York next, with 214; Iowa and Massachusetts each have 153; and Minnesota 150. Make way, I say, for the Junior movement: it bids fair to rival any of the streams of Christian Endeavor that are making glad the city of our God.

I want to make somewhat of a break right here, and refer to the work in other countries than ours. First, as to our own brethren and sisters of Canada. I have been in the Provincial conventions, and know of what I speak. Our friends are made of the right stuff, and rally with us under the blood-stained banner of the cross, with the Union Jack in one hand and the other clasped in one of ours, while we march by their side with the Stars and Stripes; and shoulder to shoulder we present a united front against the forces of sin, as soldiers of the King of kings and Lord of lords. Canadians, we salute you. Yea, verily, we will all be at Montreal in '93.

From all Canada there have been reports received from 1,377 societies,— quite an increase over the 829 societies reported at Minneapolis from within her borders. The five Provinces having the greatest number of societies are as follows: Ontario, 830; Nova Scotia, 268; Quebec, 97; New Brunswick, 57; and Manitoba, 42.

Indeed, the Christian Endeavor movement has become international in its world-wide fellowship. In Australia the growth has been phenomenal, rivalling the great strides made in this land. Last year we had 82 societies reported from Australia; to-day we have enrolled 232 societies, and more are forming each week. England, the old mother country, now has 300 societies; and her second national convention, held not so very long ago, had the true Christian Endeavor flavor and atmosphere. You will be interested to know of some of the other foreign and missionary lands. There are 32 societies enrolled from India; from Turkey, 20; Mexico, 19; the West Indies, 12; Samoa, 9; Africa, 9; China, 9; Japan, 6; and so on, from Bermuda, Brazil, Chili, Norway, Spain, Persia, the Hawaiian Islands, and from almost every land. The total from foreign and missionary lands is now 648.

The constitution has been translated, and it is printed in the following languages: German, Swedish, Norwegian, French, Danish, Dutch, Spanish, Tamil, Chinese, Japanese.

That leads me to mention one of the best features of our work. More and more are Christian Endeavor societies becoming missionary forces. I wish the time permitted me to read some of the letters that I have received from secretaries and treasurers of denominational missionary boards, which give definite information of tens of thousands of dollars added to their respective treasuries from Christian Endeavor societies. These results have been brought about very largely through the Fulton pledge-plan of giving two cents per week individually, which has been adopted so generously all over the United States and Canada. Rev. A. A. Fulton, whom we heard at Minneapolis last year while home on his furlough, is now doing hand-to-hand personal work for our Master in China. His stay here of one year was wonderfully blessed of God. His *pledge-plan* was first presented to the societies in his own denomination, the Presbyterian. Like the Christian Endeavor Society, it could not be kept in any one denomination, and now nearly every denomination is feeling the impulse of the Fulton plan. The United Society has commended the enterprise from the start, and furnishes a book free of charge to every society that makes application.

I must also take time to refer to the fact that hundreds have signed the following covenant: —

"We covenant with the Lord, and with those who enter with us into the fellowship of this consecration, that we will devote a proportionate part of our income, not less than one-tenth, to benevolent and religious purposes. And this we do in his name, who hath loved us, and hath given himself for us, our Lord and Saviour Jesus Christ."

Indeed we are to have a revival of practical Christian stewardship, and I pray for great results the coming year. *Systematic and proportionate giving to God.!* Let this be one of our watchwords to go hand in hand with "Fidelity and Fellowship." "But this I say, he which soweth sparingly shall reap sparingly: and he which soweth bountifully shall reap also bountifully. (2 Cor. 9: 6.)

The Christian Endeavor local-union idea is assuming larger and better proportions every month. It contains so much of the blessed idea of interdenominational fellowship, and its possibilities in the way of inspiration and fraternity are so large, that it is evidently an institution that has come to stay. Many of these unions are doing practical work through their missionary, executive, correspondence, lookout, press, and visiting committees. More and more are these Christian Endeavor unions becoming evangelistic forces. In passing I want to mention some of the largest Christian Endeavor city unions. The figures named include the *Juniors.* Philadelphia, the largest, and in many ways a model, is composed of 280 societies; Chicago is next, with 244; New York has 124. Cleveland has 96; Brooklyn, 95; St. Louis, 94; Minneapolis, 91; Baltimore, 81.

The annual conventions, held in the various States, Territories and Provinces, have been wonderful gatherings. They grow materially, and are becoming great springs of spiritual refreshment. Their helpfulness in the past suggests even greater fields of usefulness for the future. Shall we not, more than ever in the past, aid the officers of these various unions in their services, which are always freely and gratuitously given, — busy pastors and busy men and women, as many of them are? You have but to read the reports of the State, Territorial, and Provincial conventions held since the Minneapolis convention, from the first one of the Maritime Provincial Union to the ones very lately held in Tennesee and Ohio, to find sufficient warrant for their existence. May God continue to bless them abundantly.

The printing department of the United Society has prospered, largely through the good business management of our agent, Mr. William Shaw. Mention is made of this, as it is often asked how so large a work as that accomplished by the United Society of Christian Endeavor can be carried on without asking the societies for a penny to pay expenses from one year's end to the other, while at the same time the only source of income is from the sale of the badges and literature, and from the printing done for local societies. The answer is, that everything is conducted in the most economical way, and that very much service is rendered to the societies "free, gratis, for nothing." We do not know of any organization to which so much time and labor is gratuitously and gladly given.

One of the most important factors in the promotion of Christian Endeavor during the last few years, particularly the year just ending, is the work of the press, particularly the denominational religious press. There is scarcely a leading religious journal in the country that does not have its regular column devoted to news from the societies and to the exposition of the uniform prayer-meeting topics.

The good-literature committees have been doing a good work in extending the circulation of their denominational religious papers. The gospel can be preached with printer's ink most effectively in these days, and your own church paper contains not only denominational news and matters of denominational interest, but the gospel concerning the advancement of the kingdom of God in all parts of the earth. Why not make a resolve that before next January every family connected with your church shall be supplied with some good religious paper by which each member of the family, from grandfather to ten-year-old Johnny, shall be helped? Who knows how many souls will be won as the result of the year's work of the good-literature committee in this line?

And what shall I say of *The Golden Rule?* Occupying a field of its own, it is supplementary to all other papers. I desire to say, with all the personality I can put behind my words, that *The Golden Rule* has been always, and is to-day, a great blessing to the cause of Christian Endeavor. It has modestly made its own way, seeking to give the best methods of work to young people that are striving to work "for Christ and the Church." Its editors and the officers of the United Society have constantly said, by voice and pen, that they believed that it had its own field, and in no way made itself a substitute for any denominational paper. It desires to make itself useful to every Christian Endeavor society and at the same time an ally of every denominational paper.

This report is already too long. I have no time to touch upon some of the practical results of the work of the societies and unions. I must rapidly pass them over as they come to me. Such as an increased attendance upon the part of the young people upon all regular church services and the midweek prayer-meeting; the definite and practical work of the various committees; the acceptance of the new, revised pledge by hundreds of societies previously organized with the first pledge; the systematic study of the Bible, and an ever-increasing knowledge of its use in hand-to-hand work for the saving of souls; a vigorous attack upon all forms of doubtful amusements; open hostility to every plan for destroying in any way the sanctity of the Sabbath Day, illustrated by the united desire to exert an influence upon the directors of the Columbian Exposition that will prompt them to keep their doors closed on Sunday; aggressively waged war against intemperance and the sale and manufacture of intoxicating beverages of all kinds; a clearer understanding that the society is only a means to an end; a determination to get good and to do good; a desire for a modest and teachable spirit; hearts aflame with the love of Christ; a greater and increasing spirit of love for our church and a closer bond of union between the society and the Sunday school.

Believing that there are many matters that I have not even touched upon, let me give you the best of all the statistics I have gathered for your interest.

I have been speaking a good deal about the growth of local societies, local, State, Territorial, and Provincial unions, the forward movement denominationally, etc., and have not referred to our individual members. The importance of individualism is made manifest more and more in our work and in many ways. We do not forget our part and our work in this warfare. We believe in co-operation; and we also believe in individualism, and emphasize it prominently by accepting for ourselves, individually, definite pledged service. You will agree with me, of course, that the growth of the local societies "is marvellous in our eyes"; but what can we say when we consider some of the additions made to our churches from this rapidly increasing international and interdenominational host? Listen. God only knows all the results of our individual labors. Last year with thankful hearts we sang, "Praise God from whom all blessings flow," when we found that 82,500 of our members had become church members in the year. How much or how little of our own individual work or that of the society had influenced this blessed result, we knew not; sufficiently happy and thankful were we to know that these additions, to the number of so many thousands, had come from our membership. Another year! what would it bring forth?

How many souls could be won to the Lord Jesus Christ in the coming year? was the thought emphasized so strongly over and over again in the closing hours of the Minneapolis convention. Let me recall one scene at the closing consecration meeting. Dr. Chapman is almost through his spirited and spiritual address. He is saying, "I plead for entire consecration. In the days of old Rome, when the *sacramentum*, or oath, was given to the soldiers, the leader of the detachment that was to be sworn to live and die for the senate and the people of Rome read over to all the *sacramentum*, and then the right-hand man held up his right hand and repeated the words, 'The same for me'; and down it went along the line until the last left-hand man held up his right hand, in what he thought the most holy attitude, and swore the same oath. Are we thus ready? Who will say it? My time for God, my thought for God, my strength for God, my all, my all, my body, soul, and spirit for him, who will say it — 'The same for me, the same for me'?" You remember that the whole audience of thousands stood later, and with uplifted hands we promised that with God's help we would try to lead at least one soul to Christ during the year; and while we were still standing, Dr. Hoyt voiced our prayer of consecration. Listen. Do you not, many of you, remember the hour, as I repeat the prayer? "O Lord Jesus, thou didst utterly give thyself for us. We do now utterly yield ourselves to thee for this service. We will attempt to win souls for thee. Accept our consecration; give us souls; put upon us the power of the Holy Spirit. Be thou in us and upon us, O thou empowering Spirit, and as never before, because we consecrate ourselves to thee with earnest and full hearts. May thy kingdom come, O Lord, through us, to thy glory. For Jesus's sake. Amen."

God is answering that prayer. The thousands went home to their churches and their societies; and hand-to-hand, effective personal work has been done under God's guidance. The word, "The same for me," has been passed along the line, from State to State, town to town, society to society; and thousands of associate members have been won to him. Praises be to him, the Giver of all gifts.

At the time of the last international convention 168,162 of our membership were in the associate lists. During the last year we find that over 120,000 of our members have become church members. The past year's history has been the most notable, the growth unprecedented; and to know that, better than all that, 120,000 have joined our churches is to proclaim in the best possible way our motto, "For Christ and the Church."

You rejoice in this: well you may. God grant we may with modest and teachable spirits take up the greater work before us in the coming year. We now number 1,370,200. Think of it! 1,370,200 individuals banded together for service. Our responsibilities are equal in number to our opportunities. What shall another year bring forth? God will answer in his good time. May he give us the strength and grace needed for another year's campaign under the leadership of our Saviour King, Jesus Christ.

At the close of the reading of the report, which was frequently interrupted by applause, Rev. R. W. Brokaw read the following telegram, to be sent to Mr. Baer: —

"The Eleventh International Convention of the Young People's Societies of Christian Endeavor learns with deep sorrow of your illness. It thus expresses its sincere love and sympathy. May God speedily restore your health. We earnestly pray for you."

This telegram was accepted with unanimous and hearty approval. The congregation then sang the Doxology, and the benediction was pronounced by Rev. Dr. I. O. Adams, of Arkansas.

THURSDAY EVENING.

The evening service opened with a prayer and praise service, led by Mr. E. B. Clark, of Denver, Col., in which the great audience, which crowded every part of the building, joined heartily.

At eight o'clock the assembly was called to order by Rev. Henry T. McEwen, chairman of the committee of '92, who spoke as follows:—

Mr. McEwen: It is the duty of presiding officers to introduce men who can speak, and not to try to speak themselves. If I should begin to talk about the growth of the Christian Endeavor society, I should keep you here until midnight, and none of the distinguished gentlemen on the platform, who can perform that task better than I, would get a hearing.

But I should like to say that it gives me pleasure to note the evidences of the fact that we seem to have surprised the New Yorkers since this morning. They have been looking at the thousands of people they have met, wearing Christian Endeavor badges, with amazement, and I fancy they will be still more amazed before we go away.

When we were in Minneapolis, the committee from Montreal were anxious to have the convention of '92 held in that city. The chief argument which they urged against its coming to New York was, that New York was too big to shake. [*Applause and laughter.*] New York, it was said, was so big that the society of Christian Endeavor could not make an impression on it. Well, our chairman said, in reply, that if New York was so big, that was the very place the convention should go to. The society of Christian Endeavor, with the help of God, was ready to undertake anything — even to shaking New York. [*Cheers.*]

The committee of '92 had many obstacles to meet in making ready for this convention. You know that the reporters are thought to know everything. Well, when I told them that we would have 20,000 members of the society of Christian Endeavor at our convention, they looked at me as though I had just come out of an insane asylum — and shouldn't have come. We sent them statistics to show them that 20,000 would be here. And the next day the newspapers — to save our reputation for veracity, I suppose — stated that 10,000 would be here, and thought they had done very well. [*Laughter and applause.*]

Then there was another difficulty which we had to encounter. We couldn't get the hotel men to appreciate the numerical importance of the convention. A committeeman visited one of the hotels. He approached the young man behind the desk, and asked him if the hotel could accommodate some of the delegates.

"O yes," the clerk said, smiling blandly: "bring 'em on; we'll take 'em all."

"How many can you take?"

"Why," said the clerk, "we could take in sixteen hundred."

And when our committeeman told him that there would be nearer sixteen thousand than sixteen hundred, he only looked bland, and said nothing. [*Laughter.*]

And then there was another difficulty. We couldn't get the railroad men to wake up to the importance of the convention. We couldn't make them believe it was necessary to prepare unusual accommodations. I think they woke up this last week. [*Laughter.*]

We have not only made an impression on the reporters, coming more than thirty thousand strong — the hotel men know the society of Christian Endeavor, and the railroad men have realized its importance — but, in addition to all this, we have made an impression on this great city. The people have wakened to something of the vastness of the society's importance. They have rejoiced that so many young men and so many young women have declared for Christ. [*Loud applause.*]

The other day, when I told a newspaper reporter that there was not an office within the gift of the Christian Endeavor society; that there were no emoluments, and that the speakers got nothing for their services, except their expenses, he was not only surprised, but was profoundly impressed. We are giving to the Lord God Almighty, through this Christian Endeavor movement, the very best physical strength, the very best brain, and the very best heart of the young people of this and other countries. [*Applause.*]

Now I suppose you will be surprised that a man who has been so busy the last few weeks as I have should be a little sorry to lay down the work; yet I am. It has been an inspiring thing to sit at my desk and receive in a single mail letters from China, from India, from Japan, from Spain, from the farthest western borders of our own country, and from the far off provinces of Canada, speaking one language, stirred by one mighty impulse for the Lord God of hosts. It has been a grand thing for me to be permitted to meet and to represent the societies of New York and Brooklyn, — a loyal, loving set of men and women who have pulled together in the good old-fashioned way. You country boys and girls — and I am a country boy, too [*applause*] — remember how a team goes up a steep hill, — the whiffle tree just about straight across the tongue, now a little forward, and then a little back, but still steadily moving upward and onward. So have these societies pulled together steadily and lovingly. Although there is a bridge across the river, and the river between, the Spirit of God is more powerful than bridge and river, and makes our hearts beat as one in the mighty work which the Lord God has given us to do here. [*Applause.*] So, then, as the representative of the New York and Brooklyn Christian Endeavor societies, I bid you one and all a most cordial welcome to our beautiful cities, — beautiful in everything, and needing only the grace of God to perfect their magnificent beauty. We pray that the Spirit of Christ and his church may so permeate these cities that they shall be known in the future, not only for their wealth, for their commercial ability, for their fashion, for their intelligence, for their vice, — no, but known everywhere for their righteousness. For that end we work, and we urge you to pray for and with us, and to work with us. [*Applause.*]

About the pleasantest thing I am ever able to remember with reference to a presiding officer is that he gets the program through on time, and says very little himself. I have great pleasure in introducing to you one whom I am sure you will be very glad to meet, both because of his position and because of his personal worth. I have the pleasure and the honor of introducing to you our new Secretary of State, Hon. J. W. Foster.

As Secretary Foster stepped to the front he was received by the most enthusiastic applause and the waving of handkerchiefs.

REMARKS OF HON. J. W. FOSTER.

Mr. Chairman: — I count myself fortunate in being in New York to-day, and in having the opportunity of drawing new inspiration for duty by contact with this great army of young soldiers of Christ. We hear much, from certain quarters, in this day about the decay of evangelical religion, and of the growth of agnosticism and the various forms of disbelief which are to sweep off the earth our Bibles and our Christianity. Would that these critics might stand in my place to-night! They might be led to believe that faith in a risen Saviour and in an inspired Word of God were neither dead nor dying in this land [*applause*], — this Christian land, which owes all that is greatest and best in its past history and in its present attainment to this religion. I desire to present my humble recognition of the great work this society is doing for our country and our God, and to wish you Godspeed in your grand work. [*Applause.*]

The hymn, "My Country, 't is of Thee," was then sung with great effect, and amid much enthusiasm.

Mr. ECEWEN: I have very great pleasure now in simply stepping out of the way, that a better-known man may take my place and deliver to you an address which you are all anticipating with longing. Dr. Francis E. Clark, president of the United Society of Christian Endeavor.

President Clark then came forward to read his address, and was greeted with such an ovation as all Christian Endeavorers love to give to the honored founder of the society. At its conclusion Dr. Clark spoke as follows:—

ANNUAL ADDRESS OF PRESIDENT FRANCIS E. CLARK.

CHRISTIAN ENDEAVOR MORE THAN A SOCIETY — A PROVIDENTIAL MOVEMENT.

Is the Young People's Society of Christian Endeavor a mere society, or a providential movement? More than at first appears is involved in this question. If it is simply an organization, like one of a thousand others that exist and have existed, we can afford to disregard its principles and its progress. If it is a mere wave of foamy, youthful enthusiasm cast upon the shore of our century, we may expect it to ebb as rapidly as it has flowed, and we need not greatly concern ourselves with its past, its present, or its future.

But if the Christian Endeavor Society is a great providential movement born of God in his own good time, then we must look into God's design, and shape our course by the divine compass.

I will try to prove that the society is a religious movement, and not a mere organization. I summon its origin, its history, its adaptability, its imitators, to prove it.

To look at its origin in this light, to be sure, takes all glory from men. It makes it impossible for any one to boast. No farmer is egotistical enough to grow conceited over the seed that sprouts in the mellow soil of springtime. An architect may boast of his magnificent structures in stone and marble, but unless he is a fool, he will not boast of the oak tree in his front yard, for he did not design the tree or erect it. Equally true is it that man did not design or erect the Christian Endeavor movement. It grew from a seed, and that seed was of God's planting. No man could have hastened its growth or greatly retarded it.

It is always to be borne in mind that no ecclesiastical authority called the Christian Endeavor Society into being. No council of the Fathers decreed it. No assembly or conference said it must come. This society had the same quiet origin as the Sunday school, the missionary movement, and the temperance crusade. The world cared nothing for the beginning of any of these efforts. It knew no more of their beginning than a busy city knows about or cares for the dropping of an acorn in the forest. Ah, but there is life in the acorn, and it grows. There was divine life in this Christian Endeavor seed, and it grew. That is its history in a single sentence. Man may build a house; God builds a tree. Man may start a society; God starts a movement.

The subseqeunt history of the society makes this proposition still plainer. The means put forth to advance its interests are utterly inadequate to account for its marvellous growth. Remember that there has never been any churchly authority to force it upon the churches, no denominational pride or *esprit de corps* has been appealed to; no great corporation has stood behind it. In fact, it has made its way in spite of ecclesiastical opposition in many quarters. What, then, accounts for these 22,000 societies and a million and one-third members that girdle the earth? The visible human means are utterly inadequate to account for them. A few leaflets, a book or two; a United Society that exercises no authority, claims no allegiance, levies no taxes, accepts no contribu-

REV. FRANCIS E. CLARK, D. D.

tions; the State and local unions, which, so far as authority and control go, are equally powerless. How can we account for the unparalleled growth, for this magnificent convention which is the beautiful flower of this plant? There is only one way to account for it. *This is no man's society. This is God's movement.*

Again, the adaptability of this society proclaims it to be not a manufactured article, but God's method of reaching young hearts. A mere society might be fitted to one climate and totally unfitted to another; it might flourish in one denomination and utterly wither in another. A mere society is necessarily local and inflexible. A former honored president of the New York Union framed an epigram which will live, when he said, "The Christian Endeavor Society is as strong as steel and as flexible as ribbon."

If the representatives of the different denominations this year speak as they have hitherto declared themselves at our conventions, each one will tell us that the society is exactly in accord with the genius of his own denomination. The Methodist finds in it fire, fervency, and testimony; the Presbyterian, steadfast covenant-keeping; [*applause*] the Baptist and Congregationalist, local self-government, which, however, is not incompatible with churchly control, and voluntary individual consecration; the Episcopalian finds child-nurture and training; the Disciple of Christ, the communion of saints; the Friend, a constant moving of the Holy Spirit upon young hearts; the Lutheran, the very spirit of the Reformation. In every denomination is it equally at home, because everywhere its cardinal doctrine is loyalty, unswerving and unswervable, to the local church. [*Applause*].

It seems to bear transportation, too, and to keep equally well in every climate. The churches in Old England find here principles which they can use. Our brothers and sisters at the antipodes adopt them as eagerly as if they lived within sight of "Liberty Enlightening the World"; India, China, Japan, Turkey, South Africa, Samoa, the Sandwich Islands,—all have their Christian Endeavor contingents. "It exactly suits our particular needs," is the delightfully monotonous testimony of letters from all parts of the world.

It is flexible and adaptable, too, in its forms of opposition to evil. Protean as are the shapes of evil, this movement is always found opposed to the devil, whatever livery he wears. In Louisiana the society is anti-lottery; in Utah it is anti-Morman; at the Columbian Fair it is anti-Sabbath-breaking, [*prolonged applause*] and throughout all the land it is anti-rum.

The very names by which the pledge is affectionately called declare its flexibility and adaptability. In the Maritime Provinces it is called the "best hook to catch and hold young Christians;" in California and Montana it is called not the iron-clad pledge, but the "gold-bound pledge," and a minister of Minnesota, a wheat-growing State, originated the happy name for the pledge, "the patent Christian Endeavor self-binder." [*Loud applause.*]

The very imitators, who in large numbers have adopted everything but our name and our fellowship, prove the flexibility of the Christian Endeavor principles. But this is not a pleasant subject. I will only say that it is another proof, if proof were needed, added to the origin, the history, and the adaptability of Christian Endeavor, to show that it is not merely a society, but a *God-given, God-protected, God-advanced movement.*

If, then, it is accepted that the Christian Endeavor Society is a movement that has God's centuries in which it may develop, let us ask what are the principles which God has been able to use and bless. A great movement cannot grow without principles beneath it any more than a tree can grow without roots. It cannot long exist on froth or foam, or even on enthusiasm and youthful zeal. The time has gone by when the Society can be waved one side as the frothy product of beardless exuberance

What are these principles? It is sufficient to refer to them very briefly, for this whole convention will ring with them. Every State convention and local union emphasizes them, and every individual society that is worthy of the name in all the land exemplifies them. They are taught by no theory, but by the experience of these eleven years. These four principles, if I know anything about the matter, are PLEDGED INDIVIDUAL LOYALTY, CONSECRATED DEVOTION, ENERGETIC SERVICE, INTERDENOMINATIONAL FELLOWSHIP. These, then, are the four driving wheels of the movement, — pledged individual loyalty, consecrated devotion, energetic service, interdenominational fellowship. [*Applause.*]

The first driving wheel of the Christian Endeavor movement is *Pledged Individual Loyalty.* Every year makes the folly of trying to start a Christian Endeavor society without the pledge more evident. Every week sees societies and individuals accepting the pledge more and more heartily and unanimously, and living up to to it more strenuously. Objections and objectors have largely disappeared. Throughout Christian Endeavordom, at least, the pledge is now understood and admitted to be scriptural, reasonable, essential. One of the most glorious eras of the Presbyterian Church was the days of the Covenanters, and every church has had its covenanters. That era is not past, thank God, though the covenant may no longer be sealed in blood. The era of the Christian Endeavor Society is growing more glorious, because it is becoming increasingly and more emphatically a society of covenanters. [*Applause.*]

Notice, please, that every line of the Christian Endeavor pledge is a covenant of loyalty. In Christ's strength this covenant is made, — "Trusting in the Lord Jesus Christ for strength, I promise him that I will strive to do whatever he would like to have me do"; a covenant of loyalty in our private devotion, — "I will read the Bible and pray every day"; a covenant of loyalty to the individual church, — "I will support my own church in every way, especially by attending all her Sunday and midweek services"; a covenant of outspoken loyalty again to Christ, — "I will be present at and take some part in every Christian Endeavor prayer meeting." Not only a pledge is this, but a pledge to loyalty; not only a promise, but a promise of faithful service for some church at some particular time.

This is our bulwark, our defence, our high tower. It is not an immovable fortress in which we wait an attack; it is our *testudo,* our movable shield, behind which we move out to attack the enemy's citadels of indifference, laziness, false timidity, and worldliness.

The second driving wheel of the movement is *Consecrated Devotion.* Our society does not profess to be a religious debating society, or a literary or seriocomic club. [*Applause.*] It is not a cross between an old-fashioned lyceum and a prayer meeting. It hesitates not to say that there is but one meeting absolutely essential to a Christian Endeavor society, and that is the prayer meeting. Everything about the society centres around and draws its life from the prayer meeting. It constantly tries to raise the religious standard of the members, and leaves it to other excellent organizations to raise their literary and social standards. It continually seeks to say to them, in the ringing tones of William Carey, "Your business, young men and women, is to preach the Gospel;" and you keep store or work on the farm, go to school or do housework, as he cobbled shoes, "to pay expenses."

The third driving wheel of the movement is *Energetic Service.* It is no dreamy, introspective, hermit-like religion that is taught or practiced by Christian Endeavorers. The society believes in doing, as well as praying. It tingles with the bounding life of the nineteenth century. It not only preaches, but practices. Frequent confession of Christ is offset and balanced by constant work for Christ. Not only is there one prayer meeting every week, but from three to twenty committees are busy every day. Not only is the monthly consecration meeting essential, but the effort which alone gives one something new to consecrate is equally essential. This most excellent counter-irritant, this most admirable corrective of sluggish morals, this irrisistible stimulant for sleepy Christians, this unexcelled blister for paralyzed legs that cannot run on God's errands, and withered hands that cannot find their way to the bottom of the pocket when the contribution-box is passed — religious service — is found in these innumerable lines of committee work, which provide for every possible form of activity, and which do anything that the church wishes to have done. Cannot our local unions do more than they have yet done, grand as the work has been in some places, to shut up the rumshop and brand the saloon, to stop the Sunday baseball game, to close the Sunday theatre, and to fight municipal misrule and corruption in all its hideous forms?

The fourth driving wheel of the Christian Endeavor movement is *Interdenominational Spiritual Fellowship*. [*Applause.*] If any one thing has been made clear by the history of these eleven years, it is God's design to bring the young people of all evangelical denominations together, not for the sake of denouncing denominations or decrying creeds, but in a common fellowship that respects differences and believes in diversity. The fears of those who thought the society would destroy all distinctive beliefs, and demolish the principles for which the fathers suffered persecution, have been largely allayed, for it has come to be acknowledged that the society makes every young person more loyal to his own, at the same time that it makes him more generous toward others. [*Applause.*] As some one has wittily remarked, "it has not broken down the denominational wire fences, it has only taken the barbs off them." And O, my friends, would anything induce us to give up our fellowship and to divide ourselves into denominational clans as young people?

After tasting the sweetness of obeying our Lord's command "that ye love one another," after enjoying the fellowship which obeys our Lord's prayer "that they all may be one," after feeling the thrill of our elbowtouch as we have closed up our ranks to march against the common enemy, can anything separate us?

These four principles, then, characterize this movement. *The consecration meeting, the committee work, the pledge to outspoken loyalty, the unsectarian fellowship,* — these must be of God's ordering, because they are God-blessed. These are what make the society more than an organization, — a world-wide movement.

But, it may be said, these principles are nothing new. The church has always believed in consecrated service, in covenant obligations, and theoretically, at least, in fellowship. Such a statement is open to doubt, as the wars of the sects, the opposition to the Christian Endeavor Society, and the bitter hostility to the pledge in many places, indicate. But, even admitting that theoretically and partially they have been accepted, it can be proved that never *in their combinations and proportions* has God before brought them into a great world-encircling fellowship. Never before has he used them as the driving wheels of such a religious movement.

This movement is not the outgrowth of any one denomination. It is not due to the Methodist class meeting, or to the Baptist covenant meeting, or to the Presbyterian catechism, or to the Congregational individuality. God has doubtless taken an element from each, but he has combined them into new proportions and into a *new movement*. If this is so, then I claim that the society has a right to its history, its name, and its principles. There are a few who would deny it this right; who will not understand that it means anything, or has any rights which sectarian prejudice may not appropriate or trample upon. Its name is sometimes — not often, I am glad to believe, in these days, but sometimes — applied to a deaf and dumb, gelatinous kind of affair, without any backbone of obligation; a something called a Christian Endeavor society, deaf to the promptings of the Spirit, dumb in the prayer meeting. and with one or two feeble antennæ, instead of strong arms of committee service. Such a so-called Christian Endeavor society brings disgrace and reproach upon the whole fraternity, the only mitigating feature being that it usually dies an untimely and unlamented death. More often, these principles — with the exception of the fellowship — are all taken and the name ignored for sectarian purposes. The Christian Endeavor society antedated by years all other similar young people's societies of importance, — a fact that is sometimes denied, and often forgotten; and I say that these eleven years have given it a claim to its principles as well as to its name, and that it is not too much to ask, in Christian fairness. that its name be taken when its principles in the usual combination are taken. No patent or copyright is claimed, but is there not a moral right here? Even before the days of international copyright, no honorable publisher took another's book, made a few verbal changes in it, and gave it a new title, and published it as his own. There are other statutes besides patent laws and copyright enactments which will protect the Christian Endeavor Society in its use of its name and principles, and these statutes are called Christian courtesy and brotherly fairness. All honor to that denomination which recently decreed that when a society within its ranks took the pledge, it ought to be called a Christian Endeavor society. These unwritten statutes will keep our Christian Endeavor unions and conventions made up of Christian Endeavor societies in name and fact. They will keep the movement true to the principles of Individual Consecration, Devoted Service, Pledged Loyalty, and Interdenominational Fellowship; and these principles, thus combined, will be guaranteed by the name "Christian Endeavor." [*Prolonged applause.*]

Finally, if this is a world-wide, God-sent movement, it has a claim upon the consideration of Christian people. Not that it would force itself upon any one. Christian Endeavor never enters at an unwilling door. If there is a better way of organizing young people, we certainly wish to know it; and we will all speedily adopt it, and will take the name of the new organization with its principles. But if this is such a providential organization as we fondly believe it to be, it has the same claim upon the churches, at least to examine it carefully, as has the Sunday-school or the missionary movement.

The only ground on which Christians can unite is the practical ground of Christlike effort, — endeavor. They cannot unite on doctrinal grounds; they cannot unite on grounds of church polity. They can unite in Christian effort, which requires no oneness of doctrine or polity, no organic union, no ecclesiastical sameness. I rejoice that everywhere the denominations are accepting this thought, and more and more are recognizing the society in a broad and brotherly way, as the report of our honored Secretary shows. [*Applause.*]

Some, however, are trying now, perhaps inadvertently, to break up our fellowship by introducing into the Christian Endeavor unions various incongruous elements,— all kinds of young people's societies. A few unions have already been destroyed in this way. For this reason, to preserve the very basis of our fellowship, it is necessary to see to it in our local, State, and national unions that the name goes with the principles, and the principles with the name. [*Applause.*] I cannot do better than to quote the forceful words of another on this subject: "This plea for preserving the integrity of the Christian Endeavor name and principles is not, as some one has unfairly put it, an invitation for all the other young people's societies to come and join the Christian Endeavor Society. It is not a struggle for the credit of having originated the name. It is a modest and patient presentation of the incontrovertible fact that the only ground on which unity among Christians is at present feasible is this basis of applied Christianity, and the further fact that unity cannot be expressed by a half-dozen names: it must have one commonly accepted term. It is not an association of heterogeneous elements; it is not a congress of churches or a consensus of opinions that is wanted to express the idea of a united front to the foes of Christ; it is a common purpose expressed in a common name, and what name so fitting as 'Christian Endeavor'? There can be nothing broader. There can be nothing more really interdenominational than this." [*Applause.*]

But whether others accept these principles or reject them, whether they come into our fellowship or refuse it, our duty is plain, Christian Endeavorers,— not to glory in a name, or strive for a mere organization; the organization, without the dominating Spirit of God, is less than the least of all things, — but our duty is also our privilege: to recognize as in the past the guiding hand of God; to maintain in their integrity these principles which he has so blessed; to seek an enlargement of our fellowship on this basis of practical, pledged endeavor for Christ; to remember that our covenant, next to Christ, is with the local church with which we are connected. Then may we hope to have the closing years of this wonderful century crowned with a youthful Christian Endeavor such as the world has never seen. Then may we hope to hear, not a chorus of a million and one-third, but of many millions of youthful voices in every State and Province joining in the hymn, which shall be the battle hymn of the republic of God : —

> "Like a mighty army
>   Moves the church of God;
> Brothers, we are treading
>   Where the saints have trod;
> We are not divided,
>   All one body we;
> One in faith and doctrine,
>   One in charity." [*Loud applause.*]

This is our motto of last year voiced in one of the hymns of the ages. We cannot have a better motto for the year to come: "One is your Master, even Christ, and all ye are brethren." Will you not take it? Will you not *live* it? Then listen, my brothers, my sisters, and you will yet hear millions of youthful voices in this republic and our sister Canada, in England and Austria, in India and Africa, in China and Japan, in Samoa and Fiji, join with you in the chorus which ascribes mastership to Christ and united fellowship to Christ's brethren, and the prayer of Christ will be answered, "that they all may be one," the new commandment of Christ will be obeyed, "that ye love one another," and the mighty anthem of Christian Endeavor will roll around the world: "ONE IS YOUR MASTER, EVEN CHRIST, AND ALL YE ARE BRETHREN." [*Prolonged applause.*]

Following Dr. Clark's address the audience sang with much feeling the hymn, "Blest be the tie that binds," and also two verses of that other Christian Endeavor favorite (since the St. Louis Convention), "The Endeavor Band." Chairman McEwen then introduced the preacher of the annual sermon, Pres. J. W. Bashford, D. D., of Ohio Wesleyan University, who was likewise accorded an ovation.

SERMON BY PRESIDENT J. W. BASHFORD.

I desire to speak to you upon the conditions of successful work for Christ. I choose as the text the 6th verse of the 14th chapter of John: "I am the way, the truth, and the life."

The first condition of successful work for Christ is the mastery of the truth. A little while ago I was on the outside of this hall, and I desired very much to be

on the inside. I found a great many people who sympathized with me, but I found that that sympathy was not sufficient to get a man on the inside of this hall who was on the outside. I wanted somebody who knew the way by which I could be admitted. I finally succeeded in finding some such person. So it seems to me the first condition of success upon the part of young people who wish to lead other people to Christ, is that they themselves shall know the way to the King's high road, and be able to lead these wanderers back again. Emerson says: "That man is best heard in a public audience who knows most about the subject in hand." Socrates was accustomed to say that every man is sufficiently eloquent in that which he clearly understands. The first condition of success for our young people is a thorough mastery of the Word of God. We must study the Word more fully, if we are to be prepared to do the work which the heavenly Father wishes us to accomplish in the 20th century. A few years ago a layman went out from Chicago whose influence has reached around the globe. What is the secret of D. L. Moody's success? Surely, it is not his wonderful philosophy or his personal character, although his character is *one* of the secrets of his success. The reason that doctors of divinity and professors in our colleges and the common people sit spell-bound before D. L. Moody is, because that man has mastered, as almost no other man has, in our modern life, the Word of God, and is able to apply that to sin-sick souls. Only a little while ago we lost one of the greatest preachers of the whole world — a man who, for almost half a century, had had crowded audiences. What was the secret of Mr. Spurgeon's success? I imagine that it was his wonderful familiarity with this blessed Word of God, and his wonderful mastery of its truth. I am sure that if the young people are to do the work which the heavenly Father has in store for us, we must become, in the language of John Wesley, "Men of one Book." We must master that Book until we shall be able to apply its truths to other souls that are struggling in darkness. It is good to have a Bagster Bible under one's arm, but it is infinitely better to have the Word of God in our heads and in our hearts. So it seems to me that we need to master the Word of God in such a way that we shall get hold of its principles, and not simply be able to quote a text here and there at random. A man once asked Sir Isaac Newton the secret of his discoveries. Newton answered him: "Thinking, thinking, thinking." We need to emulate him in doing more thinking and meditating in our study of the Word of God.

But we need something more than the Word of God in our heads; we need it in our hearts, and we need to live it out in our lives. What is the reason that this age has become a scientific age? Why is it that all bow down to the name of Bacon, and honor him as the founder of our modern science? Simply because he called men back from abstract speculation and metaphysical subtleties to the test of experiment as the one method by which science was to be advanced. A skeptic said to me not long ago: "I marvel at the growth of the Christian Church in this scientific age. It seems to me to be an age of enlightenment, an age of science, an age of wonderful progress; and yet I am bound to confess that your Christian Church does make marvellous progress in this age of science. What is the reason for it?" I answered him that I thought it was because the Christian Church had applied the same method in the Christian life which Bacon had applied in the scientific age. John Wesley applied the same method of experiment in the Christian sphere which Bacon had applied in the material sphere. He found men busy with theological subtleties and metaphysical hair-splitting, and he called them back to experience as the test of the religious life. And if you and I, as young people, expect to help other young people, we must have our Bibles, not simply under our arms, and not simply in our heads, — our Bibles must become incarnate in our lives. So we shall become living epistles, known and read of all men. [*Applause.*]

What is the reason that Christianity is sure to conquer the world? We are standing face to face with Buddhism, with Confucianism, with Zoroastrianism, with Mohammedanism, and with various other forms of heathen faith. Thank God, there are members of this society in these heathen lands grappling with these great forms of error. Why is it that we are sure that Christianity is to conquer in this conflict? Simply because Jesus Christ knew the human heart, and he knew the heart of God, and Jesus Christ revealed the only principles by which modern society can live. As surely as modern society covets life more than death, as surely as we hope to grow spiritually, so surely we shall be obliged to come back to the principles of the New Testament as the guiding principles of our modern society. [*Applause.*]

Modern science has just come abreast of the Old Testament. What is the great doctrine of modern science to-day? It is the doctrine of law. Suppose that cholera, which has already broken out on the western shores of Asia, should sweep over Europe, and come here to this fair city, and suppose that we called together all the Christian men and women of the city in this great hall to hold a prayer meeting for the abatement of the scourge, and suppose that we called in our scientific friends to advise us before we began to pray! Those men would say to us, "Gentlemen, it is useless for you to pray until you have fulfilled the laws of God. Clean up the streets; make the city pure; abolish the conditions of the plague, and then, and then only, when obedient to the laws of God, can you hope to have the help of God to abate the plague." [*Applause.*] What is this doctrine of modern science but the echoing of the voice of Sinai? What is it but a reiteration of the doctrine of the law — that "whatsoever a man soweth, that shall he also reap"? The Old Testament is not a last year's almanac. It enunciates one great fundamental principle on which society lives, — the principle of law. The New Testament enunciates the other great fundamental principle — the principle of love. Give modern science another century for growth, and I imagine that she will come abreast of the New Testament and reiterate these two great doctrines — the doctrine of law, and the doctrine of love. In this way we shall solve every conflict like that which broke out yesterday at Homestead, over the details of which we have stood aghast to-day. Socialism is not the remedy, by any means. We must still reiterate the law; we must still insist on "whatsoever a man soweth, that shall he also reap"; we must still maintain that men shall have the reward of their labor. On the other hand, we must insist also on love as well as on law. Neither one of these alone will solve that problem. Only as we combine the doctrine that the laborer is worthy of only that which he can earn with the other doctrine of love for all men — only as we combine these two shall we solve the great problem between capital and labor.

So it seems to me that Christianity is sure to triumph, simply because the New Testament contains the principles on which alone society can exist.

But we need something more than the mastery of the truth. Jesus Christ had a marvellous mastery of the truth. Philosophers had been able to say in the past: " I know some part of the truth," but what philosopher had ever been able to say with Christ, " I am the truth"? But Jesus Christ did not conquer simply by his truth. He talked about God and eternity and the human soul — the most difficult and abstract subjects which can be presented to unconverted men; and yet he presented these truths in such parables and simple stories that the common people heard him gladly. We want something of the art of the Divine Master as well as the truth of the Divine Master, and that art, my friends, will only spring from love. Only as you love people will you discover the art by which you can win these people to Christ.

I think that among political speakers Henry Clay was, perhaps, the best illustration in our country of the art in his adaptation of truth to the people. I heard an illustration of this which I think I will mention, because it seems to me to convey a great truth. A gentleman from the North was on a visit to a friend in the South, residing in New Orleans. Mr. Clay was to address a jury in a noted case, and the Southern gentleman took his friend from the North into the court to listen to the famous orator. Mr. Clay spoke admirably for the first half-hour; then he repeated the argument during the second half-hour with different illustrations, and so he did during the third and fourth half-hours— repeating the argument four times before he gave the case to the jury. After the jury had retired, the Southern gentleman introduced his Northern friend, saying: " Mr. Clay, you were not at your best to-day." "What was the difficulty?" said Mr. Clay. "Why you spoke admirably for the first half-hour, then you repeated the speech three times more, and we were weary before you closed." Mr. Clay said: "Did you notice that juryman in blue jeans in that corner of the jury-box?" "No, what of him?" "Well, I saw that I had won eleven jurymen on the first presentation of the case, but one must win twelve jurymen to secure a verdict. I went over the argument a second time, and I saw that this twelfth man was dull and stupid, and partly opposed to me, but he began to waver a little. I went through the argument a third time, and he wavered still more. and I thought he was on my side. Then I went through the argument a fourth time, and that juryman in blue jeans came over to my side, and I will have the verdict when the verdict comes in." Mr. Clay won the verdict because he had tact to give line upon line and precept upon precept so that the dullest juryman was compelled to understand him. John Wesley's father said to his mother one day: "Why is it that you tell the boys over and over again, twenty times, a certain lesson?" "Because," said Mrs. Wesley, "the boys have not learned it when I have told them nineteen times." Mrs. Wesley was right. It was line upon line and precept upon precept that she trained up and gave to England two of the noblest sons of the 18th century. [*Applause.*]

I think, as an illustration of this art of adaptation, that Mr. Lincoln greatly surpassed Mr. Phillips. Mr. Phillips was the prophet of a new era. We needed, perhaps, such a man to stand upon the mountain-top, and point the American people to the heights they ought to reach, and to the depths in which they were grovelling. God forbid that the time should ever come when the memory of Wendell Phillips shall not be green in the hearts of the American people. [*Loud applause.*] Yet it seems to me that Mr. Lincoln was a greater statesman than Wendell Phillips. [*Applause.*] While Mr. Phillips stood upon the mountain height cursing the people in the valley below, Abraham Lincoln, like Paul, who became all things to all men that he might win some, Abraham Lincoln went down into the dusty valley of every-day life, not that he might abide there like a demagogue, but that he might lead the people up to the heights which Mr. Phillips occupied. [*Loud applause.*]

I am afraid that the applause is a little too hearty. Be careful that you do not carry this matter of adaptation too far. There are a great many politicians to-day who apologize for their conduct on the ground that they are trying to adapt their truth to the people. They need to aim a thousand miles higher, to reach the common sense and the consciences of the American people. Never empty your message of its truth. If there is anything that an American audience admires, if there is anything which human nature craves, it is the man who dares to stand and speak his convictions upon every subject. Speak the truth. But speak the truth in love.

We need not simply truth, not simply art, but we need personality back of both. Jesus Christ influenced the world marvellously by his truth; he influenced all the ages marvellously by his art; but greater than the truth of Christ, and greater than the art of Christ is the marvellous personality of our Saviour. We re-date our history, not from the parables of Christ, not from the Sermon on the Mount, but from the cross of our Lord Jesus Christ. Somebody said to Richelieu: "I could establish as good a religion as Jesus Christ, if I could only get a start in the work. How shall I get a start?" "I will advise you," said Richelieu, "to become such a reformer, such a leader of the race in truth, that the race will crucify you inside of three years, and then show such divine power as to rise from the grave in three days." [*Applause.*] So I am sure that it was the sacrifice of Christ that melted our stricken hearts and made us Christians. Carlyle once received a letter from a young man, saying: "Mr. Carlyle, I wish to be a teacher; I wish you would tell me the secret of successful teaching." Carlyle wrote back: "Young man, be that which you would have your pupils be. All other teaching is unblessed mockery and apery." Carlyle was right. "Every great poem," says Milton, "is the life-blood of a noble spirit." "Style," said Buffon,—"style is the man." So it seems to me it is the personality of the man breaking through his tones and his words that gives power to his speech. Who has most shaped our English literature and our mother tongue? Was it Milton? No; great as Milton was in scholarship, you must go back of him,—you must go back to Wickliffe, that man greater in character even than he was in scholarship, to find the man who has shaped our English tongue. Who shaped German literature and German speech? Not Goethe, with his breadth of scholarship and with his marvellous study of style, but Luther, infinitely greater in character than Goethe. [*Applause.*] So you will find that all permanent greatness rests not simply on greatness of talent,—it rests upon greatness of character. It is our Washingtons, and our Lincolns, and our Alfreds the Great, and our Luthers, and our Pauls,—these are the men who have shaped the destinies of nations,—not simply by what they spoke, not simply by their marvellous style, but by what they were as men. It was their character even more than their words that moved people. Jesus Christ says: "And I, if I be lifted up, will draw all men unto me." Even Jesus never dreamed that he could lift people to some height which he had not reached himself. Only as he was lifted up would he draw all men unto him. By no trick of rhetoric, by no effort to win people, by no possible use of the Scriptures, can you lift other people to some spiritual height that you have not yet reached yourselves. Jesus Christ said: "For their sakes I sanctify myself," and that is the condition upon which you are to lift other people to a larger, to a fuller life than they have to-day. A young man came to Demosthenes, and said: "Demosthenes, what is eloquence?" That grand old statesman, who had risked his life for his country again and again, saw that the young man thought that eloquence was some peculiarity of speech, and some art which he might learn from Demosthenes and practice upon the people; so he answered him in that Greek word which has been translated "action," but which simply means conduct, life, doing. The young man did not understand, and said again: "Demosthenes, what is eloquence?" But that grand old orator was determined that the young man should not be turned from the real question at issue, and again he answered: "Action." Again the young man inquired of him: "Demosthenes, what is eloquence?" and again the orator thundered back: "Action, young man." Only a dancing master or a mere rhetorician could have dreamed that Demosthenes meant "gesture" by that word "action." No! he meant conduct; he meant life; he meant doing; he meant being that which you would have others be. So Demosthenes unites with Carlyle and Jesus Christ in proclaiming, as the fundamental condition of lifting other people up, the consecration of ourselves and the transfiguration of our lives.

I believe, dear friends, that we are coming to a new age of personal development. We shall see a new humanity here upon the earth. I hope that these Young People's societies of Christian Endeavor will help to inaugurate that newer and diviner type of manhood and womanhood. Surely man's present position cannot be his final position.

An age which settles its disputes by war; an age in which Russia has half a million men idling in camp, waiting to kill their brethren, while women and children are dying by starvation; an age in which even civilized man licenses men to open places of temptation, and send their brothers reeling down to hell; an age which attempts to settle its industrial disputes by Winchesters, as we tried to do yesterday at Homestead; an age in which men are striving for their own good, seeking to heap wealth upon wealth, while others are growing poorer and poorer,— surely, in the 25th or 30th century men will look back upon this century and pronounce it a barbarous age. New light is to break out of the Word of God. When we seek to apply these commands of Christ absolutely, fearlessly, and fully in our lives, we shall see a transformation which shall make our present lives seem poor and miserable indeed. Read these marvellous promises of the New Testament. Read that promise which says: "Ye have an unction from the Holy One, and know all things." Read that other promise which says: "He that is born of God doth not commit sin, and cannot sin, because his spirit remaineth in him"; or that other promise, which says: "Be ye therefore perfect, even as your Father in heaven is perfect." What a mockery these promises seem to us in our present lives! As I read these marvellous promises, I feel like putting my hands upon my lips, and putting my face in the dust, and crying: "Unclean, unclean!" and yet I thank God that he had confidence enough in human nature to give us this divine summons — to be perfect, as the Father in heaven is perfect. Indeed, there come days when I feel that new life is flowing out of God which will enable us to realize these promises:

"So near is grandeur to our dust,
So nigh is God to man,
When duty whispers low, "Thou must,"
The soul responds, "I can."

Hawthorne tells us an Indian legend, that at one time the Great Spirit was here upon the earth. When the spirit returned to heaven he left an image of himself in the White Mountains, that men might recognize him when he came to the earth again. It is said that one Indian looked upon that image by day and dreamed about it by night. He looked longingly about in the faces of his brothers and sisters to see if he could not see in them the incarnation of the Great Spirit. One day, when the tribe had been at peace for some time and their spiritual vision had become clear, they saw in this waiting prophet's form the presence of the spirit, and they found that the Great Spirit had come to earth again in this waiting prophet's soul. What is this Indian legend but a faint attempt of a heathen race to tell of our possibilities in Christ? See how Paul makes clear those marvellous possibilities, when he says: "For this cause I bow my knees unto the Father of the Lord Jesus Christ, of whom the whole family in heaven and on earth is named." Thank God it is no petty Methodist sect, no petty Presbyterian sect, no petty Baptist sect, — " of whom the *whole* family in heaven and in earth is named, that he would grant you " — the promise is a personal one — " that he would grant *you* according to the riches of his glory " — if the grant was to be according to our deserts, we would turn our cups upside down and go out without the blessing; but it is to be *according to the riches of his glory* — " that he would grant you according to the riches of his glory to be strengthened with might by his spirit in the inner man; that Christ may dwell in your hearts by faith; that ye, being rooted and grounded in love, may be able to comprehend with all saints what is the height and depth and length and breadth, and to know the love of Christ which passeth understanding, that ye might be filled with the fulness of God." I no more understand how your poor petty soul or my poor petty soul is to be filled with all the fulness of God, than I understand how the Atlantic ocean is to be crowded into a pint cup. But that is the divine promise, "that ye might be filled with all the fulness of God." "Now unto him that is able to do 'for us" — how much? All you can ask? How infinitely our asking outruns our doing! But he is able to do all that you can ask. But that does not exhaust the divine power. Our speech is limited. Again and again as we try to speak we sit down and say, "We will never try again, because our speech falls so infinitely below our imagination." How infinitely our thinking outruns our asking! But he is able to do not only all we can ask, but all we can think. Even that does not exhaust the divine power. He is able to do abundantly beyond all you can think. That does not exhaust the divine power. He is able to do exceeding abundantly beyond all you can ask or think. "Now unto him who is able to do exceeding abundantly beyond all we can ask or think, to him be glory in the church throughout all ages. Amen." Failure! In all the infinite vocabulary of God there is no such word as failure. God has not put you in this world without giving you a special work to do. He has not, in the language of Wendell Phillips, "poured Niagara as the requiem of broken hopes, nor scooped out the Mississippi valley as the grave of a dying people. He has not piled the mountains in eternal mockery of man's impotence, nor built his home beyond the stars and left him wingless to reach that home." Be true to duty as Christ was true to duty, and you can no more fail in life than Christ himself could fail. [*Loud applause.*]

After various announcements and the singing of the Doxology, the audience joined in the Mizpah benediction and were dismissed. A great many tarried, however, and took part in the informal reception held by the trustees and officers of the United Society on the platform at the close of the service. It was supposed that the Garden would accommodate all the delegates who would be present Thursday evening, but long before the hour for opening the service the immense building was packed. Permission was secured from the city officials to hold an open-air meeting in Union Square, and five thousand people were present at that service, which was in charge of Dr. H. C. Farrar, of Albany, N. Y.

FRIDAY MORNING.

Nearly 5,000 delegates gathered in the convention hall at the hour of 6.30 A. M., to take part in the early morning prayer meeting. Mr. C. L. Stevens, of Ypsilanti, Mich., led the meeting, which was one of great interest and fervency. Brief prayers and testimonies, singing, and responsive readings constituted the bulk of the exercises.

The morning session of the convention was opened with the hymn, "Hide me, O my Saviour," sung by the congregation standing. Then all joined in repeating the 23d Psalm,— a very impressive exercise,— followed by the Lord's Prayer, Dr. Wayland Hoyt leading. Another hymn was sung, "He leadeth me," after which Dr. Clark introduced Rev. Dr. B. B. Tyler, pastor of the Church of the Disciples of Christ, New York City, who was to conduct the "Pastor's Hour," two minute speeches being in order from representatives of the various evangelical denominations.

THE PASTORS' HOUR.

Dr. TYLER: I have an opportunity this morning to make a speech, but I wont do it. Those who know me best understand the amount of self-denial involved in this decision. [*Laughter*]. Every brother is asked to make a half-hour speech in two minutes. If they don't stop I'll knock them down with this bit of granite from the foundation of Williston church. I will first introduce a tall specimen of the genus Christian Endeavor, Rev. H. O. Breeden, of Des Moines, Iowa, who will speak for the Disciples of Christ. [*Applause*].

Mr. BREEDEN: The Disciples of Christ, a million strong, hail Christian Endeavor as the promulgator of the chief principles of their own church. We see in Christian Endeavor a vivification of the principles of the Bible, a unifying of all God's forces, with no insistence on dividing dogmas, and a "missionizing" force, bearing on its banner the inscription,— nay, the prophecy, "The whole world for Christ." [*Applause*].

Dr. TYLER [Bringing down the gavel]: If I dare to knock down so tall a man, let the lesser lights look out! [*Laughter*.] We are all disciples of Christ, though some of us choose to spell it with a capital D. So, too, all of us are friends, though some of us prefer to spell it with a capital F. Rev. Levi Reese of Indianapolis, Ind., will speak for the Friends. [*Applause*.]

Mr. REESE: It is the habit of the Friends to be governed by the law of love, and the work of the Christian Endeavor societies among us is as amiable as its name. The Friends constitute one of the great branches of the Christian church, and they heartily welcome this great movement. It is not great in numbers, but it is great in the embodiment of great ideas. It is great in great names,— Penn, Clark, Whittier. [*Gavel. Applause*].

REV. B. B. TYLER.

REV. LEVI REESE

REV. C. E. DOWMAN, D.D.

REV. J. B. THOMAS.

REV. J. F. COWAN.

REV. I. F. JOHN.

REV. G. A. CONIBEAR.

REV. C. P. MILLS

REV. ANDERSON ROGERS.

REV. A. G. KYNETT.

REV. J. H. WEBBER, D.D.

REV. R. M. SOMERVILLE.

Dr. TYLER: You don't know how it hurts me to stop Whittier in the midst of his flight. [*Laughter*]. We should all be united in Christ, but some are more united than others. Rev. L. F. John, of Johnstown, Pa., will speak for the United Brethren. [*Applause.*]

Mr. JOHN: The church of the United Brethren in Christ confesses that it has been just a little bit slow in acknowledging the merits of Christian Endeavor, but it is now falling desperately in love with the fair movement. I thank God that he has prevented us as a denomination from doing so unchristian a thing as the organizing of a sectarian society. We have a union to which any young people's society is eligible. At the last biennial conference it was voted that any society taking Christian Endeavor plans should with them take also the Christian Endeavor name. Those of us who have drunk largely from the fountain of Christian Endeavor believe that before our next biennial conference it will be demonstrated that the pledge is an absolute necessity, and that all of our societies will take the pledge and be enrolled with the United Society. The Church of the United Brethren in Christ is with you, heart and hand, for Christ and the church. [*Applause.*]

Dr. TYLER: I now introduce a brother who will speak in behalf of the Reformed Presbyterian church,— thank God, there are some Presbyterians who are reformed! [*Laughter.*]— Rev. R. M. Somerville, of New York City.

Rev. R. M. SOMERVILLE: Our only satisfactory proof of the value of any instrument is that it is able to do what it is made for. In purchasing a knife, the test usually insisted upon, that the finest grade of steel is capable of a high polish, never satisfies me. I want to know whether it cuts well, and is likely to keep its edge, and so serve the purpose of a knife. I apply the same test to every new method of Christian work that puts in a claim for public favor. The question with me is not of polish or of outward display, but of efficiency. That test the Christian Endeavor society can stand. I believe that it has proved itself capable, as I for one can bear testimony, of calling forth and developing the latent faculties of the young people in our churches, and of making them feel that they are not simply alive unto God themselves, but that they are vitalizing forces in society. [*Applause.*]

Dr. TYLER: The next speaker represents the Methodist Episcopal Church, and what shall I say more? [*Laughter.*] Rev. Dr. A. J. Kynett, of Philadelphia, will now address us.

Dr. KYNETT: In this crucial hour in the history of Christian Endeavor in the Methodist Episcopal Church, in behalf of the pastors of more than two thousand societies in our midst, I desire to record the testimony that we have always found the young people of the society of Christian Endeavor intelligently loyal to church, [*applause*] to the pastor, [*applause*] to public service, to prayer and class meeting, and to our peculiar economy and our distinctive doctrines. [*Applause.*] Vital piety has been fostered without sectarian narrowness, [*applause*] broad-minded liberality without shallow sentimentality, and interdenominational fraternity without loss of denominational zeal. The letters that compose our badge have stood not only for Christian Endeavor, but for the name that at one time was given to Methodism — Christianity in earnest. [*Applause.*] We Methodist Endeavorers stand on the motto of John Wesley: "I desire a league offensive and defensive with every soldier of Jesus Christ." We rejoice that the last General Conference, while making the Epworth League the official society, has in clear terms which should not be mistaken rendered it possible for our young people to be at once true Methodists. earnest Epworth Leaguers, and loyal Christian Endeavorers. [*Loud applause.*]

Dr. TYLER: The next speaker is the Rev. Dr. J. E. Clark, of Nashville, Tennessee, who will speak for the Cumberland Presbyterian Church.

Dr. CLARK: The Cumberland Presbyterian Church has taken such advanced ground upon the Christian Endeavor question that I feel that I must say that I cannot be a good Cumberland Presbyterian without being a good Christian Endeavorer. [*Applause.*] I want to read to you the action of our late General Assembly, in Memphis, Tenn., May 29th. This resolution was adopted unanimously: "*Whereas* the Young People's Society of Christian Endeavor has become one of the established and well-recognized agencies in Christian work, therefore, *Resolved*, that we most heartily endorse this organization, and commend it to sessions and pastors of the Cumberland Presbyterian Church, and secondly, that it is the sense of this General Assembly that withdrawal from the Christian Endeavor movement and the organization of a separate denominational society would be hurtful and unwise." [*Applause.*] Some one has said that "C. E." meant "Christ Exalted"; well, "C. P." means "Christ Prominent." Some one has said that "C. E." means "Church Extended"; then "C. P." means "Church Progressive." [*Applause.*]

Dr. TYLER: We have all sorts of Methodists: some of them protest, and some of them do not. [*Laughter.*] The next speaker will represent the Methodist Protestant Church, — Rev. J. S. Cowan, of Pittsburg, Penn.

Mr. COWAN: A few years ago the question with our church was, whether we should have the Christian Endeavor society or a denominational society. Some of us were on the fence about it, but we have got down off the fence and pulled it down after us. [*Loud applause.*] Looking on the other side of it we have come to the conclusion that Christian Endeavor is on both sides of the fence. [*Applause.*] It is denominational, and it is interdenominational. The great trouble with some people is that they cannot distinguish between undenominational and interdenominational, and I sometimes wish I had a few unabridged dictionaries to hurl at the heads of such people, and get the idea pounded into them that there is a difference. You might as well try to make a train of cars out of coupling links as to try to make an interdenominational movement without the denominational first being there. [*Applause.*] Our late General Conference has made Christian Endeavor denominational by officially making it the society of the Church, and the Christian Endeavor society is just as much the young peoples' society of the Methodist Protestant Church, as the Epworth League is of the Methodist Episcopal Ghurch. [*Applause.*] The testimony of our church and of our pastors is that it is doing for us a grand and noble work. [*Applause.*]

Dr. TYLER: Methodist, in the ongoing of God's kingdom, is like steam. But you cannot keep up steam by fire alone; you want water as well. [*Laughter.*] So we need to bring our Baptist brethren to the front, and they have never been noted for being backwork in coming forward. Rev. J. B. Thomas, of Topeka, Kansas, will speak for the Baptists.

Mr. THOMAS: When it comes to the Baptist denomination, every man stands so distinctively independent and alone that he stands by himself or falls by himself. The Baptists, I believe, whatever may be their individual conceptions and their organic relations, are Christian Endeavorers. [*Applause.*] As a Baptist pastor, I want to say that the capturing idea of this age to me is the Christian Endeavor idea. Indeed, Mr. President, even the daily papers of this great city declare that this convention has captured the city. [*Applause.*] It is what it is because, first of all, it rejuvenates the world, because it matures the young, because it gives perpetual youth to all mankind. It is a threefold cord that cannot easily be broken. It is first a band of endeavorers. God cannot save a lazy man. God intended that all men should be active, with mind and might and strength for his cause. It is a band that has Christian ends in view. It declares that a man shall be pure in business, pure in society, pure in religion. And the best of all, it is a band of young people. [*Applause and laughter, as the speaker prevented Dr. Tyler from using the gavel.*]

Dr. TYLER: Ah! I'm glad he is out of the way! [*Laughter.*] The Rev. J. H. Webber, D.D., of Sunbury, Penn., will represent the Lutheran Church.

Dr. WEBBER: As the representative of the mother church of the Reformation and the largest of Protestant denominations, it affords me great pleasure to bear testimony to the beneficial results of Christian Endeavor in the Lutheran Church. I have heard the question asked, What shall we do with our young people, that they may grow in grace and become zealous workers in the Church of Christ? To-day we answer that question on the organized lines of Christian Endeavor. The Lutheran Church, from its earliest day, has advocated early Christian instruction. We find in the Junior Endeavor Society that which ably seconds the labors of parents and of pastors; and whilst the Lutheran Church insists and holds rigidly to the doctrine of justification by faith, yet she believes that faith without works is dead, and that the faith which justifies works in us is love for God and love for humanity. Hence she sees in Christian Endeavor that which directs the faith and energy of her young people to active work for Christ and the Church. [*Applause.*]

Dr. TYLER: I believe in reciprocity. So do you. There is nothing much better for Canada than to come over to the United States. [*Laughter.*] We are going to Canada, not because we must but because we can. [*Laughter.*] The Rev. Anderson Rogers, of Windsor, Nova Scotia, will speak for the Canadian Presbyterian Church.

Mr. ROGERS: It is because Canadian Presbyterians believe also in reciprocity that we have taken so kindly to Christian Endeavor. [*Applause.*] It is the written law of our church, " Let your women keep silence in the churches." It is the unwritten law of our church, " Let your women keep silence in your social service." Christian Endeavor has unmuzzled the mouths of twenty thousand young men and women, [*applause*] and never will they be closed permanently in this world or in the world to come. [*Applause.*] The Presbyterian Church thanks Christian Endeavor for overcoming the muscular resistance of twenty thousand jaws. [*Laughter.*] We thank Christian Endeavor for pointing out rational Christian work for every man, woman, and child who loves the Lord Jesus Christ. Gladly, gratefully does our church acknowledge the spirit of loyalty fostered by these societies. (*Applause.*)

Dr. TYLER: Rev G. A. Conibear, of Westerly, R. I., will speak for the Christian Denomination.

Mr. CONIBEAR: As I understand it, this is the hour given for testimonies as to the advantage and helpfulness of Christian Endeavor work. I stand here to-day representing the free Christians of this country, and I wish to say that we believe — and we show our faith by our works — in recognizing and supporting this movement. One of the most striking features of its helpfulness, to my mind, to me as a pastor, is the fact that the Christian Endeavor work brings young men and young women into contact with, and knowledge of, God's Word. The topics that are assigned for the meetings necessitate an examination of the Bible; and it is not only an acquaintance, but it is an intelligent acquaintance, that those receive who study it for these meetings. They study that they may find some appropriate expression for their Christian experience; they study that they may find something that shall bring them into harmony with truth and with one another. I find that the young men and young women in my church are growing in grace and climbing up to a higher knowledge of Christ. [*Applause.*]

Dr. TYLER: Let it never be forgotten that the first Young People's Society of Christian Endeavor was organized in a Congregational church. [*Applause.*] Let it always and everywhere be recognized that Father Endeavor Clark is an Orthodox Congregationalist. [*Applause.*] Now we will hear from the Congregationalists, and the Rev. Charles Perry Mills, of Newburyport, Massachusetts, will speak for them. [*Applause.*]

Mr. MILLS: Congregationalism, having tried the Christian Endeavor Society longer than any other denomination, and proportionately to a larger degree, has loved it from the first, loves it now, and will love it to the end. [*Applause.*] The leading principles of Congregationalism are the independence of the local church and the fellowship of all the churches; and Christian Endeavor came by birthright into its controlling features: the fidelity of the local society to its own church and to its own denomination, and the fellowship of all societies in all churches and all denominations. Broader than the hospitality of our denomination is the platform of our Christian Endeavor fellowship; for we welcome to equal rights and equal opportunity the splendid Canadians on the north, the patriotic Georgians on the south, the generous Californians on the west, and the Chinese on Gospel principle. [*Loud applause.*]

Dr. TYLER: And now one of those patriotic brethren from the South, the Rev. Dr. C. E. Dowman, of Savannah, Georgia, will speak for the Methodist Episcopal Church, South. [*Applause.*]

Dr. DOWMAN: I am only one of more than five thousand pastors, and only one of more than a million and a quarter members of this great branch of Methodism and of the Church of Christ, but I bring you the greetings of this great church of the South to-day. [*Applause.*] As a pastor I found a Christian Endeavor society already organized in the church which I am now serving, and it is still there; and, while it does the work it proposes to do and is doing there for young people of my church, it shall stay. [*Applause.*] We have four Southern Methodist churches in the city of Savannah, and I think we have a Christian Endeavor record which cannot be equalled by any other city of the same size in the South. Every one of those Methodist churches has a Christian Endeavor society. [*Loud applause.*]

Dr. TYLER: We heard a little while ago from the Reformed Presbyterians. Now we shall hear from the Reformed Episcopalians. The Rev. William Tracy, of Philadelphia, will speak for them.

Mr. TRACY: I have heard of a clergyman who was appointed chaplain of a prison. When his first service occurred, facing his audience in stripes, he looked around upon them and said: "I am glad to see so many of you here." [*Laughter.*] In the name of the Reformed Episcopal Church, I rejoice in this great assembly. We are in pronounced sympathy with the Christian Endeavor movement. We, like you, were born in a revival; we, like you, have the charm and vigor of youth; we, like you, are determined that men shall be saved and shall then become saviours, — we are determined that the old truths shall come into contact with men's hearts directly. [*Applause.*]

Dr. TYLER: Somebody has said that the Baptists are like the old fashioned way of arranging the verbs — as regular, irregular, and defective. [*Laughter.*] Are the Free Baptists defective? I do n't know; but the Rev. J. M. Lowden, of Boston, Mass., will speak for the Free Baptists.

Mr. LOWDEN: Free grace, free will, and believer's baptism are not defective. [*Applause.*] For the last ten years I have been asking this question: Is there any reason under heaven why Christian Endeavor should not be the young people's society of all denominations of Christians? [*Applause.*] I want an answer on three points: Is there any society of young people, denominational if you please, that makes the young people more loyal to the local church? There is none. Is there any society of young people, denominational if you please, that awakens and develops a greater interest in all the enterprises of the church, such as Sunday schools, educational work, and missions? There is not one.

Is there any young people's society that makes the young people of the denomination more loyal to the denomination than Christian Endeavor? There is not one. Because, then, Christian Endeavor stands for loyalty to Jesus Christ and the Church, because Christian Endeavor stands for system,— which means economy of force,— because Christian Endeavor stands for co-operation, I stand for it — first, last, and always. [*Applause.*]

Dr. TYLER: The United Presbyterians will now be heard from in the person of the Rev. Mason W. Pressly, Bovina Center, N. Y.

Mr. PRESSLY: The Presbyterians are the greatest people in the world to agree to differ. There are forty different kinds of Presbyterians in the world, and

REV. WM. TRACY.

REV. J. M. LOWDEN.

REV. MASON W. PRESSLY.

REV. A. M. PHILLIPS.

REV. J. C. KRAUSE.

REV. WILTON M. SMITH, D.D.

eight in the United States. I represent the United Presbyterian Church. [*Applause.*] We are united in the supremacy and infallibility of a God-inspired Bible; we are united in the practice of a pure worship, in the preaching of a pure Gospel, and in the maintenance of a pure type of piety. The United Presbyterian Church is popularly believed to be a church with a high wall around it — horse-high, bull-strong, pig-tight. [*Laughter.*] To a certain extent that is true. Our banner has on it "The Truth of God," but it has on it likewise "Forbearance in love to all who love God." So I am here to tell you that although we are conservative, we are catholic; we are so broad in our liberality that we have taken into our bosom the Young People's Society of Christian Endeavor, and it has been the most progressive part of our body. [*Applause.*]

Dr. TYLER: The Rev. I. O. Adams, of Pine Bluff, Ark., will now speak for the Protestant Episcopal Church.

Mr. ADAMS: I am with you, and with you to stay. [*Applause.*] I am with you because you are a body of young Christians who are to-day influencing the Christian world. I am with you because the spirit of God is with you, and I am with you on the great broad platform of Christian unity. It is an indisputable fact that while convention after convention has passed resolutions looking toward unity, the world to-day looks at this Christian Endeavor movement and says, "Here we find it; here we have it realized." [*Applause.*] I would that I had the time to present to you the many ways in which I have found this society helpful and beneficial to me. I regret that in the shortness of the time it is impossible for me to say to you here how it can be applied directly to the working of the Episcopal Church. That there are no more societies in the Episcopal Church to-day is owing, I think, not so much to the matter of prejudice as to the fact that its features are not generally known. [*Applause.*]

Dr. TYLER: We will now hear from the Canadian Methodists — the Rev. A. M. Phillips, of Toronto, Ontario.

Mr. PHILLIPS: I regard the Christian Endeavor movement as the Methodist class-meeting adapted to the circumstances and needs and advancement of this end of the 19th century. The Methodists in Canada look upon the Christian Endeavor movement as analogous to the great Sunday-school movement. Like that, it should be interdenominational. At the General Conference of 1890, while adopting the name Epworth League as the official title for the young people's organizations of our church, we adopted the Christian Endeavor Society in its entirety as the Christian Work Department, and placed a clause in the constitution to the effect that the Christian Endeavor Department shall always be regarded as central and fundamental in the organization and working of the Epworth League. Moreover, we provided that every Epworth League should have the privilege of adopting the name "Epworth League of Christian Endeavor," [*applause*] and also provided that every Christian Endeavor society, without any change in constitution, pledge, or any other part of its work, might, by adopting the name "Epworth League of Christian Endeavor" or "Christian Endeavor Epworth League," become an Epworth League of the Church, and be entitled to representation upon the quarterly board. [*Applause.*]

Dr. TYLER: The Rev. A. S. Shelly, of Bally, Pennsylvania, will now speak for the Mennonites.

Mr. SHELLY: If I cannot speak for a great body of Christians, I can speak for one man. I can speak for the person who is now the pastor of the congregation in which the first Mennonite Christian Endeavor society was organized. [*Applause.*] It is now existing, and shall exist as long as I am pastor. We are a small body of Christians, as I have said. In the great Christian family we are one of the little ones; but the little ones have promises, too, in the Bible. Our people are to a great extent a rural people, farmers and mechanics, and they are not very slow in adopting the new machinery on their farms and in their workshops; and I do not see why, in this great work for Christ, we should be any slower in adopting the machinery of the Christian Endeavor Society, — the spring-toothed harrow of self-examination and the study of the Word of God, the sowing-drill of self-consecration, and, last of all, the self-binder of Minnesota, the pledge of the Young People's Society of Christian Endeavor. [*Applause.*]

Dr. TYLER: We are now to hear from another reformed church, — the Reformed Dutch Church, the oldest church organization in this city, — represented by the Rev. Daniel H. Martin, of Newark, New Jersey.

Mr. MARTIN: It is with great pleasure that the Dutch Church welcomes the Christian Endeavor Society to Manhattan Island, for it was on this island the first Christian Endeavor society of America was started — the Dutch came here two hundred and eighty years ago. [*Applause.*] The first church was a fort; and this fort had a steeple on it. Religious exercises were held in the fort until a minister came from Holland. I know that there must have been a Christian Endeavor society here, because they got along so well without a minister. [*Applause.*] The Dutch Church has been called slow, but it is the quickest church to recognize and endorse the virtues of the Christian Endeavor movement. Why? Because the principles of the Christian Endeavor movement are best fulfilled by the ancient mottoes of the Dutch Church: "*Eendracht maakt macht*" — "In union there is strength," and "*Nisi Dominus frustra*" — "Without God, all is in vain." [*Loud applause and laughter, as the speaker finished before the bell sounded.*]

Dr. TYLER: I believe in New York, — but you don't know when or by what way you will be taken in. [*Laughter.*] Rev. Dr. Wilton Merle Smith, of New York City, will speak for the unreformed Presbyterians. [*Laughter and applause.*]

Dr. SMITH: I stand for the blue banner of the Presbyterians — unreformed, unterrified, and dead in earnest for Christian Endeavor, — the banner church of the Christian Endeavor societies. Congregationalism had the start of us; but we are leading them by five hundred lengths in the race. The blue banner is now in the smoke of battle, perhaps; but we are fighting your battles, friends, against extreme radicalism on the one side and extreme ultraism on the other. [*Applause.*] I hope that the blue banner will always be in the smoke, and at the head of the van. There is one thing we believe in, and that is the Christian Endeavor Society, because that society stands for the "high-calling" time of Christianity. What this world means is a generation of heroic Christians. Twenty years from now, if we are true to the high ideals of our society, we will have that generation, and it will do a work for the world which the generation of to-day is stumbling at and flinching from. [*Applause.*]

Dr. TYLER: I never spoke in Dr. Smith's church when he did not tell me to be brief. This is the first time I have had a chance to cut him short. [*Laughter.*] The Rev. J. C. Krause, of Pottsville, Pennsylvania, will now speak for the Evangelical Association.

Mr. KRAUSE: Among the last, among the least, comparatively unknown, — but we are here. I stand as a representative of a church that believes in organized power. We do not believe in organization without power, and we do not believe in power without organization. They must stand together. I am glad to say that we are able to report a considerable number of Christian Endeavor societies. True, we have a denominational league, but officially it is called "The Keystone League of Christian Endeavor." [*Applause.*] We believe that the young people are running this world; the old men are holding the reins. The young people are organized to carry this world for Christ and the Church. [*Applause.*]

Dr. TYLER: We are indebted, as you know, to the Moravian Church for the evangelistic zeal of the Wesleys and the great Methodist Church. We will now hear from the Moravian Church, represented by the Rev. C. E. Eberman, of Brooklyn.

Mr. EBERMAN: The Moravian Brethren Church sends its warmest greetings and its love to this great convention of Christian Endeavor, and bids it Godspeed upon its mission of aggressive and enthusiastic work. It hails and welcomes the Christian Endeavor Society as a blessed means of grace, and feels it a privilege to accept it and foster it as a divinely inspired revelation of these latter times. It stands committed by its synodal endorsement and commendation from its pastoral leaders, by its faith and its prayers, to the Christian Endeavor principles, and to its name. I firmly believe that ere another year has rolled by every congregation will have its Christian Endeavor society. [*Applause.*] We are devoutly thankful for any consecrated movement that shall help to make the kingdoms of this world the kingdoms of our Lord and of his Christ. We bid you Godspeed.

Dr. TYLER: Finally,— and this is a good place to stop,-- we have a representative of the Church of God, the Rev. J. J. Zeigler.

Mr. ZEIGLER: If there is a body of believers in all the land that ought to hail this Christian Endeavor movement, it is that body which I represent this morning. The Christian Endeavor movement has made it manifest that there is a basis upon which believers in Christ may recognize each other and work together. It is one of the fundamental principles of the body of believers which I represent, that all who by faith in Jesus Christ are children of God belong to the same brotherhood, and should be recognized upon that ground alone. If you should come to us and ask for recognition or fellowship, we would ask you but one question: Are you a child of God, by faith in Jesus Christ? If you answer that question affirmatively, we extend to you the right hand of fellowship, and accept you on that ground alone. [*Applause.*]

This closed the Pastors' Hour. Dr. Tyler, in laying down the gavel, apologized to the speakers for having compelled them to observe the time limit so closely, and, turning to the audience, he said: "Boys and girls, I thank you for being so good." The audience cheered and called for a speech from Dr. Tyler, but he declined to respond. The calls became so persistent, however, that at length he rose from his seat, and, shaking his gavel in the faces of the audience, cried, "If you don't keep still, I'll knock about ten thousand of you down!"

The hymn, "What a wonderful Saviour," was then sung, and after a number of notices had been given, Chairman H. T. McEwen, in the absence of Secretary Baer, conducted the "State Hour," responses being made by delegates as follows: —

STATE HOUR.

ALABAMA.

Rev. HORACE E. PORTER: Welcome, Christian Endeavor, to the Southland, with thy lesson of brotherhood! We had a splendid convention at Montgomery, and our dear President Clark was with us. We have made splendid progress this past year, and good work is being done, especially among our colored brethren. [*Applause.*]

ALASKA.

Mr. EDWARD MARSDEN: Not very long ago my people were in darkness. A Roman Christian general, not a Roman Cæsar, came among us not very long ago, and by the grace of God he conquered us. In a few years from now we will have the same organization of Christian Endeavor societies that you now enjoy in these United States. [*Loud applause.*]

AUSTRALIA.

Mr. HUGH JONES: Most of you have heard of the Australian kangaroo. He moves forward by leaps This Christian Endeavor society is a great kangaroo. He leaps forward on his way. Less than three years ago he leaped from America to Australia. On the spot where he first rested there were thirty Christian Endeavor members; then he sprang to over six hundred; last year he gave a mighty leap to over three thousand, and this year he is to leap further still. [*Applause.*]

CALIFORNIA.

Mr. EDWIN B. HAYES: California, the Golden State, greets you to-day with twenty thousand Christian Endeavorers and with one of the largest junior societies in the United States. We have come all the way from the Golden Gate to the gate of destruction [*laughter*] with hearts large enough and arms large enough to welcome you to California in 1894. [*Applause.*]

COLORADO.

Mr. J. W. BARROWS: Great in extent, great in natural resources, great in faith, hope, and enthusiasm of its Christian Endeavorers! We report for the year a gain of fifty per cent in active membership, of 190 societies, enrolling 4.500 active, and 1,400 associate, members, and, best of all, 500 conversions. We come to you to bring the greetings of our State, and to ask you to come to Denver in 1894. [*Applause.*]

CONNECTICUT.

Rev. H. H. KELSEY: Little Connecticut is here, 2,000 strong. We have 31,000 at home. We have not many square miles, but we have many Endeavorers to the square mile. We are trying now to do two things in the immediate future: to have a junior society wherever there is a young people's society; and for this winter to carry the Gospel personally to every unsaved young man and woman in Connecticut, in the endeavor to bring them to Christ. [*Applause.*]

DELAWARE.

Rev. GEO. E. THOMPSON: In so conservative a State, if we were simply to speak of progress it would mean a great deal. But progress has been made; new societies have been formed. Christian Endeavor is a success. Our first convention was held a year and a half ago. Our second convention pleased us so much that we determined to have another this year, and if you hear of another annual convention, you will know it is in Delaware. [*Applause.*]

DISTRICT OF COLUMBIA

Mr. P. S. FOSTER: The District of Columbia, which practically means the city of Washington, as we have but 3 societies outside the capitol city, now numbers 60 societies, with 4,000 membership, an increase of thirty-five per cent. We are doing good work all along the line; have several enthusiastic Methodist societies, and we pray God that we may never be deprived of their fellowship. [*Applause.*]

ENGLAND.

Mr. P. O. WILLIAMS: [*Loud applause and Chautauqua salute.*] Our first convention was held in June last year. We had 120 societies then; now we have 300. At the last convention we gave our message to Mr. Sankey to bring to you, and I did not expect to say anything here. [*Applause.*]

FLORIDA.

Mr. F. A. CURTIS: Christian Endeavor in Florida is five years old. We have 101 societies, with a membership of 3,000. Christian Endeavor in Florida

REV. LAWRENCE PHELPS.

REV. GEO. S. SWEZEY.

MR. J. E. THWING.

REV. E. T. FARRILL.

MR. J. D. RADFORD.

REV. W. H. HEARTZ.

MR. W. C. PERKINS.

MR. W. H. MCCLAIN.

REV. GEO. S. SYKES.

REV. H. W. SHERWOOD.

MR. V. RICHARD FOSS.

PROF. C. A. MURCH.

is progressing slowly but surely, and our watchword is, "Florida for Christ." [*Applause.*]

CHINA.

Rev. A. A. FULTON: [Cablegram] Y. P. S. C. E.'s in China send greeting. Hold fast the two-cents-a-week plan for foreign missions.

GEORGIA.

Mr. GEO. M. FOLGER: Georgia sent one delegate to St. Louis in 1890, 33 delegates to Minneapolis in 1891, and 250 delegates to New York in 1892. [*Applause.*]

ILLINOIS.

Mr. CHAS. B. HOLDREGE: Illinois is pressing on in the ranks of Christian Endeavor. The societies are growing in number and usefulness. The junior societies have increased over one hundred per cent in the past year. Illinois has to-day in its Chicago union the best organized and the largest city union in the United States. I ask of the 1,800 delegates from Illinois in this convention if I do not voice their sentiments and the sentiments of all our Illinois members when I say, there is one intense purpose in our hearts to-day, and that is on every occasion, in season and out of season, we shall use every endeavor to have the gates of the World's Fair closed on the Lord's day! [*Loud and enthusiastic applause, the Illinois delegates rising in response.*]

INDIANA.

Miss E. M. WISHARD: It was said one year ago that Indiana is a small State, but we have grown in the past year in Christian Endeavor, if not in area. To-day we report an increase of 265 societies, which gives a total of 785 societies, 83 of which are juniors. Three years ago when we came to Philadelphia there were 169 societies; to-day we have 800, and more are coming. [*Applause.*]

IOWA.

Rev. AUSTIN D. WOLFE: Iowa greets you with 30,000 Endeavorers. Iowa has not gone back on Prohibition. We have 749 societies, of which 90 are juniors; an increase of 200 societies and 5,000 members in the last year, besides a newspaper that is self-supporting. [*Applause.*]

KANSAS.

Rev. GEORGE S. SWEZEY: Kansas never does anything by halves. Her cyclones are bigger, her winds stronger, her rains heavier, her sunshine brighter, her atmosphere clearer, her sunflowers larger, her grasshoppers thicker, [*laughter*] and her Christian Endeavor spirit more enthusiastic than any in the wide, wide world. [*Applause.*]

. Rev. R. W. Brokaw here read several telegrams from South Carolina, Illinois, Russia, and California.

KENTUCKY.

Rev. G. C. KELLY, D.D.: One hundred and fifty Kentuckians are present here to bear the greetings of 147 societies containing nearly 3,000 members. Kentucky has passed into the second century of her history with a new constitution, and her first legislature has passed a bill for the Columbian Exposition, prohibiting the sale of her own spirits in the exhibits, and closing the same on the Sabbath. [*Applause.*]

LOUISIANA.

Mr. J. J. ZEIGLER: Some of us Christian people are engaged in Christian

Endeavor work in that great and wicked city, New Orleans. We have four societies, aggregating a membership of 130, all loyal workers in their churches. The Louisiana State Lottery has been crushed by the sovereign will of the people, and we are marching onward, thank God! [*Applause.*]

MAINE.

Mr. V. RICHARD FOSS: Maine raises rocks, pine trees, poets, statesmen, prohibitionists, and Christian Endeavorers. True to its motto, "I lead," the State has led in many grand movements for the weal of humanity. Maine, represented here to-day by about 300 of her best chivalry, greets you as fellow-workers in Christ, and through you the Christian Endeavor host of America. May the Holy Ghost energize this organization, which is the marvel of this age, and give you one hundred-fold results. [*Applause.*]

THE MARITIME UNION.

Rev. W. H. HEARTZ: There are 324 societies in the Maritime Provinces of the Dominion of Canada. They send their greetings to this great convention. We are loyal to the principles of Christian Endeavor, and we are glad to say that progress is the watchword with us. We are loyal to Christ and his Church, and I hesitate not to say that we are loyal to the greatest woman that ever sat upon the throne of empire. Heartily, honestly, and earnestly we sing, "God Save the Queen." [*Applause.*]

MARYLAND.

Mr. W. C. PERKINS: At Minneapolis we had 40 delegates present: to-day we are represented by 375. At our State convention in January we had 110 societies: now we have 182. During the past year the work has been characterized by the deepest spirituality, resulting in more complete devotion and more effective service for Christ and the Church; and it is our most earnest hope and prayer that there may be developed and turned into the channels of Christian activity, by and through this God-sent movement, such a band of loyal and devoted Christians as will win for Christ "Maryland, my Maryland." [*Applause.*]

MASSACHUSETTS.

Rev. LAWRENCE PHELPS: Massachusetts is here, 3,000 strong, representing 80,000 more. [*Applause.*] We hope to bring 100,000 people to Christ in his name. May God bless us. [*Applause.*]

MICHIGAN.

Mr. C. L. STEVENS: In 1891 Michigan had 201 senior societies, with 9,500 members. To-day she reports 530 senior societies, with 26,500 members, a gain of 163 per cent. In 1891 she reported 6 junior societies, with 180 members. To-day we report 60 societies, with 1,800 members, a gain of 900 per cent. [*Applause.*]

MINNESOTA.

Mr. J. E. THWING: Minnesota, the home of our beloved General Secretary, has been making rapid progress in Christian Endeavor during the past year. We have nearly doubled our societies. We have received revivals of interest in nearly all the societies of the State. In the junior work last year we had 55 societies, and to-day we have 140. This increase is largely due to the efforts of Miss Nettie Harrington, Superintendent of Junior work. [*Applause.*]

MONTANA.

Mr. JAMES D. RADFORD: Montana is among the youngest of the Christian Endeavor unions. We are two months old, and yet we are old enough to have

PARSONAGE AND WILLISTON CHURCH, PORTLAND, MAINE, WHERE THE FIRST CHRISTIAN ENDEAVOR SOCIETY WAS ORGANIZED.

developed all the characteristics of the Christian Endeavor family, — zeal, energy, and spirit of prayer. We are set in a large place. We have peculiar difficulties to contend with, and yet we remember the promise of God: "Where sin doth abound, there doth grace much more abound." As God hath permitted Montana to lead the whole United States in the production of precious metals, so he will give unto us that which is of far more value than gold or silver, even the souls of our fellow-men. [*Applause.*]

MISSOURI.

Mr. W. H. McClain: Missouri greets you in the name of 736 Endeavor societies, showing an increase during the last year of 182 societies. We have also 100 junior societies, and we have the only society in the world among soldiers. We have one society which brings with them here a Chinese representative who will address this convention. We greet you in the name of Christ, and give the report of 1,700 conversions in Missouri from Endeavor societies last year. [*Applause.*]

NEBRASKA.

Prof. C. A. Murch: "The voice of him that crieth in the wilderness, Make straight in the desert a highway for our God." From the midst of the great American desert in Nebraska 15,000 Endeavorers send you a loyal greeting. We have been pushing the work in the State, over the green hills, and through the smiling valleys. We are especially pushing the junior work, and by the help of the Lord God Almighty we will make the desert blossom as the rose. Our soil is deep, but the best part of us is above the ground. Get your ear to the ground and hear us grow. [*Laughter and applause.*]

NEW HAMPSHIRE.

Rev. E. T. Farrill: The old Granite State, 300 societies strong, brings its heartiest greetings to the great convention in whose midst we have unfurled our banner. We find on the front of one of our majestic mountains the promise of the abiding of our almighty Leader, who, as a sculptor, has chiselled in the stone the resemblance of a human face. We are going to push forward the work of training up our sons and our daughters to the resemblance of that other Face which is higher than that and is crowned with the ruby and gold of sacrifice and eternal victory. [*Applause.*]

NEW JERSEY.

Rev. G. S. Sykes: New Jersey has 564 societies, including 68 junior societies, numbering a total of 30,000 members. Christian Endeavor in New Jersey stands for the unity of the Christian Church and denominational fidelity. We believe in the brotherhood of man, and in the fatherhood of God, and in the mastership of the Lord Jesus Christ. In New Jersey, Christian Endeavor means Christianity in earnest, the Church in the world, and the world for Christ. [*Applause.*]

NEW MEXICO.

Rev. T. C. Beattie: I come from civilized New Mexico. You often think that it is the land of the tarantula and the scorpion and the snake; but in our city, the central city of New Mexico, we have 10,000 inhabitants, and we have a temperance hotel worth $100,000. We have only a small Christian Endeavor union there, including but 10 societies; yet, in the Western way, we stretch out our arm, and stretch out our index finger, and take all we can get; and so we reach down to Old Mexico and also to Texas.

NEW YORK.

Rev. H. W. Sherwood: In the language of our State secretary, New York still leads the States and Territories and Provinces in the number of societies. We have registered delegates until we have got tired and shut up shop.

REV. HORACE E. PORTER.

MISS ELIZABETH M. WISHARD.

MR. J. W. BARROWS.

MR. EDWIN B. HAYES.

MR. F. A. CURTIS.

MR. CHAS. B. HOLDREGE.

MR. GEO. M. FOLGER.

REV. A. A. FULTON.

REV. AUSTIN D. WOLFE.

MR. P. S. FOSTER.

REV. GEO. E. THOMPSON.

REV. H. H. KELSEY.

When the international convention left us five years ago at Saratoga, you had 2,200 societies, and 140,000 members. You come back and find us here in New York with 2,532 societies, and almost as many members as you had then. When you come back five years from now, we will try and have a round million in New York. [*Applause.*]

INDIA.

Rev. S. V. KARMARKAR [*Loud applause and the Chautauqua salute.*]: India is not behind America. [*Applause.*] We also have a Christian Endeavor society, not as large as this society is, but a society which is large enough to conquer the whole of India with all its millions, because that society has the power of Christ. If the number is small, we must remember that number does not tell; the power that is behind the number is what tells, and that power is Christ. Therefore, my dear brethren, I am glad to be here as the representative of my country and the great power and the great kingdom of our Lord and Saviour Jesus Christ. [*Loud applause.*]

NORTH CAROLINA.

Rev. A. C. DIXON: To set the world on fire there is only needed tar and turpentine and a blaze. North Carolina can furnish the tar and turpentine, and Christian Endeavor has applied the torch. [*Applause.*]

NORTH DAKOTA.

Judge R. W. CARROTHERS: North Dakota represents a progress of one hundred per cent in senior membership, and can boast three hundred per cent increase in junior membership. We shall have more next year. [*Applause.*]

OHIO.

Rev. W. F. MCCAULEY: The cause of Christian Endeavor is moving on, and it will move faster after we get the international convention in Cleveland in 1894. [*Applause.*] The most important thing our State union has done occurred last week, when it was recommended to all the societies in Ohio that they stay away from the World's Fair, if it was opened on the Sabbath or liquor sold on the grounds. Fifteen hundred Endeavorers rose to pledge themselves to the same end. [*Applause.*]

ONTARIO.

Mr. THOMAS MORRIS, Jr.: Ontario will have the proud satisfaction of carrying away the banner from this great convention. In Ontario, the Epworth League and Christian Endeavor societies are happily wedded; all is harmony and good will and brotherly love within our borders. [*Applause.*]

OREGON.

Rev. G. N. HARTLEY: Portland, Oregon, wants to shake hands with Portland, Maine. [*The speaker here shook hands with Dr. Clark, amid great applause.*] The waters of the old Pacific are united with the waters of the Atlantic. A short time ago we climbed to the top of Mt. Hood, and looked over to Portland, Maine, and saw the seed that was planted there, and we took some of the seed, and planted it with us; and to-day the Oregon is rolling on, and the snows of Mt. Hood are melting, and the cooling waters are going down into the valleys, and the sons and daughters of Oregon are raising their voices for God, home, and native land. [*Applause.*]

PENNSYLVANIA.

Rev. GEORGE B. STEWART: Pennsylvania salutes Ontario, and transfers the banner of the United States to England by way of Ontario. [*Laughter.*] We were glad to have had the banner. We are glad Ontario is to have it, since

Pennsylvania has lost it. Pennsylvania, the Keystone State, recognizes Christian Endeavor as the keystone in church work, and therefore she has put her seal on her keystone, and she sends that, along with the banner, to England by way of Ontario saluting the world. [*Applause.*]

QUEBEC.

Mr. HIRAM R. MOULTON : Christian Endeavor societies in the Province of Quebec are like oases in a desert of Romanism, but they are laboring to make this desert blossom like the rose with a purer and nobler Christianity. We count 75 societies, with about 3,000 members. The Christian Endeavor movement is just now rapidly growing in the country districts. A large proportion of the new societies are Epworth Leagues of Christian Endeavor. If our loyalty to our queen sometimes gets the better of us, we are also loyal to Christian Endeavor. [*Applause.*]

RHODE ISLAND.

Rev. J. B. JORDAN : The State of Roger Williams brings greetings to this great convention. We have nearly 100 societies, with about 4,000 members. We intend to double our junior work during this present year. We have hope and its anchor upon our State seal, and we have hope in our hearts for this great work. [*Applause.*]

SANDWICH ISLANDS.

Mr. HIRAM BRIGHAM, Jr. [*Greeted with the Chautauqua salute.*] : The Christian Endeavor Society of the Sandwich Islands sends greeting to this vast assembly. We have a society which was organized in 1884, beginning with 19 members. We now number almost 100. There is only one society in Honolulu, and one on one of the other islands, yet we are enthusiastic : the Spirit of God is among us, and what is the reason for this? It is because we have adopted the cast-iron pledge, or, as we call it, the verdure-clad pledge. [*Applause.*] There are hundreds of members of a Young People's society among the natives of the Group, but this does not correspond to the Y. P. S. C. E. By careful training, they may, perhaps, be brought into the Christian Endeavor fold. We are following your pledge and your motto. [*Applause.*]

SOUTH CAROLINA.

Mr. DUNBAR ROBB : South Carolina is just waking up to the Christian Endeavor movement. As far as we can learn, there are 10 societies in the State, with 343 members. At present we have no State union, but by the time the convention meets next year the delegates who are at this convention will guarantee that there will be a State union. We ask your prayers for South Carolina. [*Applause.*]

SOUTH DAKOTA.

Miss ESTHER A. CLARK : South Dakota for Christ! This has meant more to us this last year than ever before, and I thank God we are beginning to realize that to do the work as loyal Endeavorers we must have the Christ spirit, and do personal work for him, as well as make a united effort to advance his cause. [*Applause.*]

TENNESSEE.

Mr. W. L. NOELL : Down in Tennessee, notwithstanding the fact that 66 of our societies during the past year have disbanded and organized themselves into denominational societies, we have made a net gain of forty-three per cent in the senior societies, and a gain of one hundred per cent in the junior societies. One hundred and eighty-eight of our associate members have joined the church during the past year. We are marching in the front line of systematic benevolence, and nearly all of our societies have adopted Mr. Fulton's pledge of two cents a week for missions. [*Applause.*]

JUDGE R. M. CAROTHERS.

REV. J. B. JORDAN.

MR. R. W. PORTER.

MISS A. P. JONES.

MR. DUNBAR ROBB.

MISS ESTHER A. CLARK.

REV. GEO. B. STEWART.

REV. R. B. WHITEHEAD.

REV. W. O. CARRIER.

REV. H. G. SCUDDAY.

REV. W. F. MCCAULEY.

MR. THOS. MORRIS, JR.

TEXAS.

Rev. H. G. SCUDDAY: The Lone Star State, the biggest in the Union, is in the ranks of Christian Endeavor to stay, and through me she sends her greetings, and tells you that she proposes to cram every square mile of her vast territory with Christian Endeavorers. She has the prairies and the grass; the Christian Endeavor movement is the fire; and we know that enthusiasm and zeal will soon follow. Our motto is, "Our star is the star of Bethlehem." [*Applause.*]

UTAH.

Rev. B. F. CLAY: Utah has thirty-five societies and 1,000 members; every one of the Protestant churches is represented in the Union. We stand solid for Christ and Christ's church, but against Joseph Smith and Mormonism. We stand for American homes, but against Oriental harems. We put country above political party. We ask you to pray for Utah, and keep her out of the Union of States. [*Applause.*]

VERMONT.

Rev. Z. MARTIN: Not large in quantity, but for quality — oh, my! [*Laughter.*] We have lots of green mountains and green valleys, but no green people. [*Laughter.*] We have stood for more than half a century for Prohibition,— absolute, universal, and everlasting. [*Applause.*]

VIRGINIA.

Rev. T. E. COLBURN: Virginia, the mother of statesmen, the mother of presidents, and the mother of States; and if Maine had not been so quick, she would have been the mother of the grandest child of this nineteenth century, the Young People's Society of Christian Endeavor! Virginia is proverbial for conservatism, but she has at last taken hold of this work; and you know when Virginia takes hold, she never tires. [*Applanse.*]

WASHINGTON.

Mr. H. T. BUTLER: This is Washington's first report. Our State union has just held its third convention we have about 125 societies, eight local unions, and about 6,000 members. [*Applause.*]

WISCONSIN.

Rev. W. O. CARRIER: Wisconsin is a thousand miles away, but her Endeavor societies send greetings so heartily that it has required five hundred of us to bring them to this convention. We believe most heartily in the Junior work, and last year we have grown one hundred per cent in this department. Our society is going into the highways and hedges, as well as into the older and stronger churches; it is the forerunner of the church. We have one society in our State Prison, two in the Reform School, and one in the State School for the Blind. [*Applause.*]

MEXICO.

MISS DORRIE STAHL: New Mexico thought she would represent "Old" Mexico, but "Old" Mexico can represent herself. [*Applause.*]
We bring you the cordial greetings of over three hundred Mexican Christian Endeavorers. Our first society was formed a little over three years ago, and now we have twelve societies, linked together by a circular letter. We are few in numbers, but we are pushing the movement, and we are full of enthusiasm and Christian energy; and in the year 1900 we are going to ask you to come to the ancient and fair city of Mexico. [*Applause.*]

FLOATING SOCIETIES.

Miss A. P. JONES: Over two hundred members of the Floating Societies send you for the first time their greetings. They are few, but they are genuine Endeavorers. They send no trophies of grand achievements, but they can declare that Christian Endeavor is a medium through which God can work on the sea as well as on the land. The history of one society went down in a wreck. Laborers, go help these brothers on the seas, for they are all our brethren. [*Applause.*]

WEST VIRGINIA.

REV. R. B. WHITEHEAD: West Virginia, the Switzerland of America, brings to this convention her greetings. One year ago two representatives were in this body: to-day we are represented by two hundred delegates. We came to our State union with but twenty societies: we shall come this year with seventy-five, having made an increase of over three hundred per cent in our work during the year. We have ten junior societies in the State. [*Applause.*]

JAPAN.

Madam TELL SONO [*Greeted with the Chautauqua salute*]: Dear friends, I am happy to see you this morning, just as happy as I can be in my heart; I am glad to be in this beautiful building and to see this large audience of Christian Endeavor workers. I want all my young people of Japan to become Christian Endeavor workers. I am only a happy Japanese Christian; please remember me before the Lord. [*Applause.*]

SPAIN.

Miss ANNA F. WEBB [*Loud applause*]: The society of San Sebastian, Spain, sends loving greetings by me to their American friends. [*Renewed applause.*]

TURKEY.

Miss MARY MARDIN [*Chautauqua salute*]: The Christian Endeavor Society of Marash, Turkey, sends greetings to this convention. [*Applause.*]

When the roll-call of the States was about half through, Dr. Clark suggested that the delegations rise while their representatives were speaking. This suggestion was acted upon, and added an interesting feature to the roll-call. At the close, those States which had been represented previous to the carrying out of the suggestion begged that they might have an opportunity to display their forces, and the opportunity was readily granted, the larger delegations evoking much applause as they rose from their seats.

After the singing of the hymn, "Army of Endeavor," Dr. Clark took the chair, and introduced, as the next speaker, Joseph Cook, of Boston. Mr. Cook was given a very hearty "Choctaw salute," as one of the unenlightened daily papers of New York had it, and spoke as follows:—

ADDRESS OF JOSEPH COOK.

WATCHWORDS FOR THE TWENTIETH CENTURY.

God be thanked, Mr. Chairman and ladies and gentlemen, that in modern geography and in the field of Christian Endeavor there are no foreign lands. God be thanked, also, that history shows more and more clearly, as the ages progress, that the undiluted blood of Christ will not circulate freely through the wasp waist of sectarianism. [*Applause.*] And God be thanked, also, that your organization has no wasp waist.

I salute this immense delegate assembly of young Christians with reverence, as made up of the prospective Pilgrim fathers and mothers of the twentieth century, for which you are setting the keynote.

My watchword is not the sovereignty of the masses nor the sovereignty of the classes, but the sovereignty of sound opinion. This means self-surrender to the self-evident in both science and scripture, or the freely accepted leadership of a scientific, biblical, and practical church, of which your society is the youngest birth.

Your organization is yet in its early years, but your Biblical and practical pledge to watchfulness and prayer has made your society already a spiritual Colossus bestriding continents and seas. It is interdenominational and international. It is both Christian and cosmopolitan. The conjunction of these two words is an inspiring but most characteristic sign of the times. Cæsar could not drive around the Roman Empire in less than a hundred days. We now send a letter, a bale of goods, or a man around the whole world in seventy circuits of the sun. The antipodes have locked hands. The world is hereafter to be healed or poisoned very much as a whole. There can be no more hermit nations. Your field is the world. The sky is the roof of but one family. This assembly, the largest religious gathering ever held on our continent, emphasizes Whittier's words : —

> " Behold the fall of Ocean's wall,
> Space mocked and Time outrun ;
> Around the world the thought of all
> Is as the thought of one."

If your growth has already been so remarkable, how necessary it is that you should have a soul fit to animate this prodigious body. I am not here to praise you. I reverence you far too much to offer you adulation to your faces but I would, if I could, describe the soul which you ought to breathe into an age vexed with most vital perils. Not that I shall say anything new. It is the business of the Church and of your organization to echo God ; and my whole watchword is God, who was, and is, and is to come.

Face to face with an age so inadequately trained in philosophy as to be annoyed by agnostic skepticism, what shall be your watchwords in the presence of learned or vulgar infidelity, which not only denies the Christian faith, but even doubts the fact of the immortality of man's soul? It is no more wonderful that we should live again than that we should live at all. It is less wonderful that we should continue to live than that we have begun to live, and it is certain that we have begun. Organism is not the cause of life in the human body, but life is the cause of the organization of our frame. We are woven by some power not in matter. The weaver goes before the web, and not the web before the weaver. You may tear up the web, and not injure the weaver. As the weaver which we call life has existed before the web he produces, and outside of it and in total independence of it, so may he exist after it and outside of it and in total independence of it.

What should be your watchword face to face with atheism in our time ? It is a certainty that there cannot be thought without a thinker. The universe is made on a plan, and a plan must be in existence somewhere before it is executed. When a plan is in existence and has not been executed, it is a thought of some mind. There cannot be thought without a thinker, any more than a here without a there, or before without an after. There must be, therefore, a personal God, for a thinker is a person. Matthew Arnold's Eternal Somewhat, which makes for righteousness, is demonstrably an Eternal Someone who makes for righteousness, and from whom forever and forever we cannot escape. What shall you say of the conditions of salvation face to face with the limp and lavender liberalism of our times? With what watchwords as to eternal life and death will you go into the twentieth century? There is a best way to live, and it is best to live the best way. The beautiful and awful thing in man is God in conscience, intellect, and will. The axiomatic truths are the axis truths of both science and Scripture. Self-surrender to the self-evident is the beginning of the sovereignty of sound opinion. I hold it to be a strictly self-evident assertion that unless a man loves what God loves and hates what God hates, he cannot be at peace in his presence, here or hereafter. We must be delivered from the love of sin and the guilt of sin, or there is no possibility of our being at peace with a holy God in life, or death, or beyond death. You dream that there is opportunity of repentance beyond the grave; but do you purpose yourselves to go and occupy that opportunity? Not you. But a hope that you will not put under your own head as a dying pillow you ought not to put under the head of your neighbor. Let immediate self-surrender to all the light you have be your watchword, every sin against light draws blood on the spiritual retina. "Now is the accepted time, now is the day of salvation." It is never safe for any man to die in his sins. All character, by the fixed laws of the self-propagating power of habit, tends to a final permanence, good or bad; and a final permanence can come but once. The *cans* and *cannots* of Scripture are based on strictly self-evident truths. Except a man be born of water, that is, delivered from the guilt of sin, and of the Spirit, that is, delivered from the love of sin, he *cannot* enter into the kingdom of heaven. "No man *can* serve two masters." "A fountain *cannot* bring forth both sweet water and bitter." Two *cannot* walk together, unless they are agreed. We cannot enter heaven, unless heaven enters us. The kingdom of heaven is within us. Unless heaven enters the soul, the soul cannot enter heaven. We shall not find heaven around us until we carry heaven within us.

What shall be your watchword, face to face with biblical criticism in our day? The past, at least, is secure. The Bible has lifted heathenism off its hinges and turned the dolorous and accursed ages into new channels. It has done so by the doctrine that it is necessary for man to be delivered from the love of sin and the guilt of it. That doctrine will never grow old while man is man. The Bible, and it only, teaches the way of deliverance from the love and the guilt of sin. The Bible is the most inspiring book in the world, and, therefore, it is certain that it is the most inspired. The more thoroughly you insist on the vital and central truths of Christianity, the more certain you are to become the rudder of the twentieth century.

The statue of Liberty lifts up her hand in benediction over this assembly. So does the statue of Faith at Plymouth. They join hands over our heads. The statue of Liberty, as she lifts her torch to sun and moon, seems to be uttering Webster's aspiration: "Liberty and union, now and forever, one and inseparable." And the statue of Faith answers, "Liberty and union, now and forever, one and inseparable." But these are impossible, except to a people whose God is the Lord. [*Applause.*] You are proud of your youth and our national progress. Whether the best days of the world are near or remote, it is certain that *your* best days are not far distant. Man's life means tender teens, teachable twenties, tireless thirties, fiery forties, forcible fifties, serious sixties, sacred seventies, aching eighties, shortening breath, death, the sod, God. Let us strike home, for we are going home. Under this benediction of the two mighty statues of our land I would have you look up to Christ and see that all the great watchwords of science, all the great watchwords of moral reform, all the great watchwords of politics that have prolonged influence on humanity are summed up in the word Christ. He teaches the doctrines of the necessity of a new birth and of the atonement, the fatherhood of God and the brotherhood of men, the fact of immortality, the eternal judgment. But these are the wheels within the wheels; these are the truths that must lie at the centre of successful republican government.

Look on the cross, and it will become no cross to bear the cross. Total self-surrender to God makes the soul a burning glass through which Divine light and heat ignite a new life. A soul wholly surrendered to God becomes a supernatural soul. A church is a company of surrendered and supernatural souls.

I am really dazzled by the vastness of the field this audience represents. The Pyrenees here make their bow to the Alleghanies, the Alleghanies to the Pyrenees. Here the Great Lakes, the St. Lawrence, the Mississippi, the Rhine, the Rhone, the Ganges, and the Yang-tse-Kiang flow into the Hudson at the gates of the Atlantic. But let us not be dazzled by geographical greatness. Body is nothing without soul. [*Applause.*] If you can imprint upon your hearts the axiomatic certainty that unless a man is born again and delivered from the love of sin and the guilt of it, he cannot be at peace with God, here or hereafter, you will make yourselves flames of fire through which God will look in a better age and take off the wheels of the chariots of his enemies and cause them to drag heavily. [*Applause.*]

When Charles Sumner first went into the Senate, Thomas Benton said to him, "The chief questions for American statesmanship have been decided. Webster, Clay, Calhoun, have passed away; nothing great will happen in your time." [*Laughter.*] When Edmund Burke was a young man he wrote a letter to a friend stating that he had a plan to take up his residence in Massachusetts for life. He believed that this country was sure of a great future, and was, undoubtedly, that part of the world where right effort, put forth early, would be the most certain of usefulness on a gigantic scale. The Roman eagles, when their wings were strongest, never flew as far as from Plymouth Rock to the Golden Gate. The longest straight line that can be drawn inside of the dominions of the proudest of the Cæsars will not reach from Boston to San Francisco. In the nineteenth century, the political ideas of the Americans whom Washington led and whom Milton, Cromwell, Hampden, Cicero, Cato, and Phocion educated, have conquered the Western hemisphere. In the twentieth they are likely to become predominant in the eastern hemisphere also. God be thanked that we have now on this continent no slave and no king. Our only road to safe government is through self-government. I must not speak too freely in praise of America in presence of representatives of so many other lands, but this I believe most solemnly, that as the Christian Church goes, so this Republic will go, and as America goes, so the world will go. [*Loud applause.*]

Supply follows demand in history. In recent years there has been a demand for the diffusion of liberty, property, and intelligence. There will soon be a demand for the diffusion of conscientiousness, and there will come slowly and through much anguish of the ages a supply. I foresee a great day for a scientific, biblical, and practical church. It is easy to forecast an age of prodigious importance for Christian Endeavor. Wordsworth talked of an aristocracy. It will not come. Carlyle talked of a government by the best. It cannot be elected. Soon the Church, and the True Church, will be all the hope of the world. It will save the world by goodness and by truth, by practice and by doctrine also.

The church needed by the American future must be scientific, biblical, and practical.

It must be scientific by a reasonable theology, by the absorption of all established science, by intellectual supremacy over rationalism, by mental primacy in literature and art, by indisputable authority in all philosophical research, by incisive triumph over popular crudity, by courage to think syllogistically and on its knees and to the thirty-two points of the compass.

It must be biblical by the spirit of the founder of Christianity, by finding in the Holy Spirit a present Christ, by the sense that nations are a theocracy and our Lord is the world's Lord, by the doctrine of sin, by the doctrine of an atonement, by the hope of immortality, and by a far and fixed gaze on an eternal judgment for the deeds done in the body.

It must be practical, by carrying vital piety to every death-bed, every hearthstone, every cradle, by enlisting all believers in religious effort, by sleepless religious printing, by schools saturated with devout learning, by making human legislation a close copy of natural law, by leadership in all just popular reforms, by everyday integrity and "Holiness to the Lord" written on the bells of the horses, on bank vaults, and on the very dust of the streets, and by making all secular pursuits spiritual avocations.

Chauncey Depew said, when the statue of Liberty was unveiled, that he had no doubt that the spirits of the Fathers were looking down on the scene of the dedication.

When I contemplate the possibilities of Christian Endeavor, I conjoin them with the possibilities of Ultimate America as a leader of Ultimate Civilization.

Cromwell and Hampden were once on shipboard, with the purpose of coming to America for life. Their spirits seem to stand among those of our later martyrs.

Once in the blue midnight, in my study on Beacon Hill in Boston, I fell into long thought as I looked out on the sea and on the land, and passing through the gate of dreams I seemed to behold the angel having charge of America standing in the air above the continent, and his wings shadowed either shore. There were about the angel a multitude whom no man could number, of all kindreds and tribes and tongues, and they conversed of what was, and is, and is to be in the Church and State. The voices of the multitude were like unnumbered thunders, and the brightness of the face of the angel above that of lightnings.

Then came forth before the angel three spirits with garments white as light, and I saw not their faces, but I heard the ten thousand times ten thousand call them by names known on earth, — Washington, Lincoln, and Garfield. And behind them stood Hampden, and Tell, and Miltiades, and Leonidas, and a multitude who had swords and crowns. And they said to the angel: "We will go on earth and teach the diffusion of liberty. We will heal America by political progress." And the angel said: "Go; you will be efficient, but not sufficient." Meanwhile, under immigrant wharves, and crowded factories, and suffocated alleys of great cities, and scheming conclaves of men, acute and unscrupulous, I heard far in the subterranean depths the black angels laugh.

Then came forth three other spirits with garments white as the light, and I saw not their faces, but I heard the ten thousand times ten thousand call them by names known on earth, — Hamilton, and Sumner, and Irving. And behind them stood Milton, and Plato, and Æschylus, and Euripides, and a multitude who had scrolls and crowns. And they said to the angel: "We will go on earth and teach the diffusion of education. We will heal America by popular intelligence." And the angel said: "Go; you will be efficient, but not sufficient." And meanwhile, under immigrant wharves and the same places as before I heard far in the subterranean depths the black angels laugh.

Then came forth three other spirits with garments white as the light. And I saw not their faces, but I heard the ten thousand times ten thousand call them by names known on earth, — Chase, and Seward, and Adams. And behind them stood the Roman Gracchi, and the multitude who had keys and crowns. And they said to the angel: "We will go on earth and teach the diffusion of property, — not socialism, not communism, but a fair day's wages for a fair day's work. We will heal America by self-respect of ownership." And the angel said: "Go; you will be very efficient, but not sufficient." Meanwhile, in the same places as before I heard far in the subterranean depths the black angels laugh.

Then came lastly forward before the angel three spirits with garments white as light. And I saw not their faces, but I heard the ten thousand times ten thousand call them by names known on earth, — Edwards, and Dwight, and Whitefield. And behind them stood Cranmer, and Wesley, and Luther, and the goodly company of the prophets and the apostles of all ages, and the multitude who had harps and crowns. And they said to the angel: "We will go on earth and teach the diffusion of conscientiousness; we will save America by righteousness." Then the angel rose and lifted up his far-gleaming hand to the heaven of heavens and said: "Go; not in one but only in all four of these leaves of the tree of life will be found the healing of the nations, — the diffusion of liberty, the diffusion of intelligence, the diffusion of property, and the diffusion of conscientiousness. You will be more than very efficient, but not sufficient."

I listened, and under Plymouth Rock, under Lincoln's grave, under Washington's tomb, under homes and schools worthy to be called Christian, I heard no sound; but under immigrant wharves and suffocated alleys of great cities, and scheming conclaves of men, acute and unscrupulous, I heard far in the subterranean depths the black angels laugh, but there came up now with the laughter, a sound as of the clanking of chains. I speak in a metaphor, but I hope not at random.

Then I looked, and the whole canopy above the angel was as if it were one azure eye, and into it the ten thousand times ten thousand looked, and I saw that they stood in one palm of the hand of Him into whose face they gazed, and that the soft axle of the world stood on the finger of another hand, and that both palms were pierced. I saw the twelve spirits which had come forth, and the foremost of the twelve was a leader of a scientific, a biblical, and a practical church, and they joined hands with each other and with the twelve hours and made perpetually a circui around and around the earth. And I heard a voice, after which there was no laughter: " YE ARE EFFICIENT, BUT I, AND I ONLY, AND I ALONE, AM SUFFICIENT." [*Great applause.*]

The morning session closed with the usual notices, the singing of the Doxology, and the benediction by the venerable Dr. Edward Beecher, of Brooklyn, brother of Henry Ward Beecher.

FRIDAY AFTERNOON.

Promptly at two o'clock the convention was called to order by Dr. Clark, and all joined in singing " At the Cross." Then, at the request of Dr. Clark, all united in repeating the Beatitudes, and it is safe to say that those majestic sentences were never uttered more impressively, since they fell from the lips of the Saviour, than they were on this occasion. Mr. Sankey then sang " When the mists have rolled away," the choir and audience alternating in the refrain.

Dr. CLARK: One of the staunchest friends of Christian Endeavor for many years has been the Rev. W. C. Bitting, pastor of the Mount Morris Baptist church of this city. [*Applause.*] I am glad to say that he will conduct the Free Parliament this afternoon. [*Applause.*]

FREE PARLIAMENT.

Mr. BITTING: Every Christian Endeavor convention held so far has been a record breaker. If there is an institution on the face of the earth that knows how to smash records, it is the Christian Endeavor movement. Last year at the parliament we had 67 speeches in 63 minutes. This afternoon we want to increase that number one hundred per cent, at least. Christian Endeavor eloquence does not consist in rhetoric, but in fact. We do n't believe in adorn ment of our speech, but we believe in the power of true witnessing and in the strength of a magnificent testimony. We have for eleven years been raising a multitude of lords and ladies, testifying in weekly parliaments all over the world, that is unequalled by any peerage recorded in all the history of heraldry. Old mother earth is fairly freckled with bright Christian Endeavor sunspots that have been burned upon her face by the Sun of Righteousness. I believe we are seeing that time of which the laureate spoke in his dream, when he referred to the time when

> "The war drum throbbed no longer, and the battle flags were furled
> In the Parliament of Man, and the Federation of the World."

Now, in our structure we have provisions for public speaking which are equalled by no other organization upon the earth. You talk, first of all, to your

REV. W. C. BITTING.

local societies, next to the local union, next to the State convention, and next to the International assembly. Each one of us is the centre of four concentric spheres of audience, and we have only to improve the opportunity, in order to benefit the organization that we love.

Now, every Parliament must have rules, and I propose to lay down the rules here. I shall be apostolic in that I shall take a maxim which has been given to us by Paul: "Let your speech be always seasoned with salt." Now, that means we are to have nothing insipid here this afternoon; we all understand that, but I want to make an acrostic out of that word "salt."

First, S stands for *Short*. We are going to give everybody, with perhaps one exception, only half a minute in which to tell what has been done. Then again, A stands for *Appropriate*. We don't want any verbal vagrancy; we don't want any rhetorical rambling this afternoon. Go straight, don't build any switches; we don't want to get off the track. L stands for *Loud*, [*Applause*] and the man that has the iron lung and the brass throat has a good equipment for speaking to this audience; the man that fills the building will fill the bill. [*Laughter*.] T stands for *True*. What we want to know is what you have done — what your society has done for yourself, for your pastor, for your church, for your town, for your county, and for your State? We want the facts. S-A-L-T, — can we all say it together? [*The audience repeated it*] Now, we all know what it means — *short, appropriate, loud, true*. Every man that is going to speak, let him stick out his tongue right now, and let me season it with *salt* before he begins.

Now, another thing, we have rules for the audience, and I want everybody who is going to listen to lend me his ears; I want to fill his ears with salt. S stands for *Silence*; A for *Attention*; L for *Love*; and T for *Thoughtfulness*. Thus the word for this hour is *salt* — for everybody, in the ear and on the tongue; and if, as the prime minister of this parliament, I can marry the tongue to the ear, and throw a shower of salt on the happy couple, we are going to have a magnificient family of children this afternoon. [*Laughter*.]

Now, I will set you the example. To my church this society is a fountain of perennial blessing; to the sailors on the sea, a haven of superb rest; to the car drivers on the Third Avenue line in this city, a benediction and an oasis in their severe labors; to the pastor it is a dayly fountain of infinite joy and undying inspiration. There are four young men from it who are entering the ministry of Jesus Christ, and who feel towards Christian Endeavor just as their pastor feels. [*Applause*.] I want to say that as a man, and as a minister, and as a Baptist, I have the best reason for being a Christian Endeavor man all the way up, all the way down, all the way through, all the way round, from the sole of my foot to the head of my crown. [*Laughter*.] Now, any member of the parliament can bring in a bill, and we will let him have a minute to present it.

In response to this invitation replies came in great numbers from all over the house, in some cases two or three delegates speaking at once.

The District of Columbia union is just as loyal to Christian Endeavor as to the flag that floats above the dome of the Capitol.

The society at Roaring Springs, Penn., has kept a church alive for several months while its pastor was sick.

The town of Amesbury, Mass., increased its vote against license this year 300 fold, mainly because of the work of the Christian Endeavor society. (*Applause*.]

The South Chicago union has declared its purpose to do all in its power to close the World's Fair on Sundays and to stop the sale of liquor.

The society at Columbia, South Dakota, has adopted the Fulton pledge, and has two young men studying for the ministry.

The society at Joliet, Ill, has sent out two foreign missionaries — one to Syria and one to Persia.

A Florida society has sent two ministers to Africa, and has one young man preparing for the ministry.

The Stewart Street Baptist society, of Providence, R. I., is supporting a missionary in the foreign field.

A Delaware society is educating a Japanese girl to go as a missionary to her own people.

The Garfield Memorial society, Washington, D. C., organized thirteen other Christian Endeavor societies in 18 months. [*Great applause.*]

A society at Galveston, Texas, has a Chinese Sunday school, and is supporting a missionary in China.

A society at Burgess, Ontario, with 40 members, is sustaining a native teacher in the New Hebrides.

The Niagara Methodist society is educating three students for the ministry.

A society at Riverside Chapel in New York has called a pastor, and expects to organize a church and pay his salary. [*Applause.*]

Plymouth society, of San Francisco, supports three mission Sunday schools, and is educating a boy in India.

The society at Fairfield, Conn., is running a Fresh Air Home, and entertaining twelve poor children from New York city, each one of whom remains two weeks. [*Applause.*]

Salt Lake City is to have the first monument to the Christian Endeavor movement in the shape of a church built by the Endeavor society of the Disciples of Christ. [*Loud applause.*]

The Hanson Place society, of Brooklyn, gives $200.00 a year to foreign missions, and supports a girl in Syria. It has another missionary in Brazil, and holds evangelistic services in the Brooklyn Navy Yard.

The societies of eastern New Jersey and Long Island are holding religious services regularly in all the life-saving stations in their districts, and in many cases these services are springing up into religious organizations, notably at Sandy Hook, where the Christian Endeavor society preached the first Protestant sermon ever preached at Sandy Hook. [*Applause.*] Societies in all districts where there are life-saving stations are requested to extend this work.

Phillips Congregational society, of South Boston, has contributed over $200 for missions, and has two young men who are about entering the ministry.

The First Presbyterian society, of South Bend, Ind., supports an active teacher in a foreign land, and one teacher in the South, and has two young ladies preparing to enter missionary work.

The society at Putney, Vt., has established two branch Sunday schools.

The Ninth Christian Church society, of Washington, was started one year ago. To-day it has 60 members, and is carrying on a mission Sunday school.

A society at Lynn, Mass., supports one missionary, and has two young men studying for the ministry.

The society of Mr. D. L. Moody's church, of Chicago, has five young men employed as city missionaries.

New London, Ind., has a population of 150. There are 75 members of the senior society, and 18 members of the junior society. [*Loud applause.*]

A society in Bloomington, Ill., is supporting a foreign mission school in India.

Westville, Ind., has a population of 700. Over 100 are in the senior society, and 50 in the junior society. [*Applause.*]

Armour Mission, Chicago, has a boy's brigade of 220 members, which is a wonderful help and support to the Christian Endeavor society.

The East Side Presbyterian church, of Des Moines, Ia., supports a girl's brigade and a boy's brigade too.

A Minneapolis society sends over 50 periodicals every week to missionaries in the West.

A New Jersey society is valiantly fighting race-track gambling. [*Applause.*]

Mr. Shaw said that the treasurer of the American Home Missionary society, of New York, reports that he has received $43,000 from the Congregational Christian Endeavor societies. [*Loud applause.*]

Three young men of the Hough Avenue society, Cleveland, which is only a year and and a half old, have started on a ten years course for the ministry.

A Missouri society of 50 members supports a mission Sunday school, and gave last year $300 to missions.

The sailors of Snug Harbor, Staten Island, have a society of 53 members — old sailors, as salt as mackerel. [*Applause.*]

A society in Bristol, R. I., of 75 members, is sustained entirely by the young lady members — not a single gentleman member.

The Congregational society of Terre Haute, Ind., has a mission school of 100 members, and has paid $400 towards building a chapel.

The Mary Allen Seminary for colored girls at Crockett, Texas, has a society of 170 active members. It had 30 conversions last year.

Rev. HERMAN WARSZAWIAK: To the glory of Jesus, the Saviour of mankind, I am glad to report to you, brethren and sisters in Christ Jesus, that our Hebrew brothers are just now beginning to look up to Jesus as their Messiah, and I hope in a very few years all Israel will confess Christ to be their Messiah. I am glad to report that in this last year or two I have been permitted by the Lord Jesus to preach to about 50,000 Israelites in this city, and a great many of them are confessing Christ as their Messiah. We ask the Christian Endeavor societies to pray for the conversion of all Israel.

The society at Newburg, Ore., is running five Sabbath schools, and has starved its only saloon keeper to death.

Leavitt Street Methodist Church society, Chicago "We are doing our best to educate the heathen of darkest Chicago."

"Billy" Sunday, once famous as a ball player, from Chicago, said: "All the young men and women of our society have come out of the dormitory into the vineyard of Christ."

Aledo, Ill., Christian Endeavor society has supported two missionaries in China for three years. South End Tabernacle supports three native preachers in China, Japan, and India.

Reformed Episcopal Church Christian Endeavor society, of Germantown, Pa., sings and prays at the poorhouse every week.

North Liberty, Pa., sent 114 sacks of flour to the Russians.

Indianapolis, Ind., Friends Christian Endeavor society are educating a young Mexican for missionary work, and are starting a society in Alaska.

El Paso, Texas. The metropolis of the Southwest society, sends a union delegate from the M. E. Church, South, and the First Presbyterian Church. They are faithful, enthusiastic, and growing. As long as the Rio Grande flows they will be found at their post.

The society of the Second Reformed Church, of Somerville, New Jersey, is supporting a boy in India for work among his people.

Phillips Church, Boston, Mass., has given Dr. Clark to the United Society of Christian Endeavor as its president. [*Applause.*]

The Woonsocket, R. I., local union numbers 400 members, and is strong for Christ.

Duluth, Minn. First Presbyterian Church contributed to erect school for colored girls; built new church in Duluth.

Ravenswood (W. Va.) Presbyterian society is educating a native Siam boy to work among his people.

Providence, R. I., Elmwood Congregational society has bought a horse for a home missionary.

Ciudad Juarez, Mexico, Y. P. S. C. E. has fourteen members studying for the ministry.

Chicago West Division Union held sixteen missionary conferences in the past three months. As a result, six young people have given themselves to missionary work: a large number of missionary committees have been appointed: contributions to missions largely increased. They will not rest until every society in the West Division has a missionary committee, and every Christian Endeavorer is an enthusiast for missions.

Franklin, Ind. A young lady from the Christian Endeavor society of the Presbyterian Church has lately gone to Southern Africa in the interest of the temperance cause.

The Christian Endeavor society in Bombay, India, supports twelve mission enterprises in that city.

This closed the "free parliament," over one hundred delegates having taken part. The audience joined in singing "The Endeavor Band."

DR. CLARK: We must now pass on to the Junior hour and consider a department of our work which is as important to the Christian Endeavor movement as any other. Many men, from what I hear and from what I read in the newspapers, are lectured by their wives. It is not very often that a man introduces his wife to lecture to him, but that is my privilege this afternoon. Mrs. Clark is very often accused of having started the Christian Endeavor movement. She denies the charge as often as it is made; but I can assure you of this: had it not been for the constant support and sympathy and unflinching help of the pastor's wife in Williston church, I doubt very much if the first Christian Endeavor society would have been started. [*Applause.*] It is not her desire, nor is it my own, that she should speak here this afternoon, but our general secretary, in his persuasive way, has prevailed upon her to appear here in accordance with the wishes of a great many friends. In introducing Mrs. Clark to you, may I ask you to be as quiet as possible and to remember, as she uses her voice, that she is " but yet a woman." [*Applause.*]

The audience manifested their love and respect for Mrs. Clark in a very emphatic manner as she came forward to read her paper on " Junior Christian Endeavor."

MRS. CLARK'S ADDRESS.

After Christ's resurrection he still had many things to say to his disciples — words of comfort, of counsel, and of cheer. One message he brought especially for Peter, who greatly needed both comfort and counsel. Peter had sinned but he had repented, and in his sorrow he longed to do something to show his love for his Master. The loving Saviour, who saw what was in Peter's heart, came to him with a question and a message. " Simon, son of Jonas, lovest thou me? Feed my lambs." He does not ask him now to express in words his penitence, his sorrow, his purpose for the future — only this one question is necessary: " Lovest thou me?" If Peter's heart is really full of love to Christ, then he may work for Christ.

> "If Christ, the Lord, should come to-day,
> As once to Peter by the sea,
> And low and tenderly should say,
> Oh, my disciple, lovest thou Me?
> To thee and me,
> What would your answer be?"

If we can answer with Peter, " Thou knowest that I love thee," then to us also will come a message from the Master. If we love him, we may work for him, for love is the only condition of service. He will tell us what we may do, and he will give us strength and wisdom to do it. He will not give to all of us just the same work that he gave to Peter, but if we look to him for direction, we shall find the work we are fitted for.

FEED MY LAMBS.

To some of us to-day, and perhaps to some who are not expecting it, comes the same message that came to Peter: " Feed my lambs." We have heard the command and we want to obey, but how shall we do it? How shall we feed the children with the bread of life? How shall we lead them into the love of Christ, and train them for active service for Christ and the Church?

The many junior societies of Christian Endeavor that are springing up all over the land bring one answer to this question. Through this means many children have already learned to make themselves very helpful in the church, and have found many ways of showing their love to Christ. But many of us do not feel that we know much about a junior society. It seems a fitting thing, in a Christian Endeavor convention like this, to speak a few words for our little brothers and sisters, the junior Endeavorers, — for real Christian Endeavor would certainly never shut out the children, — and the same methods that have been helpful with the older people may be used for children. If so, why cannot the children be just as well cared for in the older society? Why should they have a separate society of their own?

NEED OF THE JUNIOR SOCIETY.

What is the need of the junior society? How should it be organized, and how should it be carried on? A few suggestions in answer to these questions may, perhaps, be found helpful.

We are often asked, "Why should there be a junior society?" A very little practical experience will show any one that the little children and the older boys and girls and young people cannot so easily be trained and taught together. Some of the children can, perhaps, attend the older meetings, and can be helped and strengthened and taught; but they need more than that. They need to learn how to show their love to Christ, not in words but in deeds. If they have learned to love him, they want to work for him, — they are not old enough or wise enough to do much committee work or work of any kind in the older society. For the good of the society, the work must be done by those who are older.

The children can receive help, they can be sponges and absorb; but that is not the best and wisest treatment for them. The junior society takes the little children, and keeps them and trains them and nurtures them till they are fourteen years old. By that time, if they have been wisely trained and taught, they should be ready to be really helpful, — to take part in the meetings and to give efficient service on committees in the older society, and an opportunity should be found for them there as soon as possible.

MOTHERS SHOULD ORGANIZE.

How should a junior society be organized? It would be very helpful if in some way the mothers could be organized before beginning with the children. I have never heard of a Mothers' Endeavor society, but I have thought of inventing one with a constitution somewhat changed, perhaps, and a little different object in view, but it will be real Christian Endeavor, just the same. I have not yet secured a patent on the invention, and if any one here present would like to anticipate me in this, I am willing to give the benefit of the suggestion free of charge to all whom it may concern. Of this thing I am sure, — a junior society cannot be made perfect without the hearty sympathy and cordial coöperation of the mothers.

Of course it will sometimes happen in mission work that there will be children who have almost no home training, and little or nothing can be expected from the mothers. Perhaps all the help the children will receive will be from the junior meetings. In such a case all the more time and thought must be given to plan the best ways of helping the children. In most churches, however, the mothers can be very helpful, if they will, and they should be taken into partnership at the beginning. So many mothers do not seem to understand the work of the society or the importance of the pledge or their duty in regard to it. It might, perhaps, be well to begin by talking it all over with the pastor and his wife as to having it brought before the mothers, either at the mothers' meeting or the sewing circle, or at some church sociable.

SOME GOOD ADVICE.

Have a paper prepared to be read to the mothers, explaining the object of the society, and just how it will help the children, and the importance of the pledge. Perhaps it will be well also to emphasize the fact that the mother also signs a pledge. On the junior pledge cards which are used in many societies we read these words: "I am willing that ——— shall sign the pledge, and I will do all I can to help him keep it. Signed ———."

Not long ago a mother, whose boy was a member of a Junior Endeavor society (though not a very faithful one), said to the superintendent: "I am glad to have my boy a member of the society, and I hope he will want to go the meetings, but I don't think it best to urge him too much." She was afraid he might acquire a distaste for religious things, and yet I have reason to think that that mother sometimes thought it best to urge her boy to go to school, thereby running the risk of his forming a distaste for books. I think it just possible that she sometimes found it necessary to urge him to wash his face, even at the risk of his acquiring a distaste for water. At the same time, that mother did not seem to realize at all that every time her boy purposely stayed away from the meeting he was breaking a solemn promise which she had as solemnly promised to help him keep. If he no longer wished to keep it, she should have insisted upon his returning his pledge card and getting released from the obligation. Such instances as this, and they are not infrequent, make it seem very necessary that, if possible, Christian mothers should fully understand it before their children join the society. [*Applause.*]

EXPLAIN TO THE CHILDREN.

When the children are called together, the whole matter should be very clearly explained. Read the pledge to them and enlarge upon it. Show them how much it means and how very careful they should be in making such a solemn promise. Make them understand clearly that the meetings will be prayer meetings, that they will come there not simply for a good time, but to learn about Jesus and how they may love him more and serve him more faithfully. While all this should be explained very fully and clearly, yet it need not be told in such a way as to discourage or deter them from signing the pledge.

A wise, loving leader will know how to tell the story so tenderly and winningly that the children will understand it, and know that, while it is a serious matter to sign such a pledge, yet it is a more serious matter to be unwilling to sign it, and that if they do it, trusting in Jesus for strength, he will help them to keep it, and they will be glad to do it for Christ's sake and in his name. The children should have plenty of time to consider the pledge, and should not be too strongly urged to sign it. Let them take it home, and talk it over with their mothers, and bring it back at the next meeting, signed, if they are willing, but not unless it is their own desire and choice. It is better to begin with a very few members and let the society grow slowly, than to have the children join hastily or thoughtlessly.

A VERY IMPORTANT MATTER.

It may seem to some that this would be shutting out just the ones who most need the help of the meetings. The good children will be good any way. It is the thoughtless, restless, mischievous children and those who have not much home training who need to be helped and taught and trained to Christian service. This is a very important matter, and should not be overlooked. These children certainly do need the help of the meetings, and should have it. The meetings should be free to all, and every child who is willing to come should be cordially welcomed and lovingly guided and taught, but they should not sign the pledge or become members of the society till they can do it voluntarily and thoughtfully and conscientiously.

After two or three meetings have been held, let the children choose their own officers,— a president, vice-president, secretary, and treasurer. It would perhaps be better for the superintendent to appoint the committees, one at a time, as soon as it is possible to plan work to be done and find children to do it. It is well to have as many children at work as possible, therefore as many committees should be appointed as can be wisely planned for. Usually about the same committees will be needed in the junior society as in the older one.

As soon as the society is fairly organized, it would be well to hold a special meeting for the officers and committees, to explain their duties and responsibilities to them, and to pray with and for them; and frequent short meetings should be held afterwards with each committee by itself, that the children may be faithfully and carefully taught and trained in Christian work.

HOW TO CONDUCT THE MEETING.

There seem to be various methods of conducting the children's meetings. In some societies the superintendents always preside; in others the children frequently do it. Whichever method may seem best, it should always be remembered that the meeting is a prayer meeting in which every child must take some part. A Junior Endeavor society is not a primary Sunday-school class. The object of the meeting is not mainly to teach the children Bible verses, nor to give them instruction. It should be a genuine Christian Endeavor society, and, so far as possible, should be carried on as the older society is. The meetings should be prayer meetings, where the children should be taught to pray sincerely and intelligently and trustingly for just the blessings they want, and to tell in simple, childlike words of their love to Christ and their desire to serve him. If the leader will ask a few simple questions on the topic of the day, to be answered in the meeting by the children, it will help them to learn to express their thoughts on the subject.

THE VALUE OF THE PLEDGE.

The importance of the pledge should be often impressed upon the children, and the leader can do much to help them keep it, especially the part relating to daily Bible reading and prayer. It will be well to prepare a special plan of Bible readings for the children, and to ask them each week how many have remembered to read at least a few verses every day and to think of what they have read and to pray for help to understand it and obey it.

The committee work should be genuine work in and for the church. The lookout committee, if carefully chosen, can be taught to do nearly the same work as that done by the same committee in the older society. The missionary committee can help to prepare programmes for the missionary meetings, can obtain subscribers to the missionary magazines, and can help to prepare a list of missionaries and mission stations, that each child may have his special mission station and missionary to pray for.

The scrap-book committee can look over the *Golden Rule* and other religious papers each week, and cut out whatever they find that will be helpful in any way, and save it to be read in some meeting, or to be pasted into a scrap book for the use of the society. Sometimes a letter from some other junior society, if read at the meeting, will suggest efforts, or give new enthusiasm to the children, or some hints or directions for committee work, or some helpful story will be found.

WITH LOVING CARE.

With loving care and watchfulness and patience, all the committees may be trained to do good, faithful work, and by the time the children are fourteen they ought to be ready to graduate into the elder society, and to be really helpful there, and work should be found for them there as soon as it may be conveniently arranged.

The connection between the two societies should be very close. Their relation is that of the older brothers and sisters in the family to the little ones. I know a little four-year-old boy who looks up with great respect and admiration to his twelve-year-old brother, and tries in every possible way to follow his example, both in word and in action. How very important, then, that this older brother should make his life worthy of such respect and admiration, and his example such that it may safely be followed. Is not here a hint for the young men and older boys in our societies? Should they not make their example such that their little brothers in the junior societies may wisely follow them?

THE JUNIORS OUGHT TO REPORT.

It would be a good thing for the older society to have a report from the junior society as often as once a month in their business meetings, when the various committees report. Perhaps once a year the officers and committees of the two societies might hold a meeting together to plan and pray for the work for the year. An invitation to such a meeting would certainly please the juniors, and might be made very helpful to them.

Suppose the president of the older society should take pains to find out who is the junior president, and should ask about the society and what its president was doing and planning for it, and should tell something of his own hopes and plans for the older society. Don't you think that little president would feel honored and helped by the very interest and sympathy shown, even if nothing more was done, and wouldn't he get some new ideas of what a president might be and ought to be in his society? You remember in the story of "Pilgrim's Progress" that Greatheart was appointed to lead the pilgrims to the Celestial City, and you remember that he led not only Christiana but also her four boys all the way, never leaving them till he had conducted them safely to the very borders of the heavenly country.

Christian Endeavorers, you ought all to be Greathearts travelling to a better land, guiding other pilgrims on the way, and always ready to lend a hand to help the little pilgrims over all the hard places, and to do all that you can, both by word and example, to lead them safely to the celestial city. If we think of this as a part of our work for Christ and the Church, and pray for guidance, we shall find many ways of helping these little brothers and sisters of ours; remembering Christ's own words: "Inasmuch as ye have done it unto one of the least of these, ye have done it unto me." [*Prolonged applause.*]

Dr. CLARK: I am glad to tell you that a few days after this convention is over, Mrs. Clark will start with me on a voyage to other countries. She will go, I think, in the interests of Junior Endeavor to Australia, China, Japan, India, Turkey, and Spain. [*Loud applause.*]

Messrs. Sankey and Stebbins then sang the duet, "I shall be satisfied," in a manner which greatly pleased the audience.

Dr. CLARK: I have an unexpected and a very great pleasure now before me. We are told by the wise political prognosticator that the next president and vice-president of the United States, whatever else they may be, will be good Presbyterians, [*Laughter and applause*] since the four leading candidates belong to that honored church. It is my great privilege to introduce to you one of those four Presbyterians this afternoon — our recent honored minister to the court of France, the Honorable Whitelaw Reid.

At this announcement there ensued the greatest demonstration which the convention had yet witnessed. The applause was tremendous, and as Mr. Reid came forward he was obliged to wait several moments for the enthustasm to subside, finally raising his hand to quell it. He spoke briefly, as follows: —

ADDRESS OF HON. WHITELAW REID.

Mr. Chairman, Ladies and Gentlemen: This is a most inspiring sight to which your committee has invited me. Such an organization as you are here displaying, animated by such purposes, and representing as it does thousands of individual communities all over this broad land, is an incalculable force for good, not merely to those communities, but to this metropolis and to the whole country. [*Loud applause.*] You will expect few remarks from me, and yet I cannot resist the temptation to thank you for the opportunity and for the privilege of witnessing this magnificent spectacle, of seeing something of the enthusiasm which you have brought into your great work, and of expressing my own sympathy, and more, my admiration. [*Applause.*] Only one word more, and that a recollection of a Fourth of July thought which may not seem inappropriate to you now. Our fathers who laid the foundation of the civil and religious liberty we enjoy were men who planted their fortifications on every hillside as they advanced to the conquest of the continent. You know what those fortifications were,—the school house and the church. [*Applause.*] Let us guard them as our fathers guarded them, and we shall preserve the fair heritage we have received, and transmit it in our turn, grand and beneficent, beyond their thought or ours, to untold generations of men. [*Loud applause.*]

The assembly then sang with fine effect "My country, 'tis of thee," the last verse being especially impressive.

Next came the Junior Parliament, conducted by Miss Kate H. Haus, of St. Louis. Miss Haus spoke in a remarkably clear voice, reaching every portion of the hall.

JUNIOR PARLIAMENT.

Dear Friends: We want the same "salt" in this junior parliament that we had in the senior parliament; but we want this much additional; namely, that those who do not intend to take part in this conference shall salt down their tongues and their feet and keep still until it is over. [*Laughter.*] Now, as the time is short we want to hear from you first about your helpful committees, and how you manage them; and please all remember the "salt." [*Loud applause.*]

The Woodside, N.J., Presbyterian society was 100 strong at its first anniversary.

The members of a society in Decatur, Ill., are teaching their parents to pray.

The society in Asheway, R.I., was organized April 1, and three have joined the church.

A delegate spoke of three junior societies belonging to a local union, and from these last winter 50 came into the kingdom.

The Alleghany society of 50 members is less than six months old. The children come, rain or shine, and are glad to help in leading the meetings.

A Louisiana junior society has 65 members, and is doing a grand work.

Another junior society was reported as trying to serve Christ along missionary and temperance lines.

The Central Presbyterian society, of Chicago, only two months old, has 38 members, and sends one delegate here.

The First Presbyterian society of Kansas City, three months old, with 50 members, also sends a delegate.

Bethany Church, Philadelphia, has a junior society of 150 members, and a boys' brigade of 75 members.

The First Presbyterian society at Braddock, Pa., has 60 members, and is doing a good work. They sent a Christmas box out into Indian Territory last winter.

The M. E. Church, of Greenville, N.Y., has a junior society of 104 members. The boys are interested and induced to come by teaching them the doctrines of the New Testament Scriptures, and letting them speak and pray as the old folks do.

The society at Bethany, Conn., has 72 members. The boys and girls all come alike, rain or shine, attending better than the members of the other society. Seven joined the church last Sunday. The boys divide the work with the girls.

A Nebraska society of 120 members is educating a scholar in India, paying $25 a year. Some 40 have joined the church during the past year.

An Oregon society of 115 members finds that one hour is not long enough for them to have their meeting in.

Jersey City has a junior local union of which Mrs. Alice M. Scudder is president. They have had two junior rallies, and have welcomed Dr. Clark, the president of the society.

Montreal has 10 junior societies, and will form a union next month. A Methodist society of 42 members recently gave an entertainment which netted $50, and that was paid for educating a young man for the ministry who is taking the pastor's place in his absence.

The Rochester union commenced with 7 members. To-day it has 700.

A Methodist society in New York has 80 members, and is going to make them all Methodists and every one a good Christian Endeavorer.

The Stapleton society on Staten Island is one year old, and has 100 members, and supports a sewing-class and gives instruction in dining-room work, making beds, etc. They gave an entertainment recently which netted one hundred and eighty dollars.

Miss HAUS: In the two minutes more I want to say just this: You Christian Endeavorers who have no junior society connected with your senior society, what are you going to say to the Master when you stand before his throne without one young soul that you have won to him? What will you say when he asks, "Where is that little brother and sister I gave you the opportunity of bringing to me?" Will you bring the Lord just those old ears of corn that have only two or three good grains on them? or will you bring him a whole grand army of young souls that you have won for the Master, so that when you stand before him you will have a crown that is filled with jewels composed of those young souls that you have led to Christ, while you may be able to say to him, "Here, Lord, am I and the little ones thou hast committed to my trust." Go home and do that, dear Christian Endeavorers, and inside of five years we will not only shake the city of New York, we will not only make every reporter in this grand country of ours feel the strength of Christian Endeavor, but we will shake the world, and gain the world for Christ. [*Applause.*]

Mr. Sankey then sang "Bringing in the Sheaves," adopting the expedient which was tried with so much success at Minneapolis of having the audience sing the refrain in alternate choirs. A batch of notices and telegrams were read, another hymn was sung, and then Dr. Clark introduced Mr. Sumantrao Vishnu Karmarkar, a native Hindoo, wearing his turban and silk sash, who was given an ovation by the audience. Mr. Karmarkar spoke clearly and in excellent English, his subject being "Christianity for India."

ADDRESS OF MR. KARMARKAR.

It gives me very great pleasure to represent the teeming millions of India, a land which has been famous for its profound learning, for its beautiful architecture, and for its exquisite shawls; and it gives me still greater pleasure to be here as a delegate, and to bring to you the greetings of the Young People's Society of Christian Endeavor in connection with the American Mission of the Congregational church at Bombay. We have here four representatives: one is in Philadelphia, and three are sitting here behind me, American missionaries. My wife, I am sorry to say, cannot be here this afternoon, but she joins with me in giving you the greetings of our society. This society was first formed in 1885, the first day in January, at the home of our beloved pastor, who is preacher for the Bombay church. No foreign missionary funds support him, but we support our pastor at Bombay. There we started this society, and we formulated a rule that all those who believed in the Bible could become members of the organization; also that those who were willing to work outside of their regular work could become members, and those who did not work for two months, after being notified, should be summarily dismissed. We did not want any dead members in our Christian Endeavor society. It was a great question which came before us, — how we were going to have missionaries as members of the society, because they were paid by the American church to do Christian work. But missionaries have an inventive genius; they said, we will translate the Christian Endeavor literature into Mahratti, and publish it, and in that way be of service to the society. The society has divided its work into three or four branches, — the street preaching, the house-to-house visitation, the Sunday-school work, and tract distribution. There are superintendents over each of these departments, and a committee which has to see that the members are enlisted in these various branches, and that they do their work regularly and report every month. After the society was formed, we had about 50 members in our society. We also have a department for the women, and a lady superintendent over this department, who has for her duty to see that every young lady is engaged — not in the technical sense, [*laughter*] but in the ordinary sense — in active Christian work. I was the secretary of this society from the beginning, but the year we left India, that is, in 1888, we reported that our society, through 21 of its members, had preached 600 times during the year, and that about 33 members had conducted 12 heathen Sunday schools, whose attendance was over 700 heathen children. We distributed 6,000 tracts that year.

This is the work the Christian Endeavor society is doing at Bombay. Though the membership is small, yet it is an energetic body, and the great aim of the society is not only to edify themselves, but to save souls. For that purpose every member of the society goes out and reaches those who are not saved, and those who are worshipping idols of brass, and stone, and other material. Dear friends, this society sends you its greetings. I have here a letter from the secretary of that society. He says, "Dear brother in Christ: I am permitted by the Christian Endeavor society, in connection with the American Mission church at Bombay, to inform you that you are appointed delegate from this society to the great Christian Endeavor Society convention to be held in the United States of America in July next. I have to request that you will kindly convey the Christian greetings of the society to the convention, which we hope our precious Father in Heaven will abundantly bless." These are the greetings of my own society. We now have four or five societies in the Bombay Presidency, and they are all actively at work in the cause of Christ. I believe in this Christian Endeavor movement. We believe in this organization, because it stimulates the young people of India. The young men and women are stirred up, and work actively in the cause of Christ. According to the last census, we have one million active Christians in India. [*Applause.*] I represent this body at this hour, and these young men and women of this great Christian community are to be stirred up to do active Christian work all over India. I am glad our beloved President is going to my country to place before the Bengalese, and the Punjaubese, the Mahrattis, the Tamil, and the Telugu people, the need of this Christian Endeavor society. A hearty greeting, dear President, awaits you in India. They will deck you with beautiful garlands and flowers, and not give you a piece of stone, as the people here have given you. [*Laughter and applause.*]

We need Christian Endeavor, to save the five millions of educated youths who have learned the English language, and who are imbibing the American and English infidel literature. They need our Christian men and women to go among them and lead Christian lives, and present before them the glorious cause of Christ. We need the Christian Endeavor societies for the millions of women in India. There are one hundred and forty millions of women who hold tenaciously to their idolatrous faith. You know if a woman takes it into her head to do anything, she will do it. [*Laughter.*]

Now, I want to say a last word for India. My message to this great Christian Endeavor convention is this: Lay up treasures in heaven. What treasures? No wealth, no good works, no honor, no fame will go to heaven, but precious souls will go to heaven. Thousands are dying in India. They want your sympathy; they want your help. Lay up your treasures in heaven by rescuing these precious souls from the thraldom of idolatry. Send them to heaven, and they will meet you there; lay up your treasures in heaven. [*Loud applause.*]

The missionary hymn, "From Greenland's Icy Mountains," was then sung, after which Dr. Clark introduced Mr. Jue Hawk, of St. Louis, a young Chinaman, who spoke on "Christian Endeavor for China." Mr. Hawk was also very cordially received, and his address proved to be one of the best of the entire convention.

ADDRESS OF MR. JUE HAWK.

It gives me great pleasure to appear before your convention. Indeed, I cannot express my appreciation of this privilege and my gratitude for this kind invitation to speak a few words to this vast gathering of young Christian people from all parts of the globe. This invitation indicates the broad feeling of all Christians toward one another,— a fellowship which can only come from the recognition of the fatherhood of God and the brotherhood of man. It shows that the work of Christian Endeavor is not confined to any one nation, but, like Christianity itself, is intended for all nations. I am glad to say that this society makes no distinction of color or nationality. [*applause*] but that we all believe in the Word of God,— that "there is no difference between the Jew and the Gentile, for the same Lord over all is rich unto all them that call upon him"; [*applause*] that "God hath made of one blood all nations of men to dwell on the face of the earth"; that "there is neither Jew nor Gentile, bond nor free"; that there is neither English nor German, American nor Chinese; but that we are "all one in Christ Jesus." [*Loud applause.*]

I admire the freedom which this country enjoys and which it extends to those who come to share these blessings: but when compared with the freedom enjoyed in the kingdom of God, the divinest spirit of freedom — that is infinitel greater than the freedom of this or any other government. [*Applause.*] Christ says, "Ye shall know the truth, and the truth shall make you free." This is freedom in its highest and broadest meaning. No political convention would permit a Chinaman to occupy the floor for a moment; but even the Chinese are welcome to the Christian Endeavor convention. [*Applause.*] Your great country is free to all except the Chinese; but your Christianity, thank God, is broad enough to welcome even the heathen Chinese. [*Great enthusiasm and the Chautauqua salute.*]

As I am a native of China, a disciple of Jesus, and also a member of this Christian Endeavor movement, it is my Christian duty to speak of the possibilities of Christian Endeavor work among our people at home. It is a well-known fact that the young people of any country are more impressionable to religious truth than the older people, and the people of China are no exception to this rule. Besides that, tradition and superstition have not been implanted in the minds of the young people to the same extent that they have been in the minds of older people, and for that reason the young people of China are more susceptible to the teachings of Christ. There is at present no opportunity for the people to take an active share in any religious work, such as the Sunday school, Endeavor work, prayer meetings, etc. They are taught to be entirely passive in China. All religious rites are performed by priests, and all that the people have to do is to listen. I believe that if an opportunity for religious activity were offered to them, they would gladly embrace it. Although our people are conservative in the highest degree, still, by earnest, persistent, devoted pleading, many of them, especially the young, would be led to the acceptance of the truth as it is in Christ Jesus. In view of what has already been accomplished in China through missionary efforts, it cannot be doubted that this Christian Endeavor movement has a great mission there. If the missionaries are able to do so much good and reap so large a harvest for Christ, how much more glorious the harvest would be if such a force as the Young People's Society of Christian Endeavor could be added to the other Christian agencies that are operating in that country. The efforts in Christian Endeavor work among that people are meeting with abundant success. Brethren, shall we not go in and possess the land? Tell me, does not the modern Macedonian cry come to you from China, "Come over and help us"? Since we are not permitted to come to this country, is it not all the more important that you go to China with the Gospel, and save our people? [*Loud applause.*]

The Christian world is now hastening on toward greater unity and strength, and in this I rejoice, as it is of deep interest to my native land and to all idolatrous countries. May this great movement of Christian Endeavor, through the strength of God, hasten that union and co-operation among all Christians which will win the whole world for him, so that "at the name of Jesus every knee shall bow, of things in heaven, and things in earth, and things under the earth; and that every tongue shall confess that Jesus is Lord, to the glory of God the Father." Seven years ago, before I had attended the university at Des Moines, Iowa, I was a benighted heathen, worshipping gods of stone and paper; but now, thank God, my mind has been illuminated by the Gospel and my heart filled with the love of God; and while I am in this land of liberty I rejoice in its Christianity. But when I think of my native land, of my brothers and sisters, my father and mother, who are yet sitting in darkness and the shadow of death, my heart is stirred up like Paul's at Athens, and I cry like the prophet of old, "Here am I, send me." May God help us to preach Christ and him crucified among all nations, until every nation and tongue and tribe and kindred shall join in singing "Praise God, from whom all blessings flow." [*Prolonged applause.*]

After Mr. Hawk's address, Dr. Clark announced a solo by Mr. E. F. Yarnell, of Indiana. Mr. Yarnell came immediately on the platform, and in a clear and pleasing voice, with unusually distinct enunciation, he sang without accompaniment a song entitled "There's a wonderful story I have heard long ago." The audience listened intently and applauded the singer to the echo, but there was no time for an encore.

Dr. CLARK: We have heard already in this convention from a cabinet minister, and another is to preside over our assembly to-night. We have also heard from a vice-presidential candidate. But we are now to hear from a prince, the son of an African chief,— Mr. Thomas E. Besolow, of Liberia, Africa. [*Loud applause and the Chautauqua salute.*]

ADDRESS OF MR. THOMAS E. BESOLOW.

My dear beloved: It gives me very great pleasure to have this opportunity of speaking to you in behalf of Africa. I am very much gratified to have this opportunity. My heart burns within me and my soul is melted for God and for his work. Yea, even from the very first time when my father sent me to the coast with the anticipation of my acquiring the English language, though I had never realized what Christianity was,— from the very first day I heard that marvellous story of Christ told me by a missionary from this American continent, I have ever turned my thought toward the subject and it has always been before me and it always shall be before me.

For a great many years Africa has been a land toward which we have looked to know whether her sons and daughters are capable of receiving this Gospel of Jesus Christ, whether there are men who can be truly evangelized and Christianized and take on all that belongs to Christianity and civilization, I am glad, my friends, that the day has come when men have learned one central fact — the brotherhood of man; and to-day we are drawn closer and closer- to-day we are touching shoulder to shoulder, and blessed be God, the time is coming when Ethiopia shall truly stretch forth her hands unto God. The time is approaching. Christian missionaries have gone into the dark continent for the purpose of evangelizing the land. We have had a great many discouraging circumstances about the work, but it shows one central fact, and gives ocular demonstration thereof: that in our religion there is efficacy, there is force, there is power. Where is the man or the woman who will leave this blessed continent with all the fine comfort and all the facilities of this grand nineteenth century, and, counting it nothing, go away back to that dark continent, away down to the people buried under an empty religion, and lift them up to the cross and tell them the humble story that Christ has died, and that he died for Africa as well as for every other land?

Another thing touched my heart. When I looked on my left here and saw men from China and India here to-day, I felt that the world is coming together and that we are realizing more and more the brotherhood of man. Beloved, I have not the time to tell you what has been done in the dark continent. You know yourselves what we have struggled under — slavery, the rum traffic, and all the iniquitous crimes brought upon that continent. But God has been with us; he has not forsaken us; he is with us and guiding us steadily. He has given us in recent years a man, Henry M. Stanley, who has heroically entered into the jungles and dark places of Africa and opened them up so that to-day we have more knowledge of the continent; and we Christian men and women have the opportunity to go into this dark continent and liberate these men who are under the power of a false religion and are deep down in the scale of degradation, laying aside our prejudices and differences, and bringing all these poor people into the fold of Christ. For myself, I desire no grander work than this. I was born heir to a throne. My uncle to-day sits on that throne; but blessed be God who reigns on high, I have a grander throne. [*Applause.*] Ah, beloved, when I look away back into that heathen darkness and think of the pit out of which I was digged and brought to this marvellous light of the Gospel, to my Christ and my King, I desire nothing else than to work for him as long as I live. [*Applause.*] It is my purpose in coming to this country. I have met with many obstacles and difficulties. My uncle who sits on the throne to-day is trying continually to persecute me. No longer than two months ago he planned to assassinate me, but, thank God, his plan was discovered before he could carry it out. He is a usurper; he took my father's throne when I was only a boy; now he wants to assasinate me. But the God of Abraham and of Isaac, who overrules all things in this world, shall carry me on and on until I am prepared for the work to which I have dedicated my life, and have returned to the dark continent. [*Applause.*]

This continent is a mysterious continent. That is no new topic. It was such to the men of Rome and Greece and Carthage. Africa was sealed to them, and it has been sealed ever since until Henry M. Stanley struck the knife into its very centre, and to-day it is open to us. I believe another thing, and that is that the American negro, who came to this country as a slave, and who labored here for two and a half centuries, shall play a typical part in the evangelization of that continent. [*Applause.*] Beloved, watch and see what God will do for us, for he rules all things. These men who came to this country as slaves — where are they to-day? They are being educated and prepared to go to work, not in the Southern States, but for the dark continent, for the jungles of Africa. By and by those valleys where to-day cannibalism and barbarity and all those heinous sacrifices hold sway, and the whole dark continent, shall become a beacon light to the world: and by and by, instead of having human sacrifices and the blood covenant, we shall hear the merry frolic of boys and girls going to school, we shall hear the hum of the factory, and Ethiopia shall then truly stretch forth her hands unto God. [*Loud applause.*]

The audience then joined heartily in singing "We shall stand before the King."

Dr. CLARK: We now come to an interesting exercise — the presentation of the banners to the States which have made the largest gains during the year. The one which has made the largest actual gain is not a State but a Province, — the banner goes from Pensylvania to Ontario, [*cheers from the Canada delegates*] though Pennyslvania is a good second, as we know, having formed only eight less societies than Ontario. The banner for the greatest proportionate gain goes from Oklahoma to another Province — Manitoba, [*cheers*] and again Oklahoma is only a little behind in proportionate gain. The banner for the largest number of junior societies goes to the grand State of Illinois. [*Cheers and singing of "Precious Jewels" by the Illinois delegates.*] I am sure these banners will have an added honor in being presented to these several Provinces and States by that friend of the Christian Endeavor movement, Dr. Wayland Hoyt, of Minneapolis. [*Applause.*]

ADDRESS OF REV. WAYLAND HOYT, D.D.

Christian Endeavor means the truth in love. Christian Endeavor means the truth. Christian Endeavor in no instance stands for latitudinarianism in belief. Christian Endeavor has no sympathy with the notion that it makes no difference what you believe, if only you are earnest in what you believe. I was riding once on a St. Lawrence steamboat, and I came across a man on one of the decks who bulged. He was bulged as to his hind pockets, as to his front pockets, as to his waistcoat pockets, as to ever so many canvas bags around him. We asked him what he was bulged with, and he said he was bulged with gold ore. We asked him if he would not show us a little of the gold ore; and after a while, after a good deal of persuasion, he pulled out of his vest pocket a piece of common granite and said it was gold ore. We looked at it and saw it was nothing but feldspar, and a little mica, and a little hornblende, and a good deal of iron pyrites, which shine something like gold. We said, "It is not gold." But he said, "It is; I have seen the gleam of it many a day on my farm and I am the richest man in America; I am taking this gold ore to Kingston, to have it assayed." The man's earnestness in his belief that iron pyrites was gold ore did not change iron pyrites into gold ore. It was only so much the worse for that farmer. [*Laughter.*] When men pretend to say there is no difference between the proposition that Jesus Christ was only an utmost man, the product simply of human evolution, and on the other hand that Jesus Christ is God manifest in the flesh, Christian Endeavor affirms there is an abyssmal difference between those propositions, and Christian Endeavor will never accept your poor so-called liberalistic notion of only a human teacher, for the true Scriptural idea of Jesus Christ manifest in the flesh, the divine human Saviour. [*Applause.*] Christian Endeavor stands the world around for that truth, and Christian Endeavor from it will never flinch.

Also, Christian Endeavor means truth in love. Sometimes it is hard for us to see God's love. I was spending a day in investigating the closes of Edinburgh. I went through the buildings, piled toward the blue, so closely set that standing in the midst of them you could touch them on either side with your outstretched arms. I never saw such squalor and such diseases and such various evils; and as I went on with the exploration I was constantly asking myself, How does God stand it? Why does not the heart of God break? As the shades of evening fell and I went out of that exploration and was passing along the street, I heard the scraping of a fiddle, and I turned aside to see whence the sound came. I saw standing in the gutter a little fellow scraping on his fiddle for all his life was worth. I saw that although his coat was patched, it was clean; that although his collar was worn, it was clean; and although the ribbon that held it was brown with use, it was clean; and that his boots, — or rather the one boot that he wore, for the little fellow had only one leg and was leaning on his crutch, scraping away as best he could, — I saw that that boot was blacked. I thought whence he came out of those closes, and of the mother there who kept him clean and sweet, and of the heritage of disadvantage to which that poor little fellow had come. And I said again, How does God stand it? Why does not the heart of God break? Then I saw a vision. I am not apt to see visions, but I saw one then. I saw the Lord Jesus Christ hanging on the cross, and I heard a voice, — it seemed to me as plain as I hear my own voice now, — " The heart of God is broken; it broke there on Calvary." Then I knew that God did love the world, and from my heart to the loving Christ there went out a great tide of love, and I loved Christ, and I loved all who loved Christ. And that is the meaning of Christian Endeavor. [*Applause.*]

What a blessed time we have been having here in this spiritual fellowship one with another, — though divided by continents, though divided by oceans, though divided by races, — spiritual fellowship in the Christ who loved us and gave himself for us! Last night President Clark, in his magnificient address, asked the question if we, having tasted of this sweet spiritual fellowship in Jesus Christ, would let anything separate us from it, and we did not say one word in reply. Now I want to ask that question, and I want a loud resounding "NO!" to come from all this multitude. Having tasted of the sweets of this spiritual fellowship in the Christ who loves us and gave himself for us, will we let anything separate us from it? Members of Christian Endeavor, will we? [*Cries of " No, No," from the audience.*] Say it over again, louder. [*The word was repeated louder.*] Say it over again, louder still. [*The word " NO " was still more emphasized.*] Christian Endeavor means the truth in love.

And now, in the name of the truth in love, the truth of our divine-human Saviour, the love that we all have for him and for each other, I present this banner to that State which has made the greatest absolute gain in the number of societies. The banner goes out from the jurisdiction of the Stars and Stripes and comes under the jurisdiction of the flag of the cross which waves over all the world, but it does not get outside of the universal banner of our crucified Lord and Saviour Jesus Christ. [*Loud applause.*]

Rev. J. R. Dickson, of Galt, Ont., received the banner, while Canada started "Blest be the tie," in which the audience joined.

Rev. Dr. DICKSON: This banner shows that we in Ontario believe in Christian Endeavor. We believe in it, pure and simple. We do not wish to have it mixed up with anything else, lest at any time it should be shorn of its locks. It is some time since Canada took a banner from the United States, [*laughter*] but we are very glad that the first banner in these late years is a Christian Endeavor banner. I think that this argues well for Canada's annexing the United States. [*Laughter.*] Let me say this: that so long as this banner is in Ontario, the gem of all the Provinces of the Dominion of Canada, no war shall take place between these two countries. [*Cries of "Amen" from the Canada delegates, and loud applause.*] If such a thing should happen, I may say this: that we Christian Endeavorers will enter the army and carry this banner at the front. ["*Hear, Hear!*"] More than that, let me say that you may take a good look at it now, because you will not see it for many a year. [*Laughter and applause.*]

Dr. HOYT: It is well for us always to remember that Christian Endeavor means "inter" — inter-denominational, inter-state, inter-national; and we have another opportunity of showing forth the inter-nationality of Christian Endeavor by recognizing the fact that once again Canada has captured a banner from the States, and the banner which did wave in Oklahoma must now wave in Manitoba. In the name of truth and in the name of love and as a symbol of our inter-nationality, I present this banner to the representative from Manitoba. [*Loud applause and another verse of "Blest be the Tie."*]

Miss JENNIE P. KENNEDY: In behalf of the Christian Endeavorers of Manitoba I can just say that our motto is "Manitoba for Christ." We talk much of the harvests in that country, but the Christian Endeavorers are looking for the harvest of souls. At our convention there in April the delegates decided to try and bring at least one soul to Christ during the year, and they went forth to work at once for that end.

Although there is but a small representation from Manitoba here to-day, there are many earnest, active Christians in that Province striving to bring the young people in that country to Christ; when we have brought the young to Christ, it is all right for the future of the country. [*Loud applause.*]

Dr. HOYT: Our Divine Lord and Saviour has said to us, "Suffer the little children to come unto me, and forbid them not, for of such is the kingdom of heaven." The Junior Christian Endeavor movement is only the hand of the Lord Jesus Christ himself put forth to gather into his loving and safe bosom the little children. In the Junior Christian Endeavor society in my church in Minneapolis ten of the little people came from their society into glad fellowship with the Lord's church during the last six months. So interesting was our session, that when the time for vacation came the little people pleaded for only a few more meetings, they did so rejoice in them. We who are working at this Junior Christian Endeavor idea, after all, are working at the seeds of things. Amid all the proud tablets which adorn the brow of the great State of Illinois, —

the World's Fair and the great city of Chicago and what not besides, — there is none more glorious than the fact that Illinois is pushing this Junior Christian Endeavor work. Illinois gets the banner for the largest number of Junior Christian Endeavor societies in any State. God bless Illinois. [*Loud applause and singing of " Precious Jewels" by Illinois.*]

Mr. C. B. HOLDREGE: I am most happy in the name of Illinois to receive this banner, but I desire to place it in the hands of another, through whose earnest efforts this has been secured, — Mr. Thomas Wainwright, the superintendent of junior work in Illinois. [*Applause.*]

Mr. WAINWRIGHT: Dear Christian Endeavorers: Though we have won this trophy, yet I want you to understand that Illinois is after that grander trophy, " The prize of the high calling of God in Christ Jesus." Illinois is going to capture that greatest and most glorious prize. [*Applause.*]

The afternoon session closed with the usual number of notices, the singing of the Doxology, and the Mizpah benediction.

FRIDAY EVENING.

Long before the time for opening the evening session had arrived, Madison Square Garden was packed to its utmost, save that the aisles were kept clear, in accordance with the direction of the city authorities. It was really a pitiful sight to see the crowds of delegates on the outside of the building, waiting to see if perchance there might not yet be some opportunity for admittance. Their patience was useless, however, and after a while they gradually dispersed and attended such of the simultaneous meetings as were not already over-crowded. The only way to secure entrance to the convention hall was by displaying a reporter's ticket. Even Dr. Clark himself was stopped at the entrance

until he could secure a special dispensation from within. The doorkeepers of Madison Square Garden, accustomed to managing horse shows, prize fights, etc., evidently assumed that they must be equally strict with a religious convention.

Within the hall the delegates occupied the time singing familiar hymns, under the lead of Mr. L. F. Lindsay. Punctually on the hour, Dr. Clark called the assembly to order and gave out the hymn, " Blest be the Tie that Binds," which was sung delightfully.

Dr. CLARK: The presiding officer this evening is one who has had many honors heaped upon him. We all know him as the Postmaster-General of the United States. [*Tremendous applause and the waving of handkerchiefs, with cheers.*] I do not think that it will detract from his honors, in the estimation of this audience at least, that I introduce him to you as a member of the

Board of Trustees of the United Society of Christian Endeavor,—the Hon. John Wanamaker. [*Renewed enthusiasm, bursting forth again and again.*]

ADDRESS OF HON. JOHN WANAMAKER.

My friends and fellow-members:— I was overpowered by the large meeting outside; how do you think I feel in view of the beautiful reception which you have just given me as I rose to my feet? Every heart-beat is a silent " thank you."

I believe that few men, and then only once in a lifetime, have such a privilege as is mine at this moment. As one of the original trustees, an early, loyal, loving friend, I come back to-night to see how the old plan has worked out. Looking at the original design, I must pronounce the stupendous structure still rising wonderfully like the first conception, worthy of its master workman and greatly to the glory of the Lord, whose name is or all the banners of Christian Endeavor. [*Applause.*] In the wonderful activity of the time, with great developments in science and in invention, and wondrous enterprises on every hand, the Church of God cannot lag behind. It was a wonderful discovery, this storage battery of the church, [*applause*] put into successful operation, reaching out into every quarter of the globe with its light and its joy and its blessing. Christianity is no coward. Whenever men are willing to investigate it, whenever they are ready to inquire and to give it a fair hearing, it wins its way. Day by day its friends are numbered more and more, and the procession of God's people is swinging around the world longer and stronger, and it will soon girdle the earth. [*Applause.*]

I think one of the greatest surprises that you have given to this wonderful city is the way in which you Christian men and women have taken possession of it. Who ever believed that you would march on the city thirty thousand strong?— and I think if you were to go out into the streets you would have to add twenty thousand to that figure. [*Applause.*] Surely you will when the time for the next convention comes around. [*Renewed applause.*] I rejoice to-night that the Christian Endeavor movement has brought something to this age — not a local or temporary thing, but a something that commands the heart and the good opinion of the whole world at large. Men are asking on the street, What is this movement? How did it come? There is an answer that it is the outgrowth, as I believe, of the great movement that swept over the world for young men. It was seen that what young men could do for young men the church could do for all the young people, down to the smallest boy and girl that comes under Christian influence. [*Applause.*] And so in the simplest and in the most practical and in the most common-sense way, on unsectarian lines, this, the brightest star in the Christian world, has risen, [*applause*] sending out its light and beneficence over the years of this closing century to usher in the dawn of a new century of the blessedness of Christian living all the wide world around.

I rejoice to-night in all that this means for the coming year. Every Christian Endeavor man will stand more erect as he thinks of these few hours spent together in Christian fellowship. This old flag by my side to-night [*loud applause and cheers*] and this one [*taking up the English flag amid applause from Canada*] represent the two great English-speaking nations of the world. To them more than to others is given the spreading of the Gospel over all the world. Already on other shores the Christian Endeavor movement is reaching out its arms of love and usefulness in every direction. Down on the Pacific slope, joining California and Arizona, is a great cantilever bridge, the result of

American engineering, built under the superintendence of a young Christian man. Stretching from either shore, the ends approach each other until at last the complete highway is made, and, joined with great iron bolts, becomes the highway of trade and traffic. That bridge is the type and the symbol of the Christian Endeavor movement. [*Applause.*] Reaching out from every shore, it joins nation with nation, bolting them together with faith in God; and Christian Endeavor shall bring blessing the wide world around.

"Waft, waft, ye winds, His story,
And on, ye waters, roll
Till, like a sea of glory,
It spreads from pole to pole." [*Applause.*]

But I am not down, as you see by the program, for an address. From my full heart I can only bring you this greeting. I came to stay with you for just a few moments in this place, which seems to me like a beautiful orchard where we have come at noonday to sit under the apple blossoms and hear the birds sing, and rest and enjoy good fellowship. But the clock is striking for work to begin again; and as one takes out his watch to see if it is right when the bell sounds, so let us set our souls to the right time and go back to the work, carrying this cheer and encouragment, and devote ourselves as never before to the rousing of the Church and to the speeding on of the chariot of God. [*Loud applause.*]

After the hymn, "Onward, Christian Soldiers," Mr. Wanamaker introduced to the audience Rev. Dr. Russell H. Conwell, pastor of Grace Temple Baptist church, Philadelphia, who was royally welcomed as he came forward to speak on "The Christian Endeavor Society's Place in Modern Religious Life."

ADDRESS OF REV. RUSSELL H. CONWELL, D.D., LL.D.

When great peoples declare their independence, or when any great human enterprise is put in motion, it is customary for those concerned to issue a declaration of independence or a statement of the principles which have led them to their undertaking. If individuals desire to enter into business, they give notice to the State and to the city that they are to organize for such a purpose. Such has ever been the custom of all human organizations, and they are set in direct contrast with all the organizations begun and carried on of God. Well did President Clark state yesterday, with regard to the Society of Christian Endeavor, that it was an undertaking led of God and which no human being could foresee. But we have gone on in the history of the years until at last we have reached that point where the world does demand of us, as the Postmaster-General has just hinted, a reason for the faith that is in us. The time has come when there shall be a declaration of independence. The time has come when the world wishes to know wherefore we exist, and demands an excuse for the stir that we make in a great busy city like this. [*Applause.*] When men from Wall Street, with their heads full of stocks and their hearts full of great worldly enterprises, are stopped in the great fury of their course by a crowd of Christian Endeavorers and ask, What does this mean? it is time there was made a declaration that they might understand; and the time has come when God in his providence has revealed unto us the reason for our organization ; and has shown us now why his prophet spoke as he did in the years gone by.

In the history of all the greatest movements of the earth there has always been called to the front the young man or the young woman. When Christianity was to go over into Macedonia, a young man was called, Paul by name ; and when the great reform from the curse of the Middle Ages was to come into this world, God sent the lightnings of heaven down alongside a young man, Luther, who said, "the Christian shall hereafter live by faith"; and when Christianity had lost much of its heart, God called John Wesley and Whitefield — young men : when, in England, the church had lost much of its spirit, God called Spurgeon — a young man ; and when in the great, on-going business of America we were all rushing with our hearts and souls and efforts for the accomplishment of worldly enterprise, God called F. E. Clark, [*loud applause*] and said : "Go; call other young men like unto thyself, put on thine armor and go out into the great work." But Brother Clark did not know what his work was any more than Paul knew, when he said, "What shall I do?" any more than the jailer knew, when he said, "What shall I do?" any more than any of the greatest and best and noblest of the earth dreamed of what was to be the outcome of their lives, when they humbled their souls before God. But we have found out now wherefore God called him; we have found out now wherefore God has called us.

We have found that God called the Christian Endeavor Society into being to bring happiness into the church of Christ. Oh, there were churches, — of course, not any in your neighborhood, and so don't take it as a libel, — but there were churches in some far-off distant lands where there were only old and very gloomy people. There were churches where they had nothing but long, sad, wailing speeches from the oldest and the most long-winded deacon, and where they had the most doleful and dreadful and tomb-like prayers from the most wretchedly miserable sinner in all the community, [*laughter and applause*] and the Christian Endeavor Society came to bring happiness into such churches. The Christian Endeavor Society came like the gleam of that morning sun in distant Lapland, when, after the absence of many months, it is welcomed by the inhabitants. As they see the first ray upon the snowy peaks, looking up to the crimson heaven they all lift up their hearts and praise the Almighty Being for giving to them the sunlight. So there were churches that were filled with a long, dreary night, — no conversions, no interest; the community had forgotten that there was a church in the village or city. But lo, the Christian Endeavor Society swept into that community like the coming of the morning sun to Lapland, lighting up its peaks, and beautifying its valleys; and it brought joy and peace and warmth and hope and comfort into that poor and forlorn and forsaken church. [*Applause.*] The Christian Endeavor Society comes into the church as the firelight comes into the deserted old home. Did you ever go to your old home in the mountains, where you were born and brought up, and find the house deserted and broken up, the clapboards off, and the old gate gone, and the ferns growing over the walk? Did you go inside the house, and look around where the dearest and sweetest and loveliest hours that God gives to man were yours as you stood around the old hearthstone? But the hearthstone is cold and dreary, like unto some of the churches of the world. But go and get a handful of fagots, put them on the old hearthstone, stir up the old ashes, light the fire again, bring in your loved ones, gather them around the old fire, kiss and embrace each other, cry for joy around the dear old hearthstone once more ; and it will be an experience very much like that of some of the churches you and I have known into which the light and love of the Christian Endeavor Society has come. [*Applause.*]

The Christian Endeavor societies came to bring into the church faith. It is no discredit to a church to say that it needs faith, for there is no church that has too much. But there is one shining characteristic of youth, and that is faith. It does believe ; it is filled with hope ; it is filled with the voice of the future ; it believes in great things ; it believes that God has required of us that we shall ask of him great things and undertake great things; and you have proved it in the Christian Endeavor societies. There are many churches yet in this broad Christian land where there is a marvellous lack of faith. But infuse into every such church the faith of the young,—the faith of the young man, with all life's ambitions before him, the faith of the young woman, with all the beautiful golden future already before her sight,—and, lo, faith rises in the church, and the old become young, and the young become mature, and the church is filled with faith. Whoever has faith in God will succeed in his Christian undertaking. [*Applause.*]

The Christian Endeavor societies have come to bring into the church health. They have come as the sister comes when her poor brother, emaciated, pale, trembling, coughing, lies upon his bed, and the physician says to his sister, " If he only had some healthy blood in his veins for a few days, he might overcome the tendency of the disease and come back into health and strength and manhood once more." ' And as that sister again and again bares her beautiful arm, and from its veins the physician takes the blood which is infused into her brother's system, to give him life and hope and strength, so now into the church of Jesus Christ, where it has been broken, diseased, and discouraged, there has been infused, through the Christian Endeavor societies, fresh blood—a youthful, active life principle. [*Applause.*] There are churches that you and I know which are cases of suspended animation. It is the great disease of the church in the United States — suspended animation, entire heart-failure. And yet into these churches' veins a new infusion of life has been thrust, and they have sent up to this house to-day, and to this great and wonderful city, their many delegates, to prove that they are no longer dead, but active, living churches of Jesus Christ.

And then the Christian Endeavor societies have been called of God for the purpose of bringing into the church force. Ah, the great factory is still; its wheels move not. But all the machinery is entire; the fabric is all there, and everything is ready to furnish the world with its most useful and beautiful commodities, but there is no steam. There is many a church like that. But if we could only run a steam engine through some of the churches I have seen, and stir them up, or else run over them, it would make an entire revolution for the benefit of the cause of Christianity. They need to be stirred up. We old men need to be stirred up. We are too decrepit; we have no eager ambitions. But the young people will bring into the church force; they will give to it steam and strength.

How shall we do it? By training each individual to the highest degree of his own Christian ability. There is no way of strengthening the church but by strengthening each individual. Many pastors and teachers and church-members forget that every individual is a soul loved of God, because it is a single person. But the Christian Endeavor Society notices each person, and in that is its strength-giving power. If you cultivate the best ability of each individual in the church, you will have a mighty force, and this Christian Endeavor Society has come for that purpose.

The Christian Endeavor Society has come into the church to-day for the purpose of creating union. For my own part, speaking entirely for myself, I am not afraid that the Christian Endeavor Society will break down too much the high fences that sectarian denominations have put up between each other. No; the time has come in the history of man when God says, " Unite, unite!" The world's business is uniting into great corporations and great combinations for the benefit of the world, and God is calling to us, " Unite, unite." If any denomination is afraid to have its principles come into active comparison or into active investigation, then it is behind the age. [*Applause.*] The time has come when all denominations recognize the fact that Christ is all and in all, while also recognizing that sects are of convenience, and often of great advantage. I would not for the world, so far as I can see,—I would not for the world forsake my own denomination; I would not do it for the world, but FOR CHRIST I would forsake it all. [*Great applause.*] The Christian Endeavor societies have come to put a bench alongside these sectarian fences, to enable us all to look over, [*laughter*] and to see that God has other sheep and other folds of which heretofore we have known but little.

The Christian Endeavor Society has come into the world, also, to bring to the uses of the church the highest skill. We want successful workers in the church; and as in handiwork, in manufacturing, in finance, in business, in government offices, we ought to have men and women cultivated and t ained for their work from their earliest years, so in the great work of the Christian church we ought to have individuals who have been trained from their infancy, all the way up, unto the highest degree of efficiency for the work of the Lord Jesus Christ. And the Christian Endeavor Society begins with the young, and educates them in Christian work, giving them years of training, that they may accomplish the most possible with their talents, their time, and their means.

We cultivate this individual ability in the Christian Endeavor Society by making every member sign a pledge. But there are some people so conscientious, so wonderfully pious, that they think it is wrong to sign a pledge. I knew a lady myself who always said it was wrong to sign pledges; but when a man asked her to marry him, she didn't fail to give a pledge then. [*Laughter and applause.*] I knew a man in that quiet Quaker city of Philadelphia who thought it was wrong to sign a pledge; but he signed a pledge to pay me $50, and I have got that pledge yet! [*Laughter.*] No; the Christian Endeavor pledge was brought in to reinforce the pledges which one makes before God when he joins the church. If my wife loves me, I do not care how many times a day she tells me of it. If you love God, it does not make any difference how many times a day you renew your pledge. You cannot do it too often; you cannot pledge yourself to God too much. [*Applause.*]

The Christian Endeavor Society came into the world to bring into the uses of the church womanhood. The church has not realized, until this very late day, the wonderful power that lies in the tender hands, in the affectionate touch, in the love of womanhood. The church before has not realized it, and consequently it has oft been keeping her in the background — oft saying that she shall not have equal rights with man in social life, in the church, oft saying she shall not do what she can do so effectively. I am not one of those who believe that a woman ought to sing bass, or that a woman should be a man; nor am I one of those who believe that a man should be a woman; but I do believe that every single individual under the Stars and Stripes, and under the flag of England, and under the blue heaven of God, ought to have the right to make the most of himself or herself. [*Loud applause.*] So I say the Christian Endeavor Society came into the world to bring forward womanhood to an equal place with manhood — not to give her man's place, but to give her that magnificent freedom, that wonderful liberty, wherein she can exercise all her best talents for the advancement of the kingdom of God.

The Christian Endeavor Society has come into the world for many purposes. I have not the time to recite them now; but I have rehearsed enough of them to give you a hint of the purpose God had in view when he would take these churches and revive them to fresh life, to new enterprise, to a higher hope, and to push them on, with advancing civilization, to the highest place which the church ought ever to occupy. We have learned what our duty is; we have learned that we have come into this world to bring happiness into the church, to bring health into the church, to bring force into the church, to bring faith into the church, and to bring into the church skill to develop to the highest degree the usefulness of manhood and womanhood on an equality together. We have learned that we have come into the world for these purposes. Now that we have learned it, we are in the position of that American admiral who sailed away from these shores with sealed orders, not to be opened until he reached the Island of St. Helena. When he reached the island, he opened the sealed orders, and found he was to go on to the East Indies to rescue a number of American citizens who had been taken captive there by a wild and savage tribe. He did not know until he was far across the wide sea just what his destination or duty was. When he gave out the information, some of the crew rebelled. In those early days they feared they would not get back to their homes; but the admiral said: "Here are my orders, and wherever they lead, into the sands and shoals, into the depths of barbarism, in among the savages, or to death itself, I go." We have opened our sealed orders, and we have found where God designs us to go. There are captives to be released; souls to be saved; churches to be revived; denominations to be united; and a great beneficent movement to be pushed. We have opened our sealed orders; let us be like that American admiral, and in the presence of God pledge ourselves that we will obey those orders, take us where they will, even unto death. [*Prolonged applause.*]

Dr. Conwell's brilliant address was followed by the hymn, "At the Cross." At the close of the singing a portion of the audience suddenly burst out into a furor of applause and handkerchief waving. The cause of this demonstration was immediately apparent when Mr. Depew, New York's most popular orator, came upon the platform, and took a seat near the presiding officer, cheered by the whole congregation. Mr. Wanamaker gracefully introduced him as follows:—

Mr. WANAMAKER: I sometimes have to deal with appointments. I am not proposing to allude to the letters that some of you have written to me during the last two or three years; [*laughter*] you need not tremble. Sometimes also, I have to deal with disappointments. I regret very much, to-night, that the Hon. W. C. P. Breckenridge has had need to send a telegram saying that on account of the illness of his wife it was impossible for him to keep his engagement here to-night. But there is a man for the hour. [*Great applause and cheers.*] This is not news, either to New York or to the country. You notice he comes at the moment, and whenever you touch him, he begins to sparkle. [*Renewed cheers.*] I have great pleasure in presenting to you the Hon. Chauncey M. Depew, formerly of New York, but now of the United States of Christian Endeavor.

Here there followed the most marked enthusiasm of the convention. It had leaked out before the meeting that Mr. Breckenridge, whose name was on the program, could not be present, but it was not known who would take his place. Hence Mr. Depew's appearance on the platform was a complete surprise. The audience fairly surpasssd all precedents in manifesting its delight at the prospect of a speech from the witty orator. Mr. Depew waited smilingly until the demonstration in his honor came to a pause, when he spoke as follows:—

ADDRESS OF THE HON. CHAUNCEY M. DEPEW.

Ladies and Gentlemen: — When, a few minutes ago, a trustee of this society came to my house and said I must be drafted into the service, I said, "It is a question about which I have never read anything, and about which I know nothing." My friend in the rear says that when a man talks from an empty mind of that kind, he talks without prejudice. [*Laughter.*] Since I have arrived on this platform, I understand why I came. The Postmaster-General says that the Hon. Mr. Breckenridge, of Kentucky, one of the most eloquent men in the United States, had prepared an oration which he was to deliver here to-night, but being unable to come, he sent a telegram, and then the Postmaster-General introduced me. This is the first time I have ever been flashed over the wires.

This reminds me somewhat of a convention I recently attended. [*Great laughter and applause.*] I see there are some of the brethren here. [*Renewed laughter.*] That convention did not have so many delegates.

We welcome you to New York. New York is the best watering place in the United States. Tammany Hall we have always with us, and we are pleased to have the Christian Endeavor convention as an antidote, occasionally. The advent of these fresh young girls from the country into our broad and dusty city has brought all the New York dudes back from the watering-places. They say that New York now is fresher and greener than any place in the United States. [*Laughter.*]

The beauty about your organization is that it has in it the element which is power, and which is success in any movement which is for the uplifting of the world. That power is youth. Nothing succeeds like youth, because youth is hopeful; youth is tireless; youth does not know the word fail. Alexander the Great cried because he had no more worlds to conquer at the age of thirty; Napoleon had passed his prime at thirty-six. The church to-day is a force, and political parties are progressive, not because of the old men, though they are useful, but because of the resistless rush of youth to the accomplishment of the purposes for which churches are organized and republics made. [*Applause.*] The glorious thing about youth is that it still retains its ideal. Nothing affords me so much pleasure as to meet, as I do yearly at the commencements, the young men and young women who are graduating from college and school to take their places in the world. I love to see their faith in manhood and womanhood; I love to see their belief that the world is growing better day by day; I love to see their confidence that the church is all that their ideals make it; I love to see their infatuation for the party to which they have attached themselves — its principles and its leaders; I love to hear them talk about party leaders as patriots, and to deify them into gods of unselfishness and patriotism. Contact with such things freshens up old fellows like Wanamaker and myself. [*Laughter and applause.*]

One of the best institutions ever organized in this country — and I was among the earliest members of it — was the Young Men's Christian Association. [*Loud applause.*] It was a revolt of the young men against the dry-as-dust formulas of the day. It has been the haven of young men in the great cities of the country. Your brother or your son comes to New York to take his part in the mighty rush of this great maelstrom of selfish and struggling humanity. He goes to his boarding-house, where he has no sympathy and no friends; on the street and in his place of business he has no sympathy and no friends. Youth requires companionship, affection, and confidence. The open pool room, the open saloon, beckons him on to destruction. But a member of the Young Men's Christian Association puts his hand upon his shoulder and says, "Come with me." He takes him to the hall, introduces him to his friends, gives him the gymnasium, the library, the reading-room, the prayer meeting, the church service, and he soon finds himself surrounded by the influences of his village life, and grows up according to the prayers of his mother. [*Applause.*]

It is astonishing what one person can do in this world. It has been my lot to meet with that experience time and again,— what one man or what one woman can do in this world. There came into Mr. Vanderbilt's offices at the Grand Central Depot thirteen years ago a locomotive engineer on the Lake Shore Railroad. He said: "I have established a reading-room for railroad men, under the auspices of the Young Men's Christian Association. I believe from what I have seen of its results that if it were extended over all the railroads, the effect would be most happy." We believed his story; we took up the scheme, and what has been the result? To-day, on every great railroad of the country are those reading-rooms, many of them occupying large buildings.

To-day there are tens of thousands of railroad men of the country enlisted and enrolled upon the records of this association. The railroad town has become orderly and temperate. The saloon has disappeared; the pool room has disappeared. The engineer, conductor, trainmen, and men in every part of the service are no longer throwing away their money, leaving their wives in wretchedness and their children to grow up in crime, but their money goes to the wife, and the surplus of it from the wife to the savings bank, and from the savings bank back to the home. The children are well dressed, attending the daily school and Sunday school. The church is built out of their earnings, and the railroad town becomes a light of Christianity, of civilization, and the preservation of American liberty. [*Applause.*]

Now, young ladies and gentlemen, the one thing to do in every organization is to believe that it is the best organization in the world, and that you are the most efficient and the best member of it. [*Applause.*] Nobody accomplishes anything in this world unless he has a good opinion of himself,— and Mr. Wanamaker agrees with me on that point. [*Laughter.*] In every organization you should have the same thought in regard to it that a Boston man whom I once met had in regard to Boston. He came up to Peekskill, where I was born,— Peekskill, the centre of the world!— and he addressed a Sunday-school picnic. He said: "Ten years ago I was here, and in my audience was a beautiful, flaxen-haired boy, who looked like an angel — he looked like one of Raphael's cherubs. Where do you suppose he is now?" The children cried out: "In heaven." "Oh, no," he said, "better than that — he is in Boston, a clerk in a store." [*Laughter.*] Now, you want to believe that the Christian Endeavor Society is the best organization in the world, as I believe it is. [*Loud applause.*]

I was riding in my car through Central New York last summer, sitting at my desk intent upon business matters, when the train stopped at a station. I heard the sound of a bugle outside, and a familiar hymn. I stepped upon the platform, and there was a collection of young ladies and young gentlemen, one of whom was playing on the bugle, and the others following with a hymn. "For whom is this demonstration?" I asked, and the leader, who was one of the prettiest girls I ever saw — except my wife, [*laughter*] and my wife was not with me then — said: "It is for you." "Well," said I, "are you returning from a temperance convention, or a camp meeting?" She said: "Neither, sir; we are Christian Endeavorers." [*Applause.*] Then I discovered that Christian Endeavorers on the female side were good-looking, and on the female and male sides together, were good musicians; and when they treated me that way, I knew that they knew a good thing when they saw it. [*Great laughter and applause.*]

Ladies and gentlemen, the Young Men's Christian Association is the recruiting station of the churches, but you, as a Christian Endeavor society, doing the work in the interior of your own church,— you are the citadel of the Christion camp inside the lines. [*Applause.*] You keep the weak-hearted brother from deserting, you bring the deserter back into the fold. [*Applause.*] May you increase and grow in power, recruiting from the youth with the fire of youth urging you on, with hope to be realized before you, and with heaven's gate wide open to welcome your worthy members. May your society never die! [*Prolonged applause.*]

Mr. Depew descended from the platform amidst applause, and as he left the hall many of the delegates prepared to leave also. Chairman McEwen, seeing the movement, called out: "Our splendid list of speakers for to-night is not closed. Gen. O. O. Howard has just come in." This announcement was the signal for another storm of applause, and the one-armed hero, as he came to the front of the platform, was given a splendid ovation. He contented himself, however, with only a brief word: —

Gen. HOWARD: I think, Mr. President, that you have had speeches enough; so all I can say is, welcome to New York,— a Christian welcome to New York. [*Loud applause.*]

Mr. WANAMAKER: I am not sure that you ought to excuse the general with that short speech. I never knew him to retreat before.

Gen. HOWARD: Only after the battle was over. [*Laughter.*]

Mr. WANAMAKER: General Howard's presence here to-night reminds me of what occurred in the first Y. M. C. A. convention after the war. I was then a member of the international committee. It was a question whether a convention could be held which would bring together representatives from all the country, but it was thought that if there was any place in the country to which they would come, that place was Washington. So the call went out for the convention at Washington. I had the honor of presiding, and some nine hundred delegates were present. One day a message came from the secretary of the interior asking if a delegation of Indians might not be received at the convention. The answer went back, "Yes," and in the course of the morning there came filing up one of the aisles after Mr. Delano, the Secretary of the Interior, perhaps twenty Indians,— Arrapahoes, Cheyennes, and Sioux, all in their blankets, with their faces painted and long earrings in their ears, brown-faced, solemn-looking men. They sat in a row, looking on and listening without understanding a word, but enjoying the singing and good cheer. By and by an Indian stood up and made a speech, with a little man beside him as interpreter. His speech was something like this: "We have come a long distance to see the Great Father. Some of us were never in railroad cars or on steamboats until we came here. We open our eyes with wonder at the peace, and the quiet, and the happiness, and the good looks of everybody. We live poor and in wigwams, and have no such comforts as you. We would like to understand the secret. Can you tell us what the good medicine is?" Just at that moment General Howard, who was seated just behind the chair, leaped to his feet, and with that one arm of his lifting up the blessed word of God held it aloft and said, "Tell him to go back to his people and say that the old Bible is the good medicine." [*Loud applause.*] There is the man; I wonder if he remembers that occasion?

Gen. HOWARD: Yes; I have heard that story before. [*Laughter.*]

Mr. WANAMAKER: My friends, this is the "good medicine"— this old-fashioned book, this old book of Moses and the Psalms and the Gospel. This is what we build on, and by the blessing of God we shall keep on building until the tumults of men and the strifes of sects and parties have all vanished from the world, and peace and goodwill to all men shall reign the world over. [*Loud applause.*]

The session closed with Mr. Sankey's singing of "Throw out the life-line," the audience joining in the chorus, and the benediction by Dr. Hyde.

SATURDAY MORNING.

Bright and early a large number of the delegates gathered at the Garden for the usual prayer meeting. For once there were some vacant seats in the building, although the number of those who took part in this meeting exceeded five thousand. The preliminary singing was conducted by Mr. R. V. McIlvaine, and at 6.30 o'clock Mr. E. S. Miller, of Portland, Ore., took the platform and opened the prayer meeting. The exercises were similar to those of the preceding morning, and were characterized by genuine spiritual fervor and devotion. It was good to be there.

At nine o'clock the great hall was again filled to overflowing, and the convention joined in singing for the first hymn "What a wonderful Saviour." This was followed by the repetition in unison of the twenty-third Psalm, and again every one felt the power of this mighty declaration of faith. Dr. Philip Schaff, the eminent scholar, was then announced to lead in the Lord's Prayer. Before he did so, however, he took occasion to make the following significant utterance: —

Dr. SCHAFF: The future church historian will date from the founding of the Christian Endeavor Society a new era of American Christianity, the Christianity of the rising youth which will take the lead in the coming century. I thank God that I have seen the beginning of this new epoch.

The Lord's Prayer was then recited, followed by the hymn, "Hide me, O my Saviour." The committee on nominations then reported, through Rev. H. W. Sherwood, the following list of vice-presidents of the convention: —

Alabama — Rev. Hugh K. Walker.
Alaska Territory — Edward Marsden.
Arizona Territory — Lieut. H. R. Lee. (11th Infantry, United States Army.)
Arkansas — R. W. Porter.
Australia — Hugh Jones.
California — C. J. Merritt.
Colorado — J. W. Barrows.
Connecticut — Rev. Joseph Pullman, D.D.
Delaware — Rev. George E. Thompson.
District of Columbia — P. S. Foster.
England — John Williams.
Florida — Rev. William Shaw.
Georgia — Rev. C. E. Dowman, D.D.
Idaho Territory — Rev. J. H. Barton.
Illinois — Bishop Edward Cheeney.
India — Rev. S. V. Karmarkar.
Indiana — Rev. J. A. Rondthaler, D.D.
Indian Territory — D. W. Yancey.
Iowa — Rev. Austin D. Wolfe.
Kansas — H. Roland Way.
Kentucky — Rev. George B. Overton, D.D.
Louisiana — J. J. Ziegler.
Maine — Rev. Dwight M. Pratt.
Manitoba — Joseph Ball.
Maritime Union — Rev. T. F. Fotheringham.
Maryland — Rev. O. F. Gregory, D. D.
Massachusetts — Rev. Wallace McMullen.
Michigan — Rev. C. H. Irving.
Minnesota — Rev. George H. Wells, D.D.
Missouri — Rev. J. W. Ford, D.D.

Montana — Joseph D. Radford.
Nebraska — Prof. C. A. Murch.
Nevada — Rev. F. L. Nash.
New Hampshire — Rev. E. T. Farrill.
New Jersey — Rev. J. Clement French, D.D.
New Mexico — Rev. A. B. Christy.
New York — Rev. H. H. Stebbins, D.D.
North Carolina — W. B. Stallings.
North Dakota — R. M. Carrothers.
Northwest Territory — Mr. A. H. Smith.
Ohio — Rev. W. F. McCauley.
Oklahoma — William Blincoe.
Ontario — E. A. Hardy.
Oregon — E. S. Miller.
Pennsylvania — Rev. W. H. Young, D.D.
Quebec — George R. Lighthall.
Rhode Island — Rev. J. B. Jordan.
South Carolina — Dunbar Robb.
South Dakota — Miss Esther A. Clark.
Tennessee — E. P. Loose.
Texas — Rev. H. C. Scudday.
Utah — Rev. J. Brainerd Thrall.
Vermont — Rev. Z. Martin.
Virginia — Rev. Jabez Hall.
Washington — R. L. Edmeston.
West Virginia — Rev. R. B. Whitehead.
Wisconsin — Rev. W. O. Carrier.
Wyoming — Rev. George S. Ricker.

The report was accepted and adopted. "Coronation" was then sung by the great audience, after which the program of the morning was taken up, the chief theme being missionary work in its various phases.

Dr. CLARK: Who could speak more appropriately on "Our Country for Christ" than Rev. Dr. Josiah Strong, Secretary of the Evangelical Alliance? [*Loud applause.*]

ADDRESS OF REV. JOSIAH STRONG, D.D.

If there is a discouraged Christian in New York who fears that the forces of evil are destined to triumph, any one who believes that they that be with them are more than they that be with us, I would like to take him by the buttonhole and lead him in here.

And if he were not lifted up and made jubilant by the sight of these thousands, then I would pray that his eyes might be opened to see the 1,000,000 Christian Endeavorers whom you represent, an army of the living God, which, invisible to us, is encamped round about through all the land. If a nobler, more significant audience than this ever met, I do not know where in the pages of history to look for the record of it.

I will try to show you that Christian work means more in North America than anywhere else in all the world. And secondly, I will try to show how Christian Endeavor societies can most effectively aid this work.

First, the importance of Christian work in North America is to be measured by the place which North America and her civilization are to hold in the world's future.

The committee has given to me a broad subject, — "Christian Endeavor and Home Missions." When we talk about home missions our subject is 3,000 miles broad, and when you add 1,000,000 Christian Endeavorers, it gives our subject 1,000,000 heads. It is impossible to do justice to such a subject in a single address. I can touch only the hem of its garment.

Among the ancients there were three, and only three, nations which profoundly influenced the world's history. We find their impress on all modern and Occidental civilization. These three peoples were the Hebrews, the Greeks, and the Romans, each of whom was supreme in one of the three great essential spheres of life — the Hebrews in the religious, the Greeks in the intellectual, and the Romans in the physical. It is because they were supreme in these essential spheres that their influence was supreme, and that God could use them to prepare the way for the founding of his kingdom.

If now it could be shown that those characteristics which made the Hebrews and their influence great belong to the Anglo-Saxons, it would be evidence that Anglo-Saxon influence will be far-reaching through the ages. Or if it could be shown that those characteristics which made the Greeks great belong in like measure to the Anglo-Saxon, that would afford evidence that this race is to have a profound influence on the world's future.

Or, again, if it could be shown that those characteristics which gave the Romans their mighty power all belong to the Anglo-Saxon in still greater degree, that alone would afford a presumption that the Anglo-Saxon is to dominate the world's future. What shall we say, then, to the fact that the essential characteristics of these three supreme races, those qualities which made them the great instruments of the Divine purposes, all unite in the one Anglo-Saxon race?

In the time of Abraham idolatry degraded mankind. In order to the elevation of the race man must be led to a knowledge of the one true God. To be instrumental in this was the high mission of the Hebrews. Their conception of deity was infinitely superior to that of other nations, and was worth the thousand years of schooling which it cost.

The great lesson of monotheism seems to have been fully learned in the Babylonian captivity, and then the Jews were scattered around the Mediterranean and throughout the civilized world that they might furnish in every land a prepared soil for the seed of Christian truth.

But there was to be an intellectual preparation for Christ's coming, as well as spiritual, and this was to be wrought by the Greeks. If the good news of the kingdom of God was to be widely published and men generally invited to citizenship, there must be some common medium of communication, a language generally understood, and this tongue must be a fit vessel in which to bear to the nations the water of life. No adequate language existed. There must be developed not only such a tongue, but also a civilzation capable of diffusing it throughout the civilized world.

This work the Greeks accomplished. They produced a language perfectly adapted to its destined use, and a civilization which, by their restless energy, was carried around the Mediterranean, while Alexander stamped it upon the East. Thus for a time their language gained a universal dominion.

But equally necessary was the work to be wrought by the Roman. He was to supply the necessary physical conditions, to level the barriers between different peoples by bringing them under one government, and to cast up the great highways which would facilitate the intercourse of the nations.

Thus three great lines of preparation were developed by three great peoples, and in Palestine, where their civilizations met in most perfect conjunction, appeared He whose advent Hegel calls "the goal of all previous history and the starting point of the history to come." He was to inaugurate on the earth the kingdom of heaven.

Now that that kingdom has been established, the great consummation to which we look forward and for which we labor is the full coming of God's kingdom among men. Because man has a spiritual, and an intellectual, and a physical nature, the preparation for the full coming of God's kingdom must be spiritual, intellectual, and physical.

And I believe it can be shown that the Anglo-Saxon race is as well fitted to work out this threefold preparation as were those three ancient races to prepare the world for the coming of Christ. Permit me to cite a few facts in confirmation of this view, and you shall then see how vital it is to our subject.

1. The religious life of the Anglo-Saxon (I use the word broadly, to include all English-speaking peoples) is more vigorous, more spiritual, more Christian, than that of any other. Anglo-Saxons are not righteous overmuch. They will have to answer for many sins against weaker races, but, for all that, they are a mightier power for righteousness in the earth than any other. No race has ever shown such philantropy; none is so easily moved by great moral ideas; none so capable of moral enthusiasm and disinterested endeavor. This race is forever organizing a society to help some one.

Of the 139 missionary societies represented at the General Conference of Protestant Foreign Missions in London in 1888, 18 represented all other races and 121 represented the Anglo-Saxon race. Evidently it is to this race that we must look for evangelization of the world, and to show that this is pre-eminently the missionary race is to show that it is the most Christian race, for the missionary spirit is the essential spirit of Christianity.

As the Hebrew carried his pure monotheism around the Mediterranean, so the Anglo-Saxon is carrying a spiritual Christianity around the world.

I do not forget that comparisons are odious, but our argument requires a comparison of the intellectual powers of the Anglo-Saxon with those of other races.

The highest expression of the intellectual life of a people is to be found in their literature, and more especially in their poetry. Surely no one would be so bold as to attempt to match English poetry in any modern literature. Speaking of the brightest lights of English literature, Emerson says: " I find the great masters out of all rivalry and reach."

We do not forget the precious contributions to letters, philosophy, science, and every department of scholarship made by the Germans, the French, and other races, but comparing the entire product of the Anglo-Saxon mind, as preserved in the English language, with that of all other races, can any one doubt that the destruction of these treasures would be a greater loss to the world than would the destruction of all the thought embodied in any other language? And if this be so, may we not correctly infer that on the whole the Anglo-Saxons are the intellectual leaders of the world?

Several continental races are superior to the Anglo-Saxon in speculative thought, in scholarship, in music, and in art. But these are the flowers, not the roots of life; they adorn civilizations, but do not create them. The Anglo-Saxon, like the ancient Greek, has the rare power of propagating his civilization, which, together with his language, he is carrying around the world.

At the beginning of this century French, Russian, German, and Spanish were each spoken by more people than English, but during ninety years English rose from fifth place in the point of numbers to the first. In 1800 German was spoken by 10,000,000 more people than English; now English is spoken by 36,000,000 more than German. The French was spoken by 11,000,000 more than English; now English is spoken by 60,000,000 more than French.

Travel, commerce, the missionary are carrying the English tongue to every land, but the English language is no more pervasive than English civilization. Evidently the Anglo-Saxon is doing for the modern world what the Greek did for the ancient. They each produced a civilization characterized by a high development of the individual; they each produced an unequalled language and literature; and as the Greek carried his language and civilization around the Mediterranean, so the more restless Anglo-Saxon is carrying his language and civilization around the globe.

We have seen that the Roman possessed a mastery of physical conditions and a genius for law, organization, and government unequalled in the ancient world. A glance suffices to show that in the modern world the Anglo-Saxon occupies a position of like prominence.

This is the most inventive race; more than any other it builds and owns the world's railways and steamships; it commands the world's communications; it will soon possess more than one-half of all the world's wealth. During this century it has increased more than fivefold — from 20,500,000 to 111,000,000. It has spread from its little island home until now it possesses a third of the earth and rules over 400,000,000 of its inhabitants.

No intelligent man can look at the facts and doubt that, humanly speaking, this race holds in its hands the future of the world. And the home of this mighty race of the future must be that which Prof. Bryce calls "the land of the future." Scattered as is this race, more than one-half of its members are already found in the United States. North America constitutes seven-twelfths of the possessions of this race, and here its empire is unsevered, while the remaining five-twelfths are fragmentry, and scattered over the earth.

North America is twice as large as all Europe, and fully capable of sustaining 1,500,000,000 souls — the present population of the globe. Surely this majestic continent is to be the home of this majestic race; and from this land it will mold the future of mankind.

This being true, the thorough Christianization of this country is important beyond exaggeration. The importance of evangelizing a nation is not a question of numbers. It was more important that Martin Luther should be converted than that a thousand other German monks should see the light. I do not imagine that a white skin is any more beautiful in the eyes of God than a black or yellow one. My cry is not to save America for America's sake, but save it for the world's sake. If it is important to save the world, it is important to save America, for here both good and evil have a larger leverage than anywhere else on earth.

2. How, then, can we most effectively help to save America for Christ? This question concerns every Christian in the land, but there is peculiar propriety and significance in 1,000,000 young people putting that question to themselves, because young people are capable of enthusiasm. Men in middle life and past have been compelled by experience to modify so many of their earlier opinions on a thousand subjects, that they often acquire a habit of doubt, and hold with a feeble, nerveless grasp even those things which are absolutely sure. Now, young men and women are capable of mighty convictions, and therefore of a mighty enthusiasm, - for enthusiasm is conviction on fire.

There is no country in the world where people are in such eager earnest as in our own. Whether we are seeking money or office or pleasure, as a people, whatsoever our hand findeth to do we do it with our might. A listless, perfunctory Christianity can never win such a people. We must have an enthusiasm for Christ and an enthusiasm for men, if we are to win them to him. Now, if our churches are to be fired with an enthusiasm for humanity, I believe it is the young people who must kindle the blessed conflagration.

Another reason why there is peculiar and precious significance in Christian Endeavorers asking this question is that young people are friendly to new ideas and capable of adopting new methods. Age is naturally conservative. It is only because the race has new life that it makes new growth. It is said that the growth of a tree is marked by the concentric rings which we find in its stump.

Successive generations are the concentric rings which, growing larger and larger, work the growth of humanity's tree. Death is the great reformer, or at least the John the Baptist, of all great reforms. It is the new ideas that come in with new blood which carry the race forward in the progress of successive generations.

All through Christendom, and pre-eminently in America, the Church is surrounded by changed conditions which call for change of methods; and the new methods must come in with the new blood of the young people.

I cannot discuss these changed conditions here, or even enumerate them, but I must call your attention to one which is among the most important and far-reaching of the centuries. I refer to government by public opinion. When kings and aristocracies ruled, reforms might begin at the top and work down. Now they must begin at the bottom and work up. If our rulers are not what they should be, if we wish to accomplish municipal reform, for which Dr. Parkhurst has so nobly stood in this city, we must educate public opinion. This is true of all reforms. If we wish to have the law executed or wish better laws, we must educate public opinion.

How, then, can Christian Endeavorers help to educate public opinion? You may think that is precisely what young people cannot do. Let me show you that it is precisely what they can do.

Touching religion and all reforms, we may divide society into three classes; viz., friends, enemies, and those who are indifferent. The latter class is the large class. Comparatively few are positively opposed to the Church or to any needed reform. It is from the class that don't care that recruits and victories must be won. How can this be done?

Take the temperance cause for illustration. How is a right public sentiment on the part of the indifferent to be secured? You say, by a campaign of education. True: but how is such a campaign to be conducted? You tell me, by public meetings and by means of temperance literature. But when you announce a temperance meeting, it is those who are already interested who attend, and the indifferent, because they are indifferent, stay away. That is, the meeting reaches those who need it least, and fails to reach those who need it most.

In like manner temperance books and periodicals are bought only by those already interested. The indifferent, whom we wish to influence, are precisely the ones who will not buy. How can we reach them? The answer is simple and obvious. If they will not come to us, we must go to them. This is entirely practicable and absolutely necessary, if we are to keep up with the world.

Politics, business, commerce have all been quick to recognize changed conditions and to adopt new methods. Our great railways don't wait for business to come to them: they send out men to solicit business. Wholesale houses here in New York no longer wait for Western merchants to come and buy; they send out armies of travelling salesmen, who find customers.

Politicians no longer depend on great meetings to form public sentiment: they divide up city and country into districts, and send workers from house to house with documents and arguments to influence men personally. We Christian workers must adopt the same principle. When the mountain won't come to Mohammed, Mohammed must go to the mountain.

You Endeavorers have done a vast amount of good service; but hasn't most of your work been spiritual drill? That is important; but the camp exists not for itself, but for the field of action. Isn't the work which I have described precisely the forward movement which this magnificent Christian army needs to make? It will cost some work, some sacrifice; but it wouldn't be worth doing, if it didn't. And what is more worthy of sacrifice than saving America to Christ?

It is said that Napoleon once stood before his guards and asked for a hundred men to lead a forlorn hope. He explained that every man would doubtless be killed the minute the enemy opened fire. Now, who would die for the Emperor? "A hundred men, forward! Step out of the ranks!" And not a hundred men, but the whole regiment, as one man, sprang forward and rang their muskets at his feet.

And shall Christ and country and humanity fail to command an enthusiasm which Napoleon inspired? Is there nothing worthy of supreme sacrifice to-day? There are many in this audience who would die for Christ, if need were, but in these times he calls for men and women willing to live for him. Human nature can summon itself with high resolve, and in one supreme act lay life itself on the altar. Thank God, the heroism of martyrdom has not been rare in the history of his Church, but what is needed to-day is a higher heroism, a nobler martyrdom, — even that of the living sacrifice, the sustained resolve, the renewed self-giving, the daily consecration.

Only a living society can, like Paul, "die daily." The Captain of our salvation summons his Church militant to-day, not to a forlorn hope, but to a certain and glorious victory. Oh, that every soldier of his cross might spring forward to offer the living sacrifice, until our country and the world are wholly won to his dominion!

Dr. Strong's address, which was one of the ablest of the entire convention, was accorded much applause. At its close the hymn "Revive us again" was sung, followed by a long string of notices and telegrams.

Dr. CLARK: We are now to listen to a subject allied to the one we have already had presented. Mr. R. S. Murphy, of Philadelphia, will speak on "Proportionate Giving to God." [*Applause.*]

ADDRESS BY MR. R. S. MURPHY.

Mr. Chairman and Fellow-Endeavorers: — I esteem it a great honor and privilege to be invited to give my testimony at this, one of the greatest gatherings the world has ever witnessed, on a subject which is very dear to my heart, and which I consider is one of the most important questions that confront the Church of to-day.

But at the very outset I desire to crave the indulgence of the convention in the use of manuscript, for, not being a preacher, and having always sought in our Christian Endeavor meetings to condense and be brief, when our good secretary notified me that I was to speak for twenty-five minutes, I was compelled to gather more than I could carry in my memory with other things pertaining to my daily business; but as I look into your faces there is a great fear comes over me as I realize the added responsibility that will rest upon us after this morning's service.

I must consider the necessity of my giving a clear testimony on the subject assigned to me, and your taking heed thereto as the Lord may give me utterance.

A new reformation is needed in Christendom, says the Rev. M. G. Henry. That was a grand one three centuries ago, when the Bible was unchained and opened to men of every rank, that they might learn God's wonderful plan of salvation through faith in Christ. Not less notable was that commenced a century ago in the missionary revival which unchained the Church and sent her forth anew on the mission of preaching the Gospel to every creature. And now, to complete and give full effect to these two reformations, we need another, which will unlock the Lord's money that men are holding as their own, and let it go consecrated to its proper use in sustaining the divinely-appointed agencies for evangelizing the world. [*Applause.*]

What is proportionate giving? It is conscientiously giving or laying aside a part of that which the Lord has given us, in recognition of the fact that all belongs to him. It is practically acknowledging our stewardship.

What is God's proportion? God has not left us to grope in the darkness on this great question, for as we study his Word we find that he has directly and indirectly said, over and over again, that the tenth at the very least is holy unto him.

I know some who would believe that this was a Mosaic law, and therefore is null and void in this, the new dispensation; but they have not given the subject careful and prayerful study, for if they had, they would find that the tenth principle is one of very ancient obligation. It was adopted by the patriarch Abraham, and later on by his grandson Jacob. It was enjoined on Israel by formal injunction, and the regulations in regard to it, having been framed into a law, were placed on the statute books of the nation.

It is clear, then, it was enforced under the Mosaic economy, just as was the Sabbath law; but as the Sabbath law is just as much a law of the Christian church as it was of the Jewish church, so the property law, or tenth system, is of perpetual obligation. No moral precept has ever been repealed. God's law which regulates the property trust is as strictly of a moral character as that which regulates the question of time. If, therefore, the law pertaining to the trust of time be still binding, what authority have we to declare that God's law in regard to this disposal of property has been cancelled?

These people have evidently not given the matter careful study, nor do they wish to enter into it carefully. The tenth proportion is very small, yet it is evident that from the days of Abraham this was given cheerfully. There are proofs, however, that this was never intended to be set aside. Besides, Christ said that on his advent he did not come to sweep away the old laws of the prophets, but to fulfil them. It is settled in Scripture, and it is nowhere contradicted, that we must at least give one-tenth of those gifts loaned by the Lord to us in his mercy and exceeding kindness, to his honor and to his greater glory.

They are equally parts of God's moral law, and as such stand or fall together; but they both stand, because Christ said, "I am not come to destroy the law or the prophets, but to fulfil." If I were to state some reasons for proportionate giving, I think I should give you three.

First, because of duty. "God has given us a banner to be displayed because of truth," and on the very top of it shines out the word "Duty." The Lord has said the tenth is holy unto him, and if those who have been his chosen ones in the past have given this proportion and more to him, it certainly must be our duty to follow in their footsteps. We owe it to God as obedient children. "If ye love me," etc.

If "God so loved the world," etc.— unspeakable gift, — will we not give him at least the tenth of that which he in his goodness and bounty bestows upon us?

If we do this, we lay upon our Heavenly Father the responsibility, whether we shall give little or much. It then becomes a principle of our lives, and is not left to impulse or feeling. A great many with small incomes say, "I am afraid I cannot afford it," (and this is the chief obstacle with nearly all Christians), but you can. If you will try it, you will keep it up, because you will find you cannot afford not to do it. [*Applause.*]

Yes, even in dollars and cents the objection is from a temporal standpoint, and so is the reply. The Rev. Wilbur F. Crafts, in his book entitled "God in Business," says that some years ago, in the city of Chicago, a list of 100 prominent business men was drawn up, with the following results: Seventy church members, 24 who attend church, but non-members; 3 were classed as dissipated, and 3 were Jews who were good citizens.

The percentage of Christians among the most wealthy of Philadelphia is just as good as in Chicago. The Rev. Dr. Washington Gladden is authority for the statement that about three-fourths of the business men in the city of Springfield, Mass., are actively engaged in Christian work.

Did you ever try it? Did you ever know any one who tried it and was not prospered? Did you ever hear of one? Thousands of laymen in the United States and England are practicing it; so, if there be any exceptions, they ought to be known.

Living in Chicago to-day is one who believes so thoroughly in proportionate giving that he had the following question printed and sent to thousands of ministers in the United States, namely: "Have you ever known of any exceptions to the rule that God prospers in their temporal affairs those who honor him by setting apart a tenth of their income to his service?" And during the past nine or ten years the same question has been asked of not less than 5,000,000 persons, and no conflicting testimony worthy of the name has ever been received. "Prove me now herewith, saith the Lord of hosts." [*Applause.*]

Our duty to the Church, God's chosen instrument for the spread of the Gospel and the evangelization of the world, requires that money be given to carry on the work, and that it come from God's own people. Until a very late period, I was an advocate of concerts, strawberry festivals, etc., for the supplementing of church treasuries, until a dear Christian woman and Bible student, Mrs. Agnes P. Strain, called my attention to the interview between Abraham and the King of Sodom. Did you ever read it? It is recorded in Genesis 14 : 21-23: "And the King of Sodom said unto Abraham, Give me the persons and take the goods to thyself. And Abraham said to the King of Sodom, I have lifted up my hand unto the Lord the most high God, the possessor of heaven and earth, that I will not take from a thread even to a shoe latchet, and that I will not take anything that is thine, lest thou shouldest say, I have made Abraham rich." And yet we solicit and sell our tickets to those who are not God's children. "I am debtor both to the Greeks and to the barbarians, both to the wise and to the unwise."

Those who have the Gospel owe it those who have it not. The Gospel belongs to every man. God has entrusted it to the Church for the world — for the whole world. [*Applause.*]

To keep it back from any man is to defraud him of his due. The church which does not labor to evangelize the heathen is dishonest. She is a debtor who refuses to discharge her debt. She lives in debt to the world, and is not ashamed of it, and her dishonesty is a deadly dishonesty, for men are perishing daily for the lack of that knowledge which she withholds. And as with the Church, so with the individual. Every Christian is a debtor, and owes the Gospel to an ignorant world. What are you doing to pay your debt? It is a question of duty and obligation, and not one of mere option and benevolence. "Necessity is laid upon us, and woe, woe will be to us, if we preach not the Gospel to the millions of the lost world." "Go ye into all the world!" [*Applause.*]

We say, I have not had the call, and therefore cannot go. But, my brother, from the reports of the various boards we find that there are thousands who have had the call, and are just waiting and longing for the means and the opportunity, that they may go. Oh, the responsibility that rests upon us, if we do not respond!

The heathen will rise up against us in judgment in his presence —

> "Here, in this happy land, we have the light,
> Shining from God's own Word, free, pure, and bright;
> Shall we not send to them Bibles to read,
> Teachers and preachers, and all that they need?
> Pity them, pity them, Christians at home,
> Haste with the bread of life, hasten and come."

God is not chargeable with the slow progress of the Church. He is bending with infinite concern over a dying, sin-stricken world, but his plan of operation is to save by the agency of the Church, which, alas! is only to a very limited extent imbued with the self-sacrificing spirit of Christ.

The work of evangelization progresses just as fast as the zeal, love, and liberality of the Church increase, and no faster. We hold the grace of God in restraint. Oh! what we need in these wonderful times, fellow-Endeavorers, is a complete consecration. Some of us have given our souls to him and are resting on his promises for salvation; most of us have given him our bodies. We are working night and day in his service, but oh, how few there are who have given unto him their money as they should!

We read of the Israelites when they came out of Egypt, that "not a hoof was left behind," and a redemption or consecration that does not touch everything, pocketbooks included, is a very doubtful one. If it was necessary to the Mosaic dispensation to give so liberally (and it is commonly supposed that they gave a tenth, though, if you sum up all their giving, you will find that they gave at least one-third of their income), what ought we to give?

There were the first gatherings of the harvest, estimated at one-sixtieth, and the corners of the field left in reaping. another one-sixtieth; then whatever dropped from the hand was left for the poor; and once in seven years the lands were allowed to produce spontaneously for the poor. Then there were the trespass offerings, sin offerings, half shekels of the sanctuary, and the remission of all debts every seventh year. Then came the tithe for the priesthood, one-tenth of the produce of the fields, and of what remained another one-tenth for the temple and the poor.

Oh! should it not be with shame that so many of God's children think a tenth is too much? Why, dear friends, in the light of Scripture a tenth is the very least we can give. If I had the time this morning, I could give you testimony after testimony of those who not only give the tenth, but are following in the footsteps of our blessed Master and giving their all. Listen to this one: "Sarah Hosmer, of Lowell, though a poor woman, supported a student in the Nestorian Seminary, who became a minister of Christ. Five times she gave fifty dollars, earning the money in a factory, and sent out five native pastors to Christian work. When more than sixty years old she longed to furnish Nestoria with one more preacher for Christ, and, living in an attic, she took in sewing until she accomplished her cherished purpose. In the hands of this consecrated woman money transformed the factory girl and the seamstress into a missionary of the Cross and then multiplied her sixfold. [*Applause.*]

Reason the second: Gratitude and love should make us give proportionately.

Let us for a little while this morning stand beside the Agonized One in Gethsemane. Look at those great drops of blood; follow him to the cross and listen to that heartrending cry, "My God!" and I am sure that the power which alone comes from the Cross of Christ will subdue our hearts and break all the bands of selfishness which have so long imprisoned our souls, and we will join with the Christian poet in his song: —

> "Were the whole realm of nature mine,
> That were at present far too small;
> Love so amazing, so divine,
> Demands my soul, my life, my all."

The love of Jesus transforms the matter of giving from an irksome duty into a glorious privilege, a spiritual luxury. Of all the potent forces in the universe of God to-day, love stands forth unrivaled. It will carry more burdens, endure more suffering, accomplish more work, win more victories, and it will give more money. Oh, that the love of Christ might extend the empire of its divine influence from the centre to the circumference of every one of our hearts.

"He was rich," etc. Reason the third.

The glory of God, or the results that would flow from it. I venture to say that in this great company there are comparatively few who know what it would mean if Christians everywhere tithed their incomes. What would be the result? In reply to this question I shall give you a few statistics, basing them on the reports of the Presbyterian church.

The government officials estimate the annual income of the entire population of the United States to be a little over $7,000,000,000. This gives to every man, woman, and child an annual income of a little more than $175, or 55 cents a day. Now, estimate the number of active members in the Presbyterian church at 500,000, children and adherents at 500,000 more, making a total of 1,000,000. Multiply this by 55 cents, the daily income of each, and you have the sum of $550,000 as the daily income of the Presbyterian church. One-tenth of this is $55,000. Multiply this by the number of days in the year, and you have in round numbers more than $20,000,000 as one-tenth of the annual income.

This means that the Presbyterian Church in this country should pay annually for charitable, benevolent, and Christian purposes at least $20,000,000, as no one will claim that they are below the average in wealth or material prosperity. How much do they pay? They pay for congregational purposes, which include building of churches and pastors' salaries, about $6,500,000; for the boards of the church and miscellaneous objects connected with their church work, about $2,500,000 — making a total of about $9,000,000.

Is this all they pay? No; it is safe to say that they bear their share in society of other charitable and benevolent duties, but this in the church as a whole would probably not aggregate more than $3,000,000. This would leave the immense sum of $8,000,000 yet due the Lord. These same figures would apply to our society, our part being $1,000,000 and over.

But suppose we apply the figures to the Church at large. In 1886 there were in the United States over 11,000,000 ministers and church members, which would mean $220,000,000 in the Lord's treasury, when the truth of the matter is that the very highest amount given is not over $100,000,000, leaving $120,000,000.

How long would it be before the 1,181,000,000 heathen would hear the glad tidings of the Gospel? How long before the millennium? Again this morning we hear the voice of God saying, "Bring ye all the tithes into the storehouse," etc.

These two things the world needs to-day, and God has joined them together; a baptism of unselfishness and a baptism of the Holy Ghost. [*Applause.*]

Mr. Murphy was several times interrupted by the applause of the delegates. Evidently his treatment of the subject met with much approval.

Bishop Fallows presided during Dr. Clark's temporary absence, and at this point gave out the hymn "Faith is the Victory." After the singing, he introduced Rev. Leroy S. Bean, of Gorham, Me., who spoke as follows on "Systematic Giving to God."

ADDRESS OF REV. LEROY S. BEAN.

There are no better tempered people, it seems to me, in all this wide world than our Christian Endeavor hosts. I do not think that they even allow themselves any unchristian feeling towards their old adversary, the Devil himself. They wish that he might mend his ways and cease from evil and learn to do well. But unfortunately he yet leads the mighty hosts of evil against the followers of Prince Immanuel. The Christian Endeavor hosts of this land realize that they are engaged in warfare: they have taken for their battle cry "The world for Christ," and they mean it.

But to engage in warfare requires system, movement along strategic lines, the holding of strategic points,—system that shall lead to ultimate victory and success. For success is a matter of systematic adjusting of functions and potencies to desired ends. I believe in the heroism of young people. I admire their magnificent, undaunted chivalry and knight-errantry. I believe, as Dr. Strong has already intimated, that there are multitudes who would, if it were necessary, be willing to die for Christ. If the young men of this audience were brought to the issue of confessing their faith in Christ and dying, or denying their faith in Christ and living, they would confess Christ and give the strong physical manhood of their lives to be torn by wild beasts. If the girls of our Christian Endeavor societies, tender and true, were brought to the issue to confess Christ and die, or to deny Christ and live, they would be married to the stake itself, and give their radiant forms of beauty to the embrace of the devouring flames, rather than deny their Master. But the day, happily, has passed when men are called upon to die for Christ, and a greater demand is upon us to-day, upon the Church of the twentieth century,— that we shall live for Christ. [*Applause.*] And to live for Christ means that all life bows itself under the dominancy of the Eternal thought and the Eternal purpose. It means that in every department of life and in every gift and function of life there will be reference to the high ends, not alone of personal salvation, but of bringing this world to a knowledge of Christ and him crucified. The day has passed forever when people believed that salvation was getting out of hell in one world and into heaven in another. They believe now that salvation is to face the eternities, strong in their confidence of duty to be done here and now, with their gifts consecrated to Christ. What hath one man wrought in song for the world! [turning to Mr. Sankey.] But not alone in song and speech but in the different departments of life; and if that life itself be Christ's, and if we live for him, then we are in this world to make money, if we have power to make money, for God's kingdom,— not a tenth only, but all of it.

And then system comes in in deciding what apportionment God requires for sustaining the religious and philanthropic work, and for the spread of the knowledge of the Lord Jesus Christ. I don't know how stingy anybody can be and still retain that spark of heavenly grace which makes him a living entity in the kingdom of our Lord Jesus Christ. I do not care, any more than I know, how stingy one can be and still be called a Christian. But this I know: that we are called upon to see to it that we consecrate to the Lord in his service all that life can produce, so that everywhere we touch the world,—in every place where our influence is felt *we do business for God* here in this world. We profess to believe that the kingdom of God is the great thing,—that to spread abroad the knowledge of Jesus Christ and bring the world to his sovereignty is the essential purpose for which we live and move and have our being. If this be true, the wealth and the potency of wealth must be consecrated to his service, so that out of it shall be given that which shall make the desert place to be glad and blossom as the rose, because into it have been poured the healing streams of consecrated wealth.

The cattle upon the thousand hills and the gold and the silver are God's. Let those wealthy agricultural States, upon whose plains feed countless herds, know that the cattle are his; and let the cities with their wealth — yea, let Wall Street — know that when the kingdom of Christ shall have come on earth, the gold and silver shall be acknowledged to be his also. [*Applause.*]

I am sure that there never can come a settlement of those politico-economic conditions of social life, there cannot come a settlement of the great industrial questions of America, until that settlement is along the line of consecrated wealth or capital or consecrated labor. [*Applause.*] No more until then can it be possible for the warfare between the classes to cease.

But why the need of system? Why not give in the lump? Well, my friends, we are ready to die for Christ, but Christ desires us now, instead of dying for him, — I mean, of course, physical death, — to live for him, and in living systematically to labor so that the resources of life shall be able to continually produce those beneficent functions that shall be marked in the outputting of effort to bring the world to himself. If we are going to do anything, we need to do it systematically. We need to recognize the fact that without system we are liable to be swept away by our emotions, and perhaps even impair the possibility of our doing good service in the future. I believe in the generosity of this audience. If some one should come here to plead with you to empty your pockets, leaving you enough money to keep you here one day more, and let you get out of New York and reach home safely, you would empty your pockets. But there is a greater work than that to be done. It is to resolve from this time forth, each and every one of us, that we will consider ourselves stewards of the manifold mercies of God, in wealth as well as in all other blessings of life, and from this day ever more to dedicate to the service of God a portion of

that which he has given unto us, realizing that the remainder is also to be spent in ways that will further the coming of the kingdom of God on earth.
Are we ready to do this? The Lord waits to-day for the consecration of Christian wealth. Oh, you who represent the States of this Union, what can we not do for God in America and for God in the world during the next ten years, if all these delegations go home with this resolve I will consider my life sacred to God; I will consider all the business of life sacred to him; and from this day forth forevermore I will see to it that some portion of my substance — and with increased wealth an increased portion — shall be dedicated to the spreading abroad of the knowledge of Christ and him crucified!
I am glad to remember that I commenced giving a tenth, although I would not care to bind the rule on every soul as the standard of individual duty. I think that by many much more than that might be given. I commenced to give a tenth when I was preaching on the munificent, and exorbitant, and totally unheard-of salary of $300 a year, [*applause*] and it did not hurt me a bit; and with the increase of my income there has come an increasing consciousness of ability to do more than ever in this line for the kingdom of our Lord and his Christ.
Now, what good shall it all be, if we go out from this hall and forget it all? Are we not ready just now to stand before God and say. "Some portion, at least, of my substance shall be systematically consecrated to his service, from this day forth!" There has come a request that I feel like granting — a request to know how many in all this vast audience now give some portion of their income systematically to the service of God and his Christ. How many here in all this audience to-day are giving systematically? [*Nearly the whole audience arose, and the rising was followed by emphatic applause.*] I do not see any need of talking about it longer. I was going to ask how many of you would give systematically; perhaps that is the way you anticipated it. As many of you as will give systematically from this day, please rise. [*The whole audience arose.*] Christian Endeavorers, 15,000 strong here to-day, dedicated to systematic giving for the coming of the kingdom of Christ, may the Lord bless you in the vow of this day and this hour. [*Loud applause.*]

The hymn, "At the Cross," was then appropriately sung.

Dr. CLARK: Isn't it good, my friends, that we have in official relation with one of the great missionary boards one of our own young people? [*Applause.*] We are all glad of this fact. It will bind us all, in all our denominations, closer to the missionary work to have this missionary conference which is to follow led by Rev. R. E. Speer, of the Presbyterian Board of Missions. [*Loud applause and the Chautauqua salute.*]

OPEN CONFERENCE ON MISSION WORK.

Mr. SPEER: *My beloved Endeavorers:* — I came down from the College Conference at Northfield last night to be here this morning, charged with greetings from the Seventh Annual World's Meeting of College Students to the Eleventh Annual Convention of the Y. P. S. C. E., full of love and good wishes. [*Applause.*] These greetings were to be stated in these terms: "Wherefore, seeing we are encompassed about by so great a cloud of witnessses, let us lay aside every weight and the sin that doth so easily beset us, and let us run with patience the race that is set before us, looking unto Jesus, the author and finisher of our faith, who for the joy that was set before him endured the cross, despising the shame, and is set down at the right hand of God." Also adding these words: "Love not the world, neither the things that are in the world. If any man love the world, the love of the Father is not in him; for all that is in the world, the lust of the flesh, and the lust of the eyes, and the pride of life, is not of the Father, but is of the world; and the world passeth away and the lusts thereof; but he that doeth the will of God abideth forever."

The subject that is announced for the conference this morning carries with it, as every one of us has already observed, an assumption: it takes for granted that every one of these societies is doing something for foreign missions and for home missions. Ten years ago that would not have been taken for granted: the question as it would have been stated then would rather have been: "Why should our societies do something for foreign missions?" Thank God, the ten years past have led us to see that the Christian Endeavor society that puts missions away in a corner only invites God to put it away in a corner: [applause] that every one of us has begun to realize that loyalty to one who is Master, under whom and in whom all we are brethren, calls us to loyalty, also, to his parting wish, that we should be witnesses unto him both in Jerusalem, and in all Judea, and in Samaria, and unto the uttermost parts of the earth." And it is to carry out this last wish of one whom, not having seen, we love, that we are to talk together this morning.

Did you ever notice that Jesus Christ did not say: "The hireling is a hireling because he fleeth," but he said: "The hireling fleeth because he is a hireling"? He knew that deep down in the things that people do lie the things that people are, because he knew that just in proportion as our own lives are lived in true and outspoken fidelity to him, just in that proportion are we diligent in carrying out his parting desire. So that the conference this morning is going to indicate a good deal more than what you and I think at first it is going to do. It is going to be the pulse of the spiritual life of the Christian Endeavor Society. The moment that the nerve of its energy slackens in the consecration of its efforts for missionary work, that moment does the spiritual life of the Christian Endeavor Society begin to go steadily down; so that this morning what we say is going to be to all those who listen an indication of just how warm the spiritual life of each of our societies is.

We are going to start first of all with what naturally comes first, namely: How are the Christian Endeavor societies to maintian and promote the missionary spirit in their own hearts? And we will ask, first, what our societies are doing in the line of missionary meetings. Will all of you who have missionary meetings in your societies hold up your hands? [*A good proportion of the delegates held up their hands.*] These who do not have missionary meetings, please hold up their hands. [*A much less number of hands were held up.*] There are quite a number of hands held up. You can explain it in two ways: either it is due to an unconscious thoughtlessness about something which we ought to have thought about, or else it is an illustration of the fact that many of our meetings are taken up by a selfish spirit, which finds application in other spheres of our life.

Now, how often do you have these meetings? How many have them once a month, once in two months, once in three months, or once in six months? The hands raised are pretty nearly evenly divided. How many think that holding them once a month is the best way? [*The response was almost unanimous.*] The once-a-month people have it. [*Applause.*] This gives twelve missionary meetings a year. Suppose you divide them evenly, giving half to home missions, and half to foreign missions: that gives you a glance over the wide open field of this land of ours once in two months, and gives you another glance over the wide open field of the world every two months; and less than that no Christian Endeavor society ought to take.

What do you do in these missionary meetings? [*Various responses were given:* "*We have reports from the foreign field;*" "*We have missionary tens,* and one of them reports each month;" "We have addresses by returned missionaries;" "We have a missionary catechism;" "Letters are read from a missionary supported by the society;" "We have a map of the world, and study the geography of missions;" "Our missionary committee selects different subjects, and gives them out to the members of the society."]

We have quite a good many suggestions, but there are a great many fields in the world; there are a great many missionaries' lives that have been lived counting themselves not dear to themselves, and they have passed through the gates of death and are living unto God forevermore. There are a great many kinds of missionary work. There is work among the women in the Zenanas; among the opium eaters in China, etc. You can find scores upon scores of subjects that will keep your meetings going for the whole year.

Secondly, who looks after these missionary meetings? How many have missionary committees? [*A large number of hands were raised.*] How many do not? [*Many hands were raised.*] About as many do not have missionary committees as do not have any missionary meetings. The two things are very closely connected: if you have a missionary meeting, you will have a missionary committee; and if you have a missionary committee, you will have a missionary meeting. How many members do you have on the committee — two, three, four, or five? [*The greater number of hands indicated five.*] How long does your committee hold office — for one month, three months, or six months? [*The majority was for six months.*] How many of your societies that appoint a committee for six months always make the chairman of that committee a member of the next committee? [*Only a few hands were raised.*] It ought to be done, because otherwise you have a new committee without any of the old experienced members on it. It is a good thing to put the chairman of the old committee on the new committee, so that the new committee will be tied fast to the old lines.

What does this missionary committee do? How many do not do anything but look after the monthly missionary meeting? How many do something else than that? [*Responses:* "*Our committee has established a mission.*" "*Our committee visits the sick, and distributes missionary literature.*" "*Our committee follows the two-cents-a-week plan,*" etc.] A good many of us have different conceptions of what a missionary committee is. Some think it is to do work in the locality of the society, but you ought to have another committee for that work; that work is big enough by itself. Any other things that this missionary committee does? ["*We hold a missionary social.*" "*Our committee gets the members to give proportionately to some specific object.*" "*Our committee looks after the missionary literature.*" "*Our committee has established a missionary library for the young people of the society and the Sunday school.*" "*Our committee looks after the missionary finances.*" "*Our committee corresponds with the missionaries on the field.*" "*Our committee takes special pains to make the missionary meeting doubly interesting.*"]

How many of you have a monthly concert? [*Quite a number of hands were raised.*] How many have not? [*A majority.*] A majority do not have a monthly concert. It used to be that the majority did have such a concert, and it ought to be so to-day. I will tell you another duty of the missionary committee: it ought to worry the pastor until he has established a monthly concert. There is another duty in the vast majority of our churches. A collection is taken up on a haphazard Sunday for foreign missions. If it is unpleasant, or there is some other attraction, not many people give to the object. You ought to see to it, if nobody else does, that all the members of the church each year have an opportunity, and avail themselves of the opportunity, to give something to foreign missions in that year. [*Applause.*]

Thirdly, I want to know how many missionary committees hold conferences with the missionary committee of other churches in the same community? [*Only a few hands were raised.*] Well, I do not see why not. If we are going to let down the denominational barrier on other things, I do not see why the missionary committees in each community should not come together and talk over the different plans for work.

Now, we have touched upon two things: the missionary meeting, and the missionary committee. Somebody suggested that the missionary committee must look after the matter of missionary literature. How many people here have read ten missionary books? [*About forty hands were raised.*] How many have read five? [*About the same number.*] How many have read three missionary books? How many have read two missionary books, of which the Bible was one? [*The response to these questions was not large.* A delegate asked *Mr. Speer to state what he meant by missionary books, and Mr. Speer mentioned a long list of missionary biographies.*] The missionary committee ought to see that we have a different state of affairs in this matter next year.

How many take missionary magazines? [*A large number.*] Every one of us ought to take a missionary magazine. Nearly every denomination has a missionary periodical, and they are all good ones. If you do not want a denominational magazine, you can get one or two that are excellent that will keep you abreast of the ever-widening information gathered in regard to missionary work.

A DELEGATE: What is the best magazine?

Mr. SPEER. I cannot undertake to decide that question. If you are a Baptist, take a Baptist missionary magazine. If you are a Presbyterian, take "The Church at Home and Abroad." If you are a Methodist, take "The Gospel in All Lands." If you are a Congregationalist, take "The Missionary Herald." If you want to take anything more, "The Missionary Review of the World," edited by Dr. Pierson, is an excellent magazine.

Now, we have three things: the missionary committees, the missionary meetings, and the missionary literature. Now, what about missionary giving? I am going to ask Dr. Smith, of the Central Presbyterian church of this city, to say what his society is doing for foreign missions in that way.

Dr. WILTON MERLE SMITH: We owe a monumental debt of gratitude to the press of this great city, but in one of the papers of this city there was an editorial which said that it seemed to be that the reason for the existence of this mighty organization was to combat the opening of the World's Fair on Sunday. I hope that our friends of that paper are here this morning. Whatever the Church has to do, whatever it is organized to do, the Christian Endeavor Society is to do. More than that, tell us anything more to do for Christ, and we will do it. [*Applause.*] Our home missionary in China, Mr. Fulton, suggested the giving of two cents a week for missions by every member. Christian Endeavorers have taken up that plan all over the country. In the church which I represent we tried it in a little different way. Every Endeavorer said: "Not only will I give two cents a week, but I will find four others who will give two cents a week, and hence I will stand responsible for ten cents a week." Oh, how they went for the hard-fisted men of that congregation! Men who had never given to missions before were inveigled into giving two cents a week to some beautiful girl or to some persistent young man. I said to my friend who started this movement that it looked a little clumsy and cumbersome; I did not believe he could make it work. He said they would try it. Over every ten Endeavorers they placed a collector, and the money contributed all went into the treasury of the society. When six months had passed, — I was a little suspicious of the plan, — I asked them how much they had received; I thought perhaps they had made $100. The society had 50 members, and they gathered $260 [*applause*] — $10 more than the plan called for. At the end of the year, in three months, they are going to turn over $500 into the treasuries of the home and foreign mission boards of our church. The principal thing about the plan is that it works, and for a full description of it I wish you would turn to our Christian Endeavor paper, *The Golden Rule*, page 681, for June 23, — I wish others might try the plan. It works; it has raised a large sum of money for missions. Let us give; let us all give; let us give systematically; and let us get our hands into other people's pockets. [*Laughter and applause.*]

Mr. SPEER: Before we close, suppose we sum up a few things we have looked at with reference to what the societies are to do about foreign missions. Do not forget the missionary meeting; do not forget the missionary committee; do not forget to rouse an interest in foreign missions by reading missionary books and periodicals; do not forget the hint Dr. Smith has just thrown out about giving to missions, even though it be only two cents a week, dividing the contribution between the home and foreign fields. I want to suggest two more things in closing:

First of all, how many societies regularly and systematically pray for foreign missions? [*A few hands were raised.*] Well, there are a few, but not very many. We ought as Christian Endeavor societies deliberately to apportion out the world, and see to it that Christian Endeavor societies are the greatest interceding medium in all this world; so that, as year after year rolls by, there shall not be one single missionary in the world for whom the Christian Endeavor societies do not pray. Send to your missionary board; get them to give you some single mission field, with the names of the workers; learn those names by heart, and then week after week see to it that your society is constantly praying for these workers.

Last of all, how many societies have ever sent out from their midst missionaries into the foreign field? [*Quite a large number of hands were raised.*] Well, there is a pretty good number. Every society ought to keep that as one of its goals, and never be satisfied until some life trained in its own midst goes out from that midst into the foreign field.

Having said these things, and the time being pretty much gone, it is only necessary to say this in closing: That just in proportion as our hearts grow interested in the cause of missions this coming year, just in that proportion will our Christian work at home be blessed. We never in the world shall be able to receive a blessing on the work immediately around us until we have our eye set loyally and lovingly on the uttermost parts of the earth. We need to be reminded this morning that nothing new is needed to carry on this work of the Master. We want just to return to that old conception of the Christian life that counts not its life dear unto itself, so that it may finish its course with joy in the ministry it has received of the Lord Jesus to testify the gospel of the grace of God — the life that follows in the footsteps of him who, though he was rich, yet for our sakes became poor, that we might become rich; the life that lays its honors down at his feet and only whispers "Master, behold thy servant:" the life that bows down humbly in faith, as Elisha did, praying that our eyes may be opened to catch a glimpse of the kingdom of God, when the Master has fulfilled his purpose in it; the life which is devoted thoroughly and completely to him, going out to do what he has told us to do, and to plant the standards of God on the islands of the sea, and in the uttermost limits of the earth. [*Prolonged applause.*]

At the close of this interesting conference Mr. and Mrs. Geo. C. Stebbins sang a duet, "Speed away," the sentiment of which was in close accord with the thought of the morning. It made a great impression upon the audience, who insisted upon an encore. Mr. Stebbins, however, disregarded the call and gave out the hymn "A soldier of the cross," which was sung by the congregation. Following the hymn a long list of telegrams of greeting were read from various parts of the country.

Dr. CLARK: There are many things that the management of the convention does not attempt to do. We make no demands on your allegiance; we ask no contribution; we do not ask you to follow out our plans. This is a mass meeting for inspiration and fellowship. There is no legislation here. There is nothing binding upon you when you go home except to do what your church and your pastor want to have you do. I think that the idea of this convention is sometimes misunderstood. We do not indorse organizations, but principles. [*Applause.*] This ought to be kept in mind. We have done something, we are doing something every minute of this convention, besides protesting against the opening of the World's Fair on Sunday. [*Applause.*] This morning has proved it, as has been said, and every session of the convention has proved it. The genius of the convention must not be misunderstood. It is a mass meeting for fellowship and inspiration — no axes to grind, no legislation. There will be resolutions brought in by the committee on resolutions in regard to general things that we believe in, but nothing that partakes of legislation for individual societies or individual Christian Endeavorers. But there is one thing we must do, and that is to provide for subsequent meetings. The Board of Trustees of the United Society limits itself to these two things, pretty much: publishing certain leaflets and literature, and providing for the international convention. And now we shall be told by an honored member of this board, Rev. Nehemiah Boynton, of Boston, in regard to the decision for 1894, the meeting for 1893 having already been decided upon. [*Applause.*]

ADDRESS OF REV. NEHEMIAH BOYNTON.

Mr. President, and my Good Friends: It is always a pleasant thing to be the bearer of a message, provided that message is a word of greeting and of good news. I wish that the words which I have to say this morning would fall with joy upon every ear; but I am sure that what I have to say for my brethren will be a delight to some and a disappointment to others. No word of sympathy from us for the delighted souls! We wish simply to say to those to whose wishes we cannot at present accede that we appreciate the honor which has been conferred upon this society through the generous and persistent invitations which have come to us. It requires a courage amounting almost to heroism for a company of young people from any State to come to a convention like this and discern the work which must be endured and the sacrifice which must be shouldered in order to its successful prosecution, and then appear before the board of trustees and ask that theirs may be the work and that theirs may be the sacrifice. [*Applause.*] We appreciate the invitations which have come to us, not only from the young people themselves, but from the churches they represent and the pastors thereof, from the mayors of the cities and the governors of the States, and the various boards of trade and of commerce.

We want to say to those who will be disappointed by this announcement two things: first, to ask them to remember what was the comfort of the old minister who sometimes, as he came to the close of the day with a cloud on the horizon of his life, found his consolation in bringing his trouble to the great Burden-bearer and in solacing his soul with the assurance that for him there would be another day. We want to say that we understand perfectly well the kind of young men and women with whom we are dealing, and that not only we have a company who know how to take their delights and make them tributary to their spiritual uplifting, but that we have also a company who know how to take their disappointments, [*applause*] and put them loyally in the hands of Jesus Christ, that by his supreme and divine power they may be transmuted into loving forces of spiritual life. [*Applause.*]

We have had three delightful invitations for the convention of 1894: one exceedingly fascinating invitation from the brethren and sisters of the golden gate, California; [*applause*] another from the brethren and friends of the thriving and bustling city of Denver; [*applause*] and still another from our brethren and sisters in almost the heart of the population of these United States—Cleveland. [*Applause.*] Some of us have devoutly wished that it might be right, so far as our Christian Endeavor conventions are concerned, that like all

Gaul we might be divided into three parts. [*Laughter.*] It would relieve us of a present embarassment. But we remember that "we are not divided, all one body we." [*Applause.*]

I won't tantalize you, my interested friends, by making any more of a speech. [*Laughter.*] I will simply say with these few words that the trustees have decided where the place for the convention of '94 shall be, [*applause*] and that they have commissioned me in their stead to "pass along the watchword, Cleveland, '94." [*Great enthusiasm, with cheers and the Chautauqua salute from Cleveland, the delegates from Ohio singing the words, "Pass along the watchword, Cleveland, '94," in the chorus of which they were joined by the whole congregation.*]

Now will you permit me to read the official communication entirely, before you applaud? "It has been decided that, everything considered, mainly because an international Christian Endeavor convention was never held in what is known as the central portion of our country, that the convention of '94 be held in Cleveland, Ohio. The board of trustees desire to express their heartiest thanks to the Christian Endeavorers of Denver and San Francisco for their enthusiastic invitations for the convention, and the board of trustees are prepared to say that they will pledge an international convention to the great and influential far West as soon as possible. Respectfully submitted, for the trustees." [*Applause.*]

Here ensued one of the most impressive scenes of the convention. Before the applause greeting Mr. Boynton's remarks had ceased, the Colorado delegation were on their feet and started the hymn "Blest be the tie," the rejoicing Ohio delegation taking it up and the whole audience joining. Then the California delegation proposed three cheers for Cleveland, which were given with a will, and Ohio responded with three cheers for Denver and San Francisco.

Dr. CLARK: That is a most gracious response, and shows how kindly Colorado and California accept the decision of the trustees. [*Loud applause.*] And now, is not this a happy prelude to the last address of the morning, "The Whole World for Christ," by one who has recently been around the world, and who has spent much time among the missions abroad,— Rev. Dr. Henry C. Mabie, of Boston, Home Secretary of the American Baptist Missionary Union? [*Loud applause.*]

ADDRESS OF REV. H. C. MABIE, D. D.

Rev. Dr. MABIE: Mr. President and Fellow-Workers: The time is coming, and coming soon, when such expressions of Christian fellowship and good feeling as were just voiced in that old Gospel hymn of Christian fellowship on the part of Colorado and California will be expressed by all nations of the earth, when they shall have been gathered in the one fold of Jesus Christ. I have been asked to speak for a little while this morning upon the relations of this Christian society to world-wide missions. In that open parliament in which we engaged so delightfully a few moments ago I felt as if the most practical things had been touched upon, and we had had revealed to us a marked development in the direction toward which my remarks are designed to tend. I wish simply to answer briefly the question, in what respects young people's societies, associated in such form as are the Christian Endeavor societies, may legitimately aid the great work of foreign missions in the whole world. I want to speak of four respects in which these societies may bring their influence to bear.

First of all, the societies may emphasize, in the list of the multiplied relations in which Christians stand to the world, this foreign mission relation. I prefer to speak of the foreign mission *relation*, rather than of what is sometimes called the foreign mission *cause*. Strictly speaking, there is but one cause — the kingdom of our Lord and Saviour Jesus Christ. But we stand in manifold sets of relation to that cause and that one kingdom. We stand first of all as individuals in relation to the family — a relation really ordained of God; we stand, also, in relation to the local church, and that relation this great organization fitly recognizes and encourages; we stand certainly in a vital relation to all forms of home mission work, — city evangelization and the uplifting of all classes and conditions that are gathered on the great continent on which we live. When we come to this set of relations, this great international Christian Endeavor organization may most fitly consider questions like the conduct of the Columbian Exposition that is to be held next year in Chicago. We cannot ignore or overlook these relations in their place; but we, likewise, as Christian believers and members of Christ's kingdom, stand in relation to pagan nations, who, as yet, have not the gospel of Jesus Christ. These relations are never in conflict with one another, nor need any Christian be discouraged because of the vastness and the number of these relations. The vastness and the number of these relations simply argue to the Christian, and make him conscious of his royal dignity as a disciple of Jesus Christ — as one of his junior brethren. I submit, dear friends, every believer who has partaken of Christ's nature in his proper measure stands in the same relation to all the interests of the human race as Jesus Christ, absolutely, on the human side, stood to the various portions of our race. And certainly you will agree with me in acknowledging that the young Christians of the day in which we live and of Christian America stand in greatly increased and intensified relations to these pagan peoples, as compared with the relations in which our fathers stood. By the marvellous progress of our times we are brought geographically in close touch with once distant peoples.

It was my lot within the last two years, setting sail from San Francisco, to go around this world and in about eight months to visit the great mission stations in Japan, China, Burmah, and various parts of India, and to meet face to face, in the conditions under which Christian work is carried on in those lands, more than five hundred of the representatives of the various Christian denominations in this country. In eight months of time it was possible to go safely and conveniently to all these representative missions. I stood the other day on our Pacific coast at Vancouver, the great gateway of British Columbia, and I met coming off from the "Empress of India," one of those superb ships of the Canadian Pacific line, a party of missionaries. Said I to Mr. Herring, who was one of the party just come from China, "How long since you set sail?" This was Tuesday morning. He replied, "We left Shanghai two weeks ago on Saturday." Here they were, after a journey of less than sixteen days, upon the shores of their native land. A few moments ago we saw lifted here many hands, indicating that from the various societies which you represent there have gone forth personal laborers into the various mission fields. From your Sabbath schools, from your Endeavor societies, from your Christian churches have gone forth those who, if not of your own blood, are certainly of your own spiritual nature. By all these indications you are realizing that you stand in intenser relations a hundred-fold to pagan peoples than they did in Carey's day, when he was examining the globe made of leather that hung there in his shoemaker's shop, and was reading the fresh news that was brought out in the account of Captain Cook's voyages among the South Sea islands. I was in the empire of British Burmah, in connection with my journey, and I wanted to go up to Ava and Oung-pen-la, the city of the old prison pen, where, within a century, the now sainted Judson had lain for weary months in five pairs of irons, tortured almost unto death. When Judson made his way painfully up the Iriwaddy river from Rangoon to Ava to have that memorable but disappointing conference with the Burman king, it took him six weeks in a native boat to make the journey, and he was fighting companies of robbers and bandits on the shores during the entire journey. When I went to Ava I took passage on a through train from Rangoon and made the trip comfortably in a first-class railway carriage, with all needed conveniences, in less than twenty-four hours, and I found there a great native church of Karens and Burman believers, and a score of missionaries ready to welcome me and give me an ovation as one who, representing the American Church, had come out in Christ's name to give them greeting.

This society emphasizes the foreign mission relation, as has been made plain to us this morning, especially by the fact that you do not think of conducting your work without having your missionary meetings and your missionary committees, and are beginning to offer your missionary laborers. In a great convention like this the whole forenoon is practically given to the consideration of the relations in which we stand to the nations that are yet unevangelized.

I wish to emphasize further that the Christian Endeavor societies may most fitly organize study of the mission field. Now I am glad that so great and widespread a sentiment prevails; but as we gave evidence a few moments ago, in answer to one form of Mr. Speer's inquiries, there is need yet of larger development along this line of the study of missions. Young people are largely students,— students of their time and of the forces that have entered into it. But how important, as we study the history of the world, that we should recognize those chief and foremost factors that have entered into its present Christianized and highly civilized condition through the work of the great missionary fathers. I thank God for this work in its variety and scope, representing all branches of the Christian Church. I can be thankful, and so are you, that even in one of the early centuries of the Christian era the Roman Catholic Church had in it life and missionary power enough to send Augustine across the English Channel to Great Britian to give the Gospel to our fathers, who were dancing around the altars of Druid worship in that early period, savage and barbarous to a high degree. I am thankful that even the Roman Catholic Church sent forth Augustine to introduce Christianity into the British Islands, that so ultimately it might be brought to us. Referring to Augustine as coming from the Catholic Church reminds me of a rather promising youth who, one day, looking up to his mother, said : " I say, ma, wasn't it a lucky thing for pa that he married into our family?" [*Laughter.*] If we come further down the centuries and recognize the work of Carey, and Livingston, and Moffatt, and Morrison, and Judson, and John G. Paton, and Alexander MacKay, and Joseph Hardy Neesima — that apostle of Japan, a native pioneer in the sunrise kingdom [*applause*] — in extending God's kingdom, what books are these which record their lives? Oh, my heart throbbed responsively to that of my brother, Dr. Noble, who sits on this platform, when he just said to me that within a short period he had bought twelve of the best missionary biographies he could lay his hands upon, and was personally, as the pastor of that great Union Park church in Chicago, introducing those books seriatim into the hands and hearts — and let us believe, into the lives — of the young people of his own congregation. [*Applause.*] Dear friends of the missionary committees, go home and build up that missionary library. You cannot afford to be a week older without having begun to read the life of William Carey, the boy who began in such obscurity that men despised his beginning, and that even his compeers in the church commanded him to sit down when he rose to speak in regard to giving the Gospel to heathen people; that man who translated the Bible into parts, at least, of forty languages of the earth; that man who was so recognized by Lord Wellesly and by Sir Wm. Bentinck and other noted men, that they gladly testified that he and men like him had done more for the permanency of the British empire in India than all other influences combined. You cannot afford not to fill your young hearts and lives with the inspiration that comes from men like these. You cannot afford to be a month older until you have gotten and read both volumes of John G. Paton's account of his work in the New Hebrides. Think of that man, developed, as many of you are developing yourselves, in city missionary work, beginning in one of the darkest quarters of Edinburgh, transforming brothels and breathing-holes of hell into palaces of devotion to Jesus Christ, going out after that experience to cannibal islands; and though he went through a purgatory of pain and suffering and trial during the first twelve years of his ministry there, yet he left twelve thousand of those cannibal people bowing at the feet of Christ! You who would be familiar with what is going on in the most fascinating empire outside of America that I know of — Japan — should read the life of Joseph Hardy Neesima, by Prof. Hardy, giving an account of the boy, who was a fugitive and a runaway from his own country, in order to come to a land where the Bible was known and where he might find the clue to the meaning of his life, — that youth, going through the academy at Andover, through Amherst College, and through Andover Seminary, becoming interpreter of a legation from Japan and going to the courts of Europe on two conditions: that those Japanese nobles should remove the disabilities from his own head and from his family, in case he should ever go back to Japan; and, secondly, that they should exact no official work from him on the Lord's day. [*Applause.*] Think of a youth like that going back with five thousand dollars in his hands, given to him in that historic meeting of the American Board at Rutland, Vt., and laying the foundation of the Doshisha University in Kyoto! I had the pleasure, while in Japan, as the guest of my friend Dr. Davis, a member of the theological department, to visit that college at Kyoto. I found at college prayers seven hundred Japanese youths, more reverential than I remember ever to have seen a similar company of college students at prayers in this country. On the platform were the faculty of twenty teachers, half of them graduates of Yale, and Amherst, and Williams, and other colleges, and the other half of them natives of Japan, experts in their departments as scientists, linguists, philosophers, and teachers, even, of English literature. Three-fourths of those students were Christian men, going out to labor during the summer in evangelistic work among the heathen provinces of Japan. There are thirteen dormitories for young men upon the college campus and four solid brick structures, one of them the gift of one of our noblest laymen, Mr. J. N. Harris, of New London, Conn., who in a single gift of $115,000 planted that school of science in connection with that university. [*Applause.*] Talk of romance being gone out of the history of missions! It has but begun, except that the romance is transmuted and glorified by the witnessing of the Holy Ghost into the inspiration of men who have partaken of the divine nature until these movements are the sublimest things on which the God of Heaven looks, as he scans this rolling orb in the multitude of worlds that circle about his throne. Study missions; read these biographies; fill the minds of your children with them. I have a little fellow at home, a little tow-headed shaver, and his mother spends Sunday afternoon reading stories from Paton, Neesima, MacKay, and all the rest; and the little fellow said the other day, "Mamma is getting me wound up; I think I shall go off one of these days." [*Laughter.*] Dear friends, missionary mothers, missionary sisters, missionary daughters, missionary children, they are God's greatest gifts to this sin-revolted province of God's empire!

There is a third relation in which we stand, as Christian Endeavor societies, to missions, and that is, we may plan for the support of missions. I believe that it is an accepted principle with this organization that you are to encourage your local societies to contribute to their various denominational boards. [*Applause.*] You need not form specific boards, but you are encouraged loyally to stand by your own boards. I am glad you are doing it. I tell you that the accumulations of experience that come to a mission board, as they have come to bodies like the American Board of this country, to the Presbyterian and Baptist and Methodist boards, — these accumulations of experience are in the economics of the Church of God, and we cannot afford to dispense with that accumulated experience and allow men to go off on tangents in the dark, to plan important missions, tempted to all sorts of vagaries and fanaticism; but we need to stand by these boards loyally. So in your contributions, may I throw out, in a very kindly and friendly way, one hint in regard to the matter of special contributions to specific objects. Don't insist on that. The other day I received from a devoted worker somewhere in New Jersey a letter asking me to send a list of specific causes to one of which their society might be encouraged to contribute. I did what I could. I am sometimes perplexed by these letters. Let me say to you there is a tendency just now — and I am sure my brother secretaries of other boards will bear me out — to overdo this matter of contributing to specific causes. Many people want to support a native teacher and have a letter from him about once in three months, and secure his photograph, and come into personal touch with him. Now I sympathize with the incentives that are underneath all that. You want to know and love and believe in a particular Christian worker. But, dear friends, possibly if you were to go to a mission field you would see that in some respects that sort of thing does not always work happily. Sometimes — I must confess it — that sort of treatment of a native missionary turns his head. After he has had a few letters from home and is notified that his money will come from New York or Boston, we find him some morning strutting around among his fellow-pastors, saying, "Aha, I am supported from the great America." He is a few inches taller than his brethren. It turns his head and does him an injury. For you must remember that after all these converts are but children, like the multitude that came out of Egypt under Moses. And sometimes, let me say, you are likely to take too much stock in an individual convert. Not all converts turn out successfully, I am sorry to say, on mission fields any more than they do in the churches of New York or Boston or Philadelphia. Now and then a man has a terrible fall. Now, if for a series of years your society should put all your money into one man, and then some missionary should be obliged to report that he had turned out badly, your young people would shake their heads and say, "I think I am done with foreign missions." Now suppose you were to trust your boards and trust your missionaries as a whole, and trust your secretaries who are about this time of year going over a long list of from three to five hundred of the most devoted men and women that God ever gave the church, arranging for their continued maintenance; and suppose you say, "I will take my stock in the whole mission, — in that man's salary, in that mission school conducted by that sister, in that hospital, in this native preacher, in the building of this chapel and schoolhouse." Suppose you take stock in all these; then when some one man may fail, it will not make so much as a ripple on the surface of your confidence, but you will say, "I belong to this mission cause and to the whole of it. And when some day God permits you to go out to Japan and you see the splendid missions in Sendai and Yokohama and Kyoto, you will say, "These are mine." And when you cross the Yellow Sea and meet the workers in China and go up the Yang-tse-kiang River and see those great missions at Nankin and Hankow, you will say, "These are mine." And when you go to the missions of Canton and Swatow and Foochow, you will say, "I have stock in all these." And when you go over to Rangoon or to Calcutta or up in the Punjab or down among the Telugus, or among the various missions with which your church is connected, you will say, "These are mine;" and your heart will enlarge with the divinest enthusiasm that God can give you. [*Applause.*]

My last word is this: The Christian Endeavor Society may fitly seek to recruit the mission force, — oh, so depleted again and again by failing health, by death, by the growing demand. Shall I tell you — my cheeks almost change color as I state it — that for an entire year the board which I represent has been asking for a re-inforcement of twenty-five men to go out to their great mission field in India, where God has given us more than fifty-three thousand converts within twenty-seven years, and we lack three of the men yet. The money has been contributed; it is in the hands of our treasurer; but we still lack several of those young men. How much do you think of that Christian character which does not very early in its course come to the point where at last it feels like saying, "Lord, here am I, send me"? I know he does not call you all; I know you cannot all go to these fields; but, dear friends, if the hour shall come when God opens the way for you to enter into some of these fields where you may lay the foundations of Christian empire, how great will be your privilege! Think of a man like Dr. Bunker in the heart of Burmah, — a dear friend of mine whom I saw in the midst of more than three thousand Christians won to Christ from among the wild Karens of the hill country of Burmah. I went out to a great association with him and met 1,058 delegates from 56 villages and towns in the heart of that wild portion of Burmah, and those people welcomed their missionary as an angel from heaven. They would have plucked out their eyes for him, if he had asked it. What an inspiration! I remember one sister — for women, too, are going to the foreign field — out in that Karen jungle. The man who had charge of the elephant on which she was to ride led the old Jumbo up alongside the platform on which she stood. I saw the old elephant taking in the whole situation. He lowered his head gracefully, that the lady might put her foot on his head, and then on his neck, and leap into the houdah, and then he ambled down the mountain side with that Christian sister on his back, going out for a two-month's tour in the swamps and jungles. And as she looked back and said, "Farewell; give my greetings to the women's board that sent me here," there was no tear in her eye; there was no expression of desire that we should commiserate her or awaken much sympathy for her in the churches of America. That young woman on that elephant's back, going out among those Christian believers in those jungles to win other scores to Jesus Christ, would not have surrendered that place in that elephant's saddle that day for the proudest position occupied by any queen of fashion in this world. I met Miss Guinness in the far East, at one point in China where I stopped, a woman who had travelled eight hundred miles on a single tour into the very heart of China, and who at every stopping-place found multitudes waiting to hang on her lips, which distilled the sweetness and the power of the Gospel with wonderful effect. It is not surprising that when she went home to England it seemed as though the whole of China followed her with prayers for a speedy return.

What joy comes to the pastor when now and then a young man or woman, with level head and warm heart, comes to consult him with reference to study and preparation for foreign mission work! I was pastor in St. Paul, Minnesota, and after I had been preaching on China missions, there came to me a bright and gifted young layman and said to me, "Pastor, when the contribution-box went around I had no money to put into it; but I have had this cause of missions on my heart for years, and I just deliberately put myself into the box, so to speak." [*Applause.*] When I was out there in China I saw this young man. He had just come a thousand miles from a point in the interior of China. There he stood awaiting me on the wharf, clad in the native costume, and in the native style making his best salaam to me, his old pastor. Then I praised God for the sight of his face in China. His main query was, "When are you going to send us reinforcements?" Thank God, we sent him six or eight not long ago.

Let me say to young men who are looking out into the world and asking, " Is it possible in God's great plan for me that I should find myself in some Asiatic or African mission field, or on some of the islands of the sea?"— let me say to you, from the closest sympathy and identification with those who thus work for Christ in all these pagan lands, you have my heartiest congratulation. May God multiply the number who have enlisted in the Student Volunteer movement, of those, too, who come from the churches, from the plow and from the anvil and the counter, saying, " Here am I, send me." [*Loud applause.*]

Mr. Sankey then announced the hymn, " We shall meet beyond the river, by and by," dividing up the audience into five choruses, each singing the refrain, " By and by." The benediction was pronounced by Rev. Dr. Noble, of Chicago.

SATURDAY AFTERNOON.

No session of the convention was held in the Garden during the afternoon or evening. Instead, the afternoon was given up to denominational rallies and committee conferences, and the evening to social reunions and receptions.

A large and enthusiastic meeting was held at the Marble Collegiate Church, at Fifth Avenue and 39th Street, at 1.30 P. M., to discuss Sunday closing of the World's Fair. Rev. Howard A. Russell presided, and there was considerable earnest debate as to the precise action which should be taken, though opinion was unanimous in favor af Sunday closing. Finally the following resolution, presented by Dr. Burrell, the pastor of the church, was adopted unanimously : —

Resolved, That the people assembled here to-day respectfully petition the authorities having the matter in charge to prevent the opening of the Columbian Fair on Sundays, believing that if such action is not taken, a vast multitude of the American people, particularly such as hold the biblical code of morals, would find it in conscience impossible to attend or lend countenance to the fair, and that this action be transmitted instantly to the Congressional session.

The First International Junior Christian Endeavor Rally was held at the Broadway Tabernacle at 2.30 P. M., Mrs. Alice M. Scudder, of Jersey City, presiding. The main body of the church was reserved for the little people, and the older ones found a place in the galleries,— those who found a place at all, for the church was very soon crowded to the utmost. The exercises were very interesting, among the speakers being Rev. Dr. Deems, Mrs. F. E. Clark, Rev. C. H. Tyndall, of New York, Rev. W. W. Sleeper, of Beloit, Wis., Mr. W. S. Ferguson, of Philadelphia, and Rev. H. N. Kinney, of Winsted, Ct. Miss Lillie Taylor, a little girl, recited a poem written for the occasion, and Rev. Cornelius Brett, of Jersey City, conducted the consecration service.

DENOMINATIONAL RALLIES.

A New Feature, but a Remarkably Successful One.

The denominational rallies alone would have marked the New York convention as extraordinary. Nothing like them has been attempted before, but they met with great and universal favor. They proved conclusively that there is nothing in the most hearty fellowship among evangelical Christians which can weaken the affection each has for his own denomination.

METHODIST.

The rally of Methodist Endeavorers, held at the Washington Square Methodist Episcopal Church, was a largely attended and enthusiastic meeting. Its general tenor is well shown by the resolutions adopted and the advisory committee formed. Among the speakers were Rev. G. C. Kelly, D.D., Owensborough, Ky.; Rev. Dr. Sykes; Rev. A. G. Kynett, of Philadelphia; and Rev. Charles W. Bickley, D.D., of Philadelphia. The feeling was earnestly expressed that the pastors of the Methodist Episcopal Church, who, in all love and loyalty to their denomination, wish to add the interdenominational Christian Endeavor fellowship to the strictly denominational young people's society, should have that privilege without any hindrance, expressed or implied.

We, the delegates of the Christian Endeavor Convention of the Methodist Episcopal Church to the Eleventh International Convention of the Societies of Christian Endeavor held in New York, in special meeting assembled, do desire to give formal expression to our appreciation of the action of our late General Conference, whereby is accorded to us, as Christian Endeavor societies, the right of existence in our church without interference or restriction other than that we accord with the spirit and intent of the Epworth League as expressed in its constitution — all of which we are heartily willing to do; also according us the privilege of becoming chapters of the Epworth League, thereby securing to our societies official recognition and equal status in our own church. Therefore, be it

Resolved, First, that we are profoundly thankful that in the providence of God no action was taken by our late General Conference looking toward the dissolution of the Christian Endeavor societies now in our own church, or in any wise to interfere with them, but rather according with the full official recognition upon easy conditions, with which we will cheerfully comply.

Resolved. Second, that under this permission we will proceed to strengthen and make more efficient in the service of "Christ and the Church," the Christian Endeavor societies now existing in our churches; and in those charges having no young people's societies, and where circumstances especially favor the Christian Endeavor societies, we will organize societies of Christian Endeavor.

Resolved, Third, that we here and now reaffirm our unswerving loyalty to our beloved Methodist Episcopal Church. We accept with unquestioning faith her doctrines and policy, and rejoice in the high privilege of membership in her household. By her teachings we have come to know Him whom to know aright is life eternal, and by her fostering care we have been kept from falling, and have advanced in Christian life.

We would not wilfully nor knowingly form any affiliation or connect ourselves with any organization that would in any degree alienate our affection from her or diminish our efficiency in her service. We seek no higher privilege than membership in our beloved church, until promoted to membership in the church triumphant. We will strive to cultivate in our young people the same spirit of loyalty to our own denomination, and at the same time we most heartily cherish and will earnestly cultivate that spirit of interdenominational fraternity which is so marked a feature of the great providential Christian Endeavor movement.

We have found our connection with the Christian Endeavor societies a helpful and delightful experience. It has intensified our love for the church universal. It has given us a broader and more intelligent comprehension of the scope and purpose of the Gospel. It has brought us into closer relations with young people of other denominations on the wide field of honest endeavor for our common Master.

We have come into a higher and purer affection for the "household of faith." We have come to these great conventions adhering to our denominational tenets, and we left them with no abatement of denominational zeal, and have learned through these years of delightful affiliation that there may be diversity without difference, and the most intense denominational devotion without a tinge of bigotry or narrow sectarianism. Our attachment for the Christian Endeavor movement has strengthened with the passing years, and we cherish the hope that this union of Christian counsel and Christian service may never be disrupted or disturbed.

The committee is composed of the Rev. Dr. E. K. Young, of Philadelphia, chairman; Miss FrancesE. Willard, of Evanston, Ill.; the Rev. Dr. Stone, of New York; the Rev. F. O. Holman, of Minneapolis; the Rev. N. S. Albright, of Tiffin, O.; the Rev. Dr. W. C. Webb, of Philadelphia; the Rev. Geo. T. Lemmon, of Troy; the Rev. Dr. G. S. Sykes, of New Jersey; the Rev. Mr. Coultas, of Terre Haute; the Rev. B. B. Loomis, of Lansingburg; the Rev. S. W. Gehrett, of Philadelphia; the Rev. Wallace McMullin, of Springfield, Mass.; Mr. W. S. Ferguson, of Philadelphia; the Rev. J. T. Mayer, of Abilene, Kan., and the Rev. Ezra Tinker, of New York.

BAPTIST.

The Baptist rally was held in the North Baptist Church. The great sign, "Welcome," gave its cheery greeting to a multitude of enthusiastic Baptist Endeavorers. The presiding officer of the meeting was a trustee of the United Society, Rev. John T. Beckley, D. D., of Philadelphia. In his introductory remarks he said that the Baptist denomination stood shoulder to shoulder with the other denominations in this grand work of the young people's societies of Christian Endeavor, in the noble attempt they are making to redeem the world.

An address was then made by the ever welcome Dr. Wayland Hoyt, of Minneapolis, who gave earnest testimony for the Endeavor movement and the earnest young people who are engaged in it, and predicted for them and for it a constant victory and final triumph.

The address of the Rev. W. C. Bitting, of New York, was chiefly concerned with the work of the Baptist Publication Society. He showed its deep and world-wide usefulness.

A spirited Endeavor address was then made by Rev. H. C. Mabie, D.D., of Boston. He said that this Christian Endeavor movement appeared to him to be a universal re-awakening of the people to the cause of Christianity. He saw in this movement an indication of Christ's coming triumph.

This rousing meeting was closed with capital speeches by Rev. John J. Brouner, pastor of the church, and the Rev. Dr. Tupper, of Denver, Col.

PRESBYTERIAN.

The Presbyterian rally was held in Dr. Parkhurst's church, and was exceedingly well attended. Dr. Teunis S. Hamlin, of Washington, led the meeting with great ability. The devotional exercises were conducted by Rev. J. R. Dickson, of Galt, Ontario. Rev. H. T. McEwen gave the address of welcome. He said: "I am a loyal Presbyterian. You hear of many regiments, but in the time of war we hear only of the army. We Presbyterians are a regiment, and hope to do our share of work in the great army. We hope the city missions and home missions and foreign missions and each denomination will take places side by side in the great battle."

After the hearty singing of a hymn came an address by Rev. Anderson Rogers, of Windsor, Nova Scotia. He said: "Forty-five years ago a missionary sailed away from Nova Scotia. He was a weak man, but fired with the Spirit of God. His name was Dr. John Geddie. There was then in Canada only a church here and there, but now we are a solid church, from Atlantic to Pacific. Dr. Geddie went to the New Hebrides, and when he went there were no Christians there, and when he left there were no heathen. Our second missionary field was Trinidad. The coolies there number 80,000. Our missionaries have there 50 schools and over 3,000 scholars. We have there now seven missionaries and many churches. We have a third mission in Formosa. Dr. Fraser went there twenty years ago with the forceps and Bible, and in pulling teeth and preaching he has been successful. We have now 2,500 members of the church in Formosa."

Dr. John Gillespie then spoke: "There is a tombstone at Lucknow with these words: 'Here lies Henry Lawrence, who tried to do his duty.' In life we should all do our duty.' What is the end of foreign missions? Cast your eyes upon the host of heaven, and they answer you. The grand end of missions is the glory of God, through eternity. What must be the method of foreign missions? There must be intelligence. This work requires the wisest of our men. What are the results of foreign missions? Rapid growth in India, and in every land. While you are generous to all movements, be loyal to your own special church, your own by birth and training."

Dr. McMillan then spoke, saying: "I am a Presbyterian, and my ancestors have been Presbyterians, as long as there have been any Presbyterians, and yet I love all, though I love my own a little the best. We live in peace in our town because each man loves his own family a little better than any other.

People who are not able to jump over the denominational fence will find it hard to climb to heaven. Our great home missions demand united effort of all churches. Half a million strangers come to our shores, and we require unity to accomplish the work given us. We have also the Indians to bring to Christ."

At Dr. Hamlin's suggestion the whole congregation formed a procession and visited the Presbyterian House on Fifth Avenue and Twelfth Street.

METHODIST PROTESTANT.

The Methodist Protestant rally was held at Trinity Church, Brooklyn, and was led by that earnest denominational worker, successful editor, and charming writer, Rev. J. F. Cowan. The speakers were Mr. J. F. Fulton, South Amboy, N. J.; Rev. J. H. Lucas, Brooklyn, N. Y.; Mrs. Anna Pierpont Siviter, Pittsburg, Penn.; Rev. C. F. Swift, Bellevue, Penn.; Mr. W. C. Perkins, Baltimore, Md.; Rev. J. A. Reichard, Foosland, Ill.; Mr. C. A. Dungan; Miss Jennie White, Cincinnati, O.; Mr. D. S. Stevens, Mr. G. L. Queen, Westminster, Md.; and Rev. J. S. Davis, Kansas City, Kan.

One hundred and sixty-three delegates registered, and others were present to the number of three hundred. Besides the various general interests of the church, the subjects of "Denominational Fellowship," "Conference Unions," "The Junior Mission Work," and "Young People's Rallies and Ministerial Meetings" were discussed. Trinity Y. P. S. C. E. served a lunch in the church parlors, and a social reception was held later.

Great satisfaction was expressed at the addition of this feature of denominational rallies to the convention programme, and in resolutions adopted the Methodist Protestant Endeavorers re-affirmed their loyalty to Christian Endeavor principles and name, and thanked their General Conference for its official recognition of Christian Endeavor. Measures were taken to extend the work more widely.

REFORMED (DUTCH) CHURCH.

The people of the Reformed (Dutch) Church held a most enthusiastic rally at the Marble Collegiate Church. Dr. David James Burrell, the pastor, presided in his happiest manner. The church was crowded to its utmost capacity. More than one thousand representatives of the Reformed churches from all over the land were present. It was very pleasant to see so many of the pastors present. Dr. Burrell was hoarse from his magnificent address of Friday night, and decided not to attempt a speech, but made things lively by his bright and breezy introductions of speakers.

Dr. Burrell said that the Dutch denomination was not as large as it might be, but the hearts of Dutchmen were generous and very sympathetic with those not fortunate enough to belong to the Dutch religious family. He said he was too recent a Dutchman to speak with authority upon family matters, but that he believed the past which all loyal reformers justly gloried in would be but as the purple dawn compared with the blazing brightness of the future that our Christian Endeavorers were to usher in.

Rev. DeWitt Mason, of Boonton, N. J., was the first speaker. His topic was "The Relation of Christian Endeavor to Our Reformed Church." His shibboleth was "loyalty." Christian Endeavorers should be loyal to their denominational life; their efforts should be along the line of the church's activities in home and foreign missions. Training for service is the peculiar function of the Endeavor society. This training should be accentuated along the denominational bias. If we learn to love the work in the foreign field, we should also love to know where our church is working, who the workers are, and what is being accomplished. Activity, training, enthusiasm, intelligence, — all these are Endeavor virtues, and fraught with promise of divine blessing; but we must be good stewards within our own household.

Dr. Carlos Martyn, of Newark, N. J., was the second speaker, and he brought a message of good cheer. He was in sympathy with Christian Endeavor because it went hand in hand with thorough organization and intelligent training. It was first practical, then systematic, then enthusiastic, and, of course, finally successful. The proof of apostolic succession was apostolic success, and the winning of 120,000 associate members to Christ and the Church was eminent proof of the divine origin and divine approval of this mighty factor in the universal Church of God.

Dr. A. E. Kittridge was discovered in the congregation, and was called to the pulpit. He made some witty remarks, and then gave a closing word in behalf of fellowship among the denominations. He never expected to see denominational names obliterated, but he hoped to see the day when pastors and leaders would gather together in council to plan for our one Lord and his one work.

Dr. Harsha was the last speaker. Having but just settled down in his Harlem charge, he considered himself a very young Dutchman, but judging from the fun he had been having, he felt as if he might be a hundred years old. He had a message for the Endeavorers to rise to the measure of their true responsibility. We are all witnesses for the truth: we are all priests unto God.

At the close of the speaking, Mr. Myers, one of Dr. Burrell's assistants, announced that a committee representing the Reformed churches of New York City and immediate vicinity, had prepared a beautiful souvenir to be given to all delegates representing our Reformed Dutch churches, and also to those present at the rally who had been members of our goodly fellowship, but were now in other folds. One thousand persons took advantage of the offer. The souvenir was a handsome book-mark, — a richly engraved celluloid shield mounted upon a handsome orange ribbon.

FREE BAPTIST.

The Free Baptist rally was held at the First Free Baptist Church, West Twenty-fifth Street. On the platform were seated some of the leading clergymen of the Free Baptist faith, among them Rev. Waldo Messaros, pastor of that church, Rev. J. B. Jordan, of Pawtucket, R. I., Rev. Clarence A. Vincent, General Secretary of the Board of Home and Foreign Missions, Rev. Leroy S. Bean, Gorham, Me., and Rev. Rivington D. Lord, Brooklyn.

The pastor of the church gave out an opening hymn, and then extended a hearty welcome to all present.

Rev. J. B. Jordan, who had been appointed chairman of the meeting, was next introduced, and conducted the opening service, being followed in prayer by the Rev. R. D. Lord, pastor of the First Free Baptist church in Brooklyn.

Mr. Jordan said at the very beginning of the meeting: " The Y. P. S. C. E. from the first has stood for loyalty to the local church, to the pastor of the church, and to the denomination of which they are a part. This is the reason why so many are meeting at this hour to impress upon the young people the importance of loyalty to their own denomination."

He then introduced the Rev. Leroy S. Bean, who made an eloquent address on " Denominationalism and Interdenominationalism." Mr. Bean said: —

" I am glad to see the denomination so well represented as it is to-day, small though this convention may seem compared with the greater one which has preceded it. There are people in the world who object to organizations. They are true Christian people, but seem to think that if they could only stop the organizing of individuals, it would hasten the coming of the millennium. We are social individuals, no man living to himself, and no man dying to himself. When the mind begins to grow, the man will commence to influence other individuals along the line in which his own life has been influenced. We must understand that we cannot live alone, if we want to; and we don't want to. We desire to do good together."

He then went on to speak of the reasons why we should have some definite form of organization, and declared his belief in the Free Baptist organization as being the only one (with his present enlightenment) with which he could conscientiously be identified. " The church," said he, " is something more than a nursery. The church is an organization, an organization of militant Christians. Every individual owes it to the individual church to be a living Christian; and the church owes it to the denomination to be a living church."

An eloquent speech was made by Rev. Clarence A. Vincent, in which he said: —

" England once had a golden age in literature. The Christian Church is just entering its golden age. I have been impressed more with this fact than any other during this great convention. This great movement took its birth from the missionary movement of a hundred years ago. What immense strides civilization has taken since that time! The progress has been just as great in spiritual matters — in church work. I heard a gentleman say the other day, in speaking of the history of the church during the last hundred years, ' It seems to me it is now in a perfect blaze of glory.' We want to do a great work to redeem the world in the name of the Lord Jesus Christ. We as Free Baptists want to have more self-respect. It means something to me that the Free Baptist Church was the first to stand out against slavery and to be in favor of liberty for all."

Mr. Vincent closed with a word urging the young people to take hold of the denominational work.

THE UNITED BRETHREN IN CHRIST.

The rally of the United Brethren in Christ was held at the Marble Collegiate Church. Rev. R. L. Swain, Ph.D., of Westerville, O., presided. The first address was by Rev. L. F. John, Johnstown, Penn., on " The Adaptability of Christian Endeavor to the United Brethren Church." He said : " It is adaptable to our church because of its fidelity to the local church. It teaches denominationalism, and develops church loyalty in the young people. It is adaptable because of its large fellowship, developing a broad love for all Christians. It makes our young people broader in spirit and more active in work. It adapts itself in every conceivable way. There is no limit to its flexibility in any denomination."

Next, Rev. J. H. Shepherd, Akron, O., spoke on " What Should be our Attitude toward Interdenominational Fellowship?" " The spirit of the United Brethren in Christ has always been one of fellowship. We have always been ready to give a hand, but forget sometimes to receive a hand. The Y. P. S. C. E. will advance the cause of our church as nothing else can."

Rev. M. R. Drury, assistant editor of *The Religious Telescope*, the church organ, said that fidelity is deepening, and fellowship is broadening. The Y. P. S. C. E. furnishes an admirable opportunity for training our young people in loyalty to their own church. We can't get along without it. We must have it; the more, the better.

Rev. W. J. Johnson, of Baltimore, Md., spoke on " How to advance Christian Endeavor in the United Brethren Church." " First and best, by our lives. Let us show to others that Christian Endeavor makes us more loyal to our own church, as well as helps to a greater love for all Christians. Another way is to carry the fidelity, fellowship, and enthusiasm of this convention home with us and set things on fire. Tell it to your own church, tell it to other churches, tell it everywhere. Again, a splendid way is to get as many as possible to attend the international convention. That will surely convert them. Next year let us have at Montreal a rally of at least five hundred. Let us push on, persistently, until the church is saturated with Christian Endeavor."

Rev. H. Doty, Bowling Green, O., said that Christian Endeavor was the best thing to build up a church. It made the members workers and *stickers*.

Rev. G. W. Arnold, Eton, O., said that Christian Endeavor had never failed to help him in his work. He had changed the name of one Y. P. C. U. into a Y. P. S. C. E., for he wanted the best and the original.

Prof. W. O. Krolm, of Clark University, Massachusetts, said the great principle of mutuality underlies everything in human conduct. He did not believe in freight-train religion where each was put into a box car and locked and sealed by ecclesiastical authority, with not even a bell-rope to send a signal from one end to the other. He preferred a vestibule train, where he could walk from one end to the other, shake hands, and pat people on the shoulde rand ove them. This is what Christian Endeavor is doing for the churches, — uniting them without destroying their individuality. He wanted to be in fellowship with all. He would rather be a little frog in a big puddle, than a great big frog flopping in a ditch.

Rev. B. F. Cokely, New Haven, Conn., wanted the church to stick to Christian Endeavor. Several laymen and laywomen and other pastors spoke of the great help Christian Endeavor had been to them and their churches.

A committee was appointed to memorialize the next general conference, calling on them to consider the value of Christian Endeavor, and at least put it on a level with the denominational Young People's Christian Union.

Dr. R. L. Swain said that if we were not loyal to our own local church, we should be despised by every respectable denomination. Christian Endeavor stands for a thoughtful and interested fidelity, and the broadest and purest fellowship.

CONGREGATIONAL.

The Congregational rally was held in the Y. M. C. A. hall, which was crowded with delegates. Many had to stand. Prayer was offered by Rev. S. V. Karmarkar, of India. Rev. Ralph W. Brokaw, of Springfield, Mass., who presided, made a few introductory remarks about the purpose of the rally, and introduced Rev. C. H. Everest, D.D., of Orange, N.J., who spoke in Dr. Bradford's place, Dr. Bradford having sailed for England.

Dr. Everest gave an inspiring speech, emphasizing the thought of loyalty to the common interests of Congregationalism. His subject was, "Congregationalism and Our Young People."

Rev. C. C. Creegan, D.D., of Boston, followed with a ringing speech on "Mission Work Abroad," showing our young people their opportunity, and urging them to go in and possess the land for the King. He appealed most earnestly, not only for money, but for young men and women as volunteers for service.

Rev. R. A. Beard, of Spokane, Wash., was drafted into the place left vacant by Rev. C. J. Ryder's enforced absence on account of illness in his family. Mr. Beard spoke of "Mission Work at Home," and was applauded to the echo for his manly, patriotic words. Alluding to the great problems of the day, he emphasized the solution of them all in the application of the "golden rule," which application, said he, is largely to be made by the young Christians of America.

After Mr. Beard, Rev. W. G. Puddefoot made a brief address on the same topic. It was stirring, and very enthusiastically received.

Rev. Dr. Noble, of Chicago, was present, and by vote of the audience was requested to "say a few words." He said many, and put a fitting climax on a most successful meeting, which ended with "Work, for the Night is Coming," and the benediction by Rev. Nehemiah Boynton, of Boston.

No Congregationalist who was there could fail of being a more earnest Congregationalist and a more devoted Christian, having learned to prize his interdenominational fellowship.

CUMBERLAND PRESBYTERIAN.

REV. H. C. BIRD.

The lecture room of Fourteenth Street Presbyterian Church was filled by Cumberland Presbyterians. Rev. H. C. Bird presiding. Rev. D. E. Bushnell, D.D., Chattanooga, Tenn., spoke upon the relation of the Cumberland Presbyterian Church to the Christian Endeavor movement. This church, he said, is by tradition, history, and spirit eminently fitted to receive the Christian Endeavor movement. Its broadness and progressiveness bring it into close touch with this movement, which is one of the noblest offerings of our times. He then systematically discussed his theme.

Rev. B. P. Fullerton, of St. Louis, spoke upon the question of a separate denominational organization for young people, and said there was nothing in his subject, as the General Assembly had rightly decided that we need no organization separate from the Christian Endeavor Society. He urged the giving of greater prominence to this work, through the church press and the presbyteries.

Rev. Dr. W. H. Black, of Missouri Valley College, gave an animated talk within the general discussion. The meeting adopted a resolution asking that more space in the church papers be given to this work, and that the presbyteries have an annual Christian Endeavor day in connection with their regular sessions.

LUTHERAN.

The beautiful St. James Lutheran Church, corner of Seventy-fourth Street and Madison Avenue, was filled with delegates from all parts of the country, when Rev. A. J. Turkle, of Omaha, Neb., who presided during the hour, called upon them to unite in singing "Blest be the tie," as an opening song of praise for the enthusiastic meeting that followed. The pastor, Rev. J. B. Remensnyder, D.D, in a few well-chosen words of greeting, welcomed those present.

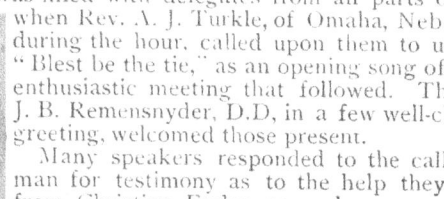

REV. A. J. TURKLE.

Many speakers responded to the call of the chairman for testimony as to the help they had received from Christian Endeavor, and many were the suggestions as to how the society might be made more helpful to the Lutheran Church. There was testimony of an increasing love of the young people for their own church. As the chairman put it, a Christian Endeavor Lutheran he had found to be a double-strength Lutheran.

Others told of the increased attendance of young people upon all regular church services. The accounts of aggressive service for the Master in conducting services and mission Sunday schools were inspiring. Rev. George Scholl, D.D., Secretary of the Board of Foreign Missions, outlined clearly a plan by which the societies might be more helpful to the church by assisting in the support of two young men whom the board was just sending to India.

There was a feeling that the young people of the Lutheran Church should be well and largely trained in the distinctive doctrines and usages of the Lutheran Church, and the sentiment prevailed that this could be done in Christian Endeavor societies as well as in a distinctively denominational society. All opportunity for teaching the noble history, beautiful polity, and various activities of the church was said to be given in Christian Endeavor; and thus loyalty to Christian Endeavor was emphasized in the Lutheran rally. The desire for the fellowship of all evangelical Christians in this interdenominational movement was touchingly referred to.

Many spoke of their desire to be the means of bringing the society to the attention of other Lutheran churches that had not yet organized a society. A greater consecration to do more for the Master in their own local churches and in the great mission field was the prevailing sentiment of the meeting.

INDEPENDENT CHURCHES.

A meeting of independent evangelical churches was held in the Church of the Strangers. Rev. Charles F. Deems, D.D., was elected president, and Rev. W. Jay Peck, of Corona, secretary.

Letters were read from ten churches. Dr. Deems gave an address explaining the object of the meeting. Rev. Eugene F. Hunt, of South Ashburnham, Mass., addressed the meeting, and made a plea for closer fellowship. George W. Smith, clerk of the Union Evangelical Church, Corona, N.Y., gave a history of the formation of his church and its growth for twenty-one years. Miss Dean, of Chicago, represented the Kenwood Evangelical Church. The Lake Avenue Union Church was also represented by Miss Dean. Miss Austin gave, in a bright paper, the history of Unity Church, of Detroit, Mich.

Dr. Deems made a report for the Church of the Strangers, and spoke of the form of its government; Rev. P. A. Canada spoke for the Christian Church, and Dr. J. B. Weston explained its character. The second meeting will be held in Montreal.

CHRISTIAN.

The Christian Church rally was held in the lecture rooms of the Fourteenth Street Presbyterian Church, Rev. J. B. Weston, D.D., of Standfordville, N. Y., in charge. After singing and the repetition of the twenty-third Psalm, Rev. G. W. Morrow, of West Randolph, Vt., led in prayer.

Dr. Weston spoke of the greatness of the meeting, and of his special joy in this movement, so thoroughly in harmony with the purposes, prayers, and hopes of his denominational fathers. Christian Unity in action is the purpose of the Christian Endeavor movement and of his own church life,—not a union in creed or polity, but in life and love. He spoke of the growth of this sentiment from the organization of the Evangelical Alliance till to-day.

Rev. P. A. Canada, of Conneaut, O., a vice-president of the Ohio State Union, then spoke of the growth of sentiment into action, and asked that an effort be made to get the statistics of this organization in all Christian conferences, and to spread the movement among his denomination.

Rev. T. S. Weeks, of Wolfboro', N. H., spoke upon "Our Idea of Christian Union," upon the basis of individualism, making each heart a unit dependent upon God for its faith, and loyal to Christ alone.

George A. Chace, Esq., of Fall River, spoke of the fellowship of Christian character in every man of every denomination, accepting all who are accepted and anointed of God.

Rev. G. W. Shane, of Troy, O., spoke of the importance of the opportunity afforded in the movement.

Rev. W. H. Hainer, of Irvington, N. J., spoke of the movement as God's answer to his people's prayers.

Mr. Herman Eldridge, of Erie, Penn., spoke of the Junior work and its work in the Erie church.

Rev. B. S. Maber, of Gilead, Me., spoke of the prohibition movement, to which Endeavorers are so true, and expressed gratitude that the fences are being overthrown by the children in the zeal for the cultivation of the whole vineyard for Christ.

Rev. G. W. Morrow, of Vermont, rejoiced in being a small part of the great convention, and told what Endeavor had done for his church, having received seven Endeavorers into his church last Sunday. Rev. W. H. Shaw, of Randall, N. Y., spoke of receiving sixty into his church within a year, largely aided by Christian Endeavor work.

Mr. Shaw, of the Church of the Evangel, Brooklyn, invited delegates to attend the Christian Church at Brooklyn on Sunday.

Rev. T. W. Howard, of Pottersville, Mass., said that the Christian Church was in full harmony with the movement.

The meeting was large and enthusiastic, and several ladies took very interesting part in the proceedings.

REFORMED EPISCOPAL.

The Reformed Episcopal delegates held a rally in the First Reformed Episcopal Church, corner of Fifty-fifth Street and Madison Avenue. They were filled with enthusiasm, and when the president of the meeting, Bishop Fallows, of Chicago, announced the opening hymn, all joined heartily in singing. After prayer by Rev. L. M. Walters, of Philadelphia, Bishop Fallows earnestly expressed his hearty commendation of the Christian Endeavor Society, and hoped before long there might be a society in every church in our communion.

The Rev. J. W. Fairley was then introduced. He emphasized the fact that Christian Endeavor demands staunch loyalty to the church. There are numerous conventions held from time to time throughout our land, but none ever attracts so great a multitude as the Christian Endeavor conventions. Does this not indicate that Christ is with us? I am proud that I am a member of *the* church among all churches which in its declaration of principles particularly emphasizes Christian fellowship. This is one of the grandest aims of the Christian Endeavor Society.

The Bishop then introduced Rev. George W. Huntington, of Brooklyn. He said, "A certain preacher took for the text of his sermon Acts 17 : 6, and made the following divisions :—
1. The world is upside down.
2. It must be turned right side up."

Application: We are the men to do it. The speaker was of the opinion that there is no question about the fitness of the "application" to the Christian Endeavor Society.

Mr. Robert L. Rudolph, of New York, was the next speaker. He said, "The initials C. E. stand for Christian Endeavor and Civil Engineer. The business of the civil engineer is to build railroads, erect bridges, bore tunnels. He has been busy making roads from North, South, East, and West that the delegates might reach this great city. So it is, too, the business of the Christian Endeavorer to prepare the hearts of men. There are prejudices to be swept away, indifferences to overcome, ignorance to enlighten."

The last address was delivered by Rev. L. M. Walters, of Philadelphia, who spoke earnestly about the work of the Holy Ghost. The speaker urged the delegates to study the Scriptures earnestly and prayerfully, and to see how much of this wondrous power is delegated to them as individuals.

In closing the meeting, Bishop Fallows took occasion to refer to the profound feeling of gratitude which fills the pastor's heart when he finds himself surrounded by an earnest, consecrated band of Christian Endeavorers, on whom he can lean, and from whom he can receive encouragement and help. He felt proud that St. Paul's Church, Chicago, of which he was rector, organized the first society of Christian Endeavor in the Reformed Episcopal Church. After prayer and the benediction, the delegates adjourned to the lecture room, where for an hour Christian fellowship was exemplified, and the delegates from Chicago, Peoria, Boston, Philadelphia, Brooklyn, and New York met each other and exchanged greetings.

EPISCOPAL.

The rally of the Churchmen was held in the Sunday-school room of Calvary Church, of which Rev. H. Y. Satterlee, D.D., is rector. About fifty persons were present, including nine clergymen. The meeting was opened with a short service from the Prayer Book, conducted by Rev. I. O. Adams, of Arkansas, assisted by Rev. Scott M. Cooke and Rev. W. Stanley Emery, both of Calvary parish.

This service was followed by an informal conference, in the course of which Rev. Mr. Adams explained the working of the Endeavor society in his own parish at Pine Bluff, Arkansas. He said that he had the usual parish guilds; but those that did the work of the parish were members of the Endeavor society, or in full sympathy with it. He found that the meetings held under the auspices of the society helped him in his own spiritual life more than all the other guild meetings in the parish. The pledge and constitution of the Endeavor society were so flexible that he found no difficulty in bringing the weekly prayer meetings of the society within church lines. The topics considered at these meetings were suggested by the Christian year.

Mr. Gallaway, a layman from St. Peter's Church, Baltimore, said that an Endeavor society had existed in that parish only one year. It was already regarded by all in the parish as essential to the success of the enterprises of the church.

Miss Gower, of London, Ontario, reported that there were Endeavor societies in four out of seven churches in that city. She was sure that the rectors of those churches would say that they could not get along without the society.

A lady from Grace Church, Chicago, said that while the St. Andrew's Brotherhood did work for men, the Christian Endeavor Society extended its efforts to both sexes; thus meeting a want which, so far as she knew, no other organization in the church undertook to supply.

Mr. Henkell, of Calvary parish, reported a society soon to be started by Rev. Floyd M. Tomkins, of St. James' Church, Chicago.

Several other clergymen expressed their interest in the movement. One from Maryland said that he had heard of the Endeavor society only two months ago. He had come to New York expressly to attend the convention and to learn something about the movement. What he had seen and heard had interested him most deeply.

The Rev. Mr. Bennett, of Grace Church, Jersey City, feared that the church would not reap her full share of the benefits of the movement. It looked as if she would come lagging along behind the other denominations. Leaflets and other forms of literature were needed to inform the clergy as to the character of the society, and to show how it might be adapted to the church.

Acting upon this suggestion, the meeting requested the Rev. Mr. Adams to act in concert with Rev. C. J. Palmer, of Lanesborough, Mass., and the United Society, of Boston, in preparing the necessary literature, and in having it published.

It was reported in the meeting that Bishops Gilbert, of Minnesota; Graves, of the Platte Mission; Jackson, of Alabama; Garrett, of Northern Texas; and Brooks of Massachusetts, were favorable to the Endeavor movement.

REFORMED PRESBYTERIAN.

An enthusiastic rally of the Reformed Presbyterian Christian Endeavorers was held in the Second Reformed Presbyterian Church, West Thirty-ninth Street. There was a remarkably large gathering of Endeavorers from all over the country, and the result of the rally was that every young person went forth more loyal to his own denomination, and at the same time more of a Christian Endeavorer, in the truest sense of the word, than ever before. We feel sure that the New York convention will have the effect of creating many more societies in the Reformed Presbyterian Church during the coming year.

Rev. R. M. Somerville, pastor of the church, presided at the meeting, and among those who made addresses were Rev. F. M. Foster and Rev. J. J. Dunlop, of New York City; Rev. J. W. F. Carlisle, of Newburgh; Rev. J. W. McElhinney, of Rochester; Rev. W. M. Glasgow, of Kansas City; the Rev. Mr. McNaughter and Miss Benz, of Sterling, Kan.; Miss Toag, of Rochester; and Mrs. T. J. Allen, of Mercer. Messrs. Alexander and Jones represented the eldership.

UNITED PRESBYTERIANS.

The United Presbyterian rally was held in the First Church, Rev. T. W. Anderson, D.D., pastor. The attendance was large, and a deep interest in the occasion was manifest. The meeting took the direction of considering the right relations of the United Presbyterian Church to the Christian Endeavor movement. Dr. McMillan, a trustee of the United Society, was the first speaker, and said this was manifestly a providential movement, and that the Lord meant by it more personal devotion to Christ, broader activity in his service, and a closer fellowship among all Christians. This last providential token of the Lord's will it is the duty of the United Presbyterian Church, and all churches, to follow, and hence this movement that expresses and cultivates Christian unity should receive their co-operation.

Miss Martha Hawthorn, of. Allegheny, Penn., gave an excellent paper on the great purpose of Christ that his people should all be one. Rev. J. O. Campbell, of Lowell, Mass., spoke of the inconsistency of any church that claims to pray for the unity of the body of Christ, and yet refuses to join in this movement that promotes unity of spirit and effort among the followers of Christ without sacrificing any conviction of truth. Rev. Mason W. Pressly, of Bovina, N. Y., thought that the Christian Endeavor movement carried its divine credentials on the very face of it, and that it is too late to raise any question concerning its claims.

Rev. T. B. Turnbull, of Argyle, N. Y., told how the Christian Endeavor organization commended itself to him the first moment his attention was called to it, as just the thing he wanted for his young people. He believed it is of God, and should be gladly accepted by all Christians as the best plan of education and work for young people, and the best basis of union among the followers of the Lord.

Rev. D. C. Stewart, of Hoboken, N. J., spoke as one who was working under the exclusively denominational organization, but extended a cordial approval to the Christian Endeavor Society. It was the judgment of all that the meeting was pleasant, successful, and useful.

THE DISCIPLES OF CHRIST.

This rally was a glorious success. The First Church of the Disciples on West Fifty-sixth Street was densely crowded. Very wisely, no formal program had been prepared, for it would have been impossible to confine the enthusiasm of the meeting within the limits of set speeches and prepared papers. The three-fold purpose of the rally was: to ascertain the present status of Christian Endeavor among the Disciples, to devise the best means for its spread, and to consider the most efiective ways of increasing the efficiency of the young people in all the general enterprises of the Church of the Disciples. W. H. McClain, the national superintendent of Y. P. S. C. E., made a brief but most enconraging report, and opportunity was then given for sentence reports from every part of the field by State superintendents and others. Scores were on their feet at once, anxious to tell of its growth and good fruits in their part of the country. Endeavor is evidently having a boom among the Disciples.

The special work which the home mission board suggested for the Endeavor societies of the Disciples is the building of a house of worship for the Disciples' mission in Salt Lake City. Rev. B. F. Clay has charge of that mission, and the enthusiasm with which he was received and the deep interest manifested in his address clearly indicated the heartiness with which the young people of the Disciples are taking hold of this great enterprise. Chancellor Carpenter, of Drake University, offered a strong resolution commending this work to all Disciple societies of Christian Endeavor, and it was adopted in a way that means success. In the foreign field, the Board of Foreign Missions has asked the societies to build a home for girls in Japan. Rev. Archibald McLean, secretary of the Foreign Christian Missionary Society, was accorded a genuine Y. P. S. C. E. ovation when he appeared to speak of this work, and before the chairman could put the resolution commending the enterprise the young people took the meeting out of his hands and proceeded to raise the money, then and there, to complete the building. More money was pledged than the secretary had asked! It was good to be there, and untold good must flow from that great rally.

THE MORAVIANS.

The denominational rally of the Moravian delegates was held in the Moravian Church, Lexington Avenue and Thirtieth Street. All the Moravian delegates were present, representing societies in all parts of the country. A large congregation, consisting of members of the churches of New York, Brooklyn, and Staten Island, went to meet them, and gave them a warm welcome.

Rev. E. T. Kluge, New York, presided, and presented the delegates with the freedom of Moravian hearts, and assured them they were indeed welcome, and especially as Christian Endeavorers. Rev. C. E. Eberman, of Brooklyn, led the "open parliament," during which every society by its delegates brought some message of greeting, or added some testimony to the blessing the Christian Endeavor Society was to their congregations. The following ministers were present, and by their earnest words served to make the meeting most helpful and inspiring: Rev. W. H. Rice, New York; Rev. E. N. Schwarze, Elizabeth, N. J.; Rev. E. S. Wolle, Philadelphia; Rev. W. H. Vogler, New Dorp; Rev. F. E. Grunert, Castleton Corners; Rev. E. S. Hagen, Stapleton, S. I.: Rev. Clarence Romig, Easton, N. Y.

Truly the enthusiasm of the great convention was felt and enjoyed in this meeting. The reports from the various societies were inspiring. One large congregation was reported as having three senior societies and two junior societies. Another has a society of over one hundred members. A pastor reported that during illness in the pastor's family the Christian Endeavor society carried on the services in the church for five weeks.

A two-fold spirit of loyalty to the church and loyalty to Christian Endeavor, with loyalty to the Master as the grand motive, was the ringing testimony of every address and report. The meeting enthusiastically committed itself to every principle, and to the very name, of Christian Endeavor.

In order to create a wider and more intelligent interest in the movement throughout the entire Moravian Church, the meeting unanimously resolved that steps be immediately taken to call together a convention of Moravian Christian Endeavor societies, for the purpose of advancing the cause. The following committee was elected to carry out the resolution and to prepare for this convention: Rev. C. E. Eberman, Rev. W. H. Vogler, Rev. E. S. Wolle, S. Grosh, F. Zulh, Cyrus Lerch.

At the close of the "open parliament," through the kindness of the congregation in whose midst the rally was held, ice cream and cake were served.

FRIENDS.

The rally of the Friends was held in the Friends Meeting House, New York, with Rev. A. C. Hathaway, Richmond, Ind., as chairman.

REV. A. C. HATHAWAY.

It was an excellent meeting in every way. The attendance was larger than expected. The spirit was excellent, for the Lord was present, and perfect unity and harmony prevailed.

The following program was carried out: "The Christian Endeavor Movement Among the Friends," Rev. A. C. Hathaway, Richmond, Ind.; "Harmony of Christian Endeavor Principles and Practices with those of Friends," Miss Matilda W. Atkinson, Iowa Falls, Ia.; "Missions and Mission Workers," Rev. J. W. Malone, Cleveland, O.; "Systematic Giving," Mrs. Phebe S. Aydelott, Fall River, Mass.

Each subject was treated very practically, and all was highly appreciated. Reports from the different American Yearly Meetings, which are the highest ecclesiastical bodies of the church, showed that eight out of ten already have Yearly-Meeting unions of Christian Endeavor, with, in round numbers, 250 societies and 6,000 members. All felt that it would advance the cause to form a bond of union, and so an "International Christian Endeavor Union of Friends" was established, embracing these eight Yearly-Meeting unions, one of which is in Canada. Rev. A. C. Hathaway was made president, and Miss Jennie A. Wing, Arlington, N. Y., secretary; and the presidents of the Yearly-Meeting unions were constituted vice-presidents of this international union.

The objects of this union are: to promote the cause of Christ by aiding Christian Endeavor, Christian fellowship, and Christian co-operation among Friends; to provide for fraternal communication between the Yearly-Meeting unions; to collect statistics and furnish information whenever and wherever needed; and to arrange for such denominational rallies or other meetings as the United Society may desire. It is hoped that this union may carry out its present promise, and prove productive of much good.

SEVENTH-DAY BAPTISTS.

The rally of this denomination was held in the Plainfield Church. As no report has been sent us, we condense the account given in *The Sabbath Recorder:* The chairman of the meeting was Rev. William C. Daland. After singing, the congregation recited the twenty-fourth and twenty-third psalms, and Rev. H. B. Lewis offered prayer. Then various addresses were delivered, interspersed with spirited singing. Miss Agnes Babcock spoke of the "Progress of the Endeavor Movement in our Churches;" Rev. C. A. Burdick, of Farina, Ill., spoke of "Our People in the West: Their debt to the Endeavor Movement;" and Rev. L. E. Livermore, of New Market, N. J., of "Our People in the East: Their Debt to the Endeavor Movement." The latter spoke most eloquently, and was loudly applauded. Mrs. O. U. Whitford, of Milton, Wis., delivered an earnest address upon "The Prayer-meeting Pledge,"—an appeal to every society to adopt the same, unaltered. Miss Alice E. Maxson, of Westerly, R. I., gave a very interesting description of Junior work. Mr. Corliss F. Randolph, of East Orange, N. J., gave a clear argument in favor of "The Christian Endeavor Movement a Conservator of Denominational Loyalty." Mr. David E. Titsworth, of Plainfield, spoke most feelingly of "The Endeavor Movement a Promoter of Interdenominational Fellowship." The last address was by the president of the "permanent committee," Rev. J. Allison Platts, whose theme was "Ideal Organization." His remarks were a fitting close to a most interesting series of addresses. After singing "God be with you till we meet again," the meeting concluded with the Mizpah benediction.

EVANGELICAL ASSOCIATION.

The meeting was held in Christ's Mission, whose pastor is Rev. James A. O'Conner. Rev. U. F. Swengel of York, Penn., secretary of the Managing Board of the Keystone League of Christian Endeavor, was chairman, and opened the meeting with religious services. Rev. J. C. Krause offered prayer. Frank J. Boyer, of Reading, Penn., publisher and managing editor of *The Preacher's Assistant*, was elected secretary.

The chairman spoke briefly of the object of the meeting, and read a personal letter from Dr. Clark in which he spoke kindly of the Keystone League of Christian Endeavor, which is the denominational union of young people's societies in the Evangelical Association. New York, Pennsylvania, Maryland, Illinois, and Minnesota were represented in the meeting. Much interest pervaded. Remarks as to the work of the Christian Endeavor movement, as to its benefit to the denomination, and as to the best methods of increasing its power, were made by Rev. J. B. Esenwein, corresponding secretary of the Keystone League of Christian Endeavor, Rev. J. C. Krause, Rev. R. W. Runyan, Rev. D. M. Metzger, Rev. A. E. Watts, Rev. Mr. Marquardt, Dr. Ziegenfus, and Messrs. W. C. Weiss and F. J. Boyer.

The following resolution was unanimously adopted:

Resolved, That we recognize the good work that has already been accomplished by the Christian Endeavor societies, and that we earnestly urge the continued prosecution of this work in the churches of our denomination.

The following committee conferences were held, reports from which were given at the Sunday afternoon session:

Lookout committee: Marble Collegiate Church, conducted by Mr. W. R. Guy, San Diego, Cal.

Prayer-meeting committee: Fourteenth Street Presbyterian Church, conducted by Rev. J. Walter Malone, Cleveland, O.

Social committee: First Presbyterian Church, conducted by Mr. G. Tower Fergusson, Toronto, Can.

Missionary committee: Second Reformed Presbyterian Church, conducted by Mr. T. P. Nisbett, Chicago.

Sunday school; Madison Avenue Reformed Church, conducted by Mr. O. M. Needham, Albion, Neb.

Temperance committee: North Baptist Church, conducted by Mr. W. D. Gibson, Appleton, Wis.

There was also a special conference of officers, held at the Y. M. C. A. building from 5 to 6 P. M., attended by about 500 officers of State, Territorial, Provincial, district, and local unions. Dr. Clark called the meeting to order, stating in his opening remarks that this conference of officers was planned for and eagerly anticipated by Mr. Baer, and his disappointment was great in that he was not able to be present. Dr. Clark then introduced Mr. A. A. Ayer, of Montreal, chairman of the committee of '93, who spoke as follows:

Mr. AYER: I like the name of Christian Endeavor. When I first heard of the society, I said to the pastor of our church in Montreal: "If there is anything in a name, this society ought to be worth something." He answered, "Amen," and we had a society of our own a couple of weeks later. Give me a man who is endeavoring to do something; give me enthusiasm. That's why I'm proud of Montreal; we have 1,500 Endeavorers there, and we have the most enthusiastic committee on the continent. [*Applause.*] Don't you think it took enthusiasm to win the convention of '93? Talking of the enthusiasm of our committee, I'll let you into a little secret. You remember how the captains of the boats on the Mississippi used, when they were racing with their rivals, to employ a staid man with a steady nerve to sit on the safety-valve to keep down the steam. Well, that's my job on the Montreal committee. I have to sit on the safety-valve to keep down the steam, and I can tell you it's a mighty big contract. [*Laughter.*]

Now, when I invite you to Montreal next year, I want you to understand that it is not, as a Southern friend of mine once thought, bounded on the north by the north pole, on the west by Labrador and Greenland, and on the south and east by unlimited icebergs, icepacks, and glaciers. Neither do its principal attractions lie, as a lecturer with a stereopticon once informed me, among the rest of his audience in Liverpool, Eng., in its being a city of the far north, where there is skating all the year round, and where the chief buildings are an ice palace, a toboggan slide, and a skating rink. [*Laughter.*]

No, Montreal is a beautiful city, full of modern comforts and of modern civilization. I am glad you are coming next year, for I want the people of the United States to know us more, for when they know us more they will love us more. Out of the 300,000 people in Montreal, but 60,000 are Protestants, and the coming of this convention among us will infallibly win many of the Roman Catholics, who form the bulk of our population, over to Jesus Christ, so that as a merchant of Montreal, and coming from the heart of the merchants' quarter there, I welcome you, praying that you bring an abiding blessing on our city and on our land. [*Applause.*]

The next speaker was Mr. William Shaw, Treasurer of the United Society, who spoke as follows:

Mr. SHAW: In the little time allotted to me I wish to ask some questions, which I leave to you to answer. The first is, Does anyone here know any reason why the Christian Endeavor unions should not be made up of Christian Endeavor Societies? Some people objected to our interdenominational fellowship and withdrew their young people, organizing a sectarian society. They now find that the spirit of the times demands this fellowship, and they are trying to get it by urging our Christian Endeavor unions to take in all kinds of societies. In some cases where this has been done the unions have been broken up, as some of the societies did not believe in our pledge and methods; but as members of the union they had the same voice in its management as the Christian Endeavor societies. Let our unions be made up of Christian Endeavor societies in name and in fact.

Now I affirm, and I am sure all here agree with me, that the Christian Endeavor Society is broad enough for any man, of whatever denomination he may be, as long as he loves Jesus Christ and admits him to be his Saviour. We welcome every evangelical denomination to our banner, but if there is any society that does not want our principles, let it leave our union and our name. But if it believes in our principles, let it take the name with them, in connection with any denominational name it may choose.

One suggestion I will throw out by the way, and it is that press committees be appointed by all the societies to give accounts of our work to the secular press. This work needs to be done persistently, constantly, and systematically. Our own papers are very well, but for sowing the seed among the barren places that need it most you must resort to the mediums that will bring the news of your work to those who are not familiar with it. I want to emphasize the fact that one paragraph concerning Christian Endeavor printed in a daily paper that is read by all is worth columns, as far as widespread effect is concerned, in a paper that is limited to Christian Endeavorers themselves.

Finally, I would remind you that the work of the year is to consist in the planting of a Christian Endeavor society in every evangelical church in the world that will open its doors to receive it.

Dr. Clark then addressed the conference as follows :—

Dr. CLARK : I want you, as leaders from whom all the others will take their tone of thought, to carry away the belief impressed on you by every handshake, by every pulse-beat, by every prayer, by every song, that this is the greatest meeting of Christians ever held. I want nothing to shake your faith in this, no jeering nor sneering from those outside the fold. You have plenty of enemies to make capital against you out of every shadow of error or mishap.

Some of the papers have said that people wearing our badges have been seen drunk in saloons and in places of doubtful amusement. One explanation of this fact occurs to me. The badges of one entire delegation — the Texans — were stolen wholesale from the hotel in which they were deposited, and it is only fair to suppose that those numerous badges, which were certainly not stolen to be immediately thrown away again, found their way to the breasts of unchristian men, who employed them as a means of mockery and malice.

I could, if I would, mention the name of one well-known man about town who, picking up a badge some Endeavorer had accidentally dropped in the street, pinned it on his coat and entered a saloon, saying : " I wonder how it feels to be a Christian for once."

The case of the unfortunate man Powell has been thrown in our teeth by some of the papers, as if, forsooth, we were harmed by his misconduct. He is probably a fraud as far as his connection with our society is concerned, and in any case, if a Christian, he wofully belies his profession. There was one Judas among twelve disciples; small wonder that there should be one traitor among 30,000 otherwise true men. Therefore don't be alarmed by these sneers, but manfully rebut them, and, above all, don't haul down your flag of interdenominational fellowship, and don't allow it to flap listlessly at half-mast, but haul it up — haul it up to the topmost peak.

And after all these " do's " I will conclude with a few " don't's." Don't introduce taxes into your State or society gatherings; let all contributions be voluntary. Let every denomination in each State have a secretary with efficient help, and a stenographer if need be, but don't let there be any scrambling after paid offices. Don't hide your business methods under a bushel. There ought to be a committee at each State convention to manage and run such excursions as these on a business principle, the accounts to be afterward audited and submitted to the public.

I say this because some of the railroad companies, in their jealous rivalry of each other, are trying to traduce us by saying that some members of the Christian Endeavor have made money for their own pockets by this excursion. You and I know this is a foul lie, prompted by the basest motives, but still, in order to avoid the veriest shadow of suspicion, let us have our accounts openly audited.

In conclusion, Dr. Clark referred to his prospective trip around the world. He asked the prayers of the delegates for God's blessing upon his journey, and Rev. Lawrence Phelps, of Chelsea, Mass., led the audience in prayer for this object. The conference closed with the hymn, "Blest be the tie that binds."

SUNDAY MORNING.

The only gathering in the convention hall Sunday morning was that of the prayer meeting at nine o'clock, led by Mr. H. B. Pennell, of Boston. The amphitheatre was full, and the delegates sang for half an hour before the opening of the meeting. Dr. Clark then called the assembly to order, and under the lead of Mr. Stebbins the congregation sang "Jesus, lover of my soul," "Hear us, O Saviour," and "He leadeth me." Dr. Clark then introduced the leader of the meeting as follows: —

Dr. CLARK: It is entirely proper and meet that our devotions this morning should be led by one who has from the first been one of the foremost in the work of this society. Eleven years ago he was a boy in the Williston Church, Portland, Me., and there he led the first Christian Endeavor prayer meeting ever held. I know why this was so: the boy's heart was touched with the spirit of God, and he was willing to do his duty, and he was led on in the work by his father. That father was the first man to sign the constitution of the society. And now I introduce them both to you — Mr. Pennell, senior, and his son, who will lead the meeting.

The two gentlemen referred to came forward and bowed, the elder returning to his seat and the younger proceeding at once with the conduct of the meeting. Several hymns were sung, prayer was offered by Rev. C. A. Dickinson, Rev. C. P. Mills led the congregation in repeating the 24th Psalm, more hymns were sung, and Rev. Mr. Karmarkar led in prayer. After the hymn, "Blessed Assurance," Mr. Pennell spoke briefly as follows, taking as his text Acts 4 : 13.

Mr. PENNELL: "And they took knowledge of them that they had been with Jesus."

This was the judgment of the world upon the disciples of Christ. It was the unwitting yet ready confession of unbelievers of the power of God to transform men into his own image. They were not raw, simple fishermen that the Pharisees then saw in Peter and John, but the symmetrical manhood of Christ, shining through redeemed and glorified humanity. This — this is the great glory of the Christian faith, — that to live with Christ makes us like Christ.

How simple and how glorious this all is. We have only to take the Saviour into our lives, and little by little our characters are purified, our manners softened, and our spirits kindled and aroused by the consuming love of God, until men, seeing in us not our sordid selves but the image of the Saviour, whisper among themselves, "He has been with Jesus."

This is the thought I would bring to you this morning as we go from this convention, this mount of inspiration whereon Jesus has been transfigured to us, and our hearts have burned within us, that men may take knowledge of us that we have been with Jesus. Let us take this enthusiasm and convert it into spiritual realities. Let us be enthusiastic Christians, energetic and wholehearted, reflecting clear and strong the perfect image of Christ in our lives. Let energy complete in us, with love and faith, the symmetry of perfect manhood.

In Christ alone lies the completeness, the fullness of our lives. The spotlessness of the Saviour's life is the pattern of the spotless life to which we must aspire. To go to him and get the perfect idea of life, and then to go forth and by his strength fulfil it — that is the conception of a strong, successful life. Let us consecrate ourselves anew to him, and one result of this reconsecration will be that we shall be enabled to find a higher idea of ourselves — that we shall be able to see our possible selves as he sees us. When we do that, we shall have but one purpose remaining in life — to realize to the fullest that new and higher idea of ourselves that we have found in him.

It certainly will be harder for us to do wrong after this consecration of ourselves to him — easier to do that which is right, harder to be selfish, easier by far to be like Christ, if we only keep the image of Christ in our hearts and our lives, and thereby strive to make our homes and our busy every-day lives a foretaste of that eternity whose promised glory is that we shall be forever with the Lord.

It is at times like the present, times of profound soul-awakening and of great inspiration, that higher ideals are formed. There opens up before us a deeper and holier and maturer region of Christian life, and we are bidden to move on, — to advance into a higher realm.

The door of a new room of life is then thrown open to us, and we are bidden not to rest satisfied with our faithfulness of service on a lower plane, but we are inspired to move to a still higher realm of life. May God give us the courage and the ambition always to be ready when the call comes and to pass on and up to a higher and a better life, to new kingdoms of heaven, as he shall open them to us, forever.

Then followed a great number of sentence prayers, testimonies, Scripture quotations, etc., interspersed with singing. Mr. Paradis, representing the French Protestant Union, spoke briefly on the work in France, and Rev. Mr. Karmarkar and his wife sang a consecration song in Mahratti. The meeting was one of the deepest interest, and when the hour of adjournment arrived the great audience went forth from the building singing " Bringing in the sheaves."

As usual, opportunity was given for all to attend the regular church services of the morning, and the delegates availed themselves of the opportunity in full force. The day was very pleasant, though warm, and the presence of the throngs of delegates at the various churches was an impressive sight to the regular worshippers.

SUNDAY AFTERNOON.

After a brief praise service, Dr. Clark called the assembly to order and Rev. Dr. G. R. W. Scott led the audience in repeating the 100th Psalm. This was followed by the singing of hymn 104, a hymn which Mr. Sankey announced was Mr. Moody's favorite. Rev. Dr. Chapman, editor of the St. Louis Christian Advocate, then led the audience in repeating the Lord's Prayer, the whole congregation standing. Rev. Mr. Eberman then read the following testimonials:

We of the press desire to express our hearty thanks and appreciation to Mr. A. V. Heely and his associates of the Press Committee, and to all the officials of this convention, for their kind, thoughtful assistance, their untiring efforts, their willing attention, their courteous and earnest co-operation, shown to the representatives of the press:

New York Times,	Baltimore American,
New York Herald,	Christian Union,
New York Press,	Philadelphia Times,
New York Sun,	Indianapolis News,
New York Tribune,	The Church at Work,
New York Recorder,	Christian Evangelist,
Mail and Express,	Decatur Sentinel,
New York City Press Association,	St. Louis Christian Advocate,
New York World,	Dayton Telescope,
Boston Journal,	The Interior,
Chicago Standard,	Zion's Herald,
Bethlehem Daily Times,	Morning Advertiser,
The Moravian,	South Bethlehem Star,
New York Evangelist,	Iowa Citizen,
New Brunswick Fredonian,	Toronto Globe,
	And many others.

The hymn, "True hearted, whole hearted," was then sung.

Dr. CLARK: Yesterday afternoon there occurred some remarkable meetings — the committee conferences and the denominational rallies. We want to hear from those meetings, as few of us could attend more than one. Mr. William Shaw, our treasurer, will conduct the reports from these meetings.

Mr. SHAW: Before calling for the reports from our friends who conducted the meetings of the several committees, I want to say just a word about the denominational rallies that were held yesterday afternoon. In every case they were large and enthusiastic meetings. In many cases the capacity of the churches where they were held was taxed to the utmost. They were full of enthusiasm, and proved, if proof were necessary, that our young people are not only intensely in love with the interdenominational fellowship of our great society, but that they are also intensely devoted to their own denomination. [*Applause.*] I may say that in one of the meetings, that of the Christian Disciples, the secretary of the foreign misssionary society reported that they needed $1,500 to complete the building of a home, and on the spot the $1,500 was raised. [*Applause.*] Not only that, but the church edifice that the Christian Endeavor members of that denomination are building at Salt Lake City is an assured fact, and will soon stand there, a monument to the loyalty of the Christian Endeavorers. [*Applause.*]

Now we will hear from what is one of the most important branches of our work, — our committee work, — and I have the pleasure of introducing Mr. W. R. Guy, of San Diego, California, to report for the Lookout Committee Conference. [*Applause.*]

Mr. GUY: Yesterday afternoon at the Marble Collegiate Church we did not take up a collection; we did not raise several hundred dollars; but we raised the roof. [*Laughter.*] The church was filled to overflowing, and many were unable to gain admittance. The conference was opened with singing and prayer, after which Mr. Guy briefly addressed the meeting, as follows: —

Fellow-Endeavorers:— Although we are a little behind time in commencing our conference on account of another meeting, yet we can easily make it up, for Christian Endeavorers can do and say more in a half hour than most people can in an hour. We have met for the purpose of considering the most important branch of all our Christian Endeavor work — that of the lookout committee. And as we look out over the thousands of Christian Endeavorers here assembled, our hearts are made to rejoice, because so many are enlisted in this grand and noble movement. And it seems to me, back of all the enthusiasm displayed, there is a firm determination not only to say but to do something for Christ and the Church. The lives of our young Christians have become vitalized and energized with power from on high, and are a potent and positive influence for good. There appears to be more individual and practical effort in the various departments of our work. It is of the utmost importance that we of the lookout committee should prayerfully and carefully prepare and plan our committee work, to the end that we may reclaim those who are drifting away, and enlist those who are careless and indifferent. We should get so full of the love of Christ that it will naturally flow out, and shed its radiant and helpful influence over all with whom we come in contact. Let us be a positive and definite force in the Christian world, and not a nonentity.

As our time is so limited, I will not detain you longer, but "come, let us reason together."

1. How many should there be on the lookout committee? Generally five. It depends largely upon the size of the society and material at hand.

2. What is the first essential for a successful committee? A good chairman. Qualifications of the chairman? Cordiality, consecration, the love of God in him, tact, good horse sense, energy, sociability, willingness. He does his work for Christ's sake, and takes time for it.

3. Who should be the other members of the committee? Same, or as nearly as possible, as the chairman — "Kindly affectioned one toward the other." Now we have our committee selected, and a most excellent one it is.

4. What shall they do? Bring in new members. Make actives out of the associates. Stir up the actives to their duties and privileges, strengthen and encourage the weak members.

5. How do you keep the members at work? Make written excuses obligatory in case of absence. If your active members lose interest and do not attend, talk with them, pray with them, pray for them, but always with a heart full of love and a head full of tact.

6. What would you do if, in a small society, there was a good lookout committee and a splendid chairman — one who had been re-elected two or more times, because there was no one competent to take his place? Re-elect him, by all means. But work new material into the committee and train them. Do not, under any circumstances, select an incompetent chairman.

The LEADER: It is now time to close this conference. I am sorry to say. And as we go out, let us remember the helpful suggestions offered. Put them in practice in your local society, in so far as they are applicable. Let there be a businesslike reality, coupled with a real devotion to our Master, in all our committee work. Chairman, frequently call together your committee for prayer and conference. Invite your pastor to meet and counsel with you. Let all work together for God, and in his name. [*Applause.*]

Mr. SHAW: We will now hear from the heart of the Christian Endeavor Society — the prayer-meeting committee, reported by Rev. J. Walter Malone, of Cleveland. [*Applause.*]

Mr. MALONE: Truly this is "the heart" of all. Yesterday's conference was a great occasion : many were the practical points given as to how to make the prayer meeting a success by the scores who took part in short, sharp shots; and undoubtedly they will tell upon the home societies. Among them we feel we must emphasize the following points: First, everybody should come bringing some fire with him — come from the closet of prayer. Our hearts went up in the prayer of the disciples, "Lord teach us to pray," and we asked him not so much to make us great preachers, or workers, or leaders, but rather to make us men and women knowing how to pray. Our prayer meetings should be soul-saving stations. [*applause*] places where people will find life, and life such as Christ came to give —"life more abundantly." A sculptor once carved a statue of Moses so lifelike that, as he gazed upon it, he wept and cried out, "Moses, why don't you speak?" And then he answered his question himself: "Because no life." So we fear some of our young people try to speak, but have no life, which is the first thing. We want not a "hope so" or "guess so," but a "know so" religion, one of those experiences of which John writes in his epistles when he uses that little word "know" over twenty times within two or three chapters. Don't let us go as Joseph and Mary of old did when leaving Jerusalem, "supposing Jesus to be in the company." Let us pray as Paul and Silas did in that jail, "until the prisoners heard them" or until God shook the foundations, and the doors were opened, and the bands loosed, and all were free; or, like Hannah of old, the mother of Samuel, who prayed with such spirit that the high priest said she was drunk. But it was the depth of her soul that formed the words of her prayers, and from the depth of that soul was born such a son as Samuel.

Our prayer meetings, too, should be more on the pattern of the one in the upper room at Pentecost — waiting until we are "endued with power from on high." The Holy Spirit, and that alone, will make strong men out of weak ones, brave soldiers out of cowards, soul-winners out of Christian Endeavorers. Seek for it; tarry in some Jerusalem till you receive it. Then we will not any more deny our Lord and Master, but be as Peter after Pentecost. Remember that God's word is true, and he says, "Ask, and ye shall receive, for every one that asketh receiveth." Now that word "receiveth" is the same one translated in other places "taketh ;" so we might read it, "every one that asketh taketh." As we pray asking God, let us learn to take from him our every need. A good model for a prayer meeting is the one at Pentecost, and being filled with the Spirit we will go out saving others. It is said that in the Beleric Isles the mothers, in order to teach their children to be expert with bow and arrow, suspend their dinners in a tree until they bring them down by severing them from the branch with an arrow. Thus our loving Father sometimes hangs over us great blessings, ours if we only pray them down. Christ spoke a parable unto his disciples to this end : "that men ought always to pray and not to faint." Lord, teach us to pray! [*Applause.*]

Mr. SHAW: We have been told over and over again that the Christian Endeavor Society is a whole man. We have heard from the eyes, we have heard from the heart; now we are going to hear from the hand that stretches up and takes hold of the cross, and the hand that reaches down and takes hold of one's fellow-man and brings him to Jesus. Our social committee will be represented by **Mr. G. Tower Fergusson**, of Toronto, Canada.

Mr. FERGUSSON: First, let us thank our friends from New York and Brooklyn for the practical illustration they have given us of social-committee work. [*Applause.*] We have come from the far South, some of us; many from the West, and others from across the line; but your heart here has been large enough to welcome us all. We have received hospitable entertainment, and we thank you for this, Endeavorers of New York and Brooklyn.

Our social-committee conference took place at the First Presbyterian Church, and it is needless to say that the church was crowded. Nor need I tell you that there was enthusiasm there: where is there not enthusiasm where Christian Endeavorers meet? The meeting took the form of an open parliament, and we had suggestions from all parts of the house. "How are we to get our associate members into active membership?" was one question. "Through the social committee," was the answer, — by sociables, and by hearty handshaking when we meet them there. But all these means must be to one end, — that they may be spiritually benefitted and become workers for Jesus Christ in this great vineyard of the world. But social-committee work does not end with ourselves. We come short in our idea of social-committee work, if we end with our associate members. I believe that the world looks at Christians and judges of Christianity much according to the spirit shown by Christians; and if any man or woman ought to be happy in this world, that man or woman is a Christian; and this happiness and joy, and this consideration for others we should be willing to show to the world. I am glad that in this great convention we have convinced the newspapers of New York, even, that our hearts are right and that we are happy people. [*Applause.*] Listen to what they say. In one paper we have this heading: "The Christian Endeavor hosts are good-natured and friendly." And then they draw this comparison: "This gathering seems strange in New York, which has become wholly accustomed to the pushing, selfish crowds which it sees everywhere going to places of amusement." Here we have ourselves compared with the amusement-loving world, and it is not to the disadvantage of Christian Endeavorers. [*Applause.*]

Now, Christian Endeavor friends, let us go home with this one idea in our social work: not to please ourselves, but that God, our great Head, may be glorified through our work, that precious souls may be brought into his kingdom, and that the world may learn from our attitude that the Christian life is the best life, and may learn to know Jesus Christ as their Lord. [*Applause.*]

Mr. SHAW: Blessed are the feet of those who bring us good tidings. Our missionary committees are spreading the good tidings in all the world. We shall be glad to hear from them. Mr. T. P. Nisbett, of Chicago, will report for that conference.

Mr. NISBETT: At the missionary meeting yesterday afternoon we heard two great calls. One of them was this: "Go ye into all the world, and preach the  gospel to every creature." We heard that call come to us — it was not to some one else. Thank God, the call comes to every true Christian Endeavorer, "Go ye, and be my witnesses." The Christian Endeavor workers in this grand movement feel that they have this special work to do for the Master. It is a work he has entrusted to our hands; and the question is, shall we ask to be excused? or shall we say, "Here am I, Lord; send me"? I think that the Christian Endeavor missionary committees realize in great part this responsibility; and yet I am sure that we cannot begin to measure the importance of this great work, — the work that he gave us to do, — to send the Gospel to one billion of people that are out of Christ.

But we heard another call coming to us, and that call was, "Help, help, help!" From whom did that call come? It came from Asia and Africa and from the islands of the sea. It came from that billion of people who are still unsaved. A few years ago, in the State of Minnesota, I had a lesson from a dear brother missionary there which came home to me very forcibly and made me say that with God's blessing I would answer that cry of help and do what I could. In riding across that great State with one of the home missionaries of Minnesota, he said to me, pointing over to a little hut across the prairie, "Nisbett, I used to live in that house, and it was near there that I received the lesson which has sent me out over this great State of Minnesota." I asked, "What was the lesson?" He said, "In coming home one night, driving across this vast prairie, I saw my little boy Johnnie hurrying away from the house to meet me. The grass was high on the prairie, and all of a sudden he dropped out of sight. I thought he was playing and was simply hiding from me, but he didn't show up after a while, as I expected him to. Then the thought flashed across my mind: There is an old well there! I hurried up to him, reached down in the well and lifted him out; and as he looked up into my face, what do you think he said? 'Oh, papa, why didn't you *hurry*?'" I tell you, dear Christian Endeavor missionary workers, the field is white already for the harvest. The cry of help comes from these people; it comes from our mission boards; it comes from all about us. You and I must respond to that cry. Our boards to-day, many of them, have young men and young women who stand ready to go to these far-off fields, but they cannot be sent because you and I are not doing our duty. God calls on us from above. "Help, help, help!" Shall we not put our hands into our pockets and give — give systematically and intelligently, teaching others to give, and showing them what a privilege it is to give? Then when we meet around his throne, we shall come bringing the sheaves with us, and we shall hear his "Well done." [*Applause.*]

Mr. SHAW: "Let this mind be in you which was also in Christ Jesus." We need not only earnestness, but we need to have our minds illumined and filled with the Word of God. Mr. O. M. Needham, of Albion, Neb., will report for the Sunday-school committee conference.

Mr. NEEDHAM: At the Reformed church yesterday afternoon about 300 — not a large number — gathered to study the Sunday-school question. I  thought of Gideon's band, and I hoped and I prayed that they might be just as good servants of God as was Gideon's band of old. We did not raise the roof, nor did we tear up the cobblestones; but I believe there was something said which will be for the Lord's glory.

I gave this thought to the conference: First, what has Christian Endeavor done for the Sunday school? next, what ought it to do? and lastly, how ought it to do it? In response, many earnest words were given. In one church 50 were brought into the Sunday school by invitations given at the doorway, and 20 out of the 50 were converted to the Saviour. Again, one society has organized a supply or a substitute teachers' class, and every Sunday there are vacancies among the teachers the superintendent gets a supply from that class. Another gives the superintendent a list of teachers for his supply. Many things were brought out in the meeting, but I cannot begin to give them to you. I wish more of the delegates had been there. I feel this much: that Christian Endeavorers are not as loyal as they should be to the Sunday school. Perhaps some of you may disagree with me, but I know what I mean when I say that the Sunday school does not receive the interest from Christian Endeavorers which it ought to receive. Some of you have been reading "In Darkest England," by Booth; some of you have been reading of darkest New York in Jacob Riis' books; and sometimes you think, "Oh, that I might do something along the line of rescue work!" But that work lies at your own doors. I go by a house every day where there are six children that are not in Sunday school. I cannot ask them to go, because I am a man and have some business as an attorney with that house. But any young woman, any young lady, could go to them. This is a work especially for young ladies. There is rescue work to be done in every hamlet. [*Applause.*]

Mr. SHAW: I want to test this question of loyalty to the Sunday school right here. Is not this a pretty representative audience of Christian Endeavorers? How many in this audience regularly attend Sunday school? Please rise. [*Apparently the entire audience rose.*] Now will those of you who do not attend Sunday school please rise? [*About twelve persons rose.*] Now will the 16,000 who attend Sunday school look after the dozen who do not? [*Laughter and applause.*] I want to know one thing more. In my church nearly every teacher in the Sunday school is from the society of Christian Endeavor. How many in this audience are teachers in Sunday schools? [*Almost the entire audience rose.*] Why, you are nearly all teachers! [*Applause.*]

Now we will "throw out the life line" and hear from the temperance committee, — Mr. W. D. Gibson, of Appleton, Wis. [*Applause.*]

Mr. GIBSON: The keynote of yesterday's conference was "gospel temperance," not political, merely. Principles: no man can lift another higher than himself; let the individual conscience be clear before trying to mold the conscience of others; the church must get right on the temperance question before it can save souls; [*applause*] no patent process — each must work in his own way; meet a man on the level and part with him on the square; don't underrate your man; drunkards are no different from other sinners; get the fine eye-sight of Jesus Christ, who saw and saved; get eyes off yourself; sympathize with and help those who break their pledge; do something as well as be temperate; don't investigate — Jesus Christ never investigated, but cured; don't wait for organized charity — do your own charity; use common things; put not less emphasis upon methods human, but more upon power divine; strive not less to remove temptations from men, but more to make men superior to temptations. Practical suggestions: Furnish social attractions surpassing those of the saloons; [*applause*] pray for and go after particular young men for weeks and months until they are saved; pray for a baptism of tact; don't work so much on the habits as upon the souls of men; get a supply of leaflets, "Ten Reasons for Signing the Pledge," etc., published by the National Temperance Society, and study them carefully before soliciting signers; let all Christian Endeavorers sign the total abstinence pledge before asking others to do so; [*applause*] add the following working pledge to the Christian Endeavor pledge: "Do all the good you can, in all the ways you can, just as long as you can, to all the people you can." [*Applause.*]

Mr. SHAW: I am sure you will agree with me that this is a most excellent report. It is not content simply to throw out one life-line, but it throws out hundreds of life-lines. I am sure that if I should ask you what is the sweetest spot in the home, you would reply that it is the nursery. We cannot close these reports without hearing from the meeting of the Juniors, and Mrs. Alice May Scudder will give us a brief report. [*Applause and the Chautauqua salute.*]

Mrs. SCUDDER: The meeting in the Broadway Tabernacle yesterday afternoon was small in numbers compared with this vast assembly. Those who attended were small in stature, but they were not small in Christian Endeavor spirit. The enthusiasm shown by those little hands and waving handkerchiefs was equal to anything that has been displayed here. We even went further, and sent up a Christian Endeavor balloon. [*Applause.*] We know how thoroughly interested you all are in the Junior Christian Endeavor work; and if there is any pastor here to-day who has not a Junior Christian Endeavor society, he should have heard the words yesterday of one of our speakers, who said, " To-day where are you without a Junior Christian Endeavor society? Our Junior Christian Endeavor Society is our rainbow of promise for the future." In only a few years, if we train the dear children rightly, you will have to leave these seats and they will take them; and I can assure you that they will do as good work and will look as well as you do, and they will carry forward the work with the same spirit.

We had earnest speakers, and many of them and all who were there went away feeling, perhaps, as one gentleman did, who expressed himself in this way: " The two happiest days of my life have been, first, the day when I united with the church, and second, this afternoon, when we see that all the churches and denominations are uniting in this beautiful spirit of fellowship, evinced even by these little ones of eight or ten years of age." [*Loud applause.*]

Mr. SHAW: I have a report from another of the denominational gatherings that you will all rejoice in. The Friends in their rally yesterday enthusiastically and unanimously formed an International Christian Endeavor Union of Friends (and we are all friends here), [*applause*] composed of Christian Endeavor unions already existing in most of their yearly meetings. Rev. A. C. Hathaway was made president of the union, with great enthusiasm. Now we will hear a word from the life-saving stations. The secretary of the People's Palace, assistant pastor of the Tabernacle Church, Jersey City, — Rev. J. Lester Wells,— will present the report.

Mr. WELLS: I am thankful to be co-operating with Rev. John L. Scudder in the People's Palace, of Jersey City, which is a life-saving station. [*Applause.*] But I am not here to represent that Palace. This great convention has endorsed the principle of giving the prayer-meeting subjects to the life-saving stations all along the coast of our country. There are 224 of these stations, and the Christian Endeavor Society is going out and holding meetings with these brave men who labor on the high seas. We want a member of this national committee on life-saving stations from every State in the Union. Every State is now represented except the following: New Hampshire, Rhode Island, Delaware, South Carolina, Michigan, California, Oregon, and Washington. We want the representatives of these States here to send one name each to be placed upon this committee, and the roll will be complete. [*Applause.*]

Here the assembly joined in singing, very appropriately, " Throw out the Life-line," Mr. Stebbins singing the solo.

Dr. CLARK: This is the only international Christian Endeavor convention, but it is not the only national Christian Endeavor convention. Our brothers and sisters in England have just held a national convention, and they have sent a letter telling us how they enjoyed the presence of their beloved brother, and our beloved brother, Mr. Ira D. Sankey, who will now present the greetings from the English Christian Endeavor convention. [*Loud applause.*]

ADDRESS OF MR. IRA D. SANKEY.

I have just returned from England and Scotland, where, with Mr. Moody, we have been holding meetings for five months continually. Thus going through that land from city to city, I have had some opportunities of seeing the progress of this society on the other side of the sea, and I am very glad to be able to report to you to-day that the institution is growing and spreading all over Great Britain, especially in Scotland, England, and Wales. I fear that Ireland alone has not had time to take up the question of Christian Endeavor. Amid her many vexations and troubles she has let the opportunity go by to study with England the great question of Christian Endeavor. I hope the time is speedily coming when that nation will have in every town and hamlet a society of Christian Endeavor, which will be to them a greater blessing than Home Rule, if they get it. [*Applause.*]

I find that the ministers of that land have come to the conclusion, as have the ministers of America, that it is a great thing to give the young people of the church some work to do, and to throw some responsibility on them; and I am glad to say that the English convention at Chester was one of the happiest meetings and one of the best meetings I ever attended, barring that at Minneapolis. I was glad to go there at the invitation of your President, Dr. Clark, to meet with them, and to speak to them about the work in this country; and I found the same spirit yonder that is here in this hall to-day. They sang the same songs of Zion; they made the same prayers; there was the same spirit of kindness, gentleness, and a preference of one for the other, as the Bible teaches there should be. Their societies are growing, and I believe that ere long the institution will fill the whole land. The English Church is very conservative, as are all the denominations in England. It takes them a good while longer to make up their mind whether a thing is good or not than it does us here in America; but when they do make up their mind that it is a good thing, they adopt it, and they stand by it longer than we do. [*Applause.*] I am glad to see these two flags in front of this desk here to-day, [*applause*] representing these two great English-speaking nations that are to lead the van of Christianity and bring light and joy to all the nations of the earth. I am in favor of every institution that will hold up Jesus Christ as the great essential magnet for both countries and for all lands. I have talked with a great many English people lately. Mothers have come to me, after having read some of the papers of the day, and said, "Do you think, Mr. Sankey, it could be possible that England and America should ever come to war?" I have replied: "No, it is not possible now; it is too late." [*Applause.*] It is too late in the centuries for such a thing to happen. As we gather together in Christ's name, the great moral, Christian sense of these two nations will say to the politicians: "No more war!" [*Loud applause.*] Why are these English mothers so anxious when the least indication of trouble appears? Because they have their sons and daughters all over our grand country here, and they feel that they belong to us and we belong to them. And is not England our motherland? Are we not the children? We shall never be separated — no, never! You know in the State of Pennsylvania to-day there is trouble. Would to God there had been two or three Christian Endeavor societies at Homestead during the last week. [*Applause.*] There can be no war where Christ's doctrines are held and believed. Jesus Christ came long ago with this blessed message: "Peace on earth and good will to men"; and I thank God that this great multitude to-day represents the same sentiment — good will to men, peace on earth, no more war. All these little affairs of difference can be settled without war, and I believe it is the Christian sentiment of these great nations that will accomplish this.

I believe that ere long they will have conventions as large as this on the other side. The movement is sweeping clear around the world; it is felt in Australia and elsewhere. The friends in England were very anxious that I should bring to Dr. Clark their warmest greetings, and to tell him to come to England again as soon as he can. They want to see him, and I hope that the day is not far distant when he shall go again, and he will find thousands upon thousands of young people ready to welcome him.

And let me say to these young Christian people here: Watch your own hearts now. Be careful; watch and pray. In the hour of your success and glory be humble and watchful. Bid godspeed to every institution that you come in contact with that is loyal to Jesus Christ. I am glad to see the demonstration to-day in regard to the Sunday school. It is the Sunday-school union in England that is conducting this movement in that country. The same officers have the oversight of both enterprises. It is a good thing that this is so, because the association of the Christian Endeavor movement with the Sunday-school Association gives weight to it.

Now, my friends, may God help us to stand true to our principles. Be humble, watchful, prayerful; and as you go back to your own homes in these various States, carry that same spirit of love and kindness and joy that you have shown here. [*Loud applause.*]

Mr. Sankey's speech awakened much enthusiasm, and at its close occurred a pretty scene. The Canadian delegates rose and sang "God save the Queen," while the audience waved an enthusiastic salute. Immediately, as soon as they ceased, the choir started "America" (the same tune), in which the audience joined, the Canadian delegates returning the salute. Then Canada started the hymn "Blest be the tie that binds," and the audience rose *en masse* and joined in the hymn with immense enthusiasm. It was one of the most striking incidents of the convention.

Dr. CLARK: There is always a place in a Christian Endeavor convention for temperance. [*Applause.*] There is always a special place for Gospel temperance. [*Renewed applause.*] We shall now hear one whom, of all others, I think we shall be glad to hear on this subject,— Mr. John G. Woolley, of Rest Island, Minn. [*Loud applause.*]

ADDRESS OF JOHN G. WOOLLEY.

For twelve months "I have thanked God at every remembrance of you." Ever since a year ago to-day, when I first felt the mighty heart-beat of the

Young People's Society of Christian Endeavor, I have believed the Church was getting ready to stamp out the liquor traffic; and I believe that to this high privilege and duty women as well as men are divinely called, to help by voice and vote.

Since last I stood in this amazing presence I have rested not one day from helping tempted men to escape to Jesus Christ; and I have seen some scores or so of clear, sure rescues. But in that same time I have seen a thousand men, and women too, make splendid breaks for liberty; and even while I watched their frantic flight, and cheered them on their way, I have seen the majestic lion of the law leap from his marble lair in the capitol and fell them by a blow of lethal velvet,— every hill and vale re-echoing his savage roar that told the lesser beasts of prey that the king would hunt that day. I have heard the saloon jackals come yelping along all the ways to shred the fallen bodies,—aye, souls too,—and, gagged by the quivering hearts of women, fly back, in awful stealth, to their screened cage to mouth them there, in catlike lust of death and blood.

And to-day, wailing through all these aisles and arches, I can hear cries of minor treble calling, "Save my father," "Save my husband," Save my child." Hear it, O friends. "It is not the will of your Father that one of these little ones should perish." Oh! hear it; and help me, for the love of human kind, to grasp the reasons why the slaughter of the weak and innocent goes on unchecked, and why God's men stand by, holding the garments of the murderers!

For nearly five years the burden of my prayer has been that God would show me why, in these great days of universal uplift, "gospel temperance" fails,—for fail it does, by every token current to intelligence. Open your Bibles at the end of Jeremiah 6 and read, "The bellows are burned, the lead is consumed of the fire; the founder melteth in vain: for the wicked are not plucked away." It reads like an invoice of the temperance cause.

"The bellows are burned." The fires of this reform are overblown. "Gospel temperance" is apoplectic with idle sentiment. Speaking broadly, temperance work is temperance meetings in which the same speakers, year after year, convince, over and over, the same people (mostly women) of the same thing by the same arguments, to the same music and the same collection. [*Laughter.*]

"The founder melteth in vain," because for three generations we have been re-smelting the same batch of overdone slag and pyrites, mourning meanwhile a discouraging lack of visible, tangible produce.

"For the wicked are not plucked away." We flux our formative citizenship with saloons, and sandwich "saving grace" with damning laws. [*Applause.*] Dram-shops are as lawful as churches, and distilleries as legitimate as public schools.

Three millions of Christian men are to vote presently, and there are but two things certain in the contest, namely: that by the vote Christian men can define the issue and determine it; and that the saloon will carry the day, and decorate its bar with Christian consciences spitted like birds on a skewer of gold.

"Gospel temperance" is an avalanche of talk upon a glacier of apathy. In its distinctively practical aspect, "gospel temperance" is congested at the little end of the subject. This is, for instance, the golden age of patent medicines. The windows of the apothecary are full of sure cures for drunkenness, and religious and reform papers fairly tumble over one another recommending substitutes for regeneration, by hypodermic injections, at a price not one drunkard in three thousand can pay.

Do I deny merit to these remedies? No. If a child and a skipping-rope combine to produce hip disease, the rationale of cure divides this way: the doctor to the hip, the child to the skip. So far as drunkenness resides in the mucus membrane or nerve ganglia or brain or blood, I say, use medicine. But, I say, drunkenness is not, by any scientific or even intelligent pathology, membranous, neurotic, or cerebral. "From within, out of the heart of men, proceed evil thoughts," and all defilement: and you could as well try to cure a runaway horse by painting the barn a quiet color as to cure an unrepentant drunkard through the skin or stomach,—though it may well happen, and does, that the cure of a disordered nerve or brain or liver often makes it easier for the penitent drunkard to recover himself. This proves medical science to be of God, and very noble, but it is not the temperance cause any more than a bakery is a market or a jail. Eighty per cent of drunkards are content so to be; and science has not discovered, and will never discover, any mineral, vegetable, or gaseous substitute for penitence and "grit." Drunkenness is sin,—not the only one nor the worst. I would as lief stagger to the gate of heaven drunk and in rags, as to go a sober, cleanly, dainty, natty hypocrite. [*Applause.*] I would as willingly roll into judgment, limp with alcohol, as to go a calm, clean accomplice of the saloon. [*Applause.*] I would go as readily, maudlin and gibbering, to my sentence, as with the shame-gold of license in my hand, or in my pocket the price of a tenement let to shame. All these are sins; and sinners need, at the last diagnosis, not salve, but salvation. [*Applause.*]

Current legislation shows the same determination to the small view, and so we have the saloon slightly restricted for free drinkers and larger patronage. No drunkard need thirst, if he has money, and no boy escape temptation. Penal statutes for the protection of life commence at shad, short lobsters, soft crabs, sitting quail, and the like, and have risen gradually as high in the scale as cattle. The same Congress that refuses even to consider the ravages of the liquor traffic appropriates a hundred thousand dollars a year to investigate hog cholera. One hundred thousand dollars' outlay to save swine from infection; one hundred millions income to spread contagion in the way of boys. God forgive us! [*Applause.*]

In local option, which is the fashionable tint this spring in political Christianity, there is just a gleam of hope for boys; but, measured by the wrong it would correct, that remedy is infinitesimal and almost contemptible.

Ask the motherhood of New York where it wants protection from the saloon. It will answer, "I want it where my sons are." Where are the sons of New York? Everywhere. That is the New York of New York mothers.

Is Christianity a smaller thing than motherhood? Is Christian duty a thing of town lines and parallels of latitude and longitude? No. Christianity has no locality or policy, waits for no growth of sentiment. A Christian is a citizen of the parish of everywhere, neighbor to everybody, stranger to nobody, brother to anybody. " Ye are the light of the world," — not of the fourth ward. [*Applause.*]

But the power of the Church of Jesus Christ appears in liquor statutes mainly as "license," — high license, high church, low license, low church, — and illustrates my thesis most disgracefully.

Our educational work is microscopic. The Sunday-school teacher explains to the children that alcohol is poison. The public school exhibits vivid charts of a drunkard's interior, to show that alcohol is poison. The temperance lecturer leaves no doubt that alcohol is poison. The preacher shows that to both body and soul alcohol is poison. The court analyzes the virus of the saloon, and pronounces it poison. The legislature does the like, and reports poison. Then they all go for more virus to analyze, and commence all over again. No wonder that the temperance lesson is marked " optional " on your lesson leaves — the thing is threadbare!

Meantime, the children see that the liquor traffic is lawful, profitable, and politically respectable. And this is called "educating the people." It *is* educating the *saloon keepers*, and the most pronounced success of it so far is that the American dram seller is the *ne plus ultra* of his breed. It has often happened in this city that a man has laid aside the linen apron of the bar for the ermine of the bench.

The negative side of the "gospel temperance" is beaten out to the last husk. The pledge is obsolete. Reformed men are praiseworthy, but negative and ineffective. The need of the world is enlisted men, wholesome, well nourished, well trained, well armed, well accoutred, stalwart, confident soldiers of Jesus Christ — like you. The men who simply "quit" begin again. Restrictive permission perpetuates the saloon piracy; and after one hundred years of negative reform, the saloon is going to enter the twentieth century in triumph, dragging the Church chained to its chariot wheels, unless *you* prevent it. [*Applause.*]

And so I offer you to-day, in barest outline, a study of the "drink" problem upon its positive and larger side. I waste no words exhorting you not to drink, not to license, not to sell. I know what you will *not* do, but I come in the name of him we serve, to ask what you entend to *do*. [*Applause.*] I spend no time haranguing you to be true to the light that enters the small end of your glass, — I know you will be; but turn it, I beg of you, and let the light enter by the larger lense.

A man is blind who sees in "gospel temperance" only the habit, influence, or welfare of an individual or a town. Duty is co-extensive with allegiance, and is as wide as life. A man is deaf who cannot hear, above the cries of the dying in the rear, the martial music of the battle front and rattling ordnance all along the line. A man is dumb who in this great debate cannot speak to the whole question. A man is a hunchback who stands to speak in these great days and cannot straighten to the plumb line that God let down over the manger of Bethlehem.

Too long we have heard and preached and lived a dwarfish and *little* Gospel, — under stained glass, in artificial heat, making nosegays of personal experience. Too long we have kept the face of Jesus Christ, like an old ambrotype in limp morocco covers, to ornament our spiritual center tables. Too long we have employed the Church as an ambulance and employed ourselves for "stretcher" service, digging graves and bearing off the dead, while at the cradle of our citizenship " license," the harlot midwife, sits and rocks and sings her bawdy lullaby. [*Applause.*]

You must add a word to your motto yonder so that it will read, " For Christ, the Church, the Country." [*Applause.*] It is time for Jesus Christ to go to Congress as well as to the slums. [*Loud applause.*] The time has come when we must stretch up to the larger life in him, or bleach to sallow, pious inefficiency; and *you* are the *arm* of the Church body.

This is a day of peril to this society. Your rise and progress have been marvellous, but you must do more than grow: [*applause*] you must step off like master masons towards God's reddering East and *build* something. The bench, bar, board of trade, caucus, convention must respect you, [*applause*] as they do *not* your fathers. The glory of young men is in their strength not in their size, shape, pedigree, or prospects. Your next move means conquest or collapse, for the devil of *sectarianism* has already shown his hated face in your great movement. [*Applause.*]

"Gospel temperance" sentiment has hung like a pearly mist over the sinks and purlieus of "the drink" for three hundred thousand mornings, but has sunk back daily into the ecclesiastical quagmire and brought no cleansing shower. But the Young People's Society of Christian Endeavor, at first no bigger than Francis E. Clark's hand, which may God nerve and bless, [*applause*] has risen straightway, gathering up a million cloudlets from a million marshes in its way. Pent up within you is a torrent of a thousand Johnstowns and the power of all God's lightning. Oh, flash! split the sky! cleave the mountains! lick up the pools! electrify the world! I said the East reddens; so it does,— with anarchy and tyranny and drunkenness and conflagration. Oh, rain! rain! rain! [*Applause.*]

Did you mean what you said on that banner, — "the world for Christ"? Up, then, and *take* the world, — [*applause*] your flag, the star of Bethlehem and the stripes of Jesus Christ. No drones, no dummies, no dunces in Christian Endeavor! [*Applause.*]

This is what I call the positive side of "gospel temperance" in the large. I believe Christian men, as such, can give and ought to give this country Gospel government. Under such government revenue laws would protect capital and labor, producer and consumer, equitably, and we should have a Gospel tariff — whatever that might be. [*Laughter.*] I am sure there might be Gospel suffrage, and under that there would be no civil difference of sex, and every suffragan would have a vote and have it counted. [*Applause.*] Under such a government I should expect the Monroe doctrine to expand to the forbidding of any foreign ship to discharge alcohol upon the American continent; [*applause*] and if one should persist in doing so and we should blow her out of the water, I would call that Gospel coast defense. [*Applause.*] And if any nation should try to force the accursed merchandise upon this hemisphere, and we should sweep the sea with shot and shell, and burn and sink and kill, I would call that Gospel war. [*Applause.*]

They tell me that the Church agrees to all this, but sticks at the *method* of doing it. But the method is the vital thing, and there can be but *one* under our form of government. Every Christian voter ought to vote so that if his ticket wins the saloon will *stop*. [*Loud applause.*] And every Christian woman, when the conscience of the country wakes to give her suffrage, ought to "fall in" with Frances E. Willard and the rest at the front of the world's work, fighting in woman's ways "for God and home and native land." [*Renewed applause.*] And every Christian citizen ought to demand of Congress, by respectful petition, a non-partisan statute declaratory of the Constitution, forever forbidding the manufacture, importation, exportation, transportation, sale, gift, or possession of alcoholic liquors, except chemically pure alcohol for scientific purposes, to be sold only by government agents, in sealed packages, such package to be registered like a bond. [*Applause.*]

Can such things be? Of course such things can be. When? Faith has no "when" in her vocabulary. God is alive. The sun stands still upon Gibeon and the moon in the Valley of Ajalon, and so will stand until this fight is over. To his saints there is no death nor failure, night nor time; only God, eternity, and victory.

Is it not true, then, that humanity is going to pieces and that Satan rules this world? Of course it is not true. Satan is the Prince of *Darkness* of this world. The Light of the world is at our head of column; and his very *name* is victory.

Are not these, then, "the last days," are not the elect nearly enrolled, and are not these nineteen hundred years to end in failure? No! No matter how you read your Bible, that is not to happen till all the world has had a fair chance with the Gospel, and that time is not now nor near.

Men who have simply heard unclean preachers speak of cleansing by the blood of Jesus; that have only heard tippling deacons talk of abstinence; that have only heard of a local-option Christianity that prohibits saloons in a village for Jesus' sake and permits them in cities for Satan's sake, have had no real chance to accept the Gospel. [*Applause.*]

Is not the Lord coming soon? He is here! I saw him down in Water Street last night; I have seen him at the Cremorne and St. Bartholomew's; at the cathedral, the church, the barracks of the Salvation Army; I see him in the faces of my wife and sons. He is here to-day! I feel him in my soul. Oh, blind eyes, open and see him! Oh, deaf ears, listen! Oh, withered arms, stretch forth to him! Oh, woman beggared by doctors and wasted by disease, press close and touch his garment's hem! Oh, widow's son, arise! Oh, Lazarus, come! Oh, ye redeemed, see him as he is and be like him! His name was called Jesus, "For he shall save his people from their sins." Oh, be saved from all your sins! God needs you, for by you he is to save this world. If it could be saved only by his coming, by his own right hand, by word of his own mouth, he would have saved it nineteen hundred years ago. Yes, he would have saved it before it fell at all. "But since by man came death, by man also comes, *comes*, COMES the resurrection of the dead."

Why, if you will hear his voice, to-day is victory. The third person of the Trinity lives in humanity, sent to us by the Lord Jesus to walk back with us on human feet to our Father's house. Up, up the mount of God winds the long column of his "whosoever" made in his image, bone of his bone, flesh of his flesh, blood of his blood," and God the Holy Spirit leading.

"Lift up your heads, oh ye gates; even lift them up, ye everlasting doors, and the King of Glory shall come in." The gates of everlasting light are "lifted" from their hinges, never more to swing. The door of heaven is an everlasting *open* door. It will never shut until the last sore-hearted, dusty-footed son of God staggers in to fall upon his Father's heart and cling forever. [*Loud and continued applause.*]

At the close of Mr. Woolley's address Mr. Sankey led the Pennsylvania delegation in singing the Pennsylvania Christian Endeavor song.

Dr. CLARK: It has been customary for the International Convention to adopt a platform of principles, that we may show to the world what Christian Endeavor stands for. This platform will be read to you by one of the oldest friends of the society and one of our most honored counsellors, Rev. C. A. Dickinson, formerly of Portland, now of Boston. [*Applause.*]

PLATFORM OF PRINCIPLES.

We reaffirm our adherence to the principles which we believe, under God's blessing, have made the Christian Endeavor movement what it is to-day.

First and Foremost. Personal devotion to our Divine Lord and Saviour, Jesus Christ.

Second. The covenant obligation embodied in the prayer-meeting pledge, without which there can be no true society of Christian Endeavor.

Third. Constant religious training for all kinds of service involved in the various committees, which, so many of them as are needed, are equally with the prayer meeting essential to the society of Christian Endeavor.

Fourth. Strenuous loyalty to the local church and denomination with which each society is connected. This loyalty is plainly expressed in the pledge. It underlies the whole idea of the movement, and, as statistics prove and pastors testify, is very generally exemplified in the lives of active members. Thus the society of Christian Endeavor, in theory and practice, is as loyal a denominational society as any in existence, as well as a broad and fraternal interdenominational society.

Fifth. We reaffim our increasing confidence in the interdenominational spiritual fellowship, through which we hope, not for organic unity, but to fulfil our Lord's prayer for spiritual unity, "that they may all be one." This fellowship already extends to all evangelical denominations, and we should greatly deplore any movement that would interrupt or imperil it.

We rejoice in the growing friendliness of Christians throughout the world. We find reason in the fact that the Reformed, Methodist Protestant, and Cumberland Presbyterian Churches, the Congregationalists, Disciples of Christ, Friends, and other denominations have, in their highest ecclesiastical gatherings, indorsed and practically adopted the society of Christian Endeavor, and that the Presbyterians in many synods and presbyteries have substantially done the same.

We rejoice, too, that the Baptist Young People's Union admits Christian Endeavor societies to all the privileges of denominational service without any change of name or principle or interdenominational affiliation; that the Free Baptists recommend that societies organized on the Christian Endeavor basis be called "Advocates of Fidelity in Christian Endeavor," the Evangelical Association, "Keystone League of Christian Endeavor," and the Methodists of Canada, "The Epworth League of Christian Endeavor," and that the United Brethren in Christ recommend that where a society takes the prayer-meeting pledge it should be called a "Christian Endeavor Society," thus guaranteeing to those who desire it our precious interdenominational fellowship as well as full denominational control.

We believe that, for the sake of Christian fairness and courtesy in all denominations and all over the world, the Christian Endeavor principles should go with the name, and the name, either alone or in connection with a distinctive denominational name, should go with the principles.

For the maintenance of these principles of *covenant obligation, individual service, denominational loyalty, and interdenominational fellowship, we unitedly and heartily pledge ourselves.*

Dr. CLARK: You have heard the platform of principles. If it meets with your approval, please manifest it. [*The vote was unanimous.*]

After another hymn, "At the cross," Dr. Clark introduced Rev. Edgerton R. Young, missionary to the Hudson Bay Indians, one whom he declared to be a modern hero for Christ's sake. Mr. Young was warmly greeted by the audience, many of whom already knew of his life and adventures in the far North.

ADDRESS BY REV. EDGERTON R. YOUNG.

Our great-hearted Master, who said: "Go ye into all the world and preach the Gospel to every creature," said a short time before that "many shall come from the east and the west and the north and the south, and shall sit down in the Kingdom of God."

Missionaries have come from the south, and east, and west, and have told you of Gospel triumphs and marvellous successes in their efforts to bring men and women to Christ in those regions where they have toiled for the blessed Master.

As a missionary from the Wild North Land, I am here by your request to tell you something of personal work among the poor Indians of the far north.

To the world's masses there is no special interest in such a work. No glamour of romance gathers round such a work.

Poor Lo has more enemies than friends, and yet in this presence there are many—may I not hope the vast majority—who believe that the Gospel of the Son of God is just the thing he needs to lift him up to a better life here, and to fit him for a bright eternity beyond. [*Applause.*]

In the eloquent official sermon of this convention, we heard that the great want of this age and world was love. No theme in Pagan lands equals that. The story of the love of the great heart of God towards humanity is always of intense interest, and readily finds listeners.

To tell of this great love of the infinite God of Love, long years ago my young wife and I, in the brightness of our happy honey-moon days, left our happy home in civilization, and went far away into the haunts and abodes of the poor Indians, hundreds of miles north of the last vestiges of civilization.

Our home was in Keweetin, the land of the North Wind, north of the Province of Manitoba. So great was the distance, joined to the difficulties of travel in those days, that we were two months and nineteen days journeying towards that land.

When we reached our destination, we found ourselves four hundred miles away from the nearest white Christian family; four hundred miles from the doctor or post office. Only twice a year did we hear from the outside world. In this far-away place and with these Indians we lived for many years.

Gathering them together, we explained the object of our coming, and told them that no matter what others might say or think about them, we were going to trust them and believe in them. So we deliberately took the bolts off the doors, and removed every fastening from the windows of our little home, and let it be known that nothing in our possession was under lock and key. As the result of this confidence in them we never, in all those years had anything stolen from us. We felt safer in our lives and property there than we have ever felt since in the so-called lands of civilization. [*Applause.*]

God wonderfully blessed our labors among them, and those of other faithful toilers, and soon there were many hundreds of converted Indians gathered into missions. Their lives are pure and true, and their every-day walk shows the genuineness of the marvellous transformation wrought by the Gospel's power.

In a land so isolated there were, of course, many trials, and some hardships. So remote were we from civilization that often, for months together, we were obliged to live as did the Indians, almost destitute of the blessings of ordinary civilized life. Fish, twenty-one times a week for six months, was sometimes our principal food. The other six months we had a great variety of game, from bear's meat to musk rat, and from venison to wild cat.

So importunate did the pagan Indians become to hear the Gospel, that in carrying the glad tidings of a Saviour's love to them I kept enlarging my mission field until it was over five hundred miles long and three hundred wide. Over this vast field I travelled in summer in a birch canoe, and in winter with my dog-trains. Our summers in those high latitudes are short and brilliant. As in my canoe, managed by my skilful canoemen, we travelled in those great lakes and rivers, we did not see a house for weeks together. The granite rocks were our bed, and the star-decked canopy of heaven our covering. Sometimes it was varied when the drenching showers fell upon us, and we were for days without a dry stitch upon us. But in patience we toiled on, and rejoiced when the blessed sunshine came out again and dried our dripping garments.

In winter we travelled by dog-train. There is absolutely no other way of travelling in that land in those long, cold, dreadful winters, except going on foot, and dog-travel means that in a greater or less degree.

As illustrated in my book, "By Canoe and Dog-Train," we harness them up tandem style, four dogs constituting a train. The sleds are sixteen inches wide and ten feet long. Generally four trains would be required for a long trip. Attended by my faithful dog drivers, in this way I have travelled thousands of miles through the dreary, pathless forests of the cold North Land. No vestige of road was there. The snow was often from three to four feet deep, and the only sign of a road before the faithful dogs were the snow-shoe tracks of the skilful Indian guide, who with unerring accuracy strode along on ahead, often at the rate of from seventy to ninety miles a day.

The cold was often terrible. Sometimes it was from forty to sixty below zero. At times every part of my face exposed to the pitiless blast was frozen.

When night overtook us on those long journeys, often, of many days' duration, we dug a hole in the snow, cooked our supper of fat meat and strong tea, fed our faithful dogs, and then after prayers wrapped ourselves up in our blankets and fur robes, and then often to the lullaby of the howlings of the great gray wolves of the north, lay down in that snowy bed, with no roof above us but the starry heavens, and tried to sleep. Often it was hard work to keep from freezing to death. Are you surprised when I tell you that once, in such a bed, I froze my nose and both ears?

But in no other way could those poor sheep in the wilderness, so isolated and so long neglected, be reached with the Gospel. These single trips often required eight to nine days, each way, of severest toil.

I was supposed to ride on my dog sled, and generally could when the way led us over the icy surface of the great lakes or rivers which constitute the good roads of the country; but when we had to push on through the dense forest regions, where the snow was very deep and the obstructions many, the missionary had to strap on his snow shoes, and in Indian file, with his faithful guide and dog drivers, help make the track on which the noble dogs could drag the sleds with their heavy loads. Your missionary had not the iron constitution of those tried, athletic red men of the north, and so, often, as he was obliged to tramp along, hour after hour, his strength gave out, and being seized by the cramps, has he fallen helpless in the snow trail. All he could do in his agony was to call out: "Boys, help me!" and quickly to his aid rush his faithful and sorrowing and dusky companions, and while one Indian seized him by his leather coat collar, another took hold of his moccasins, and pulling vigorously they straightened him out, while a third Indian sat on him to keep him straight, while the fourth Indian speedily made a fire, and boiling the kettle, made some strong tea, and warming fur robes and blankets, in which they rolled the missionary, soon got him into a sweat, and thus caused the cramps to partly disappear, so that full of pain and suffering, the missionary could resume the journey. Often the strap of the snow shoes would so chafe and injure his feet that the blood would soak through the moccasins and the webbing of the snow shoes, and the trail would be marked with the blood.

Do you very much censure him when I tell you that there were times when his heart failed him and his courage faltered? That more than once has he sat down alone, covered with snow, and chiding himself with himself, has said: "If I reach home alive from this journey, so terrible and full of suffering, I will never attempt another like it. The people who support missionaries do not ask such suffering of one of these men. My brother ministers do not ask it, and God does not ask it, and if I get home alive, I will never undertake one like it again." Yes, he has said just such things, amidst his physical agonies, and in his moments of discouragements. But he has taken them all back, and has asked forgiveness for all such foolish words. [*Applause.*]

And why he has done so we will endeavor to tell you. The welcome with which he was received by the wild Indian in the primeval forest, the eagerness with which they drank in the precious truth of the Blessed Book, the child-like faith with which they received it, and accepted it, and were saved by it, and the genuineness of their conversions, as exemplified by their devoted, consistent, honest lives, shows the reality of the work wrought in their hearts by the preaching of the Gospel and the crucifixion in the wilderness.

As I heard the happy testimony and impressioned words of how for years they had lost faith in the old religion of their forefathers, and that the religion of the Book of Heaven was just what they had been longing for, I forgot all about my chafed limbs and bleeding feet and frost-bitten face, and rejoiced that I was counted worthy to go as a pioneer missionary among so interesting a people, and see such success. I found some of these bands all pagans; they are to-day all Christians. I found some of them brutal and cruel in the extreme to the mother and wives and daughters, some of them even going so far as to strangle their own mothers to death, and then burn the bodies to ashes, for the crime of growing old and being unable to snare rabbits or build fires.

I have seen the feeble, old, and blind mother there, seated on a chair made out of the clasped hands of two stalwart sons, and with one arm around the neck of one son, and the other around the other neck, thus brought to the house of God, that she, too, might enjoy the sermons of the little sanctuary, and then when it was ended, lovingly was she carried back by those now loving, Christian sons, who, but for the blessed influences of the Gospel, would have cruelly and heartlessly put her to death for the crime of living old and helpless.

Oh, wondrous transformation! Oh, glorious Gospel, that can so change hard, cruel, callous hearts!

Fellow Christian Endeavorers, workers in God's vineyard, our mission is to see to it that in the next few years all the world has the Gospel. It is indeed a mighty task, a tremendous undertaking. But the mighty God, the everlasting Father, is on our side. The promises are all with us. The declaration has gone forth, that "to his Son shall be given the heathen for his inheritance and the uttermost parts of the earth for his possession."

To aid in this work we are toiling and ever praying. The signs of the times are all full of encouragment. In the different positions in life where God has providentially placed us, let us labor on and never give up the conflict. Never were Longfellow's words more true than now:

"Out of the darkness of night the world rolls into light. It is daybreak everywhere."

May God save us from apathy or indifference at this glorious daybreak of the bright on-coming day.

With some night visions and heart-musings from the Wild North Land, I must close.

So short are the wintry days in those "high latitudes," where for years we toiled, that on our long trips with our dogs and Indians we were obliged to rouse ourselves up from our snowy beds in the cold and dreary forests, hours before day. Aided by the light of our camp-fire we cooked our morning meal, packed up our robes and blankets, and tied them, with our provisions and kettles, on our dog-sleds. Before starting we sang in the Cree Indian language one of the sweet songs of Zion, and then bowing at the mercy-seat with grateful hearts, we offered up our prayers to the loving Protector who had watched over and shielded us from all harm, although our lodging-place was in the "forest primeval" and our bed was in the snow, with the temperature from forty to sixty degrees below zero. Our last camp duty was the capturing and harnessing of our dogs, which was an easy or difficult task according to their nature and training.

As much snow had recently fallen, we all tied on our snow shoes; then, starting our dogs, we wended our way out from the light of the camp-fire and through the weird shadows of the fir and birch and juniper trees on the vast expanse of Lake Winnipeg, across which our journey lay. The stars shone down upon us with a clearness and brilliancy unknown in lands of mists and fogs. At times meteors blazed along the star-decked vault of heaven, leaving behind them for a few seconds lines of silvery light that soon faded away. The Northern Lights flashed, danced, and scintillated with a magnificence that paled into insignificance man's most wonderfel pyrotechnic displays. Frequently a clear and distinct corona would be formed at the zenith, from which would shoot out long columns of various-colored lights, which seemed to rest down upon the snowy waste around us or on the far off distant shores. Often have I seen a cloud of light flit swiftly across these ever-changing bars with a resemblance so natural to that of a hand across the strings of a harp that I have suddenly stopped and listened for that rustling sound which some arctic travellers have affirmed they have heard from these auroral displays; but although I have often watched and listened amid the death-like stillness of this dreary land, no sound have I ever heard. Amid all their flashing, changing glories they seemed as voiceless as the stars above them. The morning crescent-shaped moon, the silvery queen of night, helped to light up our way, as through the long, dreary hours we journeyed on. If the cold had been less terrible, nothing could have been more delightful than contemplating these glorious sights in the heavens. As it was, the words of the psalmist, "The heavens declare the glory of God, and the firmament showeth his handiwork," and Job's magnificent description of that God "who is wise in heart, and mighty in strength, which alone spreadeth out the heavens, which maketh Arcturus, Orion, and Pleiades, and the chambers of the south," rang in our ears, and we were thankful that the Creator of all these things was mindful of us. Still, after all, on account of the bitterness of the morning, it being, as we afterwards found, in the neighborhood of fifty degrees below zero, there was a disposition to lose our love of the sentimental, and in almost bitter anguish to cry out to these lights in the heavens, " Miserable comforters are ye all! Can none of you give us any warmth?"

But while we journey on, a dim, faint line of light is seen in the eastern horizon. At first it is scarcely visible. The brilliant meteors seem to say, "How much more exalted and beautiful are we than that dim, faint line down there so low!" The Northern Lights appear to cry out in derision, " Who for a moment would compare us in all our ever-changing, flashing splendor with that insignificant and modest beam?" The silvery moon, the queen of night, seems to consider that eastern light as an intruder, as she gazes upon it with saucy stare. But that eastern light heeds them not. As we watch we see that it is rapidly increasing. The white line, extending round to the north and south, has risen, and underneath is one of crimson and purple. A flashing ray shoots up, and then the glorious sun bounds up from his snowy bed, "rejoicing as a strong man to run a race." Felix, my Indian guide, who ran ahead, shouted out, " Sagastao! Sagastao! " (The sun rises! The sun rises!)

The poor, shivering missionary coming next, toiling along on snow-shoes behind his dog-train, takes up the joyful sound, which is caught up and loudly shouted by William, my other Indian attendant, who at this glad sight casts off his usual stoicism and is as noisy in his words of welcome to the sovereign king of day as the rest of us. We turn our ice-covered, frost-bitten faces to the sun, and as its bright beams fall upon us like loving kisses, we rejoice that the light and brightness of another day has come, for "truly the light is sweet; and a pleasant thing it is for the eyes to behold the sun." But look around the heavens and behold the marvellous change his coming has effected. Every lesser light has gone, every competitor has left the field. The race is all his own. At first his bright rays gild the distant hill-tops, then they light up the fir-clad rocky isles which, when burnished by his golden beams, bear some fanciful resemblance to old ruined temples or vast cathedrals. And while we gaze upon them, wondering if God's footstool can be made to look so glorious, what will the throne be? The sun has risen higher, every shadow of night has disappeared, and we are deluged in his glory. I would have been but a poor lover of the world's evangelization and emphatically a poor missionary, if I could have gazed upon these marvellous transformations in the heavens and thought on the lessons they taught me, unmoved. My heart grew hot within me, and while I mused the fire burned, and then spake I with my tongue:

Meet emblem of a world shrouded in the chill and gloom of paganism seems Lake Winnipeg on this cold wintry morning. No sign of life is here. The ice and snow, like a great mantle, seem to have wrapped themselves round every thing that once had life.

The flashing meteors reminded me of the efforts of the old philosophers to reform and illuminate the world. There was a transient beauty in some of their theories, but the darkness to be dispelled was too dense, and so their lights, meteor-like, went out almost as soon as kindled. The fickle, ever-changing Northern Lights made me think of some of the various systems of false religions, or perversions of the true, which man has invented to dazzle the unwary or to lead the fickle astray. Whether it be Mormonism, or Spiritualism, or a mere sensuous ritualism, changeable and inconstant are they as the auroras. Their revelations, their spiritual communications, rapped or written, their gorgeous vestments and illuminated altars, are no more able to dispel the darkness and irradiate the world lost in sin and error's night than the auroras are to warm and comfort the poor shivering missionary and his Indian attendants, toiling through the wintry cold and longing for the morning. The crescent-shaped moon reminded me of that vast system of error which for twelve centuries has waved its crescent flag over some of the fairest portions of God's heritages. Humiliating is the thought that even in the land once pressed by the dear Redeemer's feet the baneful cry is still heard that, although "God is great, Mohammed is his prophet." But the crescent must go down before the Sun of Righteousness. As the moon is the last of the lights of night to fade before the sun, so Mohammedism, although such a stubborn foe, must eventually succumb. Once her crescent-bannered armies made all Christendom tremble; now the mutual forbearance, or rather mutual jealousies, of Christian nations keep the only great Mohammedan nation from falling to pieces.

Soon, very soon, perhaps before we expect and before we are ready to enter in, the crescent will go down before the cross, and then many more of the dark places full of the habitations of cruelty shall open for the blessed light of the Sun. Haste, happy day, day so much desired and so often prayed for, and for which we toil, when the Sun of Righteousness shall shine upon every portion of the world polluted and darkened by sin, but bought with the Redeemer's blood!

> " And shall not I, at God and duty's call,
> Fly to the utmost limits of the ball,
> Cross the wide sea, along the desert toil,
> Or circumnavigate each Indian isle?
> To torrid regions run to save the lost,
> Or brave the rigors of eternal frost?
> I may, like Brainard, perish in my bloom,
> A group of Indians weeping round my tomb;
> I may, like Martyn, lay my burning head
> In some lone Persian hut or Turkish shed;
> I may, like Coke, be buried in the wave;
> I may, like Howard, find a Tartar grave;
> I may, like Xavier, perish on the beach,
> In some lone cottage, out of friendship's reach;
> Or, like McDougall, in a snow-drift die,
> With angels only near to hear the dying sigh.

> I may — but never let my soul repine —
> 'Lo, I'm with you alway!' Heaven's in that line.
> Tropic or pole, or mild or burning zone
> Is but a step from my eternal throne."

Following Mr. Young's address, which was applauded to the echo, the audience sang "Oh, glad and glorious Gospel."

Dr. CLARK: We have heard and read a good deal about the World's Fair, but not so much about its religious possibilities. We shall be addressed on that subject this afternoon by one of our most honored and beloved friends, who is also chairman of the committee on religious congresses for the World's Fair, — Rev. John Henry Barrows, D.D., of Chicago. [*Loud applause.*]

ADDRESS BY REV. JONN HENRY BARROWS, D.D.

I deem it a great privilege to have any part in this magnificent convention, met in this imperial city, and to address the Christian youth of many lands on the majestic theme assigned me. The Columbian Exposition and the series of more than a hundred World-Congresses which are to accompany it will have a large influence over the social and Christian developments of the twentieth century. It is more than a local, it is more than a national, event. While the  patriotic pride and wisdom of America, of New York and New England as well as of the mighty West and South, are enlisted and pledged to make it the grandest and best of all expositions, while it is computed that the government, the directory, the States, and individual exhibitors, will expend more than thirty millions of dollars upon the preparation and conduct of this gigantic undertaking, nearly fifty nations, besides our own, are profoundly concerned in the coming Jubilee of Civilization. Its speedy approach causes a stir in the studios of Paris and Munich, and on the pasture-grounds of far-off Australia; among the Esquimaux of the icy North, and the skilled artizans of Delhi and Damascus. The work-shops of Sheffield, Geneva, and Moscow, and the marble quarries of Italy, the ostrich farms of Cape Colony, and the mines of Brazil, know of its coming. The ivory hunters in the forests of Africa and the ivory cutters in the thronged cities of Japan and China, the silk-weavers of Lyons and the shawl-makers of Cashmere, the designers of Kensington, the lace-weavers of Brussels, and the Indian tribes of South America, the cannon founders of Germany, the silver-miners of Mexico, the ship-makers of the Clyde, and the canoe-builders of the Mackenzie River, toil with the eyes of their minds daily turned toward the Columbian Exposition. Over the ample site on the shore of Lake Michigan, which has been transformed into a scene of more than Venetian loveliness, fall the shadows from the Alps and the Pyrenees, from the white crags of the Hymalayas and the snowy cone of the sacred mount of Japan. The buildings, planned by the leading American architects, which are to shelter not only the riches of the soil, the sea, and the mine, but also the industries and machineries and inventions of the world, which are to be crowded with the jewelled and silken marvels of Europe and Asia and the floral wonders of the Amazon, which are to be made still more beautiful by the pomp of the decorator's art and by the triumphs of the sculptor's genius, are more imposing and magnificent than any which adorned the great and brilliant expositions of London, Paris, Philadelphia, and Vienna.

But it was said long ago, on divine authority, that "man does not live by bread alone," by "things material and visible," and I am happily confident that the Columbian Exposition is to provide more amply than any previous World's Fair for the higher things of the spirit. It will be an education to every thoughtful young man and woman to become a student at this World's University, and we should be diligently eager in preparing for it. The discovery of the New World was a chief event in the social and in the spiritual progress of humanity; and the pulpits and schools of America have an unequalled opportunity of showing the providential aspects of our history,—of indicating what God has wrought through the four marvellous centuries since Columbus sighted the West Indian island from the deck of the Spanish caravel. The exposition will not only furnish an unparalleled spectacle to the eye, it will also provide for the mind an unequalled feast. It is well known that a series of world-conventions, representing the chief departments of human knowledge and effort, will be contemporaneous with the continuance of the exposition. And the chief of all these, in the importance of the themes to be treated and of the interests involved and in the period of time allotted them, will be the Congresses of Religion, extending from the closing days of August through the entire month of September. Halls and churches that will accommodate thirty thousand people will be found ready for this series of conventions.

It is expected by many of us that Sunday will be made, in certain higher respects, the chief day of the fair from the very beginning. [*Applause.*] An association has been formed to provide for great meetings on every Lord's Day, to be addressed by some of the leaders of mankind. Noble Christian music will add its attractions and its inspirations to that day which Emerson has called the "core of our civilization." The American churches and Sunday schools, whose work constitutes the nobler part of our history, will be on exhibition before the thousands who will flock to us from every peopled shore. The Gospel will be preached, by returned missionaries and others, in Turkish, Armenian, Arabic, Spanish, Greek, Italian, Chinese, and in many other of the chief languages of the world. Not only on the Lord's Day but through the week there will be tent preaching and open-air preaching near the gates of the exposition. I have no doubt that the eminently worthy enterprise, the "Hotel Endeavor," with its great convention hall and daily meetings, that the Sunday-school headquarters and Women's Temperance unions, and the rooms of the Young Men's and Young Women's Christian associations, and the tract and Bible societies, will be the centres and agencies of daily Christian activity, by means of which the Gospel of our Lord will be proclaimed to the representatives of every nation. There will also be, for the first time in any World's Fair, a material exhibit, in the splendid liberal arts building, of the work of religion, as shown by models, maps, pictures, statistics, and selected publications of the Bible, tract, missionary, denominational, and interdenominational societies, for which exhibit an area of twenty thousand square feet has been reserved. President Clark, as he carries the gospel of Christian Endeavor around the world, will make known the fact that the World's Fair is not to be a mere glorification of material achievements. [*Applause.*]

More than a year ago a committee, representing fifteen denominations, was appointed under the direction of the exposition authorities, to arrange and provide plans for a proper exhibition, by means of congresses, of the religious forces now shaping human history. Their plans have been published far and wide in modern European languages, and also in Oriental tongues, whose alphabets the committee cannot read. For more than thirty days the great halls will be thronged with the representatives of our Christian churches and of the non-Christian faiths coming from the six continents. The so-called denominational congresses will occupy a week or more. The Catholics and the Lutherans and others have already planned for conventions on an immense scale. A week has been assigned to the Evangelical Alliance, whose meetings will be of commanding importance; three days will be given to the Sunday-rest congresses, which will discuss one of the most vital themes of our times. Special days here and there will be set apart for interdenominational conventions, like those of the Christian Endeavor and other societies. The mission congresses, covering the entire field of city, domestic, and foreign missions, will occupy eight days or more, and it is the earnest desire of those having these meetings in charge to secure the presence of one active missionary from each society, and of at least one native helper, a representative of Christian conquest from every foreign land, and of one official representative of every leading missionary organization in the world. Here is an immense opportunity of showing, not only to the people of Christian lands, but to the representatives of non-Christian nations, the splendid vitality and vigor of the missionary spirit which is the grandest feature of this grandest century since Jesus commissioned his disciples to evangelize the world. [*Applause.*]

But the general committee has provided also for the most unique, interesting, and important feature of the Columbian Exposition, in a ten days' Parliament of Religions, at which, for the first time in history, the representatives of the leading historic faiths will meet in fraternal conference over the great things of human life and destiny. This parliament will be held because the committee perceived that the time was ripe for it and the opportunity golden, and because such a host of God's noblest men and women have cordially approved it. There is a general consensus of applause to the proposition that religion shall, in some conspicuous way, in this age of materialistic pride, assert its kingship over life. Since religion has been one of the chief forces of progress, since faith in a Divine Power to whom men believe that they owe service and worship, has been, like the sun, a life-giving and fructifying potency in man's intellectual and moral development, since religion lies back of Greek and Hindu literature, European art, and American liberty, and since it is as clear as the light that the religion of Christ has led to the chief and noblest developments of modern civilization, why should religion, any more than education, charities, art, or electricity, be omitted from a World's Exposition? The reply which comes to many minds is this: that religion is an element of perpetual discord, and should not be thrust in amid the magnificent harmonies of this fraternal assembly of the nations. And doubtless the animosities of the religious world have embittered much of man's past history. The event which the Columbian anniversary celebrates carries us back to an era of persecutions and of abysmal separations between Christian and non-Christian peoples. But of late years there has been a happy drawing toward each other of the Christian churches, as this society so grandly illustrates, and the disciples of Jesus have been able to study the non-Christian faiths with a desire to do full justice to all the good that is in them.

I cannot give you an adequate review of the inspiring words that have come to us from such men as Gladstone, the poets Whittier and Tennyson, from Bishops Huntington, Brooks, Whipple, and others of the Protestant Episcopal Church, from Bishops Vincent, Andrews, Foss, and others of the Methodist Episcopal Church, from the presidents of our leading colleges and universities, the editors of our leading Christian journals, great preachers like Dr. Boardman, Dr. R. S. Storrs, Dr. Burrell, Dr. Behrends, the secretaries of our missionary societies, and the eminent professors in our seminaries. In Great Britian we have the co-operation of men like the Rev. Hugh Price-Hughes of London, Wm. T. Stead, of the "Review of Reviews," Professor Bruce, of Glasgow, Professor Drummond, of world-wide fame, Professor James Bryce, Principal Fairbairn, and many others. On the Continent we are aided by men like Dr. McAll, of Paris, Dr. Godet, of Switzerland, Dr. Prochet, of Rome, the court preacher, Dr. Frommel, and Dr. Stuckenburg of Berlin, and Dr. Washburn, of Constantinople. In Canada, we have the assistance of such men as Dr. Withrow, of Toronto, Principal Grant, of Kingston, Bishop Sullivan, Dr. Macræ, of New Brunswick, and others. In Syria India, and China, and the Pacific Islands we have the hearty good will of many leading missionaries, and in the sunrise Empire — Japan — the list of those who are favorably interested has become too long to be repeated.

The Parliament of Religions is not to be a mass meeting, but rather an orderly school of comparative theology, where those who worthily represent the great historic faiths will be invited to report what they believe and why they believe it. The program will be determined and carefully arranged by the general committee, most of whom are evangelical Christians, assisted by an able committee of women, and by the wisdom of the advisory council, numbering already more than two hundred of the leaders of religious thought.

The greatest and wisest of the Mogul emperors, Akbar, who built the Taj Mahal, loveliest of all buildings, is said to have planned such a parliament in the sixteenth century. He was himself willing to learn from Christian missionaries and Moslem teachers, from Hindu scholars and Parsee scriptures. But the religion which he personally adopted had no dynamic force within it, and the parliament of which he dreamed was never assembled. I received the other day from the land which Akbar once ruled, and from perhaps the leading native Christian of India, now a British commissioner and magistrate, a cordial letter, expressing his hope of seeing our "great country and people on this special opportunity which Providence seems to have offered." He writes of his faith that this parliament, the fulfillment of Akbar's dream, will do incalculable good, and he says: "Oh how grand it will be when men from east and west, north and south, meet together, admitting the universal truth of the Fatherhood of God; and let us hope," he says, "that many will be led to the highest and most blessed truth as it is in Jesus." And after speaking of the failure of all other forces, he adds: "One thing is as certain as that the hot sun is shining over us this warm day, and that is, if there is any remedy to raise fallen man, it is in the love of Jesus. The very best of education and civilization lies in this grand secret, love, and God is love." The chief Hindu paper of southern India says that the "Parliament will certainly mark an epoch in the history of the human race," and a prominent Moslem scholar of Calcutta is bold enough to pronounce it the "greatest achievement of the century;" while leading Japanese Christians are enthusiastic in their praise of this opportunity of bringing the various faiths of the world into friendly comparison with the Christian Gospel.

I have no doubt that this phenominal meeting will make apparent the fact that there is a certain unity in religion,—that is, that men not only have common desires and needs, but also have perceived, more or less clearly, certain common truths. And as the Apostle Paul, with his unfailing tact and courtesy, was careful to find common ground for himself and his Greek auditors in Athens, before he preached to them Jesus and the resurrection, so the wise Christian missionary is discovering that he must not ignore any fragment of truth which the heathen mind cherishes, for, thus ignoring it, he makes an impassable barrier against conviction in the non-Christian mind. I believe that the parliament will do much to promote the spirit of human brotherhood among those of diverse faiths, by diminishing ill-will, by softening rancor, and giving men the privilege of getting their impressions of others at first hand. We believe that Christianity is to supplant all other religions, because it contains all the truth there is in them and much besides, revealing a redeeming God. The object of the parliament, it scarcely needs to be said, is not to foster any temper either of bigotry or of indifferentism. Each man is required to speak out with frankness his own convictions, and without compromising individual faiths all are to meet under a flag emblazoned with the words, "Truth, Love, Fellowship" rejoicing in a fraternity that involves no surrender of personal opinions, and no abatement of faith on the part of those who recognize how widely Christianity is differentiated from other systems. As any wise missionary in Bombay or Madras would be glad to gather beneath the shelter of his roof the scholarly and sincere representatives of the Hindu religions, so Christian America invites to the shelter of her hospitable roof, at her grand festival of peace, the spiritual leaders, of mankind, for friendly conference over the deepest problem of human existence. Though light has no fellowship with darkness, light does have fellowship with twilight. God has not left himself without witness, and those who have the full light of the cross should bear brotherly hearts toward all who grope in a dimmer illumination. While the apostle Paul denounced an idol worship which was devil worship, he fully recognized that heathen religion was not of that malign quality. He instructed the Athenians that he and they adored the same God, of whom all were the offspring, they in ignorance of God's full nature, and he in the blessed knowledge which Christ had given him. Rev. Thomas L. Gulick, of the Sandwich Islands, expresses his faith that St. Paul, who quotes heathen writers in confirmation of his own theology, would not refuse to confer with those whom he approvingly quotes.

And I believe that there will be furnished a grand field for Christian apologetics, a matchless opportunity of setting forth the distinctive truths of the Christian Gospel. A Parliament of Christendom is to be interwoven with the Parliament of Religions, and able Christian scholars will treat of such themes as the Incarnation, the Divine Person, the Atonement and Resurrection of Christ, and the relations of Christians to one another. Thomas Arnold has said: "Other religions show us man seeking God. Christianity shows us God seeking man." It is on this account that Christianity claims to be the true religion, fitted to all and demanding the submission of all. Christianity alone shows us a Mediator. The Church of Christ has a unique message which she will proclaim to all the world, giving the reasons why her faith should supplant all others, showing, among other truths, that transmigration is not regeneration, that ethical knowledge is not redemption from sin, and that Nirvana is not heaven. [*Applause.*]

I believe that the Parliament of Religions will be valuable to scholars and to young missionaries and to Christian people everywhere by exciting a deeper interest in the non-Christian world and a deeper respect for it. Dr. Clark, of the American Board, has well said, "that a sense of superiority or indifference to men as heathen will close the way to their hearts." I know that the worst things in pagan lands excite our horror and pity, but pagandom should not be judged solely by its worst. The more Christian a man is, as Professor Legge, of Oxford, has said, "the more anxious he will be to do justice to every system of religion." We have pitied the poor heathen so much that most Christians despise him and do little or nothing for his enlightenment. When the doors of China were thrown open to the missionary and also to the worst elements of European and American life, some people imagined that China, with her ancient and marvellous institutions, would succumb at once to our Christian civilization. But she did not, and, as Professor Fisher, of Yale, said to me the other day, "I think all the more of her for not surrendering immediately." There is tenacious and splendid material there for the future Christian Church. And on the other hand, while it would be better for Christendom to know the full truth about pagan lands, it would be vastly better for pagan lands to know the full truth about Christendom, and that cannot be gained by reading only the "Cry of Outcast London," Zola's fictions, the descriptions of American society in English magazines, the records of our crimes and divorces, the statistics of the liquor traffic, some of the newspaper pictures of Chicago, and Dr. Parkhurst's brave sermons on municipal corruption in New York. At the Parliament of Religions the nobler and grander facts of our Christian civilization will be presented to the candid judgment of the world. And yet, in the light of the discussions which may be evoked, so-called Christian nations may, in some things, stand rebuked before the non-Christian. And I, for one, shall not be sorry. The time is come when Christendom should repent in dust and ashes. Missionary progress is frightfully checked by the sins of Christian people. I need not characterize the barbarous Chinese exclusion bill; I need not speak of the rum traffic on the west coast of Africa, the whiskey and gunpowder of Christian commerce, or the forcing of the opium trade into China, or the miserable examples of greed, pride, and cruelty which have disfigured the name of Christian in India and Cathay. With Christian life as portrayed in Rudyard Kipling's pictures of British character in India before him, we do not wonder that the student of the Vedas is not altogether fascinated with Christian civilization. May it not be, under the blessing of God, a means of pricking Christendom to the heart, to see itself rebuked in "The parliament of man, the federation of the world?" [*Applause.*]

But the most cheering and valuable endorsements of our plans have come to us from missionaries in the thick of the fight; and while the Parliament will do something to promote Christian unity and bridge the chasms of separation between the disciples of Christ, it will do much, I hope, to bring the non-Christian world before the minds and hearts of a selfish and indifferent Christendom. Speaking as a pastor, living in the capital of western materialism, with all the world knocking at our doors and thronging our streets, let me here record the conviction that the divine way of building up the kingdom of Christ in America is to engage with fresh ardor in efforts to Christianize India and Africa, Turkey and China. The heart that is aglow with a wise Christian patriotism must plead earnestly for foreign missions. If this Christian Endeavor movement shall become alive with foreign missionary enthusiasm, if it nourishes the self-sacrificing and obedient spirit which heeds our Lord's command to "go into all the world," then we shall not appeal in vain for Christian work in our imperiled cities and on the vast and needy frontier. One chief hindrance to missionary progress is the misty unreality of the great heathen world. We scarcely think of them as our brethren. Many people's interest in them, judged by their gifts, is hardly noticeable. I believe they will soon be brought nearer to our thoughts; I believe that the coming event is to stir a mighty and wide-reaching interest in the study of comparative religions, thereby strengthening the faith of disciples and quickening their benevolent impulses. Biblical Christianity, exhibited by the side of the systems of Buddha, Mohammed, and Confucius, seems more divine than ever. Those who appreciate most fully the truths of natural religion are increasing their unselfish efforts to give to all the world the supreme and priceless blessings of the Christian Gospel. Professor Sampey, of the Southern Baptist Theological Seminary, Louisville, writes me: " Let an honest effort be made to get at the facts of religious experience, and the truth of God will take care of itself." Let no one fear that the solar orb of Christianity is to be eclipsed by the lanterns and rush-lights of other faiths. [*Applause.*]

I believe that the Columbian Exposition, in the general sweep of its plans, is fitted to fill our hearts with new Christian hopefulness, to stir in our souls a new sense of responsibility, and to quicken our minds with new perceptions " of the universal action and guidance and love of God." It will contribute to the great end which Prince Albert pointed out at the first World's Fair forty-one years ago, — " the realization of the unity of mankind." As I was looking the other day at the immense building for the mines and mining exhibit in Jackson Park, I was glad to see in the ornamentation of the grand southern portico the words that are stamped on our national coins, " In God we trust." And to the reverent mind, — to him who sees God and the instrumentalities for the enlargement of his kingdom in the forces of material civilization, — even these displays of human progress and achievement in subduing and transforming nature will suggest inspiring and hopeful thoughts. It would be easy for the Biblical student to find appropriate scriptural words to write on every structure in the World's Fair. Below the gilded dome of the administration building, the master-work of one of the architects of this city, I would inscribe the words of Isaiah: " The government shall be upon his shoulders;" over the machinery hall I would write: " Every house is builded by some man, but he that built all things is God;" over the transportation building I would write: " Make straight a highway for our God;" over the palace of fine arts: " The gate of the temple which is called beautiful;" over the agricultural hall: " Behold, a sower went forth to sow;" over the electrical palace: " His lightnings enlighten the world;" over the woman's pavilion: " She stretcheth out her hands to the needy;" over the horticultural building: " I am the rose of Sharon and the lily of the valley;" over the building of the United States government: " He hath not dealt so with any nation;" over the unique and beautiful fisheries building: " And the fishes of the sea shall declare unto thee;" over the mineral palace: " In his hand are the deep places of the earth;" over one of the resplendent gates to the exposition ground I would write the prophecy: " The kingdoms of this world shall become the kingdoms of our Lord and his Christ;" and over every closed gate, on Sunday morning, I would inscribe in letters of gold for all eyes to see, the immortal statute wherein is rapt up the Christian future of America and of the world: "Remember the Sabbath day to keep it holy." [*Loud applause.*]

America will be on exhibition the coming year, and especially American Christianity. Shall the nations who have heard great things of us, coming to our shores smile over our recreancy and exclaim: "How art thou fallen from heaven, O Lucifer, son of the morning." General William Booth sends word from London: "You have an opportunity of influencing the whole world with the spirit of our common Christianity without parallel in ancient or modern times." "The materials," says the English *Independent*, "have been made ready for a new world pentecost." A few years ago President Warren, of Boston, preached a sermon wherein he imagined the assembling of a great convention in Tokio, a conference of the religious leaders of the Eastern world, the Buddhist, Brahmin, Parsee, Mohammedan, Taoist, Shintoist, and Confucian, met together to discuss the great problems of faith, and to discover, if possible, the perfect religion. As the discussion proceeded they reached the conclusion that there could be only one perfect religion, that the perfect religion must reveal a perfect God, that it must assure man the greatest possible ultimate good, that it must bring God into the most loving and lovable relations with humanity, and that this could be achieved only by his taking upon himself a human form, and suffering for men. And it would have seemed that the convention was talking something ideal, something which had never been actualized, had not the last speaker, the Buddhist leader of Japan, related the story of his own long mental unrest, and how, on the day before, he had learned through the teaching of a brother, who had seen many lands, that God had really come to earth, had revealed himself through his Son, had furnished all the credentials needed by the eager intellect and the yearning heart, had centered and glorified in himself all the truths which Gautama had discovered beneath the Indian fig tree, or Confucius in his long-wandering quest, and through the cross reared on an Asian hill-top had offered deliverance from the guilt and love of sin, and had irradiated the sorrows and incompletenesses of each with sure and golden promises of celestial peace and unwasting joy. The reverent dream of the Christian soldier will soon be an august reality.

It will be a great moment in human history, as many have felt, when for the first time the representatives of the world-religions stand side by side. May the Holy Ghost be the divine apostle preaching Jesus to an assembled world! And that the fire from God may descend on these phenomenal conventions of his children, illuminating all minds and brightening all faces with gleams of that glory which shall cover the earth, should henceforth be our earnest and hopeful prayer.

"Before Jehovah's awful throne,
Ye nations, bow with sacred joy;
Know that the Lord is God alone:
He can create and he destroy.

"Wide as the world is thy command,
Vast as eternity thy love;
Firm as a rock thy truth shall stand,
When rolling years shall cease to move." [*Great applause.*]

Dr. Barrows' address was intently listened to and warmly applauded. At its close a number of notices for the evening were given, and the session closed with the Doxology and the Mizpah benediction.

SUNDAY EVENING.

It seemed to be generally understood among the delegates that the closing session of the convention would be the most interesting, and the hall was crowded at an early hour. Not even the unusually attractive programs offered at the eight or more simultaneous meetings served to diminish the throng outside the building in the least. In fact, the places where the simultaneous meetings were held were themselves crowded to the doors. As usual, those who were so fortunate as to secure seats within the Garden occupied the time previous to the opening of the session in singing. Treasurer Shaw created quite a diversion by presenting a request which had been sent to the platform that all the ladies present should take off their hats. The heat was great within the building, and apparently the ladies were very glad to comply with the request, for the hats immediately disappeared. The applause from the gentlemen following this proceeding was tremendous, and was repeated again and again. The picture was certainly a very beautiful one.

"Now," said Mr. Shaw, "as Dr. Clark isn't here, we can run things to suit ourselves for a few minutes. We would like to know how many pastors there are here. All who are pastors, please stand up on their seats." Hundreds in the audience rose, amid much applause, and Mr. Shaw said: "We want to say to these pastors that their young people are not ashamed of them. [*Applause.*] Now Dr. Beckley suggests that we have not seen the best part of these pastors. Will all the pastors' wives in this audience please rise." [*Great applause.*] Evidently the "better half" was not very fully represented, and Mr. Shaw said: "There are not half so many wives present as there are pastors. I guess it is because they didn't need this meeting so much!" [*Laughter.*]

At half-past seven the regular program of the evening began with a prayer and praise service, led by Rev. Edgar T. Farrill, of Lebanon, N. H. Mr. Farrill preceeded the hymns as they were sung with a few pertinent remarks, and prayer was offered by Rev. Sanford Merton and Rev. Dr. Dickey. The 24th Psalm was read responsively, and Mr. E. F. Yarnell sang a solo without accompaniment. The service closed with the Lord's prayer and the hymn, "Showers of Blessing."

At eight o'clock Dr. Clark introduced Rev. Dr. Beckley, of Philadelphia, who reported for the Committee on Resolutions as follows:

Resolved, That the thanks of this convention be extended to the Christian Endeavor unions of New York and Brooklyn and to the Committee of 1892 and its noble Chairman, the Rev. H. T. McEwen, who, by their energy, wisdom, and devotion, have helped to make the eleventh international convention the greatest in the history of the movement.

Resolved, That our thanks be given to the churches and the people of these cities, whose co-operation and liberality have provided for us this auditorium, the largest in which we have ever assembled.

Resolved, That we thank the officers of the Madison Square Garden Company, Mr. Sherwood, the Superintendent, and his assistant, and Sergt. Edward

M. Muret and his subordinates, for their care for our safety and their watchfulness against accident.

Resolved, That we thank the press of this great metropolis, noted for its enterprise and ability, not only for rendering faithful reports, but for its sympathetic tone and hearty editorial endorsement.

Resolved, That our thanks be given to the chorus and to the musical director, Mr. George C. Stebbins, and to Mr. Ira D. Sankey, the great leaders of Christian song.

Resolved, That we express our thanks to the Treasurer, Mr. William Shaw, for consecrating his unusual executive talent to this cause; that we remember with gratitude the services of our devoted Secretary, Mr. J. W. Baer; that we give him our sympathy in his trial and our prayers for his recovery; that we thank our President, Francis E. Clark, for the words of this year, which rang with an emphasis and power even surpassing his own previous utterances.

Resolved, That we bear to our President and his wife our hearty greetings as they begin their world-round journey; that we shall follow them, especially in their tour of the mission stations, as they carry aid and comfort to the lonely toilers who have chosen heathenism for their companionship and exile for their home.

Resolved, That we thank the United Society for its wise and economical business management, for its unselfish spirit, and for its utter refusal, now as in the past, to receive any tax or ask any allegiance from Christian Endeavor societies.

Resolved, That we again declare the pledge essential to a society of Endeavor, and that those who in any way weaken it or tamper with the principle of obligation as embodied in the covenant idea of the pledge are destroying the very foundations on which the society rests, and cannot be recognized as true societies of Christian Endeavor.

Resolved, That, as in the past, for the sake of preserving the integrity of our Christian Endeavor unions, local, State, and international, they should be composed only of Endeavor societies in fact and in name, though the name may be united with any denominational name; and no allegiance is claimed by any Christian Endeavor union or convention, all authority over every society of Christian Endeavor being vested in the local church and the denomination with which it is connected.

Resolved, That it is our steadfast opinion that in our State and Provincial unions the best service is voluntary, unpaid service. While our secretaries should have enough clerical aid, we believe that the Christian Endeavor spirit of voluntary official service in the various States should always prevail.

Resolved, That we recall with joy that during the year 120,000 members have been won for Christ, and united with the Church; that we recognize in the Christian Endeavor movement the greatest evangelistic agency of our time. It wins souls for the Master, and then educates them for service.

Resolved, That we will pray more fervently for power, and give ourselves more heartily in individual effort to win men to righteousness.

Resolved, That we emphasize the sacred cause of missions, and that we will pray for and practice a warm-hearted and broad-handed liberality.

Resolved, As we turn our faces toward Montreal, that we recognize that

Christian Endeavor is not for one nation or one people, but for the whole world.

Believing that the Columbian Exposition, in which our patriotic pride is enlisted, should be the highest exponent of our civilization, and should not be degraded by lawlessness in any form, we renew our earnest protest against the opening of the World's Fair gates on Sunday.

We respectfully petition the United States Congress to make Sunday closing a condition of further appropriations to the fair, believing that we thus express the convictions of the majority of the American people.

And we earnestly request the Board of Control in Chicago that in the management of its trust it respects the precepts of American law, the precedents of American history, the present and future welfare of the American workingman, and the sacred and perpetual rights of the Christian conscience.

Furthermore, we believe that multitudes of Christian people will find it impossible to patronize a Sabbath-disregarding exposition.

Resolved, That we declare our allegiance to the sacred observance of the Lord's Day; that we believe it to be one of the corner stones of our civil and religious institutions, and that we will, as patriots and as Christians, in every way guard its sanctity and preserve it from desecration.

Recognizing in the liquor traffic the giant evil of our day :

Resolved, That we condemn intemperance in every form; that we stand for total abstinence, for the suppression of the saloon, and for the dethronement of its power in the politics of our land.

Resolved, That we join in the petition which is being sent to the governments of the world asking them to raise the standard of the law to that of Christian morals, to strip away the safeguards and sanctions of the State from the drink traffic, and to protect our homes by the total prohibition of the curse, the heaviest that rests on our civilization.

The reading of these resolutions was interrupted by frequent and long-continued applause, and at the close they were unanimously adopted with much enthusiasm. After the singing of a hymn, "As pants the hart," telegrams of greeting were read from the Chautauqua Christian Endeavor society, and others. Rev. Mr. Karmarkar and his wife, clad in Hindoo costume, then sang a hymn in the Mahratti language, Mrs. Karmarkar playing a weird accompaniment on the organ and her husband keeping time on a curious instrument something like a pair of castanets. Dr. Clark then made the usual request — that during the rest of the program and the consecration service the audience refrain from loud applause and confine their demonstrations of approval simply to the waving of handkerchiefs.

Dr. CLARK: And now we will listen to a representative of the Methodist Church of Canada, — a church which you know has endorsed and accepted what we believe in so thoroughly, and calls its young people's societies "Epworth Leagues of Christian Endeavor," — Rev. S. P. Rose, D.D., of Montreal.

ADDRESS OF REV. S. P. ROSE, D.D.

Dr. ROSE: It is a noteworthy and significant fact that we are indebted to the enemies of our Lord for one of the acutest and most accurate analyses of Christ's life and character which have come down to us. Standing under the shadow of the cross, they exclaimed, "He saved others, himself he cannot save." And they were right. Unconscious prophets, they foretold a great truth, the meaning and depth of which we have not yet begun to fathom. Jesus could not save himself and be the Saviour of others. Only so far as he forgot himself could he remember others to their advantage. Only by refusing to save himself could he become the Saviour of the world.

This great truth reaches its climax at Calvary. But the alternative, self or others, was continually presenting itself upon Christ's conscience and heart. It met him upon the very threshold of his earthly career. St. Paul teaches that when he says, "For ye know the grace of our Lord Jesus Christ, that, though he was rich, yet for your sakes he became poor, that ye through his poverty might be made rich." The question which confronted Jesus at his incarnation was, Shall I save myself the poverty of earthly existence, or become the saviour of the world. Happily for us his grace was such that we have become rich through his poverty. But who can estimate the wealth which he resigned or the poverty which he assumed? Think of the wealth of adoration which was his! And for what did he exchange this? The hootings of an angry mob and the demand by the multitude that he should be crucified. Consider the wealth of fellowship which he resigned for the companionship of men and women the best of whom misunderstood him and misinterpreted the meaning of his mission. This problem — self or others — confronts Jesus again at that hour of his life when the curtain rises upon the temptation in the wilderness. The alternative here presents itself in three forms: First, shall I save myself the pangs of hunger, or endure these that others may have the Bread of Life? This was really the meaning of the first temptation to our Lord. The second form of this alternative appears in the temptation to bow himself at Satan's feet and worship him, — a temptation really to adopt a carnal method of accomplishing his mission, and thus to save himself the agony of a death upon Calvary. Yet again the alternative is presented to Jesus in the third temptation, which in effect suggested to him the method of saving himself from men's scorn and unbelief by means of a miracle which should compel their confidence and lead them to a faith in his divinity.

This alternative of which I am speaking was a constantly recurring one in the life of Jesus. Take two or three typical examples. It is in the second year of his public ministry, the year of popular favor. The demands of the multitude upon his time are so great that he has not time so much as to eat. He proposes to his disciples that they go into a "desert place" and rest a while. By some means the multitude becomes aware of his intention, and when Jesus and his disciples reach the place which they have chosen for rest, they find a vast company awaiting them. Does he rebuke the multitude for following him? Nay, but self-forgotten, he ministers to their necessity, even working a miracle to save them from hunger, a thing which he would not do for himself.

Stand with bared head and unsandalled feet in the garden and listen to the cry, "Father, if it be possible, let this cup pass from me." But he could not save himself the bitterness of this cup and be our Saviour, and so he drinks it to its very dregs. The hour is over, the agony of death is passed, when his enemies come up against him as against a thief. One of his disciples, in the ardor of his love to Jesus, takes his sword and cuts off the ear of the servant of the high priest. But Jesus, rebuking his follower's zeal, heals the wounded man and declares that his action is voluntary, that he accepts his fate, that we may be delivered from the evil to come. For the last time that alternative meets him upon Calvary. Standing at his feet men said to him, " Come down from the cross, if thou be the Son of God, and we will believe in thee." Some of them meant it; some of them thought they would believe. But Christ could not; he bore that awful hour, and his foes were right — he could not come down from the cross. There is no truth in the Bible more certain than that which they uttered, unconscious prophets as they were : " He saved others, himself he cannot save."

Dear friends, fellow-Endeavorers, this is my thought to-night : That very same alternative which was Christ's presses itself in upon the hearts and consciences of those who would be his disciples. You to-night must face that problem. We must find Christ our example. Salvation, if it means anything, is salvation unto Christ's likeness; and if that is to come, we must take up his mission and carry it forward. We must know something of Gethsemane; we must not shrink back from something of the bitterness of Calvary. Did you ever think of it, — that the world's greatest heroes have been confronted by that same problem, self or others, and have found for it our Lord's solution? Who is your greatest hero in the Old Testament? I cannot give your answer, but I make my confession that Moses is to me, with his peerless faith, above them all. Recall to mind that wonderful hour in the life of Moses when he stood as mediator between the people and God, and cried that if God could but forgive them, his name might be blotted out. Whom do you respect most in New Testament times, Christ excepted? I bow in reverence of thought before Paul; and if there were no Christ, I think I could worship him. Yet Paul desired that he might be anathematized, if it were possible to save Israel. You and I sit in our easy chairs, and we say such a wish is Eastern hyperbole. No, it was the facing of this problem,— this alternative,— self or others. Let me take you into my confidence so far as to say my favorite in secular history is William the Silent. You will remember how that problem came in upon his life. He could not be the saviour of the Netherlands and save himself; and so he accepted loss of place and wealth,— yea, he accepted death,—that the Netherlands might be free. And, dear friends, if you and I would be Christlike, if you and I would take up Christ's work, if we would go from this convention to make it real to the world, it must be because we are willing to consecrate self, to annihilate self, to lose self, that others may be saved. Is not that Christ's word? He says, " He that will save his life shall lose it, and he that will lose his life for my sake and the Gospel, the same shall save it." We cannot compound with duty here. We have entered upon a warfare that does not admit of buying up substitutes.

But having said this emphatically, I want to add just as emphatically that refusal to save one's self is not committing suicide. Jesus himself kept his life from harm until the hour came when he should die. Further, refusal to save ourselves may not mean death; it may mean something else than dying for people; it may mean what is sometimes a great deal more — it may mean living for people. That is a brave man who goes forth to the battlefield and dies; perhaps that is a braver man who stays at home and lives and gives out his life, though it be by piecemeal, that others may be helped.

But it is only by the application to our lives of the same rule as that which governed Jesus that we may hope to become Christlike, that we may know the meaning of salvation, that we may carry forward his work.

Some months ago, in a church of which I was then pastor, an elect lady from your own country, Mrs. Barry, representing the Woman's Christian Temperance Union, delivered an address in which she told an incident that was new to us. It may not be new to you, but if it is an old story, forgive me. Mrs. Barry vouched for the incident, which melted our hearts. It had relation to that awful period of yours which is happily becoming a memory to most, a legend and a tradition to many. A soldier found himself a prisoner in one of the prisons of the South. One day there came in an exchange list by reason of which he would be transferred from the prison in exchange for one of the opposite army. Before he went out, he went through the prison to speak to his comrades. He came to one who said to him, "I cannot help envying you. I have a mother and a wife and children at home; will you take them my greetings?" There came into the mind of that man this thought: Shall I go forth or stay? And he met Christ's problem, and found for it Christ's solution. He said to his comrade, "You go out and let me stay; you take my number, and go to those whom you love." After some persuasion the exchange was effected, and our Christian hero stayed behind. A second exchange list came in, and wonderful to relate, the name of this same man was upon it again, and again the opportunity for leaving the prison was his. He went to say good-by to his comrades once more, intending to go out, but he came to one man who was dying because of the heat of the prison and the impure air, and again Christ's problem met him, and he said to this man, "I want you to go;" and he persuaded him to take his number and go forth from the prison. Singular to say, for the third time when the exchange list came in that same name appeared. "Now," he said, "I am going; I have earned the right to go; nobody shall keep me here any longer." But there was one man in the prison in whom he was especially interested, a man who refused all overtures to lead him to Christ. So he went to him and said, "I am going to be a free man. But before I go I want to read the Bible with you and pray." His request was met with curses. The man exclaimed, "I do not believe in your Bible or in your God; I do not believe in godliness, or else there would be more of it." Then there came to our hero the thought, "I may save that man's soul by self-sacrifice;" and he said to the man, "I want you to go in my place." "What!" "Yes, I do; take my number, stand in the ranks when the list is made up, and I will stay here in your place." "Well, I will go; and since you are so anxious about it, you may pray with me before I go." He went out a free man, and when he looked up to the vaulted sky and breathed the air of freedom, he said, "I want to find out that man's God; such a religion as that means something."

Dear friends, we are going out into the world. Believe me, as we go hence we are to prove the reality of the value of this organization and of this convention by Christ-likeness; and if we have that, if his spirit is in us, we shall annihilate self, if need be; we shall be willing to die, if he so call us to do, that others may be saved. As we gaze toward these peaks of Christian living, do our brains reel and our hearts fail us from fear? No wonder; we stand at the base of the mountain upon the summit of which Jesus himself lived; but these mountain peaks do not cleave the air to be admired, but to be climbed. Jesus is not a dream of poets; Christ is our example. Calvary was not meant to save us from pain alone, nor from hell only. Calvary stands as an example, and if it be anything, it stands as an example of sacrifice to those who propose to work for Christ and the Church. Consecrate yourselves to that self-sacrifice, I beseech you, to-night. Great is your reward if you do, for suffering with him you shall also reign with him. If you pay the price of self-sacrifice, you shall gain the reward, the great reward of Eternal favor. Let me press this thought in upon you to-night; it is my message to you. God grant that it may touch your hearts! To be saved is to be Christ-like; and salvation that does not produce Christ-likeness is not New Testament salvation. To be Christ-like is to please not ourselves; to be Christ-like is to remember that if we save our lives we lose them; to be Christ-like is to breathe in the truth which the enemies of Christ proclaimed: "He saved others, himself he cannot save." God help us to understand that truth, to go forth from this hour giving ourselves to his service, whether that service be life or death. May he give us all his Spirit!

This earnest address of Dr. Rose was received with silent, yet very impressive approval, by the delegates waving handkerchiefs. After the announcement of several notices and the singing of the hymn "Christ my all," at the request of Dr. Clark the members of the Committee of '92 came forward and stood upon the platform.

Dr. CLARK: The supreme, the closing hour of this convention has almost come. The Committee on Resolutions have reported, and you have adopted their resolutions, voicing so heartily our thanks to the Committee of 1892. I am sure that it is appropriate for me, in your behalf, to add another word to theirs. My friends, [*addressing the Committee of 1892*] we appreciate your heroic efforts. I use that word heroic advisedly. We know something of the large expense and the amount of time and strength which you have put into this convention, and we congratulate you with all our hearts on the success of your achievements, and we thank you. For the dear brother who has been at the head of this coommittee I have come to have not only a profound respect but a deep, abiding affection. And for all these brothers I have the same regard, which I am sure is in your hearts. As the history of this great convention shall be written there will be inscribed across it, in letters of gold, the names of Henry T. McEwen and the members of the Committee of '92. If that be your pleasure, let them know it. [*Here followed an enthusiastic salute of handkerchiefs, led by the President.*]

Mr. McEWEN: *Dear brothers and sisters:* Perhaps this is an appropriate time for me to give you a little bit of inside history. Sometimes such conventions — I do not say Christian Endeavor conventions — are asked for because of local pride. We did not go to Minneapolis to ask for the convention because of local pride in our two great cities. We went to ask for the convention because of local need. Some people say, What is the good of a convention? Well, God found it of some use when Elijah was discouraged to tell him that there were 7,000 men who had not bowed the knee to Baal. The fight against sin and Satan in New York and Brooklyn is a hard fight. Some of the brethren, old heroes, were getting a little discouraged, and some of us younger men believed that it would be a good thing for these old soldiers to know that there was a mighty army of which they constituted but a part. So we asked you here because we believed that it was a strategic thing to do for the work of the Master, as well as a heroic thing. Now, I would like to say, with reference to our work, this: I hope you will forgive and forget our mistakes and shortcomings. Please do not think of them. We know them better than you possibly can, and we are more sorry for them than you can ever possibly be. But remember why we are here, whom we serve, and whose we are. It was not that you might see our great city; it was that all might receive the blessing of God.

And I ought to say a word for these brethren constituting this Committee of '92. A more loyal, self-sacrificing set of men never backed a chairman, and I am not willing that the praise should be put on me one whit more than upon them. I am sorry that one of my men is worn out and not able to be here.

I also would like to emphasize just one other thought, and that is, the delightful harmony with which Brooklyn and New York have worked together.

And now, if you approve of what I say, I hope you will manifest it by the waving of handkerchiefs. Our dear brother Clark, as you know, starts in a few days on his journey around the world. As chairman of the Committee of Arrangements for '92 I have thought that it might be an appropriate thing for us to send our greetings of love and affection to our brothers and sisters across the sea, in whatever land Dr. Clark may find them. If you approve of that, make it manifest. [*The audience instantly joined in the most vigorous waving of handkerchiefs.*]

Dr. CLARK: I will carry your beautiful white message, my friends. [*Salute renewed.*]

Mr. McEWEN: Just one further word, by way of explanation and apology, which I believe is your due. I could not permit the convention to close without explaining why you have heard so much from the chairman of the Committee.

COMMITTEE OF '92

1. Rev. H. T. McEwen.
2. Augustus V. Heely.
3. Josiah R. Wray.
4. J. Wilford Allen
5. Levi S. Hulse.
6. Parsells Cole.
7. M. S. Littlefield, Jr
8. W. F. Stevens.
9. Charles Caldwell.
10. Harold M. Davis.
11. J. A. Cruikshank.
12. Charles J. Frye, Jr

It has not been my wish; but when Mr. Baer found that he could not be with us, he wrote asking me if I would not stand at the desk and help President Clark. It was the last thing I had thought of doing. I had arranged to be at another desk, ready to serve you in any way I could; but when the request came from him, coupled, as I knew it was, with his great personal sorrow, I had not the heart to refuse. This explains to you why I have been so much before you when I would otherwise have been silent. [*Chautauqua salute.*]

At this point Mr. Sankey introduced Miss Ruth Thompson, of Washington, a young lady with a voice of rare sweetness and power, who rendered the hymn "Only remembered by what we have done," the audience joining in the chorus. The soloist received the heartiest approval of the audience. In connection with this hymn, Mr. Sankey referred to the incident at the Minneapolis convention when Dr. Clark read a telegram concerning the illness of Mr. Spurgeon in London, and said that he was present eight months afterward at the funeral of Mr. Spurgeon in the Tabernacle, where he sang this same hymn, surrounded by the friends of the great preacher.

Dr. CLARK: Before I go on to call the roll of the States, it is appropriate for me to say a word, I think, to this congregation — a word of grateful thanks and appreciation for your kindness to the different chairmen of these meetings. I am sure that I speak for the others who have presided as I speak for myself, from my inmost heart, when I thank you for your patience, for your considerateness, and for your forbearance. I think the patience of this great audience, their silence for the most part, and the kindness with which they have listened when it has been so difficult to hear, have been almost marvellous; and I am grateful to you for doing what you could to make the meetings what they have been. We also are grateful that no one has allowed his personal preference or his special desire for anything to be done or any measure promoted, to mar the harmony which has always marked these delightful conventions. For eleven years there has never been a single ripple of that sort; in eleven years no one has ever come here to push his own scheme, to advertise himself, to find an office, or to get something for himself or his.

A great many requests have come up from this audience, many of which could not be announced in any way. We have considered them all carefully; they have been laid before those whose duty it was to consider them; they have not been hastily put to one side. It has always been because it seemed to us impossible, viewing the best interests of the convention, to pay attention to them, that so many requests have not received the attention which some people desired. But you have not complained; you have been patient; you have been forbearing; you have endured the discomforts, and they all have been swallowed up in the magnificent enthusiasm and inspiration and fellowship of this great meeting. You have honored your badges, my friends, and the badges have honored you. I do not believe that any of you have been where you would not like to have a Christian Endeavor badge seen. I would like to have our friends of the press, who have been so very generous and kind to us, note that there are pieces of ribbon besides Christian Endeavor badges, and that they may have sometimes been seen in doubtful places; also, that some Christian Endeavor badges have not been worn by Christian Endeavorers, certainly not those that were stolen from a certain delegation. But you, my friends, have honored your badges, as they have honored you, and I think that we can thank God and congratulate this convention that throughout all the city of New York it has been what it has been during these last days — the grandest, the greatest, the most magnificent Christian Endeavor convention ever held. Is it too much to say that it has been the grandest in some respects — we would be modest — the grandest religious convention in some respects ever known in the history of the world? [*Chautauqua salute.*]

And now we come to the closing hour. What will this mean for us? We are not simply to felicitate ourselves upon the past. We are not to congratulate ourselves on these 30,000 delegates, on these eleven different meetings which are now being held in different parts of New York and Brooklyn, crowded, I presume, every one of them, as I know some of them are, to the doors. We need not say anything about all this. We are children of the future. We have our faces toward the rising sun. What about the days to come? This convention, this consecration meeting, will have something to do with the days to come. And you have a vast responsibility upon you, my friends, those of you who are here, to carry back the influence of this meeting to all the cities, to all the States and Provinces in this North American continent, and to the rest of the world. In a little while, as our beloved chairman of the Committee of '92 has stated, I start for Australia, and then for China, Japan, India, Turkey, Italy, Spain, and England, where I shall attend the English convention in '93, reaching Montreal for our convention next July. I shall take with me this most wonderful sight, these waving handkerchiefs, this message of good cheer and "God bless you" to our Christian Endeavor brothers and sisters. It is not to be a junket; it is not to be a sight-seeing tour; it is not simply a trip around the world. It is for Christian Endeavor work, and for the purpose of attending conventions that have been planned in Australia, in India, in Turkey, and in all these lands. I shall take with me your "Godspeed" and "God bless you."

And now, as we come to this last hour of the evening, let us consecrate ourselves, forgetting the things that are behind and reaching forth to those that are before. Let us consecrate ourselves to higher purposes and larger aims, to more faithful service, to more intense fellowship, and to the enlargement of our brotherhood for Christ and the Church. Brothers and sisters of the Christian Endeavor, as the roll of your States is called, will you respond in the name of Christ? Will you say individually, putting the emphasis upon the personal pronoun, "As for me, I will serve the Lord?" Let us enter upon this hour with a moment of silent prayer.

The convention joined in silent prayer, and at the request of Dr. Clark every fan, even, was kept perfectly still.

Dr. CLARK: O Lord, utterly, intelligently, and forever we would consecrate ourselves to thee through Jesus Christ, our Lord. [*The audience responded*, "*Amen.*"]

Then, in response to Dr. Clark's request, all who were pastors in the audience rose and repeated together, as their word of testimony: "I am not ashamed of the Gospel of Christ."

The choir came next, with the verse: "I will sing unto the Lord as long as I live."

All Sunday-school teachers in the audience rose and repeated the verse: "Suffer little children to come unto me, and forbid them not, for of such is the kingdom of heaven."

Then all the day-school teachers in the audience — and there were a very large number — repeated, at Dr. Clark's suggestion: "Learn of me, for I am meek and lowly in heart, and ye shall find rest unto your souls."

Dr. Clark then began on the roll of States, and this was the most impressive feature of the service. The delegations rose in their places as they were called, and repeated a sentence of Scripture or joined in a hymn of consecration. Every delegation received the salute of the audience when its testimony was concluded.

The responses were as follows :

ALABAMA: "I will say to the North, Give up, and to the South, Keep not back: bring my sons from afar and my daughters from the ends of the earth." (Isa. 43: 6.)

ARKANSAS: "This one thing I do,' etc. (Phil. 3: 13, 14.)

CALIFORNIA, COLORADO, AND NEW MEXICO: "He that dwelleth in the secret place of the Most High," etc. (Ps. 91: 1, 2.)

CANADA: Hymn, "What a wonderful Saviour."

DR. CLARK: I am only standing here as the leader of this meeting in the place of our dear friend and brother, Mr. Baer, who was to have had charge of this service. But he has not forgotten us, and he sends us this word of greeting: "At the hour of your closing consecration service I shall be telling God that I am willing to be made willing about everything; that though separated from you all, I want to add my prayer of consecration to yours: My time for God, my strength for God, my thought for God."

Mr. Sankey, at Dr. Clark's request, here led in prayer for Mr. Baer's recovery, and Dr. Clark repeated his statement that Mr. Baer would still continue his office work as secretary.

CONNECTICUT: "Our prayer is: All our associate members for Christ."

DELAWARE: "For I am persuaded that neither death nor life," etc. (Rom. 8: 38, 39.)

DISTRICT OF COLUMBIA: "I beseech you, therefore, brethren," etc. (Rom. 12: 1.) Hymn, "Consecrate me now."

FRORIDA: Hymn, "Work, for the night is coming."

GEORGIA: "The Lord is my shepherd," etc. (Ps. 23.)

ILLINOIS: "Wherefore, seeing we are compassed about by so great a cloud of witnesses," etc. (Heb. 12: 1, 2.) Hymn, "I need thee every hour."

INDIA: Dr. John S. Chandler, the veteran missionary who is about returning to India, rose in the gallery and was given a hearty ovation. Mr. and Mrs. Karmarkar on the platform repeated John 3: 16 in Mahratti, and sang a native hymn.

INDIANA: Hymn, "We'll be ready when the Bridegroom comes."

IOWA: "Stand, therefore, having your loins girt about with the truth," etc. (Eph. 6: 14-16.)

KANSAS: Original hymn, "Give me faith like Jesus."

KENTUCKY: "This one I thing do," etc. (Phil. 3: 13, 14.) Hymn, "Nearer my God, to Thee."

LOUISIANA: Recitation, "Lead us, Heavenly Father, o'er this world's tempestuous sea," etc.

DR. CLARK: We are thinking now, are we not, of those who are at home? They, too, are thinking of us. I suppose there are thousands of miniature Christian Endeavor conventions being held all over the country at this hour.

They are praying for us; shall we not pray for them? I will ask Mr. Stebbins to voice our petition for our friends at home. [*Mr. Stebbins offered prayer.*]

MAINE: Hymn. "Just as I am."

MARYLAND: "Teach me, O Lord, the way of thy statutes," etc. (Ps. 119: 33, 34.) Hymn, to tune, "Maryland, my Maryland."

MASSACHUSETTS: "Massachusetts pledges itself, by God's aid, that every one of us shall bring one soul to Christ this year." Hymn, "Bringing in the sheaves."

Dr. CLARK: In view of this pledge from Massachusetts, shall we not offer a prayer for our associate members? Dr. A. E. Kittredge will lead our petition. [*Dr. Kittredge offered prayer.*]

AUSTRALIA: "From the ends of the earth will I cry unto thee," etc. (Ps. 61 : 2.)

MICHIGAN: "I beseech you, therefore, brethren," etc. (Rom. 12 : 1.) Hymn, "More love to thee."

Dr. CLARK: These friends of ours have been living out their consecration during these days as well as singing it at this moment. Some of these States, Michigan, Georgia, and others, which have occupied seats in the rear of the hall where it must have been difficult to hear, have not made a word of complaint, to my knowledge, and they have enjoyed this convention as well as the rest of us because consecration has entered into these little things of their lives. [*Pronounced salute.*]

MINNESOTA: Hymn, "More love to thee, O Christ."

MISSOURI: "Create in me a clean heart, O God," etc. (Ps. 51: 10-13), recited alternately by the ladies and gentlemen, all uniting in the words, "Wherefore, seeing we are compassed about," etc. (Heb. 12: 1-2), and the hymn, "More of Jesus."

MONTANA: "For what the law could not do," etc. (Rom. 8: 3, 4.)

NEBRASKA: "The voice of one crying in the wilderness, Prepare ye the way of the Lord, make his paths straight." (Matt. 3: 3.) Original hymn, "Nebraska for Christ."

NEW HAMPSHIRE: "Create in me a clean heart," etc. (Ps. 51: 10.) Hymn, "I need thee every hour."

NEW MEXICO: "A little leaven leaveneth the whole lump." (1 Cor. 5-6.) "A Dios."

NEW JERSEY: Hymn, "At the cross," the delegates raising their right hands at the words, "Here, Lord, I give myself away."

NEW YORK: Hymn, "Jesus, keep me near the cross."

NORTH CAROLINA: We believe that the greatest thing in life is to be a Christian, and to this end we consecrate our lives." One verse of "Just as I am."

NORTH and SOUTH DAKOTA: "Jesus Christ, the same yesterday, today, and forever." Hymn, "Christ for the world we sing."

SANDWICH ISLANDS: "Go ye into all the world and preach the Gospel to every creature" (Mark 16: 15). "Be thou faithful unto death and I will give thee a crown of life." (Rev. 2: 10.)

Dr. CLARK: And now, in the hush of the moment, shall we unite in prayer for Christian Endeavorers in all the world, — for those especially in missionary lands? [*Rev. D. M. Pratt, of Portland, led in prayer.*]

OHIO: "We will remember the Sabbath day to keep it holy." Hymn, "Stand up for Jesus."

OKLAHOMA: "Surely God hath not dealt so with any nation." We lost the banner, but we go back to win Oklahoma for Christ.

OREGON: "For whatsoever is born of God overcometh the world," etc. (1 John 5: 4.) Hymn, "Stand up for Jesus."

PENNSYLVANIA: Hymn, "More love to thee."

RHODE ISLAND: "Fear not, little flock," etc. (Luke 12: 32.)

SOUTH CAROLINA: "Finally, brethren, whatsoever things are true," etc. (Phil. 4: 8.)

TENNESSEE: Hymn, "This is my story." Our State motto: "At least one soul this year for Christ for each active member."

TEXAS, WEST VIRGINIA, AND VIRGINIA: "Let the words of my mouth," etc. (Ps. 19: 14.) Hymn, "Consecrate me now."

VERMONT: "I press toward the mark," etc. (Phil. 3: 13.) Hymn, "In the cross of Christ I glory."

Dr. CLARK: It seems, does it not, my friends, as though the North and the South clasped hands in Christian Endeavor. God grant that Christian Endeavor may do something to bring us closer together and show us our kinship more than we have ever yet seen it. I will ask our honored friend, Dr. Philip Schaff, to lead us in prayer for God's blessing on North and South. [*Dr. Schaff offered prayer.*]

WASHINGTON: "As far as the east is from the west, so far hath he removed our transgressions from us." (Ps. 103: 12.)

WISCONSIN: Hymn, "Faith is the victory."

At this point Dr. Clark asked if there were delegates from any foreign countries who had not spoken. Immediately two delegates from Scotland gave their testimony, followed by one delegate from each of the following countries: West Indies, Persia, Spain, Russia, England, Asia Minor, China, West Africa, Assyria, Mexico and France. These delegates were received with great enthusiasm by the convention, though their testimonies were necessarily very brief.

Dr. Clark then asked all active members of the Christian Endeavor Society to rise, and nearly all the audience did so. Then he asked all who believed themselves to be Christians to join them, and a number more rose. Then he asked those who would like to join this host of active Christians to rise. Several responded to this last request, and after a moment of silent prayer Dr. Clark prayed for them. Then, while all were standing, he asked every one who would take the pledge which was presented at Minneapolis last year, to try to bring at least one soul to Christ during the year, to hold up their hands. The hands went up all over the audience, and at Dr. Clark's request every one joined in the old Roman *sacramentum*, " This for me! this for me!"

The closing hymn was then sung, " God be with you till we meet again," and with the Mizpah benediction Dr. Clark pronounced the Eleventh International Christian Endeavor Convention adjourned.

FIRST INTERNATIONAL
Junior Christian Endeavor Rally,

HELD AT THE

BROADWAY TABERNACLE, NEW YORK CITY,

On Saturday Afternoon, July 9, 1892, at 2.30 o'clock.

MRS. ALICE MAY SCUDDER, Presiding.

OPENING REMARKS.

Mrs. ALICE MAY SCUDDER: I am sure it is with great pleasure that we gather here to-day to look in one another's faces and listen to inspiring words from some of our most earnest Junior Endeavor leaders. To us has been given the special honor of holding the first Junior rally in connection with the International Convention. We do not, of course, equal in numbers the great gathering in the Madison Square Garden, but we may rival them in our earnest Christian Endeavor spirit.

This is our first International Junior rally, but it will not be the last [*applause*], for I dare prophesy that in less than ten years we shall gather by the thousands. This is even a possibility for 1893, if only this simple plan is followed: In every church where there is a senior society let there be organized a Junior Endeavor society. As the time of the convention draws near, appoint the same number of delegates from the junior as from the senior. Let one senior delegate take in charge one junior delegate, and the prophecy is fulfilled.

The Christian Endeavor of the future depends very much upon the right training of the juniors of to-day; and we should endeavor to bring them into large companies, in order that they may have the right training and enjoy Christian fellowship.

We shall open our service this afternoon by a service of song. We are very happy in having with us, as musical leader, Mr. George H. Corfield, of Jersey City, who is not only a fine musical leader and ardent lover of children, but an earnest Christian Endeavorer.

Here followed a praise service, conducted by Mr. George H. Corfield, after which the twenty-third psalm was recited, followed by prayer by the Rev. Mr. Savage.

Mrs. SCUDDER: Children, one of the greatest pleasures I have for you this afternoon is in introducing to you, perhaps to many of you for the first time, Rev. Charles F. Deems, D.D., LL. D., who will deliver the "Address of Welcome."

Rev. CHARLES DEEMS, D.D., LL.D.: I bring you most hearty welcome to New York, most hearty welcome to this Tabernacle, most hearty welcome to the first meeting of the Junior societies at an annual convention of the Young People's Society of Christian Endeavor.

I stand in this place at this hour and have a sense of sweet awfulness. I go back and remember when I was a boy like you. I was born an Endeavorer; my mother was an Endeavorer; my mother was a woman mighty in prayer. My father was a minister; my grandfather was a minister; and just as soon as I could begin to do anything, I began to endeavor, thank God.

My first endeavor was to induce my father, who was a clergyman, to sign a temperance pledge. He thought it was preposterous for him and me to sign temperance pledges, but at ten years of age that was accomplished, and my father lived and died a temperance worker. Then it was just fifty-nine years ago that I left my native city to go out to make my first public speeches, and they were both to assemblies of young people in the State of Maryland. That was my first, and I leave it to Mrs. Scudder or Mrs. Clark if that was n't a good beginning for a Junior Christian Endeavorer. The first speech was a Sunday-school speech; and boys, I have been at that temperance speaking ever since I commenced to endeavor that early.

When I look upon you and remember what your age is, and that by and by you will come to manhood and womanhood, I think what a sight you will see, what changes will come over this city and this country.

Boys, it was six years after that that I came to New York a licensed preacher and the highest house in the city was the Roosevelt house, on the corner of Sixteenth Street and Broadway. I remember there was a church somewhere down in Allen Street, and I was invited to preach there. They said a boy was going to preach, and it was so crowded they got me in at the window. My first Christian Endeavor in New York was through a window in a church, to preach the Gospel of the blessed God. That was fifty-three years ago, and from that time to this God has spared me.

I sat here this afternoon, and though I have had so many a cup of sorrow, so many a cup of trial in preaching the blessed gospel fifty-three years on four continents, my heart went up to God and said, "God, I thank thee. I thank thee that thou hast brought me to this hour, to this Tabernacle, to this scene; that thou hast conferred upon me the honor and pleasure of giving the first welcome to the first body of Junior Endeavorers assembled in annual convention." I shall thank God for it in heaven, and I forgive providence a great many things that have been very hard on me since I was a boy.

I welcome you. I welcome you, for your sakes. I welcome you because you are boys, and boys are such a wonderful institution; boys are such tremendous things; boys are such growing engines. I welcome all the boys here, because by and by the boys will all come to be men.

I welcome all the girls here, because it is not in nature to keep them back from some time being women. I welcome you: because I stand upon this elevation at this period of my life and look back and forward, and I see them coming, coming, generation after generation, first of Juniors, then of other young Christian Endeavorers, then the whole sacramental hosts of God's elect, solid, alert, powerful, with all the counsel of age and all the enthusiasm of youth; and I do not know but I shall live yet to see the world taken for Jesus. God grant I may; God grant you may! [*Applause.*]

I welcome you because I think that you are to lead the hosts hereafter. As I sat here, I thought of a little story, the story of a drummer boy. There was in the army of Napoleon a boy that was famous as a drummer boy. My boys, if you can't be the commander-in-chief, if you can't command a corps, or even a brigade, if you can't take the place of a captain in a company, at least a boy may be a drummer, and drums, boys, are wonderful for spreading enthusiasm. It so happened that this boy was in one of the battles,— I think it was on the Peninsular,—and the commander said to him: "Beat a retreat." The commander saw that the forces were going against the French and they were going to be beaten badly. " Beat a retreat." The little fellow straightened himself up, flung his drum in front of him and took hold of the sticks with which he beat his drum, and looking the man in the face, said: " I was drummer for La Paix. La Paix never commanded me to beat a retreat. But if you want me to beat a charge, I will beat such a charge as will make even the dead fall into line." And he fell to, and when the soldiers heard him, they rallied around the boy and left the commander-in-chief, and went forward so valiantly that they won the battle. Boys, boys, always learn to beat such a charge as shall make the dead fall in line, and never beat a retreat in this army. [*Applause.*]

Now, let me tell you a story about my Junior Endeavorers who meet in the church parlor every Tuesday afternoon. One afternoon I said to them: " Now, won't all you children remain, who are over twelve years of age and who would like to talk a quarter of an hour with me after you are through, and swap anecdotes, and so on." Well, all that were over twelve years did remain. We formed a little society, and one of the conundrums submitted was this: How young must a child be to be a Christian? We talked that over: and then we talked some other things over, one after another. By and by one of the little girls came up to me and said: " I want to join the church." " Certainly, my dear." And she was examined and joined the church. There was another child, a boy, who wanted to join the church, and there was a reason for his remaining over a few months. Now, those two children, I have accidentally learned by seeing a letter, happened to come together at the same watering-place — the boy that is a candidate for membership and the girl that was admitted at the last communion; and they put their heads together and said: " What shall we do now for this little town here?" And they went to the Methodist church and asked: " Mayn't we form a Junior Endeavor society here ?" There is a member of the church, and one who is not a member of the church, but both equally Junior Endeavor children, who are planning at that watering-place another Junior Endeavor society, and we will send delegates from both of them by next year to the meeting. [*Applause.*]

How many grandchildren do you think I've got? Guess. Look at me. How many grandchildren can you guess I have got? I have got some.

A VOICE: One.

Dr. DEEMS: One! Why, my darling, only one?

A VOICE: Four.

ANOTHER VOICE: Forty. [*Laughter.*]

Dr. DEEMS: Forty? Now stop right there, right between those two, because I have six in heaven and twelve on earth, and I love the whole eighteen as if they were forty. When a man has petted eighteen several and distinct grandchildren, born in the different parts of the United States, and living in different parts of the United States, don't you think he would have a right to go right down this aisle and kiss every one of you? [*Laughter.*] But that forty reminds me of a circumstance. I think I will tell it. I have a very dear little friend. I am very fond of him and he is very fond of me, and I don't mind telling you his name. His name is James G. Blaine, and he is a grandson of a former Secretary of State of this country. [*Applause.*] Since I have mentioned the name, I hope that while the children were clapping their sympathies went out to that afflicted family. Well, Jimmie Blaine, James Blaine, Jr., has great faith in me, and still more in his nurse, who is a wag of a woman. So, when the Christian Endeavorers began to pour into the New York hotel where

Jimmie and I both live, Jimmie said to her: "Fuller, what are these people making up beds for?" "Oh," said Fuller, "James, you must not ask me any questions. You see they are some more of Dr. Deems's children." He never said another word, and when I came up in the elevator James was there. "Well," said he, "Dr. Deems, there is about a hundred more of your children come to town." "Why," said I, "James, they are only Christian Endeavorers." "Yes," said he, "they are your children." "Oh, no," said I. "Yes," said he, "you must not say they are not, because Fuller says they are." "Why," said I, "James, do you think I have got 20,000 children and grandchildren?" "Yes, sir; every one of them." [*Laughter.*] That was the faith that boy has in the old man, you see.

My heart goes out to these Juniors naturally, and I have just told you these little things because I didn't care to make a set speech, and I love to talk to you in just this way. I welcome you in the name of that honored and beloved man, my friend, the sick pastor of this church, whom may God bless. Pray for him. I welcome you in the name of all these people who have taken such an interest in forming our society. I welcome you in the names of the hundreds of thousands of Junior societies that are to be formed hereafter. May God bless you. When you get to be as old as I am, may you be as happy as I am; and, when you and I pass over, may we be just as happy there as I believe my little grandchildren are, of whom I spoke to-day. God bless and comfort and help you; and if you do sing better when you cross over the river and get into the city of our God, O, children, may I be there to see you. And whoever shall go forward first of the older Christian Endeavor society or of the Junior Endeavor society, let us here pledge one another to welcome one another into the city of our God. God bless and comfort and strengthen you, and enable you to win the world for Jesus.

Mrs. SCUDDER: The Rev. Cornelius Brett, of Jersey City, has voiced the response to this hearty welcome in a beautiful poem, which is to be given to us by a member of his Junior Endeavor Society, Miss Lillian Taylor.

RESPONSE BY MISS LILLIAN TAYLOR.

A thousand thanks, dear Doctor Deems,
From every radiant eye now beams ;
Each flashing thought speech cannot find
Responsive to your welcome kind.

Never has such a youthful throng
Filled New York's streets with Christian song
As now on every side we see,
Gathering to keep their jubilee.

They come from near, they come from far,
By ferry-boat and sleeping-car,
From sunny South, and colder North,
From East and West, they issue forth.

From far Pacific's Golden Coast,
From cities of whose growth men boast,
From Canada, Victoria's Land,
A glorious "Endeavor Band."

While here, as welcome guests, they stay,
Our seniors in the holy way,
We juniors see the cross, our sign,
And heartily we fall in line.

Once on a time, the story's told,
Children of Christ, by faith made bold,
Enlisted in a great crusade,
The knights of the red cross to aid.

They gathered in a host of might,
Some armor-clad, some robed in white,
Eager to fight, and, for Christ's sake,
Mount Calvary from the Turks to take.

An enemy more fierce than Turk
On play-ground and in school does lurk;
Even the home may shut him in,
So subtle is the monster sin.

Soldiers of Christ, we rally here.
Faith is our shield, and zeal our spear;
Against our foe, with spirits brave,
We march, our native land to save.

We children, hope of Church and State,
Stand eager at the future's gate;
The seniors' place we soon must fill
Obedient to our Father's will.

The swiftly passing years move on,
Bearing us with them, one by one,
To larger deeds and purpose grand,
Still joined in our Endeavor Band.

Just for an hour we halt to-day,
Our hymns to sing, our verses say,
To wave aloft our banners bright,
And with the pledge our word to plight.

Thanks, then, to you, sir, we repeat;
Thanks, from each heart's responding beat
For greetings kind, and words of love;
May we of each most worthy prove.

Mrs. SCUDDER: You have heard a good deal about Father Endeavor Clark, and many of us in Jersey City have had the pleasure of hearing him and seeing him; but to-day we are to have the great pleasure of having with us Mrs. Clark — we may call her Mother Endeavor Clark. She is to speak to us upon the subject, "The Children for Christ." [*Chautauqua salute.*]

ADDRESS OF MRS. F. E. CLARK.

A great many, many years ago, before there were any Christian Endeavor meetings, before there was any New York, before even America had been discovered, in a country far across the sea, away in the land of Judea, there was a children's meeting held one bright day in early summer. In some respects that meeting was not at all like ours, and in others it was very much like it; but it had the same object as this, — to bring the children to Christ; and if it had not been for that meeting, perhaps this one would never have been called to meet here to-day. It was not held in a beautiful church like this, but out of doors in the country, under the green trees. You would have liked that, wouldn't you? Only a very few children were there. If they were here to-day, probably they could all be seated in four or five pews. The mothers were there too, and so there are some mothers here to-day. Some of those children were probably about the ages of those in these pews, and some were probably much younger. I have a little boy at home not quite two years old who would have liked to be here to-day, and he would have been very willing to take some part aside from singing in the meeting. I thought him rather too young to be a Junior Endeavorer, and left him at home; but if I could have gone to that meeting in Judea so many years ago, I should have been very glad to take him with me. This meeting was planned a good many weeks ago, and Mrs. Scudder has taken great pains to make it a meeting that will be not only interesting but helpful.

That meeting probably was not planned at all. Perhaps one mother thought of it and invited a few more, and that was all the planning there was. A poet has told the story of that meeting so beautifully, that I think I will tell it to you in just her words. One would almost think she had been there herself, as she tells us the story.

"The Master has come over Jordan,"
 Said Hannah, the mother, one day;
"He is healing the people who throng him
 With a touch of his finger, they say;
And now I shall carry the children,
 Little Rachel and Samuel and John;
I shall carry the baby, Esther,
 For the Lord to look upon."

The father looked at her kindly,
 But he shook his head and smiled;
"Now, who but a doting mother
 Would think of a thing so wild?
If the children were tortured by demons,
 Or dying of fever, 'twere well;
Or had they the taint of the leper,
 Like many in Israel."

"Nay, do not hinder me, Nathan;
 I feel such a burden of care,
If I carry it to the Master,
 Perhaps I shall leave it there.
If he lay his hands on the children,
 My heart will be lighter, I know;
For a blessing forever and ever
 Will follow them as they go."

So over the hills of Judah,
 Along by the vine-rows green,
With Esther asleep on her bosom,
 And Rachel her brothers between,
'Mong the people who hung on his teaching,
 Or waited his touch and his word.
Through the row of proud Pharisees listening,
 She pressed to the feet of her Lord.

"Now, why shoulds't thou hinder the Master,"
 Said Peter, "with children like these?"
"Seest not how, from morning till evening,
 He teacheth and healeth disease?"
Then Christ said: "Forbid not the children,
 Permit them to come unto me."
And he took in his arms little Esther,
 And Rachel he sat on his knee.

And the heavy heart of the mother
 Was lifted all earth-care above,
And he laid his hands on the brothers
 And blest them with tenderest love,—
As he said of the babes in his bosom,
 "Of such is the kingdom of heaven."
And strength for all duty and trial
 That hour to her spirit was given.

Would not you like to have been at that meeting? What a beautiful thing it must have been for those children to remember all their lives. Wouldn't you like to have had Jesus lay his hands on your head in blessing? Wouldn't you like to have looked right into his face as he said: "Suffer the little children to come unto me"? It seems very beautiful as we think about it, and yet in many ways you have better opportunities than those children had. They came to Jesus just *once*, and you can come to him *every day*. You cannot look into his face or hear his voice, but he can hear you, and you can speak to him whenever you will, and he will always answer your prayers. He may not give you just what you ask for, any more than he would have given those children everything they chose to ask for that day, but you can always feel sure that he will give you a blessing, and that he will give you just what is best for you; and that is what you really want, isn't it?

The disciples tried to keep the children away from Jesus then. They thought he was too busy with more important matters to be bothered with the babies and little children. Christ's disciples know better now, and they want to help the children, and show them the way to Jesus, and how they may work for him. That is just why we have all these Junior Endeavor societies. A few years ago one of Christ's disciples thought that perhaps the children did not know the way to Jesus, or what they could do for him. So one Junior Endeavor society was started, just to help the children to come to Jesus. Then other disciples heard of it, and thought it would be a good way to help other children, and so more societies were formed, till now there are a great many, and they are all for the same purpose — to bring the children to Jesus.

I suppose most of you here to-day have signed the Junior Endeavor pledge, and you have promised that all your lives you will try to do whatever Jesus would like to have you do. Now, if you go faithfully every week to your Junior Endeavor meeting, you will learn some of the things he wants to have you do, and how to do them. Whenever you are working on the lookout committee, trying to be faithful yourself and helping others to be faithful, you are doing something he would like to have you do. Whenever you are working on the missionary committee, trying to help the little children way across the sea who have never heard of Jesus, you are working for him. Whenever you are faithful to your duties at home or at school, you are pleasing him, and the more you work for Jesus the more you will love him.

As we think of all this to-day, as we look at all the children gathered here, we think once more of that little meeting held so long ago when those few mothers brought their children to Jesus. Shall we not all, old and young, come to him now, to-day, asking for a blessing, and promising better service for the future? Shall not we who are older realize our responsibility and opportunity and let our one aim and purpose be this: "The children for Christ?" Let us make the way very plain and easy for them, and may we bring them with the same loving faith that those mothers showed so long ago. And having once brought them to Christ, let us lovingly and prayerfully guide and help them, that they may keep ever in the narrow way and may live always very near to Jesus. We cannot believe that those children who really looked into Christ's face and heard his loving voice could ever wander away from him, or that they would ever forget that day, and our hearts echo the words of one who has so beautifully told the story in verse: —

> I wonder if ever the children
>   Who were blessed by the Master of old
> Forgot he had made them his treasures.
>   The dear little lambs of his fold?
> I wonder if, angry and wilful,
>   They wandered afar and astray —
> The children whose feet had been guided
>   So safe and so soon in the way?
>
> One would think that the mothers at evening,
>   Soft smoothing the silk-tangled hair,
> And low leaning down to the murmur
>   Of sweet childish voices in prayer,
> Oft bade the small pleaders to listen,
>   If haply again they might hear
> The words of the gentle Redeemer
>   Borne swift to the reverent ear.
>
> And my heart cannot cherish the fancy
>   That ever these children went wrong,
> And were lost from the peace and the shelter,
>   Shut out from the feast and the song.
> To the day of gray hairs they remembered,
>   I think, how the hands that were riven
> Were laid on their heads when he uttered,
>   "Of such is the kingdom of heaven."
>
> He has said it to you, dear children,
>   Who read it in God's word to-day;
> You, too, may be sorry for sinning,
>   You also believe and obey.

And 'twill grieve the dear Saviour in heaven
If one little child shall go wrong —
Be lost from the fold and the shelter,
Shut out from the feast and the song. [*Applause.*]

[NOTE.— It seems appropriate to have the Juniors themselves represented in the illustrations, and so, without asking permission, we have inserted this picture of Mrs. Clark and her children, two of whom are members of a Junior Society, and the others probably will be when old enough.]

Mrs. SCUDDER: To a part of this audience the Rev. C. H. Tyndall will need no introduction, for we of Jersey City will not soon forget the helpful talk on traps that he gave at our local union meeting. If he didn't set the traps of Satan in plain view to those boys and girls, they couldn't be set out; and he is going to speak to us to-day on the "Work of the Temperance Committee," and I hope the effect of it will be that not one of these juniors here will ever touch a drop of liquor.

ADDRESS OF REV. C. H. TYNDALL.

Well, how do I look, anyway. [*Laughter.*] I will tell you how I feel. I feel just as I used to imagine the Israelites felt when they were in the wilderness. When I was a little boy I read in the Bible that God said his people were a stiff-necked people, and I said to myself, "Well, they must be a sorry lot." I feel a good deal as I used to imagine the Israelites felt — a sort of stiff-necked Jew. Well, they did some very strange things in the wilderness, and I shouldn't be surprised if I did some strange things too, for I very often do very strange things.

To begin with, I want you to look very sharply at what I have in this bag here. It is not a cat, and I am not going to let the cat out of the bag; but I will show you, as I know boys and girls like to look at things rather than to just hear things. You see that is a balloon, and you know where we expect balloons to go, if we let go of them, don't you? We expect that they are going to go up. But this is a peculiar kind of balloon. You see, it has the word " Boy " on it. Now I just let go of this balloon, and you see it falls; it goes down. I let go of it again, and it goes down; and if I should let go of it, and there were a deep hole here, that balloon would go down just as far as the hole would let it. The reason for that is because it is filled with a heavy gas. It has the wrong kind of material in it to let it go up. It is like a good many boys and girls I have seen; they invariably go down. Oh, yes, father and mother think they are going to go up; the Sunday-school teacher thinks they are going to go up; but invariably, when they begin to act for themselves, they go down, just like that balloon, and they keep on going down, and I don't know as they ever stop.

I heard of a little boy who went out one day and who saw a bird's nest, and he said, "There are some nice eggs; I will have some eggs." He took hold of the nest and tore it down, took the eggs and put them in his pocket, and started home perfectly happy. At night the old birds came there, and they sat on the tree, and they chirped and chirped, and cried that their house had been torn down, everything they had had been destroyed, and they had to sit out all night, having no nest, no house to live in. The birds were made very unhappy just to satisfy the cruel delight of a little boy for a few minutes. Over in England there is a mound in one of the prison yards. Under that mound is buried the body of a man who was so cruel that he killed a fellow-man, and that murderer was that little boy. He began by being cruel. He began by going down a little like that, and he kept on going down. So we don't know when boys and girls and women begin to do sin where they are going to stop; and when they begin to be intemperate, we don't know where they are going to stop. Do you know why men and women are drunkards? Why, it is because they have the wrong kind of spirit in them, and you can't expect them to go up until they have that wrong spirit taken out of them and another kind of spirit put in.

Now, I have a different kind of balloon from that here, and I am sure you will be glad to see a real, genuine balloon, for boys and girls do not like shams any more than any body else. That is a balloon that will go up. You see I have a Junior Endeavor badge outlined on it. [*Applause.*] Oh, yes, the Junior Endeavorers go up, don't they? We expect they are all going to go up. They have got the right kind of material in them, — that is the reason. How nicely it would soar up, if I would let it. Now, we will suppose that that represents a boy, and he is a member of the Junior Endeavor society, perhaps in my church or in Mrs. Scudder's, and we will say his name is Willie. Willie says to his mother, "Mamma, I would like to go over and play with Jack." This is Jack. Jack swears once in a while, and he lies, and he thinks it is very smart to swagger, making believe he is drunk. Willie's mother says to him, "Willie, I don't think you ought to go and play with Jack, because I hear Jack is a bad boy and he says bad words." "Well, you know, mother, I joined the Endeavor society, and I am going up to heaven; I am on the right road and Jack is going down, and I think if I go over and become friends with Jack, I shall lift him up; I think I will pull him up and make something of him." The mother thinks that is pretty good logic, and she says, "Well, my boy, you may go." So he goes over and they are joined right together just as I am going to join these balloons, and I will show you the way it works. Do you know how it works? You expect, of course, that the big balloon, the one that is going up, is going to take the little one up. We will see. Ah, yes; Jack pulls Willie down. Let us try it again. "Now Jack, you must go up with Willie; you are a bad boy, but Willie has the right spirit in him; he is going to take you up." Now, we will see whether the good boy will pull the bad boy up, or the bad boy will pull the good boy down. I do it again. Invariably Jack will pull Willie down. What is to be done? I have a penknife here, and I will show you what must be done.

Ah, that is the way. Just cut right loose from the bad boys who drink and swear and lie, and think it is smart to smoke cigarettes, and then he will go up, won't he? [*Applause.*]

Well, sometimes the boys and girls really surprise us. They don't go up as well as we expect. I have a thing here under that handkerchief, and you don't know what it is, and I will just leave it here like this for a minute. I have known boys and girls, members of the Christian Endeavor society, and I was so happy when I heard they joined, and how they did go up for a little while! I didn't know how to express my feelings. But all at once they didn't seem to go up any farther. They had gotten just so far, and if they kept their pledge honestly, they were praying the same thing. I didn't understand it, and I said: "There must be something holding that boy down, something I can't see,— just as there is something under that handkerchief that is holding that little balloon down, and it can't go up. It is struggling, but it can't get up; it is being held down. I want to show you something; perhaps I might as well show you first as well as last what is keeping this down. It is a very strange thing to keep down a balloon like that. Do you see what it is? It is a wine-glass. Yes; there are Christian Endeavor boys and girls who think it is not wicked, I suppose, to drink wine; but I tell you, boys and girls, if ever you touch wine in any way, ninety-nine chances out of every hundred it will pull you down; and if you, dear friends,—boys and girls,—are touching wine, or beer, or cider, or any of those things, they will pull you down.

What do we mean by the work of the temperance committee? Why, we mean to have every boy and girl cut right loose from everything which intoxicates. First of all, have the right spirit put in his heart, cut loose from bad companions, and cut loose from that which intoxicates. I have a story here, and it is a story about some pictures, and I want to show you this picture. You cannot, however, see it very well, many of you, but I will tell you about it. That is a picture of a little boy two years old. He sits there in a chair, his two feet are firmly planted on the rounds of the chair, and his little sleeves are rolled up, his hair is curled, and he looks as if he was going to make a noble giant by and by, and he looks innocent and healthy. You would look at that boy and say, "Oh, what a fine boy he is, and how proud his mother must be of him."

Here is another picture. It is not in quite so nice a frame. That is a picture of a man thirty-seven years of age. He is the most ragged man I ever saw. I saw that man come into our church one night last winter, and something about his face struck me. He said: "Can't you help me?" I said: "We can't help people in these meetings." He just threw open his coat like that, and I was almost thunderstruck to look at him. Why, he hardly had enough rags on him to cover him. But oh, what a noble-looking face he had. I said: "Well, my dear friend, you had better stay here, and I will introduce the missionary to you." That man is that little boy thirty-five years after the time that that first picture was taken. He died one week after this picture was taken, a broken-down wreck. His father and mother never saw this picture. We wouldn't break their hearts by letting them see how their noble-looking young man died. Oh, what a wreck he was, and how sorry we felt for him. The very look of him touched my heart. When the missionary buried that young man, I saw a fine-looking man come over from a neighboring city, dressed like a gentleman, and I said, "Who is that?" "Why," they said, "he is the brother of that man— that terribly broken-down man who died recently." I said, "Is that possible? What caused it?" He was tied to that cup. He began drinking wine in a good family, and died a broken-down wreck. Oh, if he had only cut loose when he was a little boy; if he had only joined a Junior Endeavor society, and worked along the lines of the temperance committee; if he had cut right loose!

This is what he ought to have done. You see what I have there? Well, that is a good-sized pair of shears, and I have printed on one blade, "Trust in Christ," and on the other blade I have, "Total Abstinence." Now, you see if I bring "Total Abstinence" down on "Trust in Christ," it makes a very sharp thing to contend with, and it will cut right through those strings. That is what every boy and girl must do. And that is what we Juniors and Endeavorers are doing,—trusting in the Lord Jesus Christ for strength to resolve to totally abstain, now and forever. And so this is what we do: I just bring them down one on the other, so, and you notice the Junior Christian Endeavor balloon rises to the ceiling. [*Applause.*] Yes; that is just like the Junior Endeavor Society: it doesn't stop as long as it can possibly go up; and I trust, my dear boys and girls, that you will be cut loose from all those things that are holding you down, and having the spirit of Christ in you, you will just go up, and as Dr. Deems said, by and by you will see him, and see those grandchildren of his, and we will all see one another, and we will rejoice that we trusted in Jesus Christ and cut loose. God bless the boys and girls. [*Applause.*]

The hymn "Blest be the tie that binds" was then sung.

Mrs. SCUDDER: I have the pleasure of introducing to you the Rev. W. W. Sleeper, of Beloit, Wisconsin, who will speak on a "Live Junior Society."

ADDRESS OF REV. W. W. SLEEPER.

I was very much afraid that that balloon boy was going to terminate like some of the boys in the traditional Sunday-school stories. These boys that are so very good usually go up to heaven, and don't stop till they get there, and I am very glad that this little boy has stopped short enough; but how he is going to get down to earth I don't know and don't care. [*Laughter.*] I am going to tell you about a junior society that is not quite like that; but first, let me bring you greeting from the Badger State and from some of the little Badgers who are Juniors away out in the State of Wisconsin. I am sure, if they were here to-day, they would say to you as I shall say to you, "Be busy, be busy for Christ." Oh, the Juniors are busy bees, indeed, and they gather the most delicious honey out of the Christian Endeavor flowers. Be busy for Jesus is the message of the little Badgers to you to-day.

You know that once upon a time there was a very famous person, and his name was Aladdin; and when he wanted anything very nice, all he had to do was to take a lamp that he had — a magic lamp — and rub it, and presto, just what he wanted would come before him! Now, it will be very easy for me to describe a live junior society by telling you about one or two that I know of; but I am going to have you see it as well as hear about it. I have a lamp with me that is more precious to me than Aladdin's lamp, and that is this little junior badge, which I am sure you all love very much. It is a wonderful little thing, isn't it? Well, now, I am going to rub that little badge, and I am going to say "Dear Junior Society, dear live society, appear," and we will see if it will come. [*A little girl then stepped up on the platform.*] Oh, yes, I thought that this wonderful badge would bring it. [*Applause.*]

Now, boys and girls, I wish to introduce to you a live junior society. You see it all here in just one person, and you can see all the committees of the junior society, and you can see their officers. I can't tell you all about it, time won't permit — but just a little, and then you can find just such live societies in your own ranks.

In the first place, let me tell you about the lookout committee. Here are five members that I can see that belong to the lookout committee. [*Eyes and ears.*]

And then here is another member, and I can't see it, but it is right in here, [*pointing to the little girl's head*] and that is Miss Common-sense, and she is chairman, and now the lookout committee is complete.

There are some members on lookout committees in junior societies, and they are blind and they are deaf; they are just like rag babies,— they have eyes but they see not, ears have they but they hear not, and in place of brain they have bran. Oh, I have had some experiences with such lookout committees. They won't see anybody, they don't see those who want to join them. But that is not so in a live junior society, and there is ever so much real good common-sense here that you can't see, but I know it is here.

And then I see also a social committee — a very nice social committee here. and the first member of this committee that I will introduce to you is R. H. Shaker, — Right-Hand Shaker, — who belongs to the social committee, and I tell you this live junior society is giving me a real hearty shake.

And then there is another member of this committee, very important, and that is Miss Chatter. Oh, we can't have a good social committee unless we do a little talking and a little handshaking, and are glad to welcome our members and those who come into our meetings and into our society. It seems to me that a poor social committee — and there are lots of them just like wall-flowers at sociables, very beautiful to look upon, but worth nothing in the world to us — ought to apply for the position of stocking an oyster bed. Now, dumbness is very good in oysters, but it isn't good at all among boys and girls. Another member of this social committee is Miss Love, and if she were not the chairman, we should have just a mere gossip committee, after all; but with Love for chairman, and with this energetic Shaker on the committee and other shakers just as energetic, we have a most admirable committee. That is the social committee of a live junior society.

And then I see also here a missionary committee — a good one too. There are ten members to it, and they are all cousins, and they are the busiest kind of juniors too. Why, what cannot a Junior Endeavor missionary committee do? These ten members can make fancy articles for foreign mission schools, they can make all kinds of presents to send out before Christmas time for many foreign mission Sunday schools, and they can cut out and paste into scrap-books pictures for gifts for the poor children everywhere. Oh, they can do so much. I thought I would help a certain missionary committee I know once, and I gave them a lot of these little wheels; [*holding up a five-cent piece*] it is marked "five" on it, and sometimes it is called a nickle, but I call it a little wheel, because it does so much good rolling through the world. I gave to these committees these little wheels, and told them to set them rolling, and after a few months I told them to bring in what they had found, and one came in with $8 that he had made himself with this five cents, and another one had $5, and another $5, and then one had $1, and so on; and the whole together I know amounted to nearly thirty dollars. And so you see this little committee in a live junior society is a very live committee.

But they have members working on this committee too. You would have thought so, if you had been with me last Sunday evening and enjoyed a concert that was prepared by juniors, with the junior president of this live junior society in the chair. The church was filled with people, and the whole programme was given by children reciting their interesting stories, and in the choir were thirty children singing songs, and the collection was taken by the junior treasurer, a boy ten years old, but he knows ever so much about the use of money. The contribution-box was passed rather hastily along a line of children, and when the box had been passed I heard a sobbing behind me, and I looked around and discovered that a little junior was crying. I said, "What is the matter?" "Why," she said, "I didn't get a chance to put my money in." Just fancy that, crying because you haven't a chance to put your money in the contribution-box! "Well," said I, "never mind; when the box comes up to me, I will see that you have it; so when they came to me I passed the box to the little girl, and her sobs soon ended. At the same time, a little boy felt in his pockets and found he had forgotten his money, and he took his hat and darted out of the door and went home and got it and brought it back in time to put it into the box. So you see how great the work is that our boys and girls can do for Christ in this world.

But I see here a music committee, and very important it is, as you know who have listened to the singing of this committee. Here are a whole choir dressed in white, about thirty members of them, and how they do sing. Master Joy is chairman of the music committee. How he struts along like a little drum major! It is always an inspiration to hear the children singing these battle hymns and war songs of Christ, for indeed they are an army, an advancing host.

And then here is a most marvellous visiting or calling committee. I will introduce to you the chairman and his brother.— they are the Foot Brothers. Now, you see how this committee works. When the committee goes out walking, it takes the whole society with it. That is the way [*applause*] the Endeavorers make social visits,— not simply to send out one or two who come in there, and say, " I belong to the junior society, I belong to the calling committee, and I have come to see you; no, not exactly that, but one after another will come in and keep on calling, until the new member feels at home in your society. That is the way the junior calling committee works; and if you haven't such a committee in your society, be sure and give a good place on your committee to the Foot Brothers; if not, they will kick, and that is bad. [*Laughter.*] There is a chance for the feet and the hands and the head and the heart and everything in junior work; be sure and put all your material on the committees.

Now comes a very large committee,— the sunshine committee. Don't you see the sunshine there? That is the nicest committee we have there in our Junior Endeavor work. Good-will is chairman. It is a very large committee, indeed. In one society I know of, in my own church, there are twenty members on the sunshine committee, and their ages are from ten down to six, and the chairman is a beautiful young girl of ten years, whom I had the pleasure of welcoming into the church last Sunday morning, — and all the rest are going to follow her by and by. And what a great work this committee does! On Sunday they come bringing flowers into the church, and when the services are over, they carry the flowers to the sick people, and during the week they do whatever little acts of kindness they can. Their mission is to be sunshine everywhere,— and they try to be it; and when I feel a little bit glum and out of sorts, I go around to my sunshine committee, and say, " Just shine a little bit; let me bask a little in the sunshine of this committee," and they do shine, and all the shadows are chased away.

And now, one other committee I will mention, and this is the prayer-meeting committee, — the most important committee in Junior Endeavor work, as it is in senior Endeavor work; and on this committee, of course, we will place the knees, for we in the junior work are not ashamed to bow the knees before God in prayer. Also on this committee we place the voice, because, although we believe to a certain extent in silent prayer, yet, when the president calls for brief prayers from members, we do not believe in silent prayers, and we do not have them either in Junior meetings; but one after another these dear Juniors, who have received from Christ every good thing and are not ashamed to acknowledge it, lift up their voices in the sweetest and purest and most beautiful petitions to Almighty God; and the chairman of this committee is the heart.

Just one word about the officers, and I have done. I can't mention them all, but I will mention one or two. Let me say that "I will" is president of the Junior Endeavor society: " I will be a Christian" is what the boys and girls are saying,— oh, so many of them; " I will be a good faithful Endeavorer;" "I will be true, I will take the pledge, and, God helping me, I will keep it." So you see " I will " is president of the live junior society, and the secretary of it is, of course, our Lord Jesus Christ, our dear Saviour, who said, " Suffer little children to come unto me, and forbid them not, for of such is the kingdom of heaven."

Dear juniors, is your society alive? Is it fully alive? I believe it, as I look into your faces this afternoon. Then keep it so, and live for Jesus Christ, who lives for you.

Well, this Aladdin's lamp must be rubbed again, or I shall go on forever, and so I will rub it once more and this live society will disappear from sight,— but oh, how many of them there are here. [*Applause.*]

Mrs. SCUDDER: I have the great pleasure of introducing next to the audience Mr. William Ferguson, of Philadelphia, who has very kindly aided me in preparing for this meeting which has given you so much pleasure Twice has he come over from the Quaker City to give his wise counsel and confer about the work; and I know I am speaking the truth when I say that there is not in all the United States one who loves, or who would sacrifice more for the Junior Endeavor work. I have great pleasure in introducing to the children this afternoon, and to the others, Mr. William Ferguson, of Philadelphia. [*Applause.*]

ADDRESS OF MR. WILLIAM FERGUSON.

My dear little Juniors : — I love you all as well as I do the Junior union of the city of Philadelphia, and from them this afternoon I bring you fraternal greetings,— the greetings of sixty-seven societies, with almost 5,000 boys and girls.

This is the second happy day in my Christian experience. The first great happy day was when I stood behind the pulpit in the church of which I have the honor to be a member and looked down upon 1,014 boys and girls who had pledged themselves for Christ and the Church. Now, boys and girls, you know there is always a dry crust to every custard, and that is on the outside; and that is my part of the work. I have got to give you the dry part of the Junior Endeavor work; but I am going to try and make it just as moist as I can for you. To do that, we will class ourselves as soldiers in an army and will fight a battle this afternoon. It is a fierce battle, and we will maintain it until Jesus says to you and me, "Come up higher."

Now, in order to protect ourselves from the enemy we must build a fort. Satan is watching us even now, yes, he is watching us while I am talking to you, and his eyes are glaring at us, and he says, "Don't you come here." Yes, we are, we are going into his country and take possession of it, and then by and by the time will come when we shall say to him, "Get you hence," and he shall flee. We are going to throw up a fort this afternoon, as we have all taken upon ourselves this little pledge, and with the stones that are in that pledge we are going to build the fort.

The first stone will be *Trusting* — the very first word. We are going to build this fort with books. There is the first one, and that is *Trusting* — trusting in the Lord Jesus Christ. What a big stone this is in the world. We could'nt get along unless we trusted each other. We are walking along one beautiful afternoon with papa and mamma, but by and by the sun begins to go down, and it gets dark, and we begin to feel afraid, and all of a sudden we take hold of papa and mamma and go right along just as nice as possible. We don't have to be afraid. Why? Because we have got some trust in our papa and mamma. But dear little friends, when we sign that Junior pledge we take the Saviour by the hand, and oh, how he loves us : no matter how much the devil tempts us to do wrong, so long as we have hold of the Heavenly Father's hand, we can't wander.

Now, we men who are in business get along by trusting each other. A man says, "I want twenty-five cases of goods," and he puts his name down on a piece of paper. We say, "All right," and we send them to him, although he has not given us a cent of money. Why? Simply because we trust him. That is what the Saviour wants us to do,— to trust him. Do we trust him this afternoon? Oh, yes, I know as I look down into your bright, smiling faces that certainly you trust him. That is the great big stone that we will put there for the first one in our fort, for we trust in the Lord Jesus.

Now, the next big stone we will put in will be *Promise*. That is a great big fellow that comes alongside of *Trusting*. If you were soldiers and digging a trench, it would be solid all along, and you would pile it up and make it higher than your head. Let us see what the Bible says about promising. If you will look at 1 Kings, you will find, "Blessed be the Lord, that hath given rest unto his people Israel, according to all that he promised: there hath not failed one word of all his good promise, which he promised by the hand of Moses his servant." I have that marked in my Bible; that is the promise verse. Oh, there is where we get the promise, right in this Book, and while I am talking about the pledge this afternoon, let us study this Book, and that will help us keep our promise. The very first promise we made in our lives was to our papas and mammas, and yet we find parents who won't let their boys and girls sign this pledge. "I don't want Katie to bind herself down to anything," and yet you say to them, " John don't you dare to touch those things," and he is compelled to promise. And yet when we come to you with our loving hands and sympathies, and want to save John and Katie and Clara and Joe, and want you to let them sign that pledge, you don't want to let them do it. Parents, don't forget that God gave you those children, and if you don't take care of them, he may come and knock at their little hearts and say, "Your mother and father don't take care of you, and I will take you up here." That is the second stone.

Let us get another one — *Whatever*. That is a great big fellow. We have promised to do whatever he would like us to do. "Now, Katie, won't you go upstairs and mind baby brother while I go to attend to the dusting?" "Mamma, won't you send Clara? I want to go out to play." Yes, we pledge ourselves to do *whatever*. When you are helping mamma and papa and your big brother and sister to do something in the home, that is one of the *whatevers*. Those are the little things we have to do —*whatever*. I know a little girl in Philadelphia who takes her Bible on Sunday afternoon and goes to visit an old lady who can't see, and reads to her. That is one of the *whatevers;* anything we can do to make anybody else happy is one of the *whatevers*. Oh, I look into your little faces while I am talking to you, and I know you are saying, " I will do it, —*whatever*."

I have something here which I want to show you: it is in my pocket, and I think a good deal of it. It is a watch. I got that watch for making a promise, and I am here to tell you this afternoon about it. My father said to me one day, "Will, if you don't drink any liquor until you are twenty-one years of age, I will make you a present of a watch." I joined the church when I was fourteen, and I remember when my dear father placed this watch in my hand. I have carried it a good many years, and a good many years have rolled by since, and every time I open it I read what is on the face of it: " I promise my father that I won't drink any liquor." Oh, boys and girls, every one of you, promise that you will never touch a drop of liquor in any shape or form. That is the thing that is cursing this country of ours to-day, and is driving us away — away from God. [*Applause*.] I wish, Christian friends, this afternoon that the people who say, "I am a member of a Christian church" would solemnly promise in their hearts, "I, who am a member of the church, will not drink any liquor." How long do you suppose it would be that we should have to wait for prohibition in this country? Why, until the sun rose in the east and went down in the west. I know that hundreds of thousands of people, when you come into their house, will say, " Won't you have a little wine?" Oh, I want to see boys and girls who will say, "No, I will not drink any wine." Let God read it upon our hearts. [*Applause*.] It is one thing, my dear boys and girls, to make a promise, and it is another thing to keep it. Now, the promise that we read in this blessed Book keeps you and me. That is the kind of a promise I like to take — one that keeps me. The promises of God are sure — they never fade away.

Now, let us get another stone into our fort, after our *whatever*, and we will call this stone *Prayer*. "We promise that we will pray." Yes, but my dear little friends, there is a good deal of difference between praying and saying prayers. Now I doubt not I am correct in saying that every boy here this afternoon has some time in his life made an effectual prayer and one that has brought what he wanted.

Now, let us see what the next stone is in the fort. Before I pass from *Prayer*, however, let me say that prayer is the brightest stone in all this fortification. Why? Because "Satan trembles when he sees the weakest saint upon his knees." When Satan sees you and me upon our knees, he goes away. He will come right close up to us when we are saying our prayers and saying, "Jesus, dear Saviour, hear me," or that little prayer, "Now, I lay me down to sleep, I pray the Lord my soul to keep; if I should die before I wake, I pray the Lord my soul to take;" but he won't bother us. When you and I feel that Satan is tempting us, if we say a little prayer, he will leave us.

Now, the next stone we want to put up there is *Read*. These are the days of knowledge, and the boy who hasn't got knowledge doesn't amount to anything. There are plenty of good books to read, but when we see this terrible literature and all these horrible stories, we ought to avoid them. There was a boy in our society that I caught with a book in his pocket that I didn't think he should read, and I told him to read the Bible. He said, "We have got a Bible home under a glass case," and I told him where to look in the Bible. That night four or five boys were in the house, and he said, "Say, father, won't you get out that Bible and read?" and so his father got out the Bible and turned to a place, and I guess it was about the first or second time that this man had read the Bible, and he read it with the boys. The prayer-meeting committee were busily praying for this man, and he got his Bible and commenced to read one chapter, and then said to the boys, "Do you believe that?" "Our superintendent said it is true; I guess it is right." Then he said, "Boys, come in to-morrow night, and we will read some more." Well, it wasn't long after that before we saw that gentleman stand before the chancel with his little son, and ask to be taken into the church. That is the book that is to convert the world, and you and I are to help to convert the world, every one of us. Let us work hard and earnestly.

The next stone in our fortification is *Present*. I see the time is going, and I don't want to keep you little folks too long. After we get all these stones together in the fort, what is the fort for? It is to protect somebody. Whom? You and I, and I use this watch to represent us. There we are in the fort, and we have got all these words and all that I have been talking about this afternoon in that Bible.

I want to tell you a little story about a boy who lived in this great city of New York. He was a little fellow, and had a nice father and mother, and lived in the upper part of the city some years ago. But it wasn't long before his father began to drink, and their nice home went, and they had to go down in the lower part of the city to live. And by and by what little they had there went, and after that they came down to one single room, and there this little boy and his father and mother lived together. One day his mother was taken sick, and when his father came home his mother was lying down; and his father went up to her and said, "Why haven't you got some supper?" And she couldn't do anything, so he struck her a blow, and away he fled. She called her boy to the bedside and said, "Harry, I am going to die, and I want you to make me a promise," and she put her loving arm around his neck and said, "Harry, I want you to make me a promise;" and the tears were running down his little cheeks while his mamma said, "Promise me you will never touch a drop of liquor." And he said, "Mamma, I won't," and the next morning the Saviour came and took her home, and the people from the society came and took the body and put it into a rough coffin and took it away and buried it. What became of Harry? Why, for weeks and months Harry slept in a box in an entry way — yes, right in the great city of New York, and they do it in Philadelphia, too. Poor little fellow, he was almost starved to death, when, one day, walking along a wharf, a man said, "What do you want?" He said, "I am looking for a job." The man said, "I think you want something to eat," and he gave him something to eat and gave him some clothes; and he said, " I will take you on board my vessel; I guess we will make a sailor out of you." So he was enlisted on board that sailing vessel. They had only been out to sea two days when an ugly mate said to the captain, "This young wretch won't drink any grog," and he had a tin cup in his hands. The captain said, "You young rascal, you must drink it." The boy said, "I can't, sir." The captain said to the mate, "Give him that rope," and the mate picked up the rope and beat him unmercifully. Then the captain said, "Drink that grog." The boy said, "I can't, sir." "Well, if you can't drink it, you must go aloft and sleep there all night," and the boy climbed up and sat on the topmast, and had sense enough to tie himself to the mast. When the morning light came he was summoned to come down, but there was no answer, and they thought he was dead. A sailor went up for him and carried him down, and after they had revived him there stood the captain with the cup in his hand and told him to drink it, but he still said, "I can't, sir." Then he told the captain his story, — how his father had struck his mother and how she had died, and how he had gone away. And there stood a man with tears rolling down his cheeks, and he said to the boy, "Harry, where is mamma?" "She is dead." And in a minute Harry was in the arms of his father who had gone away, and the captain and the men who stood around were in tears. And the captain said, "Bring all the rum that is aboard this vessel on deck;" and they brought it up and knocked in the heads of the barrels and poured it into the sea, and to-day that vessel sails the ocean, but without any rum on board. [*Applause.*]

Boys and girls, let us intrench ourselves behind this fort. This promise that we have taken is our fort, and while we are there we are there. "Trusting in the Lord Jesus Christ for strength, I promise him that I will strive to do whatever he would like to have me do; that I will pray and read my Bible every day; and that just so far as I know how I will try to lead a Christian life." Oh, I am so glad that I have had this privilege of talking to you, that I have had the opportunity of looking into your faces, and with this one little verse I close: —

> Keep your colors flying, all ye Christian youth,
> To Christ's call replying, full of grace and truth;
> Rise in strength and beauty in life's morning glow,
> Answer to each duty, onward, upward go.
> Keep your colors flying, stand for God and Truth,
> Keep your colors flying, all ye Christian youth. [*Applause.*]

Mrs. SCUDDER : I wonder if there is anybody here who knows where the first Junior society was organized. If there is, will you speak? Well, I will tell you one thing that we did n't know when we came here : it was organized in Iowa, and I asked the pastor of that church to speak to us to-day, but he could not come. However, he has sent me a note and this greeting, which I will read : —

"The Junior Society of Christian Endeavor, of Tabor, Iowa, sends greeting. More than eight years of work in this line have but increased our faith and our enthusiasm. The boys and girls of to-day are the church of to-morrow. Let us fit the coming church to the pressing need of our time, earnest, consecrated men and women. To this end, let us teach our boys and girls to think for Christ, speak for Christ, act for Christ. And may the blessing of him who loved the children be on the convention and on all faithful workers, giving wisdom and courage and patience. So shall we 'Be strong in the Lord' and have 'good success,' through the good hand of God upon us." [*Applause.*]

The audience then sang "The Endeavor Band."

Mrs. SCUDDER : We shall hear now from one of Connecticut's best parsons. Connecticut is a small State, but it has some of the finest societies in the United States, and has, I think, some of the largest conventions. We are very proud of Connecticut. [*Applause.*]

ADDRESS OF REV. H. N. KINNEY.

The Juniors At Work.

I have wondered why you wanted to hear from a Connecticut speaker, but perhaps on the top of your splendid custard which has been so long in the oven you desire a little nutmeg. I do not believe I shall ever be like the apostle Paul. Though I am a man, I have not put away childish things. For five years I have been a member of the Junior Endeavor Society, and have not missed a meeting when at home. Instead of speaking *to* these boys and girls who have sat still so long, I am going to speak *for* them to the older ones. And I have a further right to do this because, as a pastor, I consider the Junior Endeavor Society the dearest, drollest, and most interesting department in the whole work of the Church.

And, first, we boys and girls are glad we were born in America and about the time the Junior Endeavor Society came into existence.

Girls have often been considered a nuisance. An Arab father, if he has no boys in his family, will say: "I have no children, only girls." A tribe in India till recent years had a way of preventing old maids; it killed the extra girls when babies. Boys have often been considered a nuisance: by some of the girls, by ancient Greece and Rome, by the early Christian Church, and by venerable lady school teachers in my early days, who for nothing used to make us sit on nothing.

But now we are having a grand good time. You older ones have taken us into your arms, and we have climbed up on your shoulders, and in Church and State are riding pigback. In Holland, Servia, Spain, and Persia, and in your hearts, a child is king or queen to-day — Junior Endeavor is not all. Not only are "Chatterbox" and little "Tommy Tucker" now in the prayer meeting but "Toddlekins" and "Baby Bunting" are pattering in to "see the wheels go 'woun." Cradle Endeavor is coming! Indeed, societies are already forming for children from three to seven as well as from seven to fourteen. It is as if the cherubs of Raphæl and the winged-headed children of Sir Joshua Reynolds in their paintings, and all the lovely bas-relief children of Luca, Della Robbio, and Donatello had swarmed down from their frames and panels, and, joining hands with the "Five Little Peppers," the "Prudy Book," "Kate Greenaway," "Walter Crane" and "Brownie" children, and the children of the "old woman who lived in the shoe," were romping through the world on a new crusade.

To see the juniors at work, look into our meetings. A cooking-school is going on. It will be like looking into the kitchen of the monastery, illustrated in one of the pictures of the Louvre. The cook, a monk, has been called of God away. But those who depended on that kitchen fared better than before. Angels came down with sleeves rolled up, scrubbed pots and kettles, and baked in the oven. They made angel cake, I suppose; and that is what pastors and churches are living on to-day who have Junior Endeavor societies.

A writing lesson is also in progress. The Junior society is making capital C. E.'s. When the members join the older society or the church, after thorough training they will know how to "mind their P's and Q's."

The Juniors are making clinkings, too. This is a term not found in Webster, but refers in "stone-masonry" to the little stones used to fill the chinks or gaps in building a solid stone wall.

If a regular Y. P. S. C. E. is true to its object, it will train its members for work elsewhere, and so in time will lose them. In my own society, out of 134 members in 1888, less than 20 are members now; out of 40 at organization in 1885, less than five are resident members to-day. Graduating juniors are the best ones to take their places. This is the simplest method of keeping full the ranks.

The Juniors are making many prayers. Some of them of course are funny. Here is one which came into a Junior meeting: "O God, give baby brother a high chair — he has a cradle and baby-carriage." "Do you suppose God caught on to that?" said a boy, after stumbling in his prayer once or twice.

A little boy was sent up to his room for punishment. When his mother arrived she heard him praying: "O God, if ever you wanted to help a little boy, now's your chance." His prayer was answered.

But then prayers are solemn, too, as when one society knelt in prayer at the bedside of a dying member and prayed for her; or when the Juniors repeat, after sentence prayers, the following morning prayer: —

> " Father, we thank thee for the night,
> And the pleasant morning light;
> For rest and food and loving care
> And all that makes the day so fair.
> Help us to do the things we should,
> Be to others kind and good,
> In our work and in our play
> To grow more like thee every day."

You will find the Juniors at work at their place of meeting, in the chapel lecture-room, day-school house, or pastor's study, on the stairs in house-cleaning time; out of doors, too, in summer time, on lawn or beach.

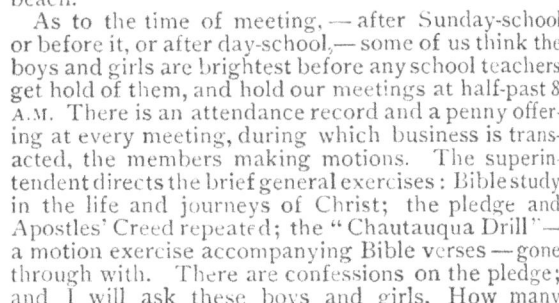

As to the time of meeting, — after Sunday-school or before it, or after day-school, — some of us think the boys and girls are brightest before any school teachers get hold of them, and hold our meetings at half-past 8 A.M. There is an attendance record and a penny offering at every meeting, during which business is transacted, the members making motions. The superintendent directs the brief general exercises: Bible study in the life and journeys of Christ; the pledge and Apostles' Creed repeated; the "Chautauqua Drill" — a motion exercise accompanying Bible verses — gone through with. There are confessions on the pledge; and I will ask these boys and girls, How many read the Bible every day? [*Nearly all the hands go up.*] How many pray? [*All the hands go up.*] How many pray in the morning as well as at night? [*Not so many.*] Well, pray in the morning as well as at night, we say to all. When asleep, of course we are good; awake, we need God's help to keep us from mischief.

There is a roll call of church attendance at every meeting. We believe every Junior Endeavor member should be at church on Sunday morning. By going, many of them have learned to love to go, though the preaching be still beyond them. Bibles reward the faithful at the end of the year.

We learn at the Junior Endeavor meetings each week one or more of the church hymns to be sung in church next Sunday, so that we can all take part in the worship there. The Junior society aims to make good church members.

After the leader — always a boy or girl — has opened the Junior prayer meeting, all the Juniors take part in order, beginning at the right. There are thus no long pauses or gaps. When one is through another begins. No one is allowed to sit when taking part, or to speak indistinctly, or to merely read a verse. Any one who takes part carelessly must do it over again. We allow no one to graduate into the older society until he promises in that society, too, to do as well as in the Junior.

We — but my time is up. I have many more things to say of what the Juniors do. But a good motto for every Junior Endeavor speaker is to be brief, bright, and brotherly. I will close.

ADDRESS OF MRS. ALICE MAY SCUDDER.

"All Ye Are Brethren."

When Jesus said to his disciples "All ye are brethren," he did not intend to say that they all had the same father and mother, but rather that they all had the same purpose and interest at heart. Children, if Jesus were here with you to-day and should say, "You are all brothers and sisters," it would not imply that you all *looked alike;* to be sure, there are often strong family resemblances, but many times members of the same family do not look at all alike. These two Juniors from my society are own brother and sister, and yet there is no marked resemblance in their *faces*, but at *heart* their interests are one.

We here to-day are all brothers and sisters; we may not have exactly the same church form, but the good Book says, "If one is your Master, even Christ, then are ye all brethren."

I hold in my hand twenty-three pinks, no two of which are alike, and yet any of you will say that they are all pinks; perhaps you cannot tell the name of each variety when I hold them closely together, but if you will examine them singly you will find their points of difference. This is exactly the way it is with us to-day. We know we are all Junior Endeavorers, and yet we cannot tell which are Methodists, or Presbyterians, or Congregationalists, or Baptists, until we question each other closely, or look at our pretty badges; then we can be classified.

Who can tell how many States there are? Forty-four. What are these States called? United States. Yes, and by that word "United" we become one nation, with one president. Notice, however, that each State still retains its own government, even though it sends representatives to Washington to help plan for the good of the entire nation. Exactly so is it in our Christian Endeavor work. We are one society with one president, and yet at home we govern and work for our own church and our own denomination; but we send our representatives to local and State unions and to our international conventions to talk over the interests of the *entire* church. There is one thing, children, that I wish to emphasize so forcibly that if you forget all else you will remember this. It is never intended that you will cease to be a Baptist or a Methodist, a Lutheran or a Presbyterian, when you become a member of a Junior Endeavor society. Dr. Clark never intended to weaken the denominational feeling; on the contrary, he expects that the Christian Endeavor spirit — which is loyalty to Christ and loyalty to the Church — will make you far more earnest for the welfare of your own denomination. Meeting in convention with those of other names will not make you love your own less, any more than visiting a cousin would make you less interested in your own brothers and sisters. Having different denominations gives great variety, for if we were exactly alike in all our church ways, we should be too much like a paper of pins or needles. The denominational feeling is all right, *provided it does not drive out the Christ like spirit which makes us all brethren.*

I have here a large wheel which will further illustrate this thought. I will call it my Christian Endeavor wheel. The hub represents the Christian Endeavor Society, and the spokes the different denominations. The outer band we will call Christian fellowship. Let us see how many denominations are thus happily bound together: —

Presbyterian, Union, Congregational, Methodist-Episcopal, Cumberland-Presbyterian, Baptist, Friends, United Presbyterian, Reformed Presbyterians, African-Methodist, Seventh-Day Baptists, Primitive Methodists, Reformed Episcopalians, Evangelical Lutherans, Methodist Protestant, Methodist South, United Brethren, Lutherans, Free-Will Baptists, Epworth League of Christian Endeavor, besides public institutions of various sorts.

What a strong band, then, this outer band of fellowship is; and when we see how many denominational spokes it binds together, we can well say: —

> " Blest be the tie that binds
> Our hearts in Christian love;
> The fellowship of kindred minds
> Is like to that above."

In some of our great tropical forests there are creepers that pass from bough to bough and from tree to tree, binding all together in a network of green which is strong enough to hold up the giant trees, even though their roots are undermined or they are rocked by a hurricane. Even so, if the Christian Endeavor spirit can thus interlace the churches of America, we need have no fears for the future, for no political undermining or infidel cyclone can overthrow the Church of God.

I was thinking, as I sat listening to the beautiful music which Dr. Penfield brought out of yonder organ, that an organ is truly a Christian Endeavor instrument. Perhaps you do not know, children, that it is made up of pipes and reeds, which are brought into use by what are called stops; when the organist has decided the kind of musical sound he wishes emitted, he draws out a corresponding stop, and that is the way we manage our Christian Endeavor organ. When we wish bright, lively music, we draw out a Congregational stop, and Mr. Sleeper speaks to us. Later on we shall want something solemn, and we shall draw out a Dutch Reformed stop. Dr. Brett will lead the consecration service. But when we wish to get the full volume of Christian Endeavor sentiment, we pull out all the stops and unite in a song of fellowship, the grand harmony of which might delight the angels of heaven.

I hope, children, that I have made very clear to you this beautiful idea of Christian brotherhood. We may have our external differences, but at heart we must be one in Christ. The Bible urges this idea, and Peter summed it up in the true Christian Endeavor spirit when he said, "Finally, be ye all of one mind, love as brethren, be pitiful, be courteous."

There arrived a year or two ago, in Chicago, one early morning, an immigrant family from Denmark,— fifteen, they numbered in all. When the father and mother alighted from the car, they each held an infant in their arms, and were closely followed by the eleven other children, who were joined one to the other by a small rope fastened about the arm. All the way from Denmark these little ones had come in close fellowship. None was lost, for not once in their long journey were they separated from each other. Think how much anxiety those parents were spared, and think of the freedom from worriment that the children enjoyed, knowing that they could not go astray while thus lovingly bound together. This simple method of union originated by Danish peasants clearly represents the work of our Junior Endeavor societies; the dear children in them are going from an earthly to a heavenly country, and we who guide them ought to link them together with this strong cable of Christian Endeavor fellowship, in order that in the many changes of life not one of them may be lost. [*Applause.*]

Mrs. Scudder then thanked those who had sent the beautiful flowers with which the pulpit was decorated, and those who had sent flowers to Mrs. Clark and herself. She also thanked the pastor of the church for the use of the beautiful building, and Mrs. Smith of Bridgeport for her kind and generous gift which helped to meet the expenses of the convention, and also the audience for its attention.

She then introduced the Rev. Cornelius Brett, of New Jersey, who conducted the consecration service, which consisted of prayer and the reciting of Scripture quotations by the children, and also the Junior Christian Endeavor pledge.

The audience then joined in singing "God be with you," and the services closed with the Mizpah benediction.

SIMULTANEOUS MEETINGS.

Marble Collegiate Church, Fifth Avenue and Twenty-Ninth Street.

FRIDAY AFTERNOON, 2 O'CLOCK.

Rev. R. L. Swain, Ph. D., of Westerville. Ohio, presided. Mr. H. C. Lincoln conducted the musical services. The meeting was opened by a service of song, followed by a short prayer service. The chairman then introduced, as the first speaker. Rev. J. B. Thomas, of Topeka, Kansas.

ADDRESS OF REV. J. B. THOMAS.

This service is entirely impromptu, so far as I am concerned. Just before the announcement was made this morning Dr. Clark came to me and asked me if I would be at this meeting. I read this forenoon, somewhere, I think it was in Jeremiah, that it was said that the streets were full of boys and girls. I am quite sure it was a prophecy of the streets of New York City to-day, for I tried my best to get my dinner in time to be here by two o'clock, but I had to go nearly to Castle Garden in order to get it. It is all Christian Endeavorers everywhere. I do not believe that New York City ever saw anything like what it is seeing to-day. I do not believe that the Christian world ever saw anything like what we see here to-day. Not thirty thousand — I believe there are fifty thousand Christian people who have come up to this city from all over this country. And what an education! I sat in the depot at St. Louis on Tuesday evening and saw those twenty odd cars packed in there like sardines — like silver spoons in a box — with Christian workers, exchanging ideas and thoughts and prayers and songs all the way through. You know just how you did it; and as you go back you will have new friends all over this country. I believe that not only this life, but heaven itself, is going to be brighter because of these happy times we have here. Is there any place where God's people can have such Christian fellowship as when they have assembled together as we are assembled together here to-day throughout this entire city?

I said this morning in the pastors' conference that this was a wonderful organization because it rejuvenated the older class of people. Look at the gray hairs before me! On the train coming from St. Louis, there was an old man who was very lame, but he had a great big Christian heart in him. He was coming from Kansas with his old wife to attend the convention of the Young People's Society of Christian Endeavor. What do you call that? I call that a rejuvenation of the older people, don't you? It is remarkable how God puts a mature head on young shoulders. He enables young people to look with a broader forethought and a deeper conception of life now. I don't believe I had it when I was young. I do not feel that those who were brought up ten or fifteen years ago had the opportunities for Christian culture that we have to-day. Then, too, it is to be a perpetual youth. There is no growing old in this army. I was away last summer, out on the Western coast. Some of you have been out over the plains of Arizona. You remember it is sandy and windy and disagreeably dusty. The dust seemed to come in between the twofold glass of our sleeper until we were most suffocated. One afternoon they brought in a poor young woman upon a stretcher and laid her down upon one of the berths. She was accompanied by her husband and four children. At half-past ten o'clock that night a certain Christian Endeavorer went to the man and looked at the woman's eyes, and they were setting in death. He said, " May I speak to that woman just a minute?" Obtaining permission, he spoke to the woman about her soul's welfare. The next morning she was dead. They arose from their sleeper berths that night at three o'clock, and the Christian Endeavorer took the husband and four children, and, kneeling down with them, asked God Almighty to spare the boys and girls for himself, and to save that man. Then he threw his arm around the man and said, "Dear friend, are you a Christian?" And he said, "No, sir; but I had a noble Christian wife." And again he knelt and prayed for him.

And what that Christian Endeavorer was doing out there in Arizona, they are doing in Maine and throughout the entire civilized world. I say, brethren, it never was known in this wise before. A Christian Endeavorer came and sat by me on the train. I was dressed a good deal like a western drummer; and the very first thing he did was to show me a little testament like that [*indicating*] and he said: "Is the man who sits by me a Christian man?" And we had a blessed time. All the way through there is this magnificent good being done for God. [*Applause.*]

A certain insurance agent a few days ago went down into Southern Illinois to fix up a little matter. A man's barn had been burned, and the man hated to see the insurance agent come around, for he had not a very good opinion of insurance agents; and the agent opened up his gripsack, and the first thing that lay on top of the grip was the Bible. The man looked up and his eyes bulged out and he said: "What! an insurance man with a Bible!" and he replied, "Yes, I love the Bible;" they read the 23rd Psalm together, and the man said, "I know now I will get paid for my barn."

I rejoice that I am a Christian Endeavorer. I rejoice first that I am a Christian man. Let us have Christ before any organization on top of God's earth. Do you believe it? If you do, say so, and say so with your lives.

I believe the time is coming when every Christian man must stand out and out for Jesus, or get out. The time is coming when the Church must dictate to the world, and no longer allow the world to dictate to the Church. The time is coming when we must study more carefully this word of God and we must abide by it. And you, Endeavorers, are to accomplish this work.

Down in the machine shops in the town where I am living I have done for the last few noontimes a little Christian work. There was an old infidel down there that I had had my eye on for some time, and on this particular day this fellow made up his mind he was going to have a right nice little tilt with me, and I didn't mind it myself, as I felt first-rate that day. He came up to me and said, "I want to ask you one question;" and I replied, "Let me ask you one question first. Do you believe that is God's word?" he said, "Yes, but did God make everything?" "Yes," I said, " the Bible says he made the heaven and earth and all that in them is." "And he also makes the whiskey, doesn't he?" I said, " There is a devil, and he has got hold of you." Just then there were three hundred boys and men around us, and I took out my Bible and I said, "Fellows, did you ever see a dying man or woman call on infidelity for comfort at the time of death?" And they shouted, "No!" And I said, "Did you ever hear of a Christian man, with the Gospel of Jesus Christ, taking comfort at the time of death?" And three hundred hats went off and three hundred voices shouted, "Yes!"

Now, brethren. I believe before God, as Christian workers, what you and I need is not to deal with criticism, either higher or lower. Let us know our Bible, and let it rest right there. The only refutation in this world for infidelity or for agnosticism is the Bible. You must have your hold on your Bible thoroughly, and you must let your Bible get a good, square, solid hold of you. It is one thing to hold on to the Scripture and know where to find it; it is another thing to let the Scripture burn in your heart. [*Applause.*]

The audience then sang Hymn No. 111, after which Chairman Swain introduced Rev. H. C. Farrar, D.D., of Albany, New York.

ADDRESS OF REV. H. C. FARRAR, D. D.

I am glad I belong to the winning side. It is ever so much better to be on the winning side than on the losing. I am glad I am connected with an organization whose "tramp, tramp" is tremendously onward and upward and outward, and it will not be long before it will roll up into the millions. It is almost a million and a half now — very nearly one million four hundred thousand, lacking only a very few hundreds of that number. It is wonderful how this organization has grown. There is nothing like it. It could not have grown only as it sprang from the Word ministered to by the Holy Ghost and striking into the very heart of the Church. And I am glad that this grand organization touches so many young people, — the best young people of America; the wisest, the sharpest, the keenest, the most upright boys and girls of this country. They are all falling rapidly into line with this young people's movement, and who can forecast the result of an organization like this on this great land of ours in the next century? It is simply an unsolvable problem. And yet we know enough of it to know that it is going to reach over into the twentieth century and lay its hand upon law, on politics, on science, on the school, on the Church, and on everything that is American, and lift it to a higher plane and make it of a higher, better character. [*Applause.*]

Stop and think a moment. Nearly a million and a half of young people! These young people are to be married. These young people are to have homes. Out of these newly organized homes are to come a crop of children. We are coming to understand that the old Methodist revival system has almost lost its force in America, and that we can raise a better crop of Christians by Christian culture, taking the boys and girls young, than we could by the old method. If I could get the ear of every Christian Endeavorer in the United States of America, I would say two things; and the first one is, By all means pack your associate list with the young people of your church. Then I would say another thing. In our Sunday schools of this country we have fifteen millions in the Protestant Sunday schools of America. It is a wonderful thought when you get hold of it, and it inspires. But there is one tremendous fact that comes in just there, — that almost one-half of the boys and the girls that are in our Sunday schools are lost out in the period of their teens. Why are they lost? For half a dozen reasons. First, the inefficiency of superintendents, and more particularly the inefficiency of teachers, and more particularly the inefficiency of pastors. What I say to you is, Your field is in the Sunday school; the primary department of our churches is the most important part of our churches to-day. I would that every teacher and every worker in the Sunday school could understand that he must give his most important service to the Sunday school, this primary work of the Church. What becomes of nearly two-thirds of the membership of our Sunday schools? They must be brought into the Society of Christian Endeavor and developed gradually into the activities of the Christian Church. You are solving the biggest problem of Christianity to-day, how to save the boys and girls. It is a tremendous question. Nearly fifty per cent of the boys and girls are lost from our Sunday schools, and the majority of them are lost to the Church. Up yonder, between the city where I live and Troy, there were, the other Sunday, fifteen thousand young men that went to the ball games. Not ten per cent of the young men of America are members of the Church, and only about fifteen per cent attend the church at all. What is the matter? Why do our Sunday-school members drop out? Because of the namby-pambyism in our Sunday-school teaching. Teachers stay at home for lack of something fashionable to wear and other light excuses. O Lord, give us Christian Endeavor teachers, fashion or no fashion! Think of a pastor that would'nt go to his church because he did not have a gilt-edged sermon!

I have started trains of thought that I hope you will carry out in your Sunday-school work. Start a Junior organization at once. Pack your associate list with the boys and girls; and get them to quote Scripture; get them interested; get them turned that way; and then pray with all your might, and live better than you pray, and you will sweep them into the kingdom and save them to Christ and the Church.

Then just look at this organization of two millions — it represents that to-day — of the best-cultured, best-brained, best-hearted, best-charactered young men and women in the world. Who can tell its influence on politics? Who can tell its influence in shaping judges and juries and everything else that is characteristic of America? Who can tell its influence in keeping and preserving for us the grandest flag that ever kissed the heavens and shook out its folds to the breezes? Who can tell the power of these young men and women in taking care of that grand old flag that means so much to us? Some one over at the Garden to-day called our iron-clad pledge the "verdure-clad pledge." That is to say, a fellow that keeps it is perpetually green. There are a good many dried-up old Christians in our churches whom we dare not move out to South Dakota, lest the cyclones blow them away. We want green, fresh, earnest, enthusiastic, hearty, consecrated young men and women to take that old pledge. What does it mean? "I will read the Bible every day." I thank God for what another speaker said, that from lid to lid the Bible is inspired. I have no sympathy with the nonsense of the so-called higher criticism or higher scepticism. I love that grand old Bible, and I am pledged by all the power that is in my manhood to read it every day. And then I am pledged that every day I will look into the face of my King and get his image transformed into me and receive an inspiration to go out into the world and learn how to live. I tell you, two or three millions of young men and women face to face every morning with the King, bending over that Holy Book, catching its inspiration, and walking out and keeping their lives clean and pure, — what a thought! There is no room for tobacco, no room for sin, and no room for iniquity of any kind. [*Applause.*]

After the singing of a hymn the chairman introduced the assistant pastor of the church, Rev. Alfred E. Myers.

ADDRESS OF REV. ALFRED E. MYERS.

I remember a few years ago, on my return from the other side of the Atlantic, watching the pilot scaling the side of a ship. We were twenty-five or thirty feet above the water, and the pilot came alongside with his skiff, and then, catching the rope as his skiff swung on a favorable wave, he jumped on to the rope ladder and scaled up the side of the ship and piloted us into the harbor of New York. As I looked at him, I was glad that he had it to do and not I, for he was accustomed to that difficult kind of ship-side scaling. I was thinking this afternoon how it used to be in the old time — more or less old — about young people coming into the Church. It was a little of the process of the pilot scaling the side of the ship. It was somewhat difficult, — not intended to be so by the fathers, not intended to be so by the ministers, but actually so in its practical effect upon the minds of the young. They felt themselves far off and low down, and they looked up at the side of the ship and at the church members as they looked down at them; and they may have said, "I wish I had courage to go up the side and get into that ship of the Church."

But now, dear friends, in this Christian Endeavor movement the ship is alongside of the wharf, and we have great, broad gang-planks for people to get into the ship by, and there is no more scaling of the side of the ship from the skiff that is dancing up and down upon the waves. That is one thing that this Christian Endeavor movement has helped forward, and I bless God for it.

Now, dear friends, how many of us are there who, if we were to describe ourselves as Christians, would say, "Well, at any rate, I do want to live a Christian life; I do want to give my life to Jesus Christ, my body to be his in purity and vigor, my mind to be his in intelligence and consecration; and my whole body and soul and spirit to be sanctified to his praise and to his service." You are hungering and thirsting after righteousness. Yes, we are Christian Endeavorers, and we will do our best to increase the membership of the Christian Endeavor Society and encourage young Christians — children, boys, and girls — to come and confess Jesus, with faltering accents, in the Christian Endeavor experience meeting. And so we let down that still lower gang-plank of the associate membership, and encourage every one to come and learn that there is more and more of the water of life that Jesus has provided. I thank God for the new day in which we live, when the young have such great encouragement to serve Jesus Christ.

Sometimes, in the presence of a tremendous movement like this, I permit myself to indulge in an imagination of the very opposite of such a movement. I dare not follow out that imagination; but just for one moment let your thoughts dwell upon the possibility of the young people of America being in a movement against Christ and the Bible. With what horror we look over such an abyss, and how it makes us thank God more that this great popular movement is a movement of Christian Endeavor.

Some years ago I had the privilege of looking upon a great sweeping salt river, running between two continents. The hills on either side belonged to Europe on the one side and Asia on the other. The waters of the Black Sea come down from the North, and the waters of the Mediterranean sweep up from the South; and the city of Constantinople stands at the meeting of the waters. In that city, as you traverse its streets, you hear every language of the whole world spoken. You hear Turkish, Armenian, Greek, Italian, Arabic, French, German, and all other known tongues. It is the meeting of the waters of the people that are there as well as in that mighty Strait of the Bosphorus. So, I think America is the meeting of the waters. I think God has sent the people of many nations here to work out his great design. And it seems to me that in this last decade God has raised up the Christian Endeavor movement with reference to the fact that here in America are meeting all the forces of the whole world for a great moral and spiritual conflict. Who knows but this Christian Endeavor movement is raised up and brought into this prominence at this time with reference to this mighty action of opposing forces in this our country?

I look forward to great results from this Christian Endeavor movement, for several reasons. One is, because it is based upon Christian experience. It goes right back and encourages and draws out that little spark of love to Jesus Christ and the desire to lead a Christian life that is in the boy's heart and the girl's heart, and fans it into a flame; and so from the very beginning it is based upon personal Christian experience. No religious movement is good for anything, unless it is based upon personal Christian experience. What are all theories and all theologies worth, unless they come back to that initial, personal experience of conviction of sin, of repentance for sin, and of faith in Jesus Christ as a redeemer and of the hope of eternal life through him. And so I have great hope of this Christian Endeavor movement, because it is based upon a personal Christian experience.

I have great hope of it, too, because it is so strongly marked by a mutual support among Christians. Here we are in a Christian Endeavor meeting.

Here are those who are glad and anxious to speak a few words for Jesus Christ; here are others who in the darkness of their hearts find some little stray beam of light, coming like a ray through a chink in a dungeon wall, and they are stretching out their hands feebly toward that light, and that light is what they want. And so we are looking for a great future from this grand system of mutual support and encouragement in Christian life.

And then I look for a great future for this movement because of its demonstration and actualization of Christian unity. We ministers who have been in church courts for so many years past have had experience in attempts at ecclesiastical church unity. We have had overtures sometimes sent to us from other Christian bodies that would have in them some condition with which it was impossible to comply, and then the thing would drop. But while the church courts are sending their letters to and fro, and sending their delegates to represent each other, — a glorious work in the line of God's providence, yet a very slow process, — God's Holy Spirit, outrunning the councils of men, outrunning the decisions of church courts and travelling faster than delegates can go from one church council to another by swift express trains, — God's Holy Spirit comes into all parts of this great land and touches the hearts of Christian young people who will be the people of the churches in ten or twenty years, and brings them together, — not in theory, but in fact, — brings them together in their hearts. And when Christians are brought together in heart, then all intellectual understanding, all ecclesiastical co-operation, all creed unity, and all other things will and must follow, because out of the heart are the issues of life. We know that when hearts are once united, they cannot be kept apart. Well, it is just as true in that higher realm of Christian affection as it is in the affections of the heart that lead to the establishment of the family. This is God's way; and God was surely leading Francis E. Clark when he established his little society of boys and girls in Portland, bringing on this great consummation the unity of the Church of Jesus Christ. [*Applause.*]

After singing " Hide me," the meeting adjourned.

FRIDAY EVENING.

The praise service was conducted by Mr. J. W. Jones, of Jamaica, L. I., and prayer offered by Rev. W. H. Albright, of Boston, Mass. The presiding officer, Rev. James L. Hill, D.D., of Medford, Mass., then spoke as follows :—

Dr. HILL: I want to express, first, my profound sympathy for all the delegates who are not in this room to-night. I pity those who have been obliged to go to any other meeting than the one we hold. Talk of speakers! Why, there are no speakers besides those we are to have in this church to-night. [*Applause.*] When Senator Sumner was pleading the cause of the negro in the United States Senate, somebody said to him : " Why, you want to hear the other side." " There is no other side." [*Applause.*] When you have the founder of the United Society with you, and such an array of splendid talent as will be introduced to you, — indeed, every one of them is a compressed convention, and no two of them were ever brought together before [*applause*] — you will be surprised to find how much bottled eloquence is done up in these men. All I have to look out for is the gilded ceiling when I uncork the bottle. [*Applause.*] I am very glad to say that the new wine is in new bottles, lest the bottles would be made worse.

If I were to suggest a theme to-night, I would say to the brethren: "Say to these young friends, who are gathered from over the sea, and from over the land, just those things that you would be glad to have them carry home."

The agent of the down-town office of the New York Central Railway said to-day that there were in this metropolis of America 60,000 young people who have come here upon our tickets. [*Loud applause.*] Since our little planet was sent spinning on its way, I need not remind you that all Christian history shows no evidence of such an assemblage as this. It stands alone in the history of the world, and it is no small privilege for us to be spectators of it. If this thing goes on there will not be much room for Satan in this world. [*Applause.*] And I want to tell you that coming to this great city — I have no doubt it is a great city — we will not discuss the character of the city. [*Laughter and applause.*] I never like to begin an argument I can't carry through — we will let the character of the city go; but I would like to say this, that since we have been here Satan has been put on the defensive.

It is understood that a half-million young men come to vote every year; that in every presidential election a million and three-quarters of young men cast their maiden votes; and if these young people, young men and young women, should stand together in a solid phalanx, and stand for one thing, there is no abuse that they cannot correct [*applause.*]; there is no reformation that they cannot achieve; there is no government but that they themselves could influence. Oh, that this company may stand together for Christ and the Church! [*Applause.*]

I want to introduce to you a gentleman who has bottled up in him a St. Louis convention, a Chicago convention, a Minneapolis convention, and a part of the New York convention. He is the gentleman who wrote the platform of principles that you find so admirably stated in the souvenir that you are to carry home. I am proud to introduce to you the orator of many a convention, Dr. Wayland Hoyt, of Minneapolis. [*Loud applause.*]

ADDRESS BY REV. WAYLAND HOYT, D.D.

Mr. President, dear Brethren and Sisters in Christian Endeavor: — This thing is going on, and we are going to crowd the devil out. [*Applause.*] I propose to be practical. I think we ought to be in our great gatherings. That was a good suggestion: "Say what you would like to have taken home." I want to speak a practical word or two for and about the lookout committee.

Let us enter a poor, dim room, perhaps in Ephesus, perhaps in Corinth. As we enter, and our eyes get accustomed to the dim light, we see, poring over a parchment scroll, a small man, much bruised and battered, but nevertheless with a brow on which the highest sort of intellect is taking its seat, and with that singular lustre on his face which speaks of a peaceful and of a rejoicing heart. And as our eyes get further accustomed to the light and we look at him, we see that it is with great difficulty that he can do what he is doing, for his eyes are perpetually and chronically inflamed. I think that was the "thorn in the flesh" that troubled him when, and about which, he prayed so earnestly, and which he accepted so joyfully when he discovered that it was his Lord's will that that thorn in the flesh should pierce him. And as we look further, we see that there is many a mark upon him and that age has told upon him. And as we read the little sketch of autobiography about the number of times that he was stoned and shipwrecked and cast into prison and beaten we do not wonder that his hand trembles a good deal and that writing is a difficult thing for him. But here he is in this dim room, and with these blurred eyes writing, toiling over the parchment scroll. I wish you would think about him a minute writing there.

Now, to whom is he writing? He is writing to the Galatians. And who were the Galatians? Why, the Galatians were the Frenchmen of the New Testament, and the Celtic characteristics were in them. When this man who is now writing made his first missionary journey among them, they received him with such enthusiasm that, as he says, they would have plucked out their own eyes and given them to him. There never was such a welcome as this writer got in Galatia. But you will remember that the steps of this writer were always dogged by enemies. He didn't have the pleasantest time in the world. He preached a grand, free Gospel. He said, "There is therefore now no condemnation to them that are in Christ Jesus." He said that all the Mosaic ritualism was finished, just as the scaffolding is finished when a building is put up. But you know that there were Judaizers who dogged his steps and who preached a narrow Gospel, and were Christ's in a sense, and yet were saying that you must submit to the Mosaic ritual, in order that you might enter into the true Christianity. And these Judaizers have been among these Galatians, and these Galatians, after their unstable fashion, having welcomed the apostle so splendidly, welcome now the Judaizers, and are going over to this narrow, silly, heretical Gospel. I wish you would notice that this man who is writing in this dim room is not a man who in any way thinks doctrinal defection is something that does n't amount to anything. He thinks doctrinal defection a most mighty trouble; and now, while doctrinal defection is seizing these Galations, he does what he has not done in any other case. He is a prolific writer, but in every other case he has dictated what he had to say to an amanuensis, and then he has made it his own by signing his name. But now he won't commit the matter to an amanuensis; and notwithstanding the dim light and the blurred eyes and the trembling hand, he is himself with his own hand tracing every word upon the parchment scroll. And as you look over his shoulder, now that your eyes have become accustomed to the light, and notice what he is writing, you see that he himself describes his writing very accurately when he says, "Ye see how large a letter I have written unto you with mine own hand," or to translate what he says accurately, "You see with how great and scrawling characters I have written unto you with mine own hand." It is Paul, the apostle, with his own hand writing to the Galatians in a time when special difficulty was confronting the Galatian Church.

What is the lesson for you and me? Why, it is plain enough. The lesson is this: The time of special difficulty ought to be the time of special painstaking. What has that to do with the lookout committee? It has a good deal to do with it. Do you know that the most wonderful organization of young people on this planet is the Christian Endeavor organization? But do you know that there is here a spot and there a spot where the working of the organization is, to say the least, now and then just a little difficult?

The backbone of a Christian Endeavor organization is the pledge. If any one of you is a member of a Christian Endeavor society so-called, that blinks the pledge, don't flatter yourself; you are not Christian Endeavor, and you can't be. [*Applause.*] The backbone of the Christian Endeavor Society is the pledge. But a pledge not lived up to is a broken backbone, and that is a very poor thing. [*Applause.*]

Now, you know when Christian Endeavor was originated, just that difficulty was foreseen. It is a mighty and a splendid thing for young Christians to stand together and, with right hand uplifted toward God, take the *sacramentum*, the oath, and say, "I swear that I will do for Jesus Christ, my Lord and Saviour, this thing, and that thing, and the other thing." But do you know there was a man once leaning against a tavern door-post. He leaned there a great deal; he spent most of his time leaning there; and he was leaning there one afternoon, and some friends of his drove by in a buggy, and they stopped and looked back at him, calling out, "Tom, what makes you so confoundedly lazy?" And he lifted himself, swingingly, from the door-post, and swayingly stood forth, and said, "Lazy? I am not lazy; I was born tired." (*Laughter.*) Have n't you known a good many Christians who were regenerated tired? And do you know that there are some Christians who were regenerated tired even in a Christian Endeavor Society : and after they have taken the pledge, somehow or other, once in a while. — I think the number comparatively is very small, but it is large enough to talk about, — once in a while, somehow or other, they sort of get tired and lose their grip on the pledge? What is the business of the lookout committee? The business of the lookout committee is to hold those tired Christians steadily up to their pledge, and see that they keep it. [*Ap-*

plause.] And do you know that it isn't always just the pleasantest duty in the world? And do you know that sometimes members of lookout committees sort of draw back and shirk and don't do it, and let it go, and say, "We are getting on pretty well"? "Pretty well" will never do for a Christian Endeavor society [*applause*],— never! You are never to be satisfied until you do strictly well. [*Applause.*]

And now remember the picture I have drawn of the apostle in the time of special difficulty taking special pains, and be sure, members of Christian Endeavor, in the time of special difficulty gathering about the lookout committee, that you then and there, for the Lord's sake and for the sake of those banded with you in Christian Endeavor, make that very place of special difficulty the place of special painstaking. Do it, and do it now. Don't put it off till next month, and then till the month after, and then till the month after. When you find members of your society not appearing in the consecration meeting, and not sending written excuses, do you go for those members now, this month. Here is a jingle that has helped me. It is not poetry, but it is jingle. Perhaps it will help you.

> "Where 'er a duty arise for nee
> With sober judgment view it,
> And do not idly wish it done —
> Begin at once and do it.
>
> "For sloth says, idly,
> 'By and by will be as well to do it.'
> But present strength is surest strength;
> Begin at once and do it.
>
> "And find not lions in the way,
> Nor think if thorns bestrew it,
> But bravely try, and strength will come,
> For God will help you do it."

Members of Christian Endeavor lookout committees, remember this: The place and time of special difficulty is the place and time of special painstaking.

And now, God bless you, and may we have even better lookout committees in Christian Endeavor than we have ever had before. [*Applause.*]

The chairman then introduced as the next speaker, Rev. William E. Park, of Gloversville, N. Y.

ADDRESS OF REV. WILLIAM E. PARK.

As I left the house of a friend yesterday, the last thing I did was to stand in a group with others upon his door-step, where we were photographed. We may  have been careless in taking our positions, and not thought much about them, but our features and positions are stamped upon the paper forever. The historian is a man with a camera, and the scriptural author took an awful picture about 1850 years ago. It is a picture that photographs every element of society forever, and in that picture we have our places. The group taken in the picture was on a mount. Oh, how many great things have happened on hills and on mounts! The central figure of the picture is a beautiful youth; but ah! he is not standing erect in his manhood; he is writhing on a cross. He represents everything that is grand, everything that is beautiful, everything that is desirable, the *summum bonum* of life, the rise of expectancy of the fair state of man, struggling and dying. Around him in awful distinctness are represented the characters of the world. There were the scribe and the Pharisee, who represented a kind of stupid and malignant conservatism in the church, jealous of any interference and selfishly hating any one who aspired to usurp their authority. There were the disciples, who reasoned, "He is crucified, and therefore he will die, and no man has survived death before except Elijah. Therefore he will not live." They were right according to human logic, but sometimes there is a precedent that surpasses all logic. There were the weeping women, who symbolized the sentiment and the great heart of woman-kind, love, — love that surpasses all reason, love that is victorious over logic, — they believing that in some way he would rise again and come back. And they had the best of all of them.

There was the Roman centurion, who represented the imperial power of the day and generation, the mailed representative of Tiberius, far away on the rocks of Capri. There were the brutal executioners, representing the stupid brute force by which Rome executed her behests. There were the rabble, who cried "Hosanna" one day and "Crucify him" the next, — the dillydallies, whom the leaders of parties have always talked with one way and another and secured to their respective standards. In the meantime, while man is indifferent and is exulting over the misery of the Crucified One, nature declares herself. The sun concludes that he will give no more light to shine on such abominable villany, and he withdraws in darkness and lets them get their light where they can. The stupid, senseless stone bursts asunder and cannot abide the sight of so great a wrong. The earth rocks and reels in terror, and yet does not shake the cross down. The linen that made the shroud of death bursts asunder, and whatever the living thought, the dead could not abide it. The corpses arise from their graves and are seen of man. But the meanest and smallest feature is yet to be. In that awful darkness, in that silence that stifles the very soul of nature, I hear two sounds. The one is the feeble voice of a gasping, dying man, "*Eli, Eli, lama sabachthani?*" and the other sound is the little rattle of dice. In the darkness of the passion the soldiers are shaking dice in a helmet to get the robe of the One that is crucified. I hear them talk. They give a shake. "Five and three; that is a good throw." "Six and five; we have just about got it." "Double six; you can't beat that. I have got it; give it to me." And while all that is good in the universe is writhing in the agonies of death, and while nature darkens the earth because she cannot abide the unutterable horror, they are fuming and bickering to make as much money out of the thing as they can.

Dear friends, I won't say to Christian Endeavorers, "Thou art the man;" but if there are persons here not connected with the Christian Endeavor Society, I would like to say to them that if you won't work for the cross, if you won't work for the Christ, if you won't work for the Church, if you won't work for the Christian Endeavor, that is just where you are, making gain out of Christianity instead of contributing to it. [*Applause.*]

Let me explain myself. I said the Man on the Cross represents everything that is good in the universe. He represents the eternal and the chronic spirit of his followers — Christianity incarnating itself in living man. Struggling, dying, it gives birth to a present state, wrestling, talking, toiling, battling for the human race, and everything that is good in the world comes out of it. Everything that is good in the world comes out of it, do I say? Yes, materialism comes out of it, wealth comes out of it, prosperity comes out of it, — not only things spiritual but things material. "Seek ye first the Kingdom of God, and all these things shall be added unto you." And when I look at the stupendous progress of modern invention, when I see the locomotive shooting across the continent from the Atlantic to the Pacific at the rate of fifty miles an hour; when I behold the steamship tearing across the Atlantic in five days and eighteen hours, the old voyage that used to be four months at times; when I behold the printing press rolling off the sheets that are disseminated by the lightning; when I think of the stupendous banking systems of England and America; when I see the whole earth and the sea, under the sea and over the land, turned into a whispering gallery by the telegraph and the telephone, I behold the indirect consequences of the death of Jesus Christ, and we Christian Endeavorers will make no mistake about it. The world is not to be renovated by theological speculations; the world is not to be renovated by little whimsical, riffle-raffle ideas of a second probation. No; Heart of the eternal, mighty, glorious Gospel of Jesus Christ, thou dost do it! As William II. said to William of Orange, when he left him at Flushing, in 1791. never to see him again, "The discontents of Holland are owing not to protests, not to the natives; it is to you, you." The character of our country is not owing to genius, to industry, to mechanical invention: glorious Gospel of Jesus Christ, it is to you, *you*, YOU.

Now I want to say that the individuals who get the benefit of this Gospel of Jesus Christ and do not contribute to it are robbing it. If, my friend, — Christian friend I hope, and my friend in any case, — you are advancing, you are prosperous, vast advantages are given to you by the structural character of society. But I want to say that without the influence of Christianity, you would have no opportunity to advance yourself in life. Without the productive power of Christianity, no man would be able to produce anything, and no'man would have any money to buy with. Without the power of Christianity, there could be no contract. Unless there were moral character and principle generated by Christianity behind the signature, the promissory note of no man in the universe would be worth the paper on which it is written. It is independence by dependence on Christianity that you get the vast advantages that life gives you; and if you contribute to Christianity itself, you are men, and if you refuse to do it, you are become robbers and plunderers of the institution that has built you up. For commerce floats upon Christianity as upon a sea, and if you do not, like men, toil and work for Christianity, you are only robbing it, and the text in the Bible describes you: "They parted my garments among them, and for my vesture did they cast lots."

Oh, there is something pathetic in the appeal of the Church! Think of the money that is squandered in vice; think of the money that goes to pampered appetite and luxury, and the humble demands of charity! The Church appeals to us, and she says, "Ninety million dollars are raised for me, and nine hundred million dollars for ardent spirits, and six hundred millions for tobacco." The Church declares that the missionary societies of the Congregational, the Presbyterian, the Methodist, and the Baptist churches together in all this country receive five and one-half million dollars, and Christianity says, "Oh, give me the means to evangelize the world. Let me have a little of the money of which I am the producer. Oh, give it me. All I ask is a little fragment of the wine bill, a small percentage of the charge of pampered luxury, a little fraction of the expense of vice. Oh, let me have that!" And the church-building society appeals, and the church-missionary society appeals, and the benevolent organizations of the day appeal, and they say, "Oh, give to me that which is my portion, and let me have the means of carrying on the work for which my Redeemer died, and in your service I am dying also! Oh, let me have more than the one-sixteenth part of one per cent that the world gives to the cause of vice! Let me have more than the one dollar in every fifteen hundred and eighty-four dollars now contributed to advance the Christianity of the world." But "No; "says one: "I want to get more honor;" and "No," says another; " I want to get more gain. I can spare but little for the great cause that is evangelizing the world." And again I listen, and I hear the rattling of the dice under the cross, — "And they parted my garments among them, and for my vesture did they cast lots."

Now, I want to advance the idea that the non-consecrated labor and the non-consecrated gain is only a labor and a gain that is in itself a robbery. The whole earth belongs to the Lord and the fulness thereof, and a non-consecrated property is a refusal to give back his own. No matter whether it be an original Rothschild, an original Vanderbilt, an original Astor with vast commercial genius sweeping in the great sums of the revenues of the world. Because the business is done with genius and power it does not alter its moral character. No matter whether it be a Cæsar or an Alexander, if the business be done with a selfish spirit, the Lord looks upon it only as the conduct of the smallest person, and a false and mercenary action. It is defrauding God of his rights and a taking away of that which belongeth to the Master. It is only a form of grasping the robe of the great Master Spirit and making money out of the great kingdom of his faith. [*Applause.*]

Christian Endeavorers, I look upon this audience with pride and pleasure this evening, as I think the magnificent life of the young Church is coming forward to consecrate itself. We go directly onward with the grandest object that human life or society can attain, and the young, strong, vigorous life of the Church, the power that shall ultimately control it, is consecrating itself to its Master, and advancing to do the great central work that is given to human nature. I used to learn in my philosophy that the centre of gravity of the body is that part of it which, if supported, causes the whole to remain at rest. We put the love of the Gospel directly under the centre of gravity, and we seek indeed to raise the whole world with us. Our aim is the noblest and the grandest. We work not for profit; we work not for glory; we do not want to get the cast-off garment of the Master Spirit, but rather enter into his love, that our existence may be hid with Christ and in God.

Let us consecrate ourselves unto Christ this evening. In the picture that we have seen, let us take the place of the women, — faithful at the cross of Christ, faithful in the ranks of his followers in Christian Endeavor to-day. Love is the mightiest power in the universe. Say what you will, love understood and followed the Redeemer to the end, and saw him rise again from death. In the words of the poet: —

> "Love took up the harp of life,
> And turned it in his glowing hand;
> Every moment, like his self,
> Ran itself in golden sands.
>
> "Love took up the harp of life,
> And struck upon the chords with might;
> Smote the chord of Self,
> That, trembling, passed in music out of sight."

May that love, may that faith, be ours forevermore. The world may fly off into tangents; it may clasp what vagaries of theological opinion are satisfactory to it; but as for ourselves, we believe in him denied, by Pontius Pilate crucified. [*Applause.*]

The CHAIRMAN: We know that God sometimes elects a man and chooses him to be instrumental in fulfilling his purpose. In this movement he found the man to hold the die while he struck the blow, and from that die there has been no considerable change until this moment; and when you take the hand of Dr. Francis E. Clark, the founder and the President of the United Society, you take the hand that held the die while God struck the blow. It is my great pleasure to introduce to you the Rev. Dr. Francis E. Clark. [*Applause.*]

ADDRESS OF PRESIDENT FRANCIS E. CLARK, D.D.

My friends in Christian Endeavor [*Applause*]: — I remember that the last time I had the honor of speaking in this beautiful church we were asking ourselves what would be the outcome of the year of preparation which the New York City Union and the Brooklyn Union had been through. We were looking forward with some anxiety and a little trepidation to these days. We did not know exactly what God had in store for us. We had some nervous anticipations, perhaps, that this Eleventh Annual Christian Endeavor Convention might not reach the high-water mark in Christian Endeavor, as we hoped and believed it would. But I am sure that now, on the second night of this convention, all these fears are dispelled, and we are already, though the convention is yet not half-way through, prepared to sing " Praise God, from whom all blessings flow." [*Applause.*]

I remember, at that meeting we were wondering what would be the outcome of the convention. A gentleman said to me in the vicinity of New York a little while ago, " The Christian Endeavor convention will not make a ripple in the city of New York, and you needn't think it will. There is no convention of a religious kind that ever can make a ripple in New York or make an impression upon New York." Is that so? [*Cries of,* " *No!*"] I think not. I came from the Overflow Meeting a little while ago, the meeting into which the people who couldn't get here had to go, you know [*laughter*], and the Postmaster-General of the United States, when he made a few remarks in presiding, said that he thought that this magnificent convention was the most wonderful surprise that had ever come to the city of New York. He said he understood there were 25,000 people in attendance upon this convention, and when he was corrected and was told that it was 30,000, he said that he hadn't the remotest doubt that it was true, and that he thought, as he tried to get into the hall, that we might add 20,000 to that 30,000, and not come very wide of the mark. He said that he thought it had made a ripple in the city of New York, and that it had made an impression upon this great business metropolis. I believe that we can think so too, and that this impression is a distinctively religious inpression, — that this impression is one made for the Lord Jesus Christ, and that this convention will hold high above all its methods and all its plans and its name and everything else, the uplifted cross of Jesus Christ, our Lord.

I remember that I ventured to say when I was here before, if I am not mistaken, that I thought this convention would teach us a lesson in geography. Some of you, I know, were present during the session to-day in the Madison Square Garden when we heard from all parts of the world, — when the Chinaman, and the African, and the Hindoo, and the individual from Turkey and the one from Alaska, and the one from Manitoba, and from California, and from Texas, and from every State and Territory and Province in North America, and from old Mexico to the South, and from Australia, and from England, and from Scotland, and from every land where our missionaries have gone, — when those representatives came on the platform and told us that they were Christian Endeavorers, and that they were working as we are working, for Christ and the Church, I am sure that it taught some of us a lesson in geography ; and when we saw the banners, so gracefully presented by our brother, Dr. Hoyt; when we saw that from the little Territory of Oklahoma, the latest arrival of this family in the family of States and Territories, the banner was transferred to the Province of Manitoba, equally new; and when we saw the other banner go from the great State of Pennsylvania to the great Province of Ontario, I am sure that we felt there were links in this chain of Christian Endeavor that we had not known much about before, and that in all parts of this country, geographically, are these friends of ours. [*Applause.*]

Another thing: Hasn't it taught us something about young people? Young people! This audience is full of them — this audience is made up of them. There are three other audiences in New York City at this moment made up of them — thousands, actually tens of thousands, of young people. And what have they come here for? What could induce them to spend their money? Why have they taken these long railroad journeys? Why have they been willing in these hot days of July to give up the comforts of the seaside resort or the mountain pleasure resort, where they were expecting, perhaps, to spend their vacation, for the sake of coming to this crowded metropolis? Ah, friends, this has taught us something, and it will teach the city of New York something, and it will teach the United States of America and the world something about the character of young people : that there is something Christ-like within them, that there is something heroic within them, that there is something of true religious fibre found in every one of them, and that they are attracted by nothing else in this world as by Christ and the cross.

And one other thing: This convention, I believe, will teach us and has taught us the strength and power of the religion of Christ. I went out on the Pacific coast a little while ago, and in the city of Tacoma I saw a tabernacle that had been built for the Rev. B. Fay Mills out of trees that three weeks before my arrival in Tacoma were growing in the forests of Washington. And they said that this tabernacle that seated 4500 people was built in ninety-six hours of working time. It was built for a religious convention; it was built for evangelistic work; it was built that in this tabernacle might be told the "old, old story," that has been told so often in all the past. Oh, there is nothing so attractive as the religion of the cross; there is no such magnet in all the world as the cross of Christ. What is it that could have brought these young people together? Let me ask you once more — perhaps I asked you when I was here before, but we can ask to-day with redoubled emphasis — what else could have brought these young people together? I do not think that there is anything in the world. There is no theatre company; there is no opera troupe; there is no base-ball aggregation; there is no circus; there is no hippodrome; there is no political convention; there is nothing that we can think of in this world that would have brought 30,000 young people to the city of New York except a convention that was based and planted on the religion of Christ, except a society that had for its dearest motto our motto, "For Christ and the Church," except an organization that believes in the Fatherhood of God and the brotherhood of man; that says to you here and to a million and a third of Christian Endeavorers all over the world, "One is your Master, even Christ; and all ye are brethren." [*Loud applause.*]

The chairman then introduced the Rev. David James Burrell, D.D., pastor of the Marble Collegiate Church, New York City,

ADDRESS OF REV. D. J. BURRELL, D.D.

The man who would n't have any enthusiasm in his heart in looking over such an audience of young people as this is, as Shakespeare said, "Fit for stratagems and spoils;" and the minister of the Gospel of Jesus Christ who, looking down to faces like yours, could not make a talk that would raise the temperature a bit, ought to go and join a deaf and dumb asylum. [*Laughter and applause.*] If I were a Methodist, I would say, "It is good to be here;" and I will say it anyhow. I feel like adding what Philip Phillips said when he went down to the State Prison of Joliet: he looked around him there in the chapel of the prison, and said, inadvertently, "I am glad to see so many of you here to-day." [*Laughter.*] I am just in from the country, and coming down through Harlem last night I got into an elevated station. I happened to know that the gateman there is a good Roman Catholic, and I just overheard him saying, as I passed by, "Yes, sir; as sure as you live, there is more Christian people in New York City to-day than there ever was before since the sun began to shine." [*Loud applause.*]

But I began to talk about this superior audience. It is good to look into the faces of some earnest young men and women — there are so many good-for-naughts and ne'er-do-weels. We ministers look into so many stolid faces, — I don't in this church, but so many of them do, — so many people who look as if they were carved out of wood; and there are so many young men and women who do not seem to have any *raison d'être*, or something of that kind, I think the French call it. They don't know why they are here, and we don't, either. They don't seem to have any visible means of support, as they say about a vagrant in the police courts. The same is true of the young women, plenty of them, who are living for nothing, apparently, and who, when they die, will not have accomplished anything, and all that they leave behind them will be a fragrant memory and some fancy work, — a few tidies hung over the backs of the chairs to crawl down the back of the minister when he comes to make a pastoral call [*laughter and applause*], and some more or less indifferent oil pictures around the walls, and some bundles of old letters tied with pink ribbon and smelling of rose leaves, and a mound in the graveyard, and occasionally somebody standing by it, saying, "Sweet girl; she was a sweet girl;" and that is the end of it. What is the use of living that way?

And then the young men! I wish they could pair off properly, but they do not. [*Laughter.*] There is very often a misadjustment. The young men that my dear friend Wayland Hoyt talked about a moment ago were born tired, — the cane chewers and the dog leaders, the young men who get their bread by the sweat of their fathers' brows, — I call them ne'er-do-weels, bi-furcated things who haven't anything in the world that is so much to them as a trousers stretcher. Now, I want to come out of an audience of people like that we meet almost anywhere except in this church, — some portion of our audience is made up in that way, — and to look down in the faces of young men and young women of whom we know to a certainty that they know what they are doing, and that they mean business, and that they do mean to spend their lives and make the most of themselves for the glory of God. Oh, it is like catching a cool breeze from the King's garden on a summer night. I am glad to be here, and notwithstanding Philip Phillips, I am glad to see so many of you here too.

We are living in the century of new forces. One of these days, a man will write the history of this century, and he will call it the period of new forces. When my friend, who didn't know that he was my friend until I introduced myself to him a moment ago, — Dr. Park, whose father I used to hear preach years ago when I was in Phillips Academy, — when he was talking about the telegraph and the telephone and similar improvements and all that sort of thing, — the new forces, the new explosives, and the new projectiles that are making war impossible, because, if you take a handful of dynamite, pretty soon you can blow up a whole division of an army, and there is no use of making war after that, — I say, when he was talking about the new forces in the material and the industrial world, I was thinking that in the presence of spiritual things there are new forces that abundantly match them in these times. For this is the century of magnificent Sunday-school work. It is only a hundred years ago or thereabouts when Robert Raikes was going about the streets of Gloucester offering a shilling to women to come in and teach the children in his ragged school. It is in this century that the missionary enterprise has taken its great impulse; it is within this century and the latter part of this blessed nineteenth century that woman has assumed her proper place in the vanguard of the progress of the Church of Jesus Christ. [*Applause.*] It was in a synagogue in Capernaum that the Lord looked down one day into his congregation, and he saw a woman all doubled, as it is said, with an infirmity of I know not how many years, so that she could by no means lift up herself; and he looked at her pityingly, and said, "Woman, be loosed from thine infirmity;" and she straightened herself up, and took her place where a woman ought to be. That didn't happen eighteen hundred years ago only; it has happened within my memory. I have heard the Lord speak the word to the crooked woman, and I have seen her straighten herself up and take her part in the work of evangelizing the world, and God be praised for it. That is another of the new forces.

But among all the spiritual forces of this blessed nineteenth century, I believe there is no one that is for a moment comparable with the blending of the youth of all Christendom in this mighty Endeavor movement; and I am glad to participate in some slight measure in this important work. I did not always feel that way. I had to be converted, like Saul of Tarsus. It was about ten years ago. The thing had been going on for about a year, and I didn't half believe in it, till it seemed to me as if there wasn't any use; it was going on anyway, and I might as well get in. I felt like a man trying to stop a cyclone, and it was of no use, and I heard God say, "It is hard for you to kick against the pricks," and I told him I wouldn't do so any more. That was the way I was converted to the Christian Endeavor movement. [*Applause.*]

Now, I believe in Christian Endeavor with every drop of blood that is in my body. [*Applause.*] I believe that it is the great movement of this age, and of the whole history of the Christian Church. That sounds immensely large, but I believe that we can substantiate it, and before we get through there will not be anybody to doubt it. In less than a hundred years I do believe all the people in the Universal Church of Jesus Christ will be looking back, and they will not be saying so much about my dear brother Clark here, but they will be saying, "Oh, what a time that was when the youth of Christendom rallied to the help of the Lord against the mighty." [*Applause.*]

Now, I want to give three reasons for the faith that is in me. I believe in the Christian Endeavor mission, first of all, because of the immense significance of that cabalistic word "Endeavor." It is a great time for the Church of our Lord Jesus Christ when the people who profess to be consecrated are ready to prove their consecration by endeavor for the Master's sake.

The most pathetic picture in all Scripture, outside of Golgotha, is that of the Church sleeping in the city gates when the Lord, the bridegroom of the Church, comes that way and finds her sleeping with the dust upon her and manacles upon her hands and fetters upon her feet, and, bending over her, tries to awake her, crying to the Church, to his sleeping bride, "Awake, awake, O daughter of Zion, put on thy beautiful garments, shake thyself loose from the dust of the earth, unloose thyself from the bonds of thy neglect, O captive daughter of Zion. Arouse thyself and awake, O daughter of Zion."

If endeavor means anything, it means that the bride of Jesus Christ is stirring in her sleep, and presently will awake, and when the Church awakes, and when the people are in earnest, and when you and I and all the other servants of our blessed Lord are ready to endeavor for his sake, then presently we will be at our avocations one day as usual and will look into each other's faces and look aloft, and we will see the heavens rend asunder and roll up like a scroll, and he will appear, and we will say to one another, after looking with unspeakable joy for a time, "Maranatha; it has come at last; the Lord is here." That is when the Church awakes; that is when the Church shall hear the voice of the bridegroom crying to her as she lies sleeping in the gate. Always self-reliant,—that is what this Endeavor movement means,—though I believe that shibboleth belongs to the Methodist church, but it has got so in these days that we are all robbing each other of our best shibboleths. God be praised that denominationalism in its worst aspects is pretty nearly over. Every man doing his own part! Man there is generic. So to speak, man embraces woman in that phrase. Every one doing his part,—that is the meaning of the word "Endeavor." Let us carry it home with us, and let us endeavor in the name of the blessed Lord as we never have hitherto. I wish we could catch some of the spirit of dear Dr. Guthrie, when he used to look down in the cow gate, as he worked among the "submerged tenth." He used to call it his "golden field." If you have ever stood on one of the bridges running into the city of Edinburgh, and have ever looked down into the cow gate there, you know what he meant when he spoke of his "golden field." No, there is no place that I ever saw where it is so manifest that it is a "submerged tenth." But I was going to say: Dr. Guthrie in that hard field of his, when he went about visiting the people in their squalor and in their abject misery and poverty and shame, used to help himself by repeating now and then, to enhearten himself, these words, which have been a strength to me, and which possibly may be a help to you. Down into the cow gate he looked as he said it:—

"Sin worketh: let me work too
Sin undoeth: let me do;
Busy as sin my work I will ply
Till I rest in the rest of eternity.

"Death worketh: let me work too;
Death undoeth: let me do;
Busy as death, my work I will ply
Till I rest in the rest of eternity."

That is what Endeavor means. I love the Christian Endeavor Society for that. Then I will love it and believe in it thoroughly and to the very centre of my heart and life, because it means not merely endeavor, but skilled endeavor. It is a school for apprentices; it is a place for training the servants of the living God. How in the world have we ever gotten thus far in the Christian Church without a training-school, and without devoting any attention, as it were, to the preparation of the young men and young women for the duties and responsibilities of the Christian life?

It is a great thing to know how to do anything. If you ever tried to cook rice without having learned how, as I have done in camping, and had to gather it up from all the surrounding territory while all the rest of the campers were laughing at you, you would know then that there is a great deal in knowing how to do a thing.

If you take a little sawdust and a little nitric acid and a little glycerine and throw them together, you can hammer them with a battering-ram and they will not do any harm; but if you know how to do as well as those fellows do who down at Homestead are hurling this mighty explosive at Pinkerton's men, — if you know how to put them together as they do, — you can touch your nitric acid and your glycerine and your sawdust with a toothpick, and you can make an earthquake out of it. It makes a tremendous amount of difference whether or not we are skilled workmen, — whether we know how to do a thing.

Before St. Cloud there was a military school just beyond Paris, and there were a lot of boys there who were accustomed to keep step in their march, and to train their sight; and one of them was a little Corsican. They used to carry a flag around with them on which was written, "Tremble; we are growing up." And many people laughed when they saw it. But the boys went on keeping time, aiming at the bull's eye, carrying their banner, till one day the little Corsican stood out in the front of the Invalides, on the great open plaza, the Imperial Guard his immediate guard; before them was the mob, the French people with their red caps, coming on with a quick step, — a mighty, murderous mob. And here a little group of armed men, the old school of St. Cloud, and half a dozen great guns. The little Corsican had grown up. "Watch them," he said; "let them come near, nearer. Now, fire!" Oh, but that was a harvest field! Down they went, men and women of Paris; down they went, like wheat before a sickle. They knew how to do it. There is a vast difference between the mob that has been working for 1800 years without training, and the church that is drilled at St. Cloud, getting ready its guns and coming up to the help of the Lord against the mighty in the next quarter of a century. [*Loud applause.*]

The Lord himself was an apprentice. He never mended a plow for a farmer in Judea until he learned how to do it; he never tinkered a chair for a mother in Nazareth until he learned how to do it. The best picture of Jesus that ever was made is that of Holman Hunt, representing him as standing with the chips and shavings around his feet and the implements of his trade on the bench before him, and behind him, in the rays of the setting sun, the shadow of the cross thrown against the workshop wall. He not only learned how to do good carpenter work, — and he did honest work as long as he was a carpenter, — but he trained himself for the higher work that was to find its confirmation in the glorious act of divine self-denial, which is the most human thing that Christ ever did, when he died for us on the accursed tree. He trained himself for it, was all the while getting ready for it, — getting so nervous now and then, and retaining, as it were, no heart when the Greeks came up to see him. "Now is my soul troubling me, and what shall I say? Father, save me from this trial, from the shadow of this dark effigy, this cross before me? Nay, nay; but for this cross came I into the world. Father, glorify thyself." He was always getting ready for it, serving his apprenticeship, growing in stature and in wisdom and in favor with God and man, till he was able at last to work his masterpiece. So young men and young women ought to train for service as Jesus Christ trained for his cross and for the divine self-denial that gave us spiritual and eternal life.

I remember so well the old village church. Nobody there might do anything except old father Brewster, over in yon corner, and old father Buckley over in that corner; and when they prayed, the thing was done, and then, if the women had anything to do, it was dear Mrs. Cary who led the way, and if she didn't do it, it wasn't done. As Mrs. Beaks used to say when she was asked to do anything, "Yes, certainly, there is only a few of us; them as will, may forever; them as wont, need n't never." And that is the way it used to be before the days of Christian Endeavor in all our churches; and it must be so as long as there is no apprenticeship. A woman does not know how to speak. It is not because a false interpretation of an old passage keeps her silent in the churches; it is because she does not know how to open her mouth and say anything for Christ. She has not trained herself to it. She will get up to it in about ten years. That is about the time I think you young ladies will be in the forefront of the Church of Jesus Christ. But in the old time, why, if a woman straightened herself up, I declare the old folks scarcely knew whether it was the woman or the talker that was doing it. [*Laughter*.]

There is one thing more to say. I love the Christian Endeavor movement, first, because it means Endeavor, and second, because it means trained Endeavor, and third, because it means international, interdenominational Endeavor. [*Applause*.] I do not think it means non-denominational Endeavor [*applause*]; and I am very glad it does not, because I could not be in such hearty sympathy with it. I am a denominationalist; I believe in the denomination that I belong to. I came out of the Presbyterian Church after I was in it twenty years and crossed the lowest kind of a fence into the Reformed Church, and here I am a little bluer than I ever was; for in this church we believe that what is to be will be, whether it comes to pass or not. [*Laughter and applause*.] And it would n't do for me to talk about non-denominationalism. I do believe that fences make good neighbors; but then I do not believe that any fence can ever be made so high that my dear brother Hoyt (Baptist as he is all over) and I can't come out on a bright morning and shake hands across the top railing and say, "It is a bright morning; God bless you." [*Applause*.]

All the quarrelling in these days is not between the churches, but inside them. The Presbyterian Church is having a wholesome little racket of its own [*laughter*]; and the Episcopal Church is having the nicest sort of a little quarrel — a triangular quarrel between high church and low church and broad church, and all the people are standing up and telling us all that there is n't any dispute at all, and all the churches are having their own amusements, except the Reformed Church of America. [*Applause*.] But there is no quarreling between the churches. The time was when you Methodists used to hang your banners on the outer walls, and when the Presbyterians used to plant their great guns to "prove the doctrine orthodox with apostolic blows and knocks," and when all the denominations were making war on one another. But that has gone by; the churches have n't anything against one another any more, and I bless God for that. We are ready for interdenominational work. We are going to shake hands across the fences now and forever more — not take them down. [*Applause*.] We are not going to take them down, for do you know, I believe we are to have them in heaven. I do not think heaven is going to be such a neutral-tinted sort of a place that some of us ministers can't get together and have a good quarrel on theology when we want to. [*Laughter*.] What sort of a place would it be, if we could n't sit down and differ with one another. We are going to differ on the non-essentials up there, but we are going to agree on the things that we hold at one in the Christian Endeavor. I want you young Christian Endeavorers, — if that is the word that is going into the dictionary, — I want all Christian Endeavorers the world over to stand for two great truths, in spite of all theological division. One of them is the incarnate Word, the other is the written Word, — one as inerrant as the other, and each of them as absolutely perfect as it came from the hand of the living God. [*Applause*.] We can have our quarrels as much as we please. If we stand by the Lord Jesus Christ, first, last, and all in all, and if we stand by the dear old-fashioned Book that our fathers touched with reverent hands and our mothers stained with their last kisses, — if we save Christ and the Bible, — let the rest go; and I pray you young men and women never be moved from your loyalty to Joachim and Boaz, the two great pillars, — the written Word and the incarnate Word, all one in the revelation of God, — the two pillars which, with united strength, uphold the porch of the temple of the living God.

Now, the last word, and I am done. I greet you, Christian Endeavorers, all in the name of our common Lord, in the name of the denomination that I represent; and may I not venture to greet you in behalf of this congregation that tenders you hospitality to-night, which is the oldest evangelical Christian organization on the American continent to-day. [*Applause.*]

Do you remember the story of Æsop? An old man, burdened with his years, bowing to earth, he drew his gray locks back, and hugging his chilled old body, fell asleep upon the earth. And the witch Medea came that way and saw the old man sleeping and dreaming, and she distilled a magical decoction of herbs, and injected some of the magical mixture into the old man's veins. He moved in his sleep, opened his eyes, rose and looked about him, and drew back his locks, — and they were black as a raven's plume, — straightened himself, and the chill of old age was gone and his blood was flowing with the warmth of youth. He rose with his old-time vigor, and was a new man. Not the witch Medea, but the youth-giving spirit of the living God has been this way, and in this last decade has infused the elixir of life into the veins of the old Church. These are the days of renewal of youth. I praise God that I have lived to lift my hand and lift my voice for the mission of youth in behalf of the cross of our Lord Jesus Christ. We have come to the day at last when the dream of Ponce de Leon is realized, for the bride of Jesus Christ has found at last the long-sought fountain of perennial youth. [*Applause.*]

After the singing of hymn No. 209, Dr. Park pronounced the benediction.

Madison Square Presbyterian Church.

FRIDAY EVENING.

The praise service at 7:30 was led by Mr. S. V. Hoag, Brooklyn. Rev. G. R. Alden, of the District of Columbia, then offered prayer. Rev. N. Boynton, of Boston, presided.

REMARKS OF REV. N. BOYNTON, OF BOSTON,

My dear friends in Christian Endeavor: — It is a sincere joy which is mine to-night, — that of greeting you in this place. There are many meetings of Christian Endeavor being held in this grand metropolis this evening, but there is no place where Christian Endeavor can be more appropriately heard than in this house of God, where faith and earnestness strive so mightily together for those things which are pure and blessed and uplifting and Christlike. [*Applause.*]

One of the papers of the city, in giving to us a very pleasant editorial notice to-day, remarked that probably the great reason of our strength inhered in our social organization, — the fact that we were friends and that there was a sort of an *esprit du corps* of sociality which ran from one to the other and made us true and powerful and strong. Christian Endeavor does not underestimate the power of society. We know how souls which are severed are preserved by the fraternal relationships of life; and still if there is any one thing for which our society does not pre-eminently stand, it is the social idea. We are first and foremost a spiritual organization. "One is our Master, even Christ, and all we are brethren." It is the spiritual power which is underneath this organization of ours which gives it its hold upon life and its promise for the days that are to come. It is the fact, not that we are primarily in league one with another, but that we are in league with our Lord and Saviour Jesus Christ, which makes it possible for us so to move by our presence this great metropolis.

I remember that on one occasion an artist went into a church to see a fresco which had been painted by a friend of his. He at once discerned certain defects in it, and instead of anathematizing the work of his friend, he simply took a crayon which was at his disposal and upon the walls drew the outlines of a fresco of his own and went his way without a single word. A friend asked him the reason for his strange procedure, and he said, "I criticise by creation." That is the mission of Christian Endeavor to the life of the present. Not ours to defame, not ours to anathematize. Ours to criticise by creation, ours to lift the world nearer Christ, by first of all ourselves going and dwelling in his immediate presence; and we are to have our power and our great influence in these days and the days that are to come just in proportion as the created work of our individual lives shall present Jesus Christ in fairer outlines to the world about us than any light which it knows.

But I remember just here that it is the characteristic of a good waiter to speedily bring to his guests that which has been ordered for them, and I suppose that one of the greatest troubles of a hungry individual is to be compelled to wait an undue length of time for that which has been promised him upon the printed bill of fare. Therefore, let me try to be to-night at least a good waiter

The chairman then introduced the Rev. Edgerton R. Young, of Toronto, Can. [*See Mr. Young's eloquent speech, in the report of the Madison Square Garden meetings.*]

The CHAIRMAN. — There are some people in the world, I am sorry to say, who never have a good word for Chicago. They are the people either who have never been there, or who have no friends in the city whom they desire to visit next year. [*Laughter and applause.*] Christian Endeavor has been to Chicago; we know the character of her hospitality and the hearts of her loyal men and women, and boys and girls. Some years ago, when Christian Endeavor was young, it was with great difficulty that we were able to secure for our platform upon public occasions representative men. But there was one man whose voice had already been heard throughout our land, who even in those young days gave to us his loyal support. His voice was ever employed for our defence, and his pen was always ready for our needs. Is not the man who stood for us in the gray of the dawn worthy to stand before us in the radiant glory of the morning? His speech is silver, his spirit is golden, — the Rev. John Henry Barrows, D. D., of Chicago. [*Applause.*]

ADDRESS OF REV. JOHN HENRY BARROWS, D. D.

The Trustees of the United Society, at our meeting last year at Minneapolis, gave me the honor and privilege of announcing to you that the next convention would be held in the city of New York, and I was brave enough to make the prophecy at that time that 25,000 delegates would come up to this imperial city, — if I had said 75,000, I think I should have been nearer the mark, — and I was saying to Brother Young that if he will go out in the street in front of this church and tell some of the stories he told in my church, he will have an audience of 50,000 in the course of an hour.

This convention seems to me not only the culmination of all our conventions, but of the Christian development of eighteen centuries. It is likely to become a turning point in the deliberations of our times. There is no question about the character and sweep of the Christian Endeavor movement, and I may add that there is no question about the high and noble quality of the Christianity it represents; but it is my hopeful prediction that this movement, while remaining always loyal to its original purpose, while proving to be in every church the pastor's strongest ally and a wholesome school of discipline for the young people, may touch with regenerating power the life of communities and nations.

In the excellent New England Magazine of a few months ago, the editor, my friend Mr. Mead, of Boston, in a friendly way suggested that our societies should be more generally and earnestly active in Christian beneficence. I believe that we have always, as societies, been eager to show our faith and to prove it by an abundance of good work. I believe that we have wisely gathered our many-sided activities around the prayer meeting, from which springs the inspiration of our efforts. Still, the suggestion has clung to my mind that this majestic movement must come to represent in all respects the Christianity which is needed by our time and by all times. We sometimes speak of it as the new Christianity. It does not beat itself against evangelistic dogma, it does not oppose the teachings of history; it confirms and proclaims them. It is not a Christianity of denials, but rather of abnegation and self-denials. It would see the cross not only lifted on church spires, not only exalted in our studies of theology, not only graven on sword hilts in the hour of battle, — it would see the cross borne upon the heart of every disciple in the essential spirit of it. [*Applause.*]

Now, the new Christianity, while proclaiming the Gospel, must have a record for righteousness. While preaching Jesus and salvation and faith in him, it must not forget other things. Since the perils of our time are striking at the purity and existence of our nation, we must proclaim that those perils spring from disregard of the words of everlasting rejoicing written by God's finger on the tablets of Mt. Sinai. Finding in mammon and not in Jehovah the Supreme Being, with Sabbath desecration inviting a judgment of God against our land, with licentiousness rampant, with theft sheltered under the disguise of respectability and carried on under laws which executives were appointed to execute, with murder making our daily calendars as red as the rubrics of hell, and the lying exalted into a place of chief power in national political contests and not deprecated by one party or the other, it sounds not strange to hear unbelief saying that the Frenchman's dream of liberty, equality, and fraternity is an advance on the decalogue.

Oh, my friends, the trouble with religion in America is that it has got beyond the Ten Commandments, or, in other words, that it has'nt yet come up to them. Men leave the commandments behind them when they enter into business or political life. The teaching that all is fair in politics or business, and that there are spheres in human life into which the Bible cannot enter, is the teaching of devils. If our land is to be the abode of God and not ultimately a lair of ravening and roaring tigers, then, my friends, we must stock our boards of trade, our caucuses, our halls of legislation, and our executive mansions with good old-fashioned rejoicings, fresh from Mt. Sinai. We must see to it that delegates who are sent to select candidates for the chair at Washington do not disgrace themselves and their party and their nation, as did the delegates to the recent political conventions in Minneapolis and Chicago, by drunkenness and disorder. [*Applause.*]

I am told that the saloon-keepers of Minneapolis, at the time our Christian Endeavor convention was held there last year, complained that they got no profit in our coming [*applause*], and I suppose their brethren in New York will make the same complaint; but that complaint was not offered by the saloon-keepers in Chicago and Minneapolis at the recent political conventions.

All Christianity needs is to catch the inspiration of John Knox and of Oliver Cromwell. It needs the unflinching tongue with which Paul made Felix tremble, and the unflinching eye with which John the Baptist stood before Herod.

It needs to breathe the atmosphere of old Israel, and I believe that Christianity has been re-embodied in the great preacher who in this pulpit has denounced the great evils in this city. [*Applause.*] It will be a great mistake in this magnificent convention if we do not carry home the resolve that this mighty Christian Endeavor movement, and the young manhood and young womanhood represented by it, shall feel its responsibility to shape with moral influences the life of our land. It will be a great mistake if we do not feel our obligation to cherish and illustrate the loftiest Christian patriotism. [*Applause.*]

The grandeur of America is not our territorial bigness or the swiftness of our national progress. Whatever wealth and greatness we have gained has sprung from integrity, from intelligence, from respect for law, from a reverent obedience to the statutes of the Almighty that are recorded in the Word of God. I know some people read our great history and miss all the nobler elements of it. There is a truer and a nobler side to our past and to our present. I know there is another side to it. I know there is an America which is condemned the wide world round, — the America of the municipal boodler, the hoodlum, the politician, and the unscrupulous money-getter; but you and I know there is another America. While our nationality is looked upon by the eyes of the world as the seat of municipal corruption and domestic scandal, we know there is a truer and a nobler America. The true America is well represented here by this magnificent convention representing the young manhood and the young womanhood, by the thousands who have come up to us from the East and the West, and the North and the South. I claim that the true America is represented by our great statesmen, by our patriots, by our great soldiers, and by our Bible-reverencing and law-abiding common people; and this is the America that should be heard of by the public. The public-school teacher, even though she is so modest that she is not always recognized by our politicians, is the lawful ruler of this world, that world which the Spaniard thought to be a golden continent of light and wealth for the aching hearts of mankind.

The true America came across the Atlantic in the Mayflower, the dearest seaweed that ever floated to an unknown shore. The true America is well represented in the common schools. The true America is found in the order of General Washington requiring the observance of Sunday by the continental army [*applause*], and the order of President Lincoln, requiring the observance of the nation's rest day by the armies of the Union. The true America rang out in the voice of General Hawley when he said, "Before God, I am afraid to keep open the Fair gates on the Sabbath." [*Applause.*] The true America found expression in the petition of the Woman's Temperance Union, representing a constituency of nearly a million, asking that the gates of the World's Fair be closed on the Sabbath day, and in the repeated protests of the Young People's Societies of Christian Endeavor, who have demanded the same thing. [*Applause.*]

Our American people, and especially our American churches, are very slow in rising and stirring themselves. We showed this with regard to slavery, intemperance, municipal licentiousness, and the Louisiana lottery. Slavery is dead, the rum power is broken; municipal corruption is to be attacked in the next generation and even in this as the most flagrant evil in our times, and the Louisiana lottery dies by the good people of the Pelican State, a congress, a postmaster-general, and a Christian President. [*Applause.*] The Louisiana lottery has been defeated and is ready for burial in a scoundrel's grave. [*Applause.*]

However, we from every part of the republic, representing these better elements, ought to lift ourselves to a new conception of what God means by America and a new conception of that Christianity which is required by these times. If our courage has not utterly oozed away, then we should resolve that the laws restraining and punishing crime should be thoroughly enforced, and that our city should not be given over to shameless gangs of boodlers, compared with whom the hordes of robbers of the middle ages were bands of missionaries. We should be as ashamed to crouch and cringe in the presence of the rumseller, the gambler, and the monopolist, as our fathers would have been to yield to George the Third. We should resolve, not only to carry the Gospel to the poor Indians of the North and the new world, but we should resolve to carry it to the slums of our own city, and to fight the conditions which make the slums possible. We should resolve, not only to carry the Gospel into our workshops, but to fight those conditions that make possible the shameful riots at Homestead. [*Applause.*]

Let us, my friends, overturn every soldier's monument in the cemetery of Arlington, let us destroy everything noble that Lincoln and Washington accomplished, let us make a gaming table of Plymouth Rock and cover Boston Common and Central Park with gin mills and turn the shaft of Bunker Hill monument into a distillery, before we succumb to the present powerful and un-American haters of our freedom and of all that is noblest in our past. [*Applause.*] Oh, for a whiff of Nasby, to sweep away all this chaff from the Lord's threshing-ground! Let us not forget that our freedom is strong only in righteousness, in self-rule, and in obedience to the laws of God. Let us not only carry the Gospel to every nation, but let us buttress the august fact of our American nationality with institutions of religion and of learning, with self-discipline and obedience to law, until the prophetic view of our greatest American stateman is realized, and each honest man shall have his vote, and each child shall have his school; for what availeth anything for light or love, if freedom fail? And may the God of Columbus and of Washington, the God of our fathers, protect us through all the enlightened future of the republic. [*Applause.*]

THE CHAIRMAN: There are some good people in the world to whom we cannot be introduced. They are our friends. We may have never seen their faces, and still we hold them in our thought. Among those whom we love to call by that precious name of friend, I am very sure that the lady whom I am about to present to you this evening cannot be unnoticed. You may never have seen her face, but who has not read "Pansy," [*applause*] and who would not like to see "Pansy." I have great pleasure in introducing to you Mrs. Isabella M. Alden, who will read us a short story.

Mrs. Alden then stepped forward and read the story of which the following is an abstract:—

ONE DAY'S ENDEAVORING.

The young girl, one day of whose life I want to photograph for you, could never be called pretty. Her eyes, a good honest grey in color, had nothing remarkable about them, and her face was freckled. Her dress was very simple, her only ornament being a very small pin marked with the initials, "C. E." As to her surroundings, she occupied a very small room in a fourth-rate boarding-house, her room only being furnished with a cot and a tin toilet service.

Maria was an orphan, her only connection being an uncle in the country, of whom she knew very little, and a step-aunt, whom she did not know at all. They were willing that she should try to earn a respectable living as a salesgirl.

What is there interesting about Maria?

I think it was because in the early summer morning she knelt in front of her window, with her head bowed, and prayed — because of this I want to photograph bits of her day for you. Her reading this

MRS. ISABELLA M. ALDEN.

morning had been part of a chapter in Galatians, and the verse was, "As we have therefore opportunity, let us do good unto all men."

After putting her room in order, she slipped across the hall, and took care of the sick baby of a poor woman whom she sent out to get some breakfast, allowing her own to get cold. But the woman was grateful, and Maria was satisfied. She later had the woman and child sent on an excursion. On her way down town in the crowded car she gave up her seat to a woman with a heavy bundle, and to another wretched woman she gave a spray from some flowers that had been given to her, and felt herself amply repaid by their earnest thanks. She would like to have read a new book from the Christian Endeavor library, but remembering her motto for the day, — "As we have opportunity," — she loaned the book to a friend, who was reading a story which Endeavorers had been earnestly urged to avoid. The morning was a busy one in the store, but at noon Maria had another opportunity, taking the place of a girl who wished to go home to see her sick mother. And then she sent word to the lookout committee to come and look after a dissipated young man. But she had one hard trial in the insulting attentions of another young man; but she spoke to him in a way that made him regret his remarks, and apologize. Her next customer was a member of the Christian Endeavor Society, and she asked him if his lookout committee was looking after this young man. The good gentleman was startled, and said he thought the Christian Endeavor and Clarke Dixon had nothing in common, and advised her not to have anything to do with him. Maria said she was not proposing to, but thought the committee should have something to do with him; and the gentleman said finally he would see what could be done.

Perhaps the giddiest clerk in the store, and also the one in whom Maria had most interest, was silly little Minnie Baker, who was always good-natured and careless and unselfish in her way, and was always getting into trouble. During a lull in business she opened a note which a messenger boy had brought, and gave a little squeal of delight over its contents. "Oh, look at this, Maria. Joe Hendricks has asked me to go to the open-air concert; and it happens that I want to go out to-night."

"O Minnie! You said you would not accept Joe Hendricks's invitations."

"Bother! I can't be squeamish all the time, just to please you. Joe is awfully swell; some of the society girls go with him whenever they get a chance, and he is real jolly company. I don't see any harm, Maria."

A somewhat prolonged and on Maria's part very earnest conversation followed. She had only too good reason for dreading the young man's influence on the giddy and pleasure-loving Minnie; yet how could she plan about keeping Minnie from going? If she had the money, she would suggest a carriage for meeting Minnie's sister at the depot,— as Minnie said she would not go with Joe, if it wasn't for having to meet her sister, and she had to have some one to go with her. She finally persuaded Minnie to wait an hour before sending a note to Joe, hoping that in the meantime something would happen by which her sister could be met, as in that case Minnie would decline the invitation. Absorbed as Maria seemed to be in serving customers, she was earnestly praying for help. There lacked but fifteen minutes of the hour, when Miss Angell entered the store and made her way directly to Maria's counter. Miss Angell was at the very height of the wealthy and aristocratic world. To win recognition from her was enough to settle the standing of any person who aspired to be known in society. She was more than this, — she was a veritable daughter of the King. Greeting Maria cordially, she said she had known of her, and that they ought to know each other.

"But, how tired you look! Would you like to have a ride? I am looking about for company."

There was such a flash of delight in the grey eyes that Miss Angell stopped, well pleased with the effect of her invitation. But Maria's first words surprised her.

"Do you think, Miss Angell, that God really sends people nowadays to answer one's prayers? It is very wonderful? May I tell you about Minnie Baker?"

Miss Angell listened thoughtfully, nodded her appreciation, and finally said, "And you want me to take Minnie in your place? I am wondering what the poor girl could have done under the circumstances; I suppose such emergencies arise often; among our young Endeavorers, too. Introduce me to your friend."

The introduction was made, Maria in a glow of satisfaction over the thought of the delight it would be to Minnie Baker to be introduced to the elegant Miss Angell. Then she left them and went back to her work. Minnie came to her presently, a curious smile on her face.

"The impossible happened," she said demurely; "the angel came, and brought an elegant span of matched ponies, and a carriage that I said the other day I would give up my eyesight for a week for the privilege of stepping into just once. I am to drive miles with her. Think of it! You are a queer girl, Maria Streeter; I never knew one like you. My sister Kate will be met in a style that will frighten her; but we will neither of us forget it. As for Joe Hendricks, I'll send him word that I don't go to concerts in street cars. Honestly, Maria, I will be good after this, if I can, just to please you and the angel."

The day was done at last. I have only given you a touch of its history. There were other people, dozens of them, with whom the quiet, unpretending shop girl came in contact. She stood during most of her journey home, because there were old people needing her seat. To a worn old man she gave a card with this verse: "Come unto me, and I will give you rest;" to a schoolboy in military dress she gave one which read, "Put on the whole armor of God;" and to a young mother in deep mourning, another with, "He shall gather the lambs with his arms, and carry them in his bosom." She scattered her seed as she had opportunity, and knew not which of her efforts should prosper, whether this or that.

It was lonely in her room that night. She could know nothing of the happiness her efforts of the day had given to those she had helped, nor about the winning words spoken by Miss Angell that evening. There were many things which she did not know. If she had, — if she could have looked down the near future and seen the forces which her simple, commonplace endeavoring had set in motion that day; if she could have looked down the ages and seen the far-away, wonderful end, — I am not sure but she would have been half frightened at life and its responsibilities. As it was, she was only a poor, homely, unknown salesgirl at the "notion" counter, very tired with her long day's work, and very warm in her close back room. Yet withal she was very quiet and happy as she knelt once more, this time in the moonlight, and thanked God for that day's opportunities, and asked to be forgiven wherein she had failed in doing just as Jesus would have her do.

She afterward moved about preparing for rest, and singing softly: —

> "Oh, blessed work for Jesus,
> Oh, rest at Jesus' feet!
> There toil seems pleasure,
> My wants are treasure,
> And work for him is sweet.
> Lord, if I may,
> I'll serve another day."

The audience then joined in singing hymn No. 211.

The Chairman then introduced Rev. Geo. H. Wells, D.D., of Minneapolis, Minn.

ADDRESS OF REV. GEORGE H. WELLS, D.D.

Well, dear Christian friends, I feel a good deal mixed, a little doubtful about my personal identity, a good deal confused as to the locality from which I come and to which I belong, completely carried out to sea by the figures and suggestions which your presiding officer has just made. He has gone beyond all my experience. I wish, when people talk to me, that they would talk about things with which I am acquainted. [*Laughter.*] I don't know how he gets hold of those things, unless he has had personal experience. [*Laughter and applause.*]

And now, to stand before a Christian Endeavor meeting and to be introduced as coming from Minneapolis, I don't know whether it is I or some other fellow. I had been so long at Montreal, had come to be so frequently and familiarly called and introduced as "Wells, of Montreal," that I began to consider it a part of my patronymic, and expected to go down to posterity and slumber in the grave remembered by an affectionate and faithful people as one to whom my brother has referred always as "Wells, of Montreal." But whatever doubts may enter into the situation of to-night in my own mind, there is none in connection with the grand object that we have met to promote and to carry forward. This is undoubtedly a Christian Endeavor gathering; it could not possibly be mistaken for anything else under the sun; for it is *sui generis*, new, original, American, unheard-of before in the world's history to have a movement like this Christian Endeavor movement, and a convention like the convention of this body.

They say that honest confession is good for the soul, and I want to begin by confessing a little. Some of you who were at Minneapolis last year heard me speak, and know the stand I took and the earnest advocacy that I made for the meeting of the convention in 1892 over on the north side of the line of 45, in that fair country, beneath those clear skies, where I lived so long and that I still love so well. Some of you know that I didn't enjoy the medicine that was administered to me when our big sister from New York came in and presented her claims and took the prize away from us on that occasion, and I was so far inclined for once to sulk in my tent that I predicted only disaster and failure from the course then pursued. I said, "New York! What will it care for a Christian Endeavor convention and what will it know about it? New York will go on its accustomed way of business and wickedness and pleasure, and scarcely know or appreciate, so much as a flea-bite, that the Christian Endeavor convention has been held within it." I take it all back to-night. [*Applause.*]

I have been doing what naughty boys do sometimes, — I have played truant to-day, and instead of being a faithful Christian Endeavorer, attending all the meetings and applauding every speaker, I have been out on the bay catching some of that delicious air of which we just heard from our fascinating speaker, and there I noticed some of the busy tugs and steamers flying about the harbor of New York, and I saw some, with newly-painted chimney stacks, and upon those the magical letters, " C. E." [*Applause.*] I wondered what new company, what business corporation or railway association that was, until it dawned upon my mind at once that Christian Endeavor was being written upon the very steam-tugs in New York harbor; and I suppose it is a sort of beginning of the fulfilment of the prophecy that in the good times coming "Holiness to the Lord" should be written upon the very bells of the horses.

Well, as one Irishman said to the other, you know, in regard to that heavenly ceremony, when his brother was impressed with the glory of the consecration service, — " Why," he said, " Mike, bedad, this beats the divil," and says Mike "That is the intintion of the business." [*Applause.*] That is the very intention of the Christian Endeavor convention in coming to New York. It is on purpose to "beat the divil." We have taken the old negro's advice for once, and gone where there was the most devil possible. We have come down here, and I tell you we are impressing New York,— we are moving it as it never was moved before.

I came up on a street-car. There was a crowd upon it, and when we got to Union Square there was a great open-air meeting; and some one said, "What is it?" "Oh, it is a political meeting." Just then we heard singing, and it was "All hail the power of Jesus' name, let angels prostrate fall." The man almost split his ears with listening, and his eyes nearly came out of his head with astonishment. He said, "The likes of it was never seen in New York before."

We came a little further up the street, and Broadway was fairly choked on both sides with the crowds marching down the street who hadn't been able to get into Madison Square Garden at all, or into the Madison Square church, and who were seeking some place where they could hold a meeting; and the man said, "Where is this thing coming to; if it goes on, what is to become of the Salvation Army?" I said, "My friend, that isn't the question; we are not going to hurt the Salvation Army; the question is, what is going to become of some other institutions that have been very well known in New York?" [*Applause.*]

Well, one's faith grows very radiant and strong, and one seems to come up to the mountain-top and stand upon the radiance of hope and of expectation, when we see such signs on such occasions; and we seem to lay hold upon the exceeding great and precious promises that are given to us that not one word of God shall pass till all shall be fulfilled. My friends, believe me, I feel deeply the fact that this is a most significant, a most inspiring occasion and event in the world's history. It is something in the height of summer to draw from the remotest portions of this great country of ours train-loads such as I have seen converging from every portion of this continent upon New York, paying their own expenses, asking no favors of anybody, but rather having them thrust upon them, and singing the praises of Jesus Christ. I tell you it is like the prophecy again: "There shall be a way and a highway shall be there, and the ransomed of the Lord shall return and shall come with singing unto Zion." [*Applause.*] "Everlasting joy shall be upon their heads, and sorrow and sighing shall flee away."

The only question in my mind, the only thing that gives me anxiety in the face of this demonstration of the Christian Endeavor movement, is whether we shall read all the signs of the times, whether we shall recognize the greatness and the glory of our work, whether we shall in faithful obedience to our motto and our pledge consecrate our lives, our influence, our power, our labor, all that we have and all that we can do, to the Master, and use it for his kingdom and his cause.

Unfortunately, Dr. Barrows spoke before me. Now, I have always tried to speak kindly of Dr. Barrows. I have known him a good while. I met him first in Paris nineteen years ago this summer. Arriving in that modern Babel on Saturday night, the first place that I went to on Sunday morning was the American Chapel, in the Rue de Paris. I doubt not many of you know it well. I knew something of the pastor of that church at the time, and I knew when the minister arose in his place that it wasn't the pastor. Who it was, I didn't know; but I found a friend from New York in the congregation, and I said to him after the service was over, "Who is that who preached for us this morning?" He said, "That is Barrows." "What Barrows?" I said. He informed me that it was the young man who had been recently settled at Springfield, Ill. I said, "I am going to stop and see him." I introduced myself at the close of the service, and the result was an intimate acquaintance and companionship with him for a week, and we managed to see Paris together. We didn't see everything they sometimes tell about, but we saw a good deal and had a good time, and from that day to this we have been very good friends, whenever in the providence of God we have met in our fields of labor. But he did me a very bad turn to-night. He made my speech. I am not so young as the chairman would have you think when he speaks of our juvenile brother from Minneapolis; but I am too old a speaker to endeavor to repeat what Dr. Barrows said so eloquently and truly and magnificently. He pointed to the vast fields, the gateways that are opening to us on every side, the doors on golden hinges swinging before the coming of Christian Endeavor feet, inviting them forth into all the fields of usefulness and of aggression in regard to good citizenship and sound Christianity, as so well illustrated by himself in his pulpit in Chicago and by the pastor who preaches in this pulpit here, Dr. Parkhurst. [*Applause.*]

I am not going to say that over again, but I want to take up that thought and carry it a little further. People sometimes say, "What is Christian Endeavor for, anyway?" and I have heard different answers given. Christian Endeavor is to promote the religious interests of the young people in our congregations; it is to help young Christians into ways of usefulness for Jesus Christ and their fellow-men. Christian Endeavor is to man certain committees, that they may always keep a lookout at the prayer meeting and the Sunday school. Yes, it is for all that, and it is for a great deal more. What is Christian Endeavor for? It is to bring glory to God in the highest, and on earth peace, good-will to men, — that earliest angelic definition of the Gospel that sounded over this earth of ours the morning the stars shone over the fields of Bethlehem. It is to do that; it is to take young people and build up their characters; it is to open wider the eyes of their understanding; it is to consecrate to all noble and elevated objects the most sacred treasures of their being; it is to link them together in bonds that bring them into closer sympathy, that train them to the wisest co-operation with one another; and so to send them forward, not as distinct persons making so many separate efforts and onslaughts against the great enemy, but as one disciplined, united army, one army of the Living God, marching beneath his banner to do his work upon this earth of ours. That is what Christian Endeavor is for, — in the home, in the family, in the church, in the city, in the State, in the nation, in the world, until it shall lift up its voice in every quarter of this entire world of ours, singing praises to God and good-will to men everywhere. That is what Christian Endeavor is for.

Now, I am anxious about Christian Endeavor. I am almost dazzled by its successes in the past. I can do nothing but thank God and take courage in thinking of what it has accomplished. But I am inexpressibly anxious that it shall not be satisfied with the past, that it shall not rest upon the laurels it has already won, that it shall not think that it has as yet been made perfect, but forgetting the things that are behind and reaching forth to those that are before, it shall press towards the mark for the glorification of God and Jesus Christ. That is the magnificent call that comes to us from the spirit of this grand mount of transfiguration and revelation upon which we stand here in this convention, and from which by and by we are to go down to our different and distant homes.

I suppose there are representatives here to-night, perhaps, that span the entire distance between the Atlantic and the Pacific, and that reach from the inhospitable and frozen regions of the North to the tropical zones of the South. Let us take with us to our homes this thought: That great as have been the achievements of the Christian Endeavor movement in the past, wonderful as is its present size, and power, and influence, these are but promises of encouragement and inspiration. As yet, we are only sowing the seed in the early springtime; the glory of the summer and the fulness of the autumn are yet to come. We are going to discover new uses for Christian Endeavor, and are going to enter new fields of effort and labor that we have not touched as yet. And as the years go by and our Brother Clark, the father of this Christian Endeavor movement, passes onward into maturity and by and by into old age, may God grant that to him and to those who are his fellow-laborers and fellow-helpers in the great work there may come increasing wonder and an ever-deepening gratitude to God for their widening sphere of influence, until Christian Endeavor shall stand for "whatsoever things are true, whatsoever things are honest, whatsoever things are pure, whatsoever things are lovely, whatsoever things are of good report." If there be any praise, and if there be any virtue anywhere upon this earth and in the Church of Jesus Christ, it shall be understood and taken as a matter of course, not needing proof or affirmation, that Christian

Endeavor is synonymous with all that is great and good, with everything that is pleasing in the sight of God, and everything that can bless our brethren on the earth. [*Applause.*]

The audience then sang hymn No. 209, after which Rev. Dr. Young pronounced the benediction.

Union Square.

FRIDAY EVENING.

Prof. W. W. Andrews, of Sackville, N. B., presided and opened the meeting with prayer, which was followed by singing. Mr. Andrews called upon the various gentlemen who had been appointed to speak to come upon the platform, so that they might be on hand. He first introduced Rev. Stanley Roberts, of Bethany Presbyterian Church, Utica, N. Y.

ADDRESS OF REV. STANLEY ROBERTS.

Fellow-Christian Endeavorers: It is a grand and inspiring thought that we can gather in the midst of this busy mart and lift up our voices in praise and thanksgiving to the Redeemer of our souls. It is one of the most inspiring things we can conceive of to come into the presence of our daily press, as we have this day, and read from its pages the words that come to us and give our hearts so much cheer. When the daily press asks the Christian Endeavorers to march up and down the streets of the metropolis of this great country, to give a practical demonstration of what the young Christian life and thought is in this nation, it is an honor conferred that we cannot but receive with gratitude and with thanksgiving. When the great press, that has so much influence in this nation, recognizes a power like Christian Endeavor and speaks of it in such a way as we have read to-night from its pages, we may well say that the day is hastening when every knee shall bow and every tongue shall confess the Lord Jesus Christ to the glory of the Father, as he has given us power to do. This evening, as we are come together, let us remember that the Garden is full to-night of Christian Endeavorers; that Dr. Parkhurst's church is to-night filled even to overflowing with Christian Endeavorers from all over the world, and that up yonder, that grand old church, the Marble Collegiate, that stands as the representative of the Dutch Reform idea of this country, is to-night filled with Christian Endeavorers; and here Union Square might be filled with them, if we could gather together those who are wandering about our streets seeking to find a place where they may listen to the words that shall enthuse their hearts in the line of Christian Endeavor work.

Friends, we are here not for show, we are here not for parade, we are here not for music, we are here not for oratory, but we are here to demonstrate the power of the living God in the hearts of the young people of this nation, the young blood that marshalls again to the cause of liberty and righteousness, as it has been already marshalled on many a plain and field, for victory, and righteousness, and liberty. Let us remember, friends, that Martin Luther was a young man when he nailed the thesis on the door that spoke to the world of justification by faith. Let us remember that John Calvin was a young man, scarcely twenty-six years of age, when he wrote those Institutes that thundered forth the liberty of the Christian Church. Let us remember that John Wesley and Charles Wesley, his brother, who sang the Christian anthems through the world, were young men. Let us remember, also, that when John Knox stood fearlessly before Mary Queen of Scots, he also was a young man, and dared the powers that be in the name of righteousness. And let us remember that we can furnish young men in this generation, who thunder against wrong and who speak the truth fearlessly in the face of the Tammany Tiger or anything else in the world. For have we not our Parkhursts, and have we not the magnificent pastor of the Twenty-third Street Baptist Church, in this city, to tell the truth for righteousness and Jesus of Nazareth, to stand in the presence of corrupt governments and speak the words of power that shall thrill this nation and bring it forth to a broader plain of liberty than it has yet occupied? We are here under the influence and power of the Holy Spirit, and we hope to place side by side with the starry banner of the free — yes, above it, towering over it — the white banner of the cross of the crucified Nazarene.

As we listened in that great meeting to the voice that came to us from India, abounding with Christian principle; as we listened to that voice that came to us from far-off China, insisting upon the faith and works that give salvation; as we listened to the other voices that came to us from the uttermost parts of the earth, all fired with the same eloquence and spirit, our hearts could not but lift up an anthem of praise unto God. That is what we came here for, friends,— to demonstrate the fact of the power of the spirit of God. Last year it was my privilege to stand in that magnificent hall in Minneapolis and listen to that strong, moving address of Rev. Dr. Chapman, of the Bethany Presbyterian Church, of Philadelphia, when he urged us to consecrate ourselves to God, and for the year to come to make it the endeavor of every one to lead one other soul to Christ. Brethren and sisters in Christ, have we carried out that pledge? Looking down from that platform upon that vast assemblage, it seemed to me as though another benediction had fallen upon the hosts of Christianity, and that the cloven tongues of fire were touching those people. It was a glorious sight as they came forth, a living stream, from that meeting-room, singing their songs,—" Nearer my God to thee," " At the Cross," " Blessed Assurance," " Jesus is mine," " Shall we gather at the river?" I thought, as I saw that stream of inspired humanity coming down from that place, blessed be God, this is the river of God going out into the world; and there shall be opened up, through Christ, the plains, the hillsides and the valleys of America, and through America, of the world, "for Christ and the Church,' teaching the people, touching their hearts, making them better and nobler, causing them to live up to a higher standard of righteousness, against personal vice, against the saloon, against gambling dens and brothels, against the iniquity of ignoble living, and lifting up the white banner of the cross, for victories in the name of Jesus. [*Applause.*]

A hymn was then sung, after which Professer Andrews introduced Rev. W. N. Paige, of Leavenworth, Kan.

ADDRESS OF REV. W. N. PAIGE.

When the Rev. John A. Anderson, a Presbyterian preacher of Kansas, was elected to the Congress of the United States, he began his first address in Congress with something of this kind: he said he came from a State that was 200 miles broad, 400 miles long, 8,000 miles deep, and reached unto the stars. Now, I thank God to-night that we represent an institution — an organization — that is 8,000 miles broad, is as high as heaven, and I may say as deep as hell, for it has gone down by its mighty power into even the depths of hell, and rescued already thousands from its grasp. It reaches into heaven, because there are in heaven to-night thousands and tens of thousands who are rejoicing over the power of the organization in its active, spiritual, soul-saving work - that of the Society of Christian Endeavor.

While I am from Kansas, I am a New Yorker by education and by a lifelong living and service for the Lord Jesus Christ. I am carried back many years as I look in your faces to-night. The last time that I stood in the Union Square Park — the last time that I gathered with a body of young men here — was in 1862. It was not a body like this. We wore the blue. We were camped here upon this very ground. We heard the sound of fife and drum upon every side. Our blood beat in our breasts, our hearts throbbed and thrilled with power. We reached forward for a battle — not a battle for the cross, but a battle for the country. Oh, I remember how many thousands went with me, and how few came back! The country is strewed with their graves, that are green to-day — men who laid down their lives for this country that is ours. But it is my pride and joy, by the providence of God, now in middle life to remember and believe and know that to-day I am a soldier, — a living, working, fighting soldier, — in an army greater than that of 1862, with a higher inspiration than that which they ever possessed, with a nobler cause even than that of saving this loved country of ours. But I know this: as I look into the faces of the young men and the young women before me, that there are here as loyal hearts beating and throbbing and thrilling with loyal blood, — loyal to the country, but beyond that and better than that, loyal to the Lord Jesus Christ. Oh, if we can but consecrate the hearts and lives of the young men and young women of this land for Christ, if we can fulfil our motto, "For Christ and the Church," if we can send forth these companies, regiments, and batallions of young men and young women into the highways and by-ways of this country under the blood-red banner of Jesus Christ, seeking and saving those that are lost, high heaven shall sing it as it never sang before. [*A voice, "Amen."*] It was my lot, not long since, to stand in the church at St. Ursula, in the city of Cologne. They have there, they claim, I think it is, some 13,000 skulls of the maidens who a thousand years ago, according to the legendary statements of history, followed St. Ursula in a loyal service, following her to death for Christ and the Church. The Catholic Church shows there to-day, with pride and glory, the skulls of those who laid down their lives for Christ. Thank God the Society of Christian Endeavor can show thousands and tens of thousands of living souls that are living for Christ and that in his hands are being used for the salvation of other precious souls.

Let me say to you, this movement is not of man. It is of God. It did not originate with Dr. Clark, as he himself said so eloquently last night. It is to-day the inspiration of the tens of thousands of young men and young women gathered here. God Almighty is in it. It is one of the marvellous instrumentalities of his that he is using to-day for the enthusiasm, for the inspiration, for the Christian culture, for the Christian development of mankind, and for the salvation of America, and through America, of the world. [*Applause.*]

Now, I verily believe that while it is a common thing for us to-day, we are glad that we are living in the nineteenth century, and I am profoundly glad that I am living in it, — and that we are glad that God has given us a part and parcel in this great work. I tell you that I believe the cause of profoundest gratitude is that God Almighty has raised up this agency, organized and set it at work here, and that he has given us something to do in the cause of Christian culture in this country. It is through this organization, I believe, that the young people are to be reached, by being organized and re-organized, and that through America the world is to be redeemed.

I remember in the old Spartan history we are told that a certain teacher took before his scholars, in order to teach them a lesson, a dead body, and held that up before them, and set it upon its feet; and it tipped over. Then he took it and set it up again, and it tipped another way. Finally he put it upon its feet again, and it tipped upon its face. He turned from it to his scholars and said, "Something it wants — it lacks something." Aye, it wanted something; it wanted the spirit and inspiration of life in it.

Now, I say I believe that the cause of Christ, especially among the young, had come to that point, in the history of America, where it was almost like this dead body — young men and young women full of pleasure, full of amusement, full of everything but Christ. They wanted something. They were spiritually dead. And the Lord God Almighty, by the power of this organization, has put in them that which they needed, — the power and spirit and inspiration of Christian culture and Christian work for the salvation of souls through the Lord Jesus Christ. I read somewhere, I think it is in the "Schöenberg-Cotta Family," a simple story that illustrates to me what will be, under Christ, the work of saving souls through this organization. You may remember it if you have read that book — it is a long time since I have read it. I believe it runs something like this: There was a certain lord living in a grand castle, and he had a wife, as lords were apt to have in those days, and he kept her very strictly, as lords were wont to do in those days; she was a gentle woman, a lovable woman, and a charitable woman; and when the lord, noble, or knight, whatever he was, was away on his warlike forays, she was in the habit of taking fragments of bread from the castle, going down into the valley below, and feeding the poor. He found it out when he returned one time, and he forbade her doing it. But her great heart was so full of love for the poor and the hungry and the needy that she must needs disobey her lord and master, and the next time he went away her loving heart led her to do this thing again. The legend is that he came back and found her feeding the hungry — feeding them with crusts of bread. Going to her, he demanded what she had. She was frightened, and she said "Flowers, my lord — simply flowers." The legend said, marvellous to relate, when he tore her apron open, indeed God Almighty had changed the fragments of bread into beautiful flowers. However this may be in the old legend, it ought to lead to the inspiration of every young man and woman here to-night to go forth with the spirit of Jesus Christ. Take your humble means, take up the work in some small place, take it up with some little influence. However small, however humble the piece of bread that you carry to the hungry and the cup of cold water you carry to the thirsty, and however small the portion of the bread of life you carry to the dying, by the inspiration of God it shall change into flowers that shall bloom in countless souls and adorn the paradise of God.

Hymn No. 111 was then sung, after which Professor Andrews introduced Mr. William McNeil, of Chicago, a brother of Rev. John McNeil, the famous London preacher.

ADDRESS OF MR. WILLIAM McNEIL.

I am glad, my dear Christian Endeavorers, that I am permitted to-night to speak on behalf of the Christian Endeavor Society for my Lord and Master Jesus Christ. I am proud to be called a Christian Endeavorer, because it has been one of the first things in my life that brought me out as an active worker in the cause of redeeming souls to the honor and glory of my Master. There are hundreds in this city, yes, thousands of young fellows like myself who can trace back their career of active work to that day and that moment when they signed the Christian Endeavor pledge out and out and became what that signifies. I am glad that I am a pledged member. I believe in pledges. [*Cries of "Amen."*] I am first of all a pledged Scotch Band of Hope boy. [*Cries of "Amen."*] I then became a pledged total abstainer. [*Applause.*] I don't believe in moderatism of any kind, anywhere. You can no more cure drunkenness by moderatism than you can eat salt herrings and not be dry after it. And in this great city of New York you can no more whitewash the drink traffic in its damning influence on the hearts and the souls of young men than you can perfume an ash barrel. [*Applause.*]

I believe, then, in Christian Endeavor societies because we are forced out into the field in order to work to redeem ourselves, if we have signed the pledge conscientiously before God and our fellow-men. And again, I believe it is the greatest privilege which God Almighty has given us that he has called us to be co-workers and laborers together with God in his vineyard, that is to say, this world. If he had stopped short of asking us to be laborers together, we would have missed our fellowship with Jesus Christ in the one greatest of all joys, namely, that of leading poor, perishing souls into the light and the liberty of the glorious Gospel of our Lord and Master.

And again I believe in the pledge because we are bound thereby to stick to it and to keep our promises. You all remember that little story that John P. Gough was so fond of telling about the mouse and the cat, — and it was in those days so long ago when mice and cats could talk. That honor has now fallen upon the biped race, and I don't know whether we do it any better now than they did then. But anyway, this mouse happened to be caught in a great big beer vat, and was being slowly suffocated as well as being madly intoxicated by the poisonous stuff. In its dilemma it appealed to a cat that was passing by to rescue it from this intoxicating grave. The cat said, "Well, but you know if I take you out of that stuff, I am going to eat you." "All right," said the mouse: "I had rather be eaten by a decent cat than starved and drowned in this horrible stuff." [*Applause and laughter.*] "Well," said the cat, "I will get you out." And the cat did it. And immediately the cat put the mouse on the floor, of course the mouse ran into a hole. And the cat went after it and said, with a very gruesome face, "Why, did n't you promise me that if I took you out of that beer vat, I might eat you?" "Oh, yes," said the mouse, "I promised that; but don't you know that when I promised that I was under the influence of intoxicating liquor?" [*Laughter.*] Now, the Christian Endeavor pledges are not taken under the influence of any liquor of any kind, unless it be the influence of the Holy Spirit of God and of fire. I believe in that kind of inspiration and enthusiasm which not only backs it up by shouting and cheers, but which goes forth into the slums if need be, with arms bared up to the very elbows in the desperate attempt to bring sinners of any kind into the fold of our Lord and Master. And, therefore, I would leave you to-night with this watchword ringing in your ears: "Watch ye, stand fast in the faith, quit you like men, be strong." [*Applause.*]

After another hymn. Rev. Frank Fannon, of Tonawanda, N. Y., was introduced.

Mr. ANDREWS: All of you who have New York blood in your veins will be glad to hear, with the rest of us, from the Rev. Frank Fannon.

ADDRESS OF REV. FRANK FANNON.

I believe in prayer; I believe in a God whose ear is open to the petitions of his people; and while I stood in the presence of that grand assembly last evening, when it seemed that the girdling string of the skies had drawn its canopy and was huddling the stars close together, and moon and sun had lent their attractive splendor to witness and to give light to the beautiful, enchanting scene that fell from it upon the hoards of people from all parts of the nation, it seemed that truly some power outside that of man had drawn this great assembly of people, — those hosts with wondrous enthusiasm, — to the great city of New York, for the praise and glory of God.

I felt to-night the disadvantage which you feel; I felt the same disappointment when I turned away from the place in which we thought such good times were to be had to-night, and there came this thought to me: "God doeth all things well." And my mind went away back to my boyhood's State of Iowa, over into those plains of Kansas, into the West yonder, where some mother to-night kneels by the bedside, — she who so many nights ago had followed her boy to the city, where some hundreds of them, perchance, to make their living in this land, had gone with the thought that there were so many advantages in the city, and night after night had been petitioning heaven for the guidance of her boy. I thought that perhaps in that village, in that little home, in that little cottage of the farm, those prayers were heard and all the inconveniences were but God's answer to the prayer of that mother and that father, — that perhaps some wayward man, some wandering woman, might hear again the old story, might hear again the old song, might feel again the presence that was over them in the trundle bed, and that here to-night, going back and forth in the midst of this mighty metropolis, some song might touch their hearts, and from dissipation they might come to think of God — their mother's God — and of the crucified Christ, — of him whose name is borne above all other names, and so come to loyalty to that Christ and his Church. And I thought, this may be the means of saving them; it may be that those inconveniences are but the means God is using for the answering of those tender prayers. May God grant that that shall be the mission; and if that man or that woman or that wanderer is here to-night, may they remember that these thoughts and inspirations are by God's directing, that they may hear of him so dear to us, to whom we have pledged ourselves in this loyalty for his cause and for his Church, and finally for that which he has prepared for us.

More singing followed.

Mr. ANDREWS: We shall now hear from Mr. W. H. Pennell, who is known as the man who first signed a pledge in Christian Endeavor circles.

Mr. PENNELL: Brother Andrews has very kindly introduced me by what has almost become a chestnut to a great many; and yet there was one time, just for a moment, when there was only one man in all the world, so far as I know, pledged as a Christian Endeavorer. It happened to be me. [*Applause.*] It just simply happened, that is all; it was an accident. But it was one of the happiest accidents, so far as I am concerned, that I ever met with, and I have met with a good many. [*Applause.*]

I came down here to-night to enjoy the outdoor meeting. I had tried to enjoy the indoor meeting, and had been most sadly disappointed. But when I think of what Christian Endeavor has done for me, for my children, for our church, for all churches, for this United States, and for all the world, I just want to say, "Thank God, from whom all blessings flow," for it is from him — from God himself — that this work was inaugurated, instituted, brought forward, and helped forward, and is held forward now until it is the foremost work in all the world in all denominations. Think of the result of one year's work, — a hundred and twenty thousand young converts brought from our membership into the Church in one year's time! That is what the Society of Christian Endeavor has helped to do during the last twelve months. What it will do in the next twelve months God himself alone knows. He has a mission for it — a mission for each one of us. Humble it may be, and yet there is a mission for every one of us, — something for each one to do, — and to do it and do it well will be to the glory of Almighty God, and will be to glorify the name of our Redeemer and make the world better — the world for which Jesus Christ died.

Now, brethren and sisters, I thank you very kindly for listening thus to what I had no idea of saying, but what I am glad to say, — that Christian Endeavor is the joy of my life. [*Applause.*]

One verse of "Nearer, my God, to thee" was then sung.

Mr. ANDREWS: We shall now hear from one who last year described himself as the Scotch-Irish-Canadian-American, Rev. William Patterson, of Toronto, Ontario. [*Applause.*]

ADDRESS OF REV. WILLIAM PATTERSON.

Well, brethren, we are all here, because we could not get any place else. [*Laughter.*] And I must say that I was disappointed to-night, but am glad now that I had the privilege of hearing McNeil, because if the Lord spares him he will be older yet, and I believe he is one of whom Scotland will be proud. [*Applause.*] Now, when I say we are all here, of course I do not mean that we will all stay here. We will all be out of here before long. Before many days we will be scattered over many parts of the land; and the question is, When we get back what are we going to do? Are we going back to be more active and more zealous in this work in which we are engaged? We have not long to live, but let us make the best of the time we have.

There are one or two things I wish to say about Christian Endeavor and about Christianity as to what they will do for men. First of all, they will knock the selfishness out of men, and that is the thing that is killing a lot of people. There are men in New York, and I suppose there are some of them in Chicago too, who are so selfish that if they had an orange they would suck the whole orange, and then would give the skin to somebody else, if they did n't need it. [*Laughter.*] Well, now, we want men to be unselfish, and Christianity is one of the things that will knock selfishness out of them. We want men, — men that have got backbone, men that are going to stand up for their rights; and that is what Christianity will do. Some people imagine that Christianity is all right for old women and for little children and all that kind of people, but not for young men. Well, it is an easy thing for a man to go down a stream, but it is a hard thing to go against it, and let me tell you it takes a man to be a Christian. A nonentity will go down the stream and float with the tide. Show me a young fellow in New York who gets around him a lot of chums who drink and whose ways are not straight, and it is an easy thing for him to drink the glass that is proffered him. It is a harder thing but a grander thing for him to say, "I shall not do this," "I will not do that." That is the man — the man who will stand up against all opposition. Christianity will make such men. And, do you know, the reason there are so many drunkards bothering these policemen is simply because they have not got backbone in them. That is what Christianity will enable them to get. I heard a man one time — I don't think he was married, and I was going to say he never had a mother; but if he had, she died when he was young, and his girl must have left him — well he said a young lady's biography might be written with a few words: "She was born; she lived; she chewed gum; she died." I don't believe that about the girl; but I do believe that there is many a young man whose biography you might write by saying: "He was born; he lived; he smoked cigars; he advertised goods for a dry-goods establishment; and he died; and that is about all he did." Now, we don't want that kind of people. We want men and women — women that are going to do something for this world and men that are going to do likewise. How are you going to get such? By simply giving them the Gospel of Jesus Christ. When the Lord sent out the disciples, he did n't send them out to defend the Bible or religion, but he said, "Go ye into all the world and preach the gospel to every creature." It is the newest thing in the world, it is the grandest thing in the world, and it is the most powerful thing in the world.

There are some young men, of course, who have intellectual questions. They believe in Darwinism. Well, if I ever meet a man who tells me that his ancestors wore long tails and were monkeys, I say, "All right, my friend, you keep by your kin and I'll keep by mine." If a man wants to claim these things for his ancestors, he can go down to Central Park to-morrow and take a long look at his grandfather. I never try to argue with these men. [*Applause.*] Then there is another thing; when you see young men that way who have intellectual doubts, what does it mean? It means that they believe their minds to be greater than the mind of a Shakespeare or a Milton or a Gladstone, or some of the great and glorious names that adorn the pages of the history of this great republic. Let us remember that a man who has not any weight of brain may say he doesn't believe these things. Any poor fool may burn a house, but it takes a man to build one. And so don't let us waste our time with these things, but let us go on with the Gospel of Jesus Christ. The Gospel was the power of God in Rome; it was the power of God in Paul's time; it is the power of God now, and always will be. When men get into their minds the Gospel of Christ, then they become men like Paul; and I want to know who are the men who will not lie — men who can stand up against all the people? You remember they said to Peter what they might say to young McNeil: "You have got the Galilean brogue." Poor Peter was more than annoyed. But after that how many and many a time he spoke — he was almost constantly before thousands, speaking in the name of Jesus.

And let me just say one word now about associate members. If a thing is worth doing, it is worth doing well. If it is worth being a Christian Endeavorer, it is worth being the right kind of a Christian Endeavorer. People sometimes say, "We don't want to go into the Endeavor society or into the church, because there are so many hypocrites." Lord bless you, we don't want you to be hypocrites, but we want men to come in even if there are hypocrites, and show them what genuine Christianity is.

To-day I went down to get a drink of soda water. I gave in payment a silver quarter, and there had been a piece of lead put into it, which I knew nothing of, though of course the woman that received it saw it at once. Now, suppose that woman had said, "I got a bad quarter from a traveler; therefore from this day forward I will have nothing to do with travelers." Neither would it be any more fair for a man to say that because he comes across an individual Christian who does something bad, he will have nothing more to do with Christians. Let us come out and do the square thing and the right thing, and let us live for Christ and humanity.

Mr. ANDREWS: We shall now hear from Rev. G. C. Kelley, D. D., of Owensburgh, Kentucky.

ADDRESS OF DR. G. C. KELLY.

The greatest thing about this convention is the convention itself. It rises above the personality of any man, however great his personality or however great his position. I have been impressed with this, that perhaps nothing has transpired in the history of this country better calculated to bring Christ and the Church before the American people than the gathering of this great convention. In this day we are learning that Christ, though unseen, is laying hold of all forces and all influences to carry on his work in the world. We have had the grand spectacle of the young people of these United States chartering trains and having the right of way through the midst of commerce. We read in the papers of this city this morning that no meeting that has ever gathered in New York has made the impression and attracted the attention that this Christian Endeavor convention has. [*Applause.*] We see thousands at this hour standing at the gates of Madison Square Garden seeking admission, when there are 16,000 or 18,000 people inside. We come along by the churches and we see hundreds coming away unable to get a hearing; and here in one of the central parts of the city we see gathered a great multitude to hear any speaker who has a word to say for Christ, the Church, and Christian Endeavor. A gentleman upon the rear of this platform said to me a moment ago, " All the speakers who have spoken thus far have addressed themselves to Christian Endeavorers; it would be well for some one to address the people who are without." Although he is an intelligent gentleman, and keeps himself abreast of the movements of the day, he says he knew nothing of this movement until a week ago. I suppose there are very few people living in the city of New York who a week hence will not know there is such a thing as a Christian Endeavor society. We see the badge in all the hotels and boarding houses, and overflowing every place and in every street. In every place of interest we see them. What does this mean? It means that the Lord Jesus Christ is silently and yet forcibly present in our American life, in our American churches, and especially in the young life of America [*applause*]; and if any man has any misgivings concerning the future of our great republic and of our great cities, which are said to be the storm centres, let him take courage as he looks upon this gathering of young manhood and young womanhood, for I tell you that as a result of the workings of this society we shall have better city government as well as broader, more catholic Christianity. [*Applause.*]

Mr. ANDREWS: We will now have to bring our meeting to a close, and we will do it in a true Christian Endeavor way. We have been glad, those of us upon the platform, to look into your faces, and to have you look back into ours. We hope that some seeds of thought have been sown which will bear fruit in other days. We have been here enjoying ourselves; we may never meet again. Let us therefore sing with one voice, " God be with you, till we meet again ; " and after that we will have the Mizpah benediction.

Marble Collegiate Church.

SUNDAY EVENING.

The opening praise service was conducted by Mr. J. W. Jones, Jamaica, L. I. The Scriptures were read by Rev. Palmer S. Hulbert, assistant pastor of the Marble Collegiate Church; prayer was offered by Rev. Frederick A. Noble, D. D., Chicago, Illinois.

Rev. Charles A. Dickinson, of Boston, who presided, then spoke as follows: —

My friends of the Christian Endeavor: — I have no elaborate address to give you myself to-night. I am here rather to introduce others, and yet I cannot refrain from speaking of two things that come up before me as I look into your faces. I am reminded of a scene about eleven years ago, when in the good old city of Portland by the sea I attended the first Christian Endeavor convention. I think there were about one hundred and twenty people present. It was in Williston Church, and there were about four or five societies represented at that time. We thought it was a great convention then, and we took heart and prophesied even great things for it in the State; but we had no idea in those early days that Christian Endeavor was soon to girdle the globe.

I remember well the first time I ever heard about Christian Endeavor. It so happened that in the providence of God I was a pastor in Portland at the same time that Dr. Clark was pastor of Williston Church. He and I had been boys together, and we had known each other for many years. We had conferred together about a great many things, and after he had started this Christian Endeavor Society, he came down to my house one day and wanted to know if I would walk out with him. I remember we walked arm in arm down Congress Street, and after chatting about some other matters, he said: " I have got something in my church that I think you want in yours." I said, "What is it?" He said, " It is a society that we call the Christian Endeavor Society, down at Williston." Then he told me about how it started. He had had a revival there among the young people, the boys and the girls, and he had been puzzled as most of us ministers have been puzzled again and again, over the problem of shepherding the little ones. He didn't know how he could get them in touch with the church and develop their Christian life; and it was while he was praying and wrestling over this problem that God gave him this wonderful thought of the Christian Endeavor movement, and he started that little society in that humble way in that beautiful church by the sea. Well, I said I didn't believe I wanted anything of the kind in the Second Parish Church; I had a young people's prayer meeting, and they were doing finely, and I didn't want to disturb them. So I let the matter pass until one of my young men came to me and said:

" Mr. Dickinson, have you been down to the Williston Church to see the Christian Endeavor society?" I said, no, I hadn't. " Well," he said, " I wish you would go down there some time to one of the meetings. They are having a grand time; I wish we had something of the kind here." Well, I let it pass on for a week or two, and one of my young ladies came to me and said, " Mr. Dickinson, I wish we could have a Christian Endeavor society in the Second Parish Church." Then I began to think it was worth talking about. You notice that the Christian Endeavor Society spreads not usually through the pastors, but through the young people themselves. That has been the history of this movement from the very beginning; it has been the work of the young laity; it has started in one church, and then it has kindled in the ranks of another church, and another church, and so it has spread from State to State, and through the country.

I went down to Williston, one evening, and took a back seat in the church, contrary to my usual principles,— I think people should take front seats,— and I watched the proceedings of that society. I saw the boys and the girls, one after another, stand up and give their simple testimony for Jesus Christ, and I tell you my heart began to melt and the tears came to my eyes before I got through with that meeting, for one after another of those young Christians stood up, and in an unmechanical, loving, earnest way, gave either their simple interpretation of some passage of Scripture, some impromptu sentence, or some word of prayer for Jesus Christ. " Well," I said "there is something here that I haven't got, certainly; I will investigate it." I talked with Mr. Clark, and he proposed we start a society in the Second Parish Church. So after a little conference with him, we started a small society. I supposed for a long time I had the honor of starting the second society in the country, but have since heard that Brother Mills started the second one in Newburyport.

A few of us in that vicinity at once saw what we believed to be the possibilities of the movement in that district, and we believed that perhaps it would go outside of New England; so we had that first Christian Endeavor convention. I remember it so well, and I remember how after the close of the convention we got together and congratulated Mr. Clark and the society for having done so much in a year, and having stirred up the churches. Well, what the history has been, you know well. You know how the Christian Endeavor movement spread out of that State and down into Massachusetts, and from Massachusetts out through New England, and then to New York, and then from America over the sea into China, Japan, England, and Scotland, and that to-day the blessed sun doesn't set on the name of Christian Endeavor. God bless every man and every woman who has in his heart the interests of the young people. God bless every man and every woman who is doing what he or she can to cultivate and discipline the young Christian life. We praise God for Robert Raikes; we praise God for Mr. Williams, who started the Y. M. C. A.; we praise God for every earnest, hearty, intelligent man who, in the providence of God, has been prompted to give to the world something that has helped to better it and to lift mankind to a higher level; and we all join to-night in hearty thanksgiving for the gift of Christian Endeavor, and for the great work which has come through the unconscious invention of this constitution, which to-day stands almost as it originally stood, and which is represented in so many churches of so many denominations.

We who have come to New York came, of course, expecting to meet with a great many disappointments. We expected to be disappointed in a good many ways. We expected, possibly, that we should meet with some mishaps, that we should miss some of the meetings, that we should get crowded out of the Madison Square Garden. Well, a good many of us have been crowded out several times and have been obliged to take ourselves to some of the smaller churches; but I presume we have solaced ourselves with the thought that some of the best things are done up in the smallest bundles, and I have no doubt that those of you who have come to-night will be amply repaid for coming here and for finding yourself in this presence.

As I came into the church to-night and looked down Twenty-ninth Street and saw that magnificent sunset which made the street look very much like the pathway to the celestial City, I was reminded of that picture of the sunrise in the north land which a dear brother gave us in the great building this afternoon, and I was glad in my heart to think that he was going to be present here to-night to speak to us again. We have here a man whom I am proud to honor with the name of a missionary, — Rev. E. R. Young, from the north land among the Indians.

ADDRESS OF REV. EDGERTON R. YOUNG,
American Indian Missionary.

A few years ago, at the close of one of your western Indian wars, some of the generals who had been conducting the campaign against the Indians thought it would be a good idea to take some of the captured warlike chiefs to Washington and through this great country, to give them some idea of the might and power of the United States nation, of the multitudes of her people and their resources and wealth and so on, and thus convince these poor Indians of the absurdity of continued hostilities against the whites. These chiefs were brought down here to New York and Brooklyn and Washington and other places, and were shown a great many things, and in their Indian way were considerably impressed, although, Indian-like, they did not want to show it. Among other places in Washington they were taken into some of the art galleries and shown some of the beautiful historic paintings there. Four of these paintings very much impressed the Indians. The first one represented a scene in the life of the Pilgrim Fathers. It was a time of want and suffering to those heroic men, and the picture represented them looking gaunt and hungry, while coming to them were Indians with abundant supplies of food. The Indians looked at this picture with delight, — Indians feeding white men. The next picture they looked at with a great deal of interest was that of William Penn, quietly and peaceably making a treaty with the Indians. The Indian chiefs decked out in their finery were there, and the venerable Quaker stood in their midst. The picture was explained, and gave a great deal of satisfaction. The next picture they looked at with interest was that of Pocahontas saving the life of Captain Smith. That pleased them, when it was explained to them. The fourth picture represented Daniel Boone standing with his rifle in his hand, and one foot on the prostrate body of a dead Indian, and that also interested them. They put their heads together, did these chiefs, and they summed up the whole matter. They said, "Yes; in these pictures we see the white man and the Indian and the white man's dealings with the Indian. In the first picture Injun gave white man food; in the second picture Injun gave white man land; in the third picture, Injun saved white man's life; in the fourth picture, white man kill Injun." And that is just about the way it has been.

I am not here as a special apologist of the Indian as being better than any other sinner. Nothing of the kind. He has his defects and blemishes and crimes and faults. The trail of the serpent is over the Indian tribes as well as over the inhabitants of China, India, or Africa. But you and I believe that the Gospel of this book is just the thing to lift him up and save him; and oh, how grandly it can save him! Let me give you an illustration. On those journeys I tried to talk to you about a little this afternoon, as I travelled through my great field in the far North in the summer in a birch canoe, and in winter with a dog train, — on those journeys my good wife did not accompany me in winter, on account of the terrible cold; but sometimes in the summer time she went with me. One summer we were going in a skiff on a great lake. Our boat was manned by skilful Christian Indian oarsmen. We camped for dinner on a little tongue of land that ran out into the lake. While my boatmen were carrying the driftwood and cooking the dinner, the Indians on the shore saw the curling smoke going up, and wishing to greet us, they launched their birch canoes and came as hard as they could paddle. We didn't intend to call at that point going down, expecting to visit them on our return trip; but as they drew near I saw one canoe with an old man and his wife in it, and I said to my good wife, "My dear, you go and talk to that old man. Get down into his heart and hear him talk about Christ as his Saviour, and I will talk to these other Indians." She went over and chatted with them. She talks the language like a native. After a while our men on the point of land had dinner ready, and they shouted, "Dinner is ready," and I went over, calling to my good wife, but she wouldn't come. Then I went over and said, " My dear, come; dinner is ready, and the Indians are scanning the threatening clouds and say we must go on. If we are caught in a storm here with nothing but this skiff, it might be very dangerous. Come, my dear." But she said, "Let me alone; I would rather talk to this grand old man than go and eat my dinner." But I said, "You *must* come;" and I had to use a good deal of entreaty to induce her to start with me. She got up and her face was flushed and her eyes bright and she said, "He is one of the grandest old men I ever talked to. I am so delighted that I have met such a man: he has made my heart glad, as he talked to me of the things of God." And she went on and talked so fast that I couldn't get in a word edgeways until she lost her breath, and when she did, I said," My dear, he is all you have said he is; he is one of the grandest Christians I have ever met. But, my dear, listen to this: he was once a cannibal, and he ate his first wife." "Oh, dear me," she said; "oh, dear! Well, I am so glad I didn't know it before I went to talk to him; I am afraid I shouldn't have so enjoyed the interview. But he is a grand man, anyway." And so he is.

Benjamin Cameron, long years ago when he was a wild Indian, took his young wife and went out into the woods to begin their hunting. They pitched their tent, set out their traps and snares, and tried to shoot the reindeer, or find the dens where the bears were sleeping through the long northern winter. But they couldn't find many of the animals, and so it looked as though they were both going to be very hungry, and perhaps even starved. And one day as Benjamin stood there, thinking about the scarcity of food, he said to himself, "What is the use of both of us starving?" And he picked his rifle up and fired the death-dealing bullet, and killed his own wife. Then he put the body upon a staging, where it froze in that bitter land like marble; and when he could find the reindeer, or the beaver house, or the bear's den, to dig out those animals and live on them, he did so; but when that supply failed he went to her, and during the winter he ate his own wife.

By and by a missionary came along with this blessed Book, and whenever he could find Benjamin Cameron at the camp fire, or out beside the river in the short summer time,—he would go and talk to him. He talked and pleaded with him. At first the man said, "He did not come to me. That book is the white man's book; it is not the book for the poor Indian." Then, after he was shown it was for all, he said. "No; it is not for the man who took up his rifle and shot his poor wife, and then ate her; it is not for him." And then, when he was shown how great was the love of the Saviour who prayed for his own murderers, and for the dying thief on the cross, he by and by came to think that perhaps he could be saved. Then the devil tempted him awhile, to make him believe there was no salvation for him; but after a while the Holy Spirit came in his blessed voice and power, and that man was enabled to look to the cross, and the burden fell. The dark condemnation, the dreadful state in which he had been, changed to one of brightness and joy, and Benjamin Cameron for many years has been one of the grandest Christians I have ever met in any land.

I want to give you another incident to encourage you for work. You don't always do the grandest work for the Master when you have the biggest crowds. Sometimes, when you go to your Sabbath school or your Christian Endeavor society, when you have a headache or when it is raining hard, when you think very few will be there but it is your duty to go and you will go,—that is the time that God permits you to sow the seed that brings the harvest. And in my work some of the grandest successes were at times apparently the most discouraging. The last Sabbath that I spent on one of the long journeys I took with a number of missionaries to the wild north land was the mightiest day of which I have any recollection. We were travelling over the western prairies of Dakota, very near the border line of the British possessions. As Christian missionaries, we rested on the Sabbath day and had service. The minister who was to have preached that hot Sunday was a man portly and fleshy, and he felt the heat so that he said, "I am so prostrated by it, I can't possibly preach." "Well," I said, "I preached last Sunday; it is not my turn;" and the other ministers said, "It is not our turn;" and it seemed as though we would have no service. So my conscience condemned me a little, and I said, "Well, if you will gather around the front of my canvas-covered wagon, I will stand there behind the dash-board under the canvas roof, and you can make yourselves comfortable seated on the prairie grass with your umbrellas and sun-shades up, and I will hold a short service and preach a short sermon." So they gathered around. In addition to the missionaries and teachers, and the few friends of our party, we were joined in Minnesota by some wild Sioux Indians. They had been implicated in that terrible Sioux massacre of a few years before in which nine hundred people had lost their lives,—a war which cost the United States thirty millions of dollars in the effort to crush those wild Indians who went to war because they were robbed and swindled out of their treaty money by white men. Well, we were joined by a few of the wild fellows who had an idea that the government was seeking for them to hang them, as they were undoubtedly the authors of some dark, terrible crimes. With one of them only we have to do this evening. His name was Joe. He was just about the wickedest man, white or Indian, that I ever came across. The fact is, he could swear the most glibly and the most uniquely and the most continuously of any man that I ever met in any land, either side of the Atlantic; and he did all his swearing in English, for Indians never swear in their own language. If a wicked Indian wants to swear, he learns our language and swears in it. But Joe was an awful fellow, and was very wicked; and whenever morning and evening prayers were held, as we journeyed on, Joe would get out of hearing, and on the Sabbath he would take his gun and go off shooting all day while the rest of us were holding service and resting. But this hot day, as I got up there in my wagon, Joe was lying there in the grass on his back, with his hands under his head, and his old Indian hat over his face; and when I opened the Book, I thought, "We will lose him." But whether it was the intense heat, or the Spirit of God, something detained him, and there he remained. When I saw that we had him within range for the first time, I prayed a prayer to our Father in heaven. I said, "Lord, give me a message for Joe. I don't care for the doctor of divinity and these other missionaries and schoolmasters just now, but give me a message for Joe, the wicked Indian, who for the first time is within range." So I forgot all my elaborate preparations to preach a learned and finished and exquisite discourse, and I turned to some sweet passage in the Word of God referring to the love of the Father and of the Son, and I went on and preached and made it very simple. I remember I kept saying, "Lord, help me to make it simple, so he will understand." He had quite a knowledge of English, and I remember how, as I kept on preaching, his black, snaky eyes looked up at me under that old Indian hat of his. The whole service did n't last an hour, and then broke up.

Day after day we journeyed on, and a few days after our party broke up,— some to go west to the shadow of the Rocky Mountains in the great Saskatchewan country, some to remain and begin work in Manitoba among the white settlers who were then crowding in, and my young wife and I to go far away to the north land, away up among those regions northwest of Hudson Bay. Joe went on to the Saskatchewan. His idea was to join the wild Black Feet and go on with his wicked course of scalping men, stealing horses, and so on. As he was travelling along the prairies one day, driving his cart, a teacher came along, and Joe said to him, " Mr. Snyder!"

"Well, Joe!"

" Did n't that missionary tell a lot of lies, that preached that hot Sunday?"

"Why, no, Joe; that was true."

"Did n't he tell a big lie when he said the Great Spirit loves the Indian as well as the white man?"

"Why, no; the Good Book says, 'God is no respecter of persons.'"

"Well, but did n't he tell a big lie when he said the Great Spirit died for the Indian as well as the white man, — was n't that a lie?"

" No," said the teacher; " Jesus Christ, by the grace of God, tasted death for every man."

"Well," said Joe, not yet convinced, "did n't he tell a big whopper when he said the Good Spirit had opened the place he called heaven for the good Indian to go in as well as for the good white man? Was n't that a lie?"

" No, Joe; that is true. John says, 'After this, I beheld, and lo! a door was opened in heaven;' and, Joe, that door is opened for you as well as for me, if you will be good."

"Well," said the Indian, "if I could believe that, I would be a Christian."

Then they talked to him and helped him along, and when they reached our first mission on the South Saskatchewan, Joe said to our missionary, "I like to stay here and go to school; I don't feel like going to join the Black Feet and kill people and steal horses. Something has got into my heart that says there is better for me." He was encouraged and he went to school, and he learned the wonderful Indian characters in which we had the Bible printed. Oh, I wish I had the time to tell you how we can teach an Indian, in two or three weeks, to read that blessed Book. Ninety per cent in some of our missions are reading the Word of God in their native language. Well, Joe went down and learned to read the Bible, and a few months after there was a blessed revival among the Indians and scores were converted, and among them Joe gave his heart to God. His testimony was beautiful and clear, like that which we hear in our Endeavor society meetings. Everybody loved him; he was a changed man.

The next year that awful disease, the smallpox, broke out among those wandering tribes; it went from tribe to tribe, and hundreds — yes, thousands — died. It was an awful plague. It got into the mission at Victoria, and five hundred of our Christian Indians there died. It entered the home of McDougall, our missionary, and five of his loved ones were down with that loathsome disease. O friends, I do want you to pray for missionaries when sickness enters their homes. You are here, some of you, in the habiliments of mourning, telling us eloquently of times when the dark messenger came to you, and the hearts of your loved ones were pinched by the icy fingers of death, and you were full of sorrow; but your sorrow was mitigated by a great deal that missionaries don't have. Loving friends came in to nurse your sick; skilful doctors were able to do everything that medical science could do; while faithful friends came and read that Book and prayed with you, and neighbors and friends sympathized with you. Look at that mission room, a thousand miles from the nearest Christian family. When those loved ones, five men and women, were down with that loathsome disease, there was only the father and the son, both missionaries, to attend to them; and when one of them died, the father and son had to put a log upon a staging and saw out the boards and make the coffin and dig the grave and bury their own dead. Have you ever been as badly off as that, without a soul to guide you or sympathize with you? That was the condition of that family.

Mr. Snyder was away 140 miles teaching school when he heard of this pestilence, and he came back and was a great comfort in that sorrowing home. One day an Indian came running in and said, " Mr. Snyder, out down below the fence, on the trail, there is a sick Indian, and he says he wants to see you." Mr. Snyder took his hat and hurried down. He came to the fence, and just as he was getting over he started back; there was something that terrified him, accustomed as he was to sad scenes in that time of plague. There, lying in the grass, on the other side of a fence, was a man in the last stage of the smallpox. His whole face was one mass of corruption, both eyes were gone, and but for the fact that his breast rose and fell with his heavy breathing, my friend would have thought he was a putrid corpse. But as he saw that he was breathing, he leaned over on the fence and said, " Are you the man who sent for me"? " Oh, Mr. Snyder," said that sick man, " I am so glad you have come; I heard you had come to the mission house, and I tried to crawl from my wigwam, but I couldn't get over this fence. Then somebody passed and I heard them, and I said, ' Tell Mr. Snyder to come; I have got a message.' I am glad you have come." " Who are you?" " Why, I am Joe." " Joe! you poor fellow." Mr. Snyder had learned to love him. " I am sorry to see you here. What can I do for you? Can I help you back to your wigwam? Can I get you a drink of water?" " No," said he; " it is all right; let me die here. I couldn't get any farther; I wanted to get to the house to give you a message, and when I give it, it is all right, and I shall be glad to die." " What is your message, Joe? I will do anything for you?" The poor fellow said, " Mr. Snyder, if ever you see that missionary who preached that sermon that hot Sunday, tell him that sermon made me a Christian. Tell him I thought he was telling lies. You know, Mr. Snyder, as we walked along the trail, I asked you if he wasn't telling lies; but I know, tell him, it is all true. I know now that the Good Spirit loves the poor Indian, — that he loves poor Joe. Tell him I know he gave his Son to die for the Indian, and that I have something here that tells me he died for me; and tell him that I have something inside that tells me the gate is open and I am going soon to enter in. And tell him I am so glad he made it so simple that Joe could understand." " Why, I will tell him, of course," said Mr. Snyder; " but can't I do anything for you?" " Oh, no," said he; " it is all right, Mr. Snyder. I can't see you; my eyes are both gone with this terrible disease, but I see Jesus with other eyes, and I shall soon be in his presence. Mr. Snyder, will you tell that missionary when you see him that I am going to ask the dear Jesus in the years to come, when that missionary comes up and comes in through the door of heaven, — I am going to ask the dear Jesus to let me find him out, and I am going to thank him myself that he preached that hot Sunday and made it so simple that I could understand. Good-by, Mr. Snyder, good-by," and in a minute or two he was gone.

Oh, friends, fellow Christian Endeavorers, I am going to find out Joe, and I want to introduce some of you to him. Will you let me? O blessed thought! In the mansions of the city of our God, on the golden street, in the by-ways of paradise, seated on the banks of the river, we are going to meet where Joe is. Would you like to see that wild Sioux Indian who gave his heart to God and died there in the prairie-grass and went home to heaven after leaving a message of thanks for the poor missionary who had preached so simply and plainly that he found the Saviour? Glorious as this gathering is, there is a greater one by and by. Shall we all be there, and shall we come bringing in our sheaves, and as we receive our crowns, will they be decked with stars, radiant, flashing, brilliant, beautiful, each representing some soul saved through our instrumentality? God grant that it may be so, amen and amen. [*Applause.*]

A duet by Mrs. Anderson and Mr. Philip was sung, followed by the hymn "Blessed assurance."

Mr. Dickinson then introduced Mr. John G. Woolley, of Rest Island, Minn.

ADDRESS OF MR. JOHN G. WOOLLEY.

When the brother read the Scripture, I made up my mind what I should speak upon. I think it was the last verse he read: "Ye shall receive power after that the Holy Ghost is come upon you, and ye shall be witnesses unto me." That struck me, I suppose, because that is my business, — being a witness. I am not a preacher; I don't know anything about theology, and to tell you the real truth I don't care much about it. I know almost nothing about dogma, but I know Jesus Christ, and he is my theology.

One night five years ago, down here in New York City, a poor, wretched, wandering, outcast, bankrupt man, without any hope in the world; a man to whom there was not a door on the face of the round world that would longer open; a man shelterless, but for God's sky that shelters everybody; a man whose wife — and he loved her, too, — sat way yonder, 1,500 or 2,000 miles away, in that awfullest widowhood where the husband is not dead at all, but lives on in everlasting pain and sorrow and disgrace; whose children — and he idolized them — waited yonder in the shame of having a drunken father, worse than orphan children, because their father was an outcast, a wandering, hopeless, drunken man, — on this winter night, five years ago next January, groping, dazed, and bruised, and broken-hearted amongst the wreckage of as sweet a lifeboat as ever put to sea in all the world, in a perfect chaos of loss and pain and shame, this man, myself, staggered up against Jesus Christ. He went home with me and sat beside me while the devils of drink tore me but went out of me, and since that night he never lets me go alone anywhere, and he never lets me fall. I am not going to tell you much about it; it is a long story, pitiful and sinful, but it ends well. That is a great thing about a story. But ever since that night I have been a witness for him. I made up my mind that night that I would never engage in any business, but would travel from place to place, wherever men and women would listen to me, and stand up wherever opportunity offered, and tell what I knew about the power of Jesus Christ to cleanse a drunken man.

Power! That is what I want. The verse struck me again, I suppose, for that reason. Power is the prayer of every heart that is good for anything. The desire for power develops very early, even in children. I remember when I first started out in this work, I was gone eleven months. My boys were up in Maine, in the family of a Quaker preacher; and when I got a chance to go and see them, oh, how my heart swelled! My wife and I went up into Maine to see the boys, and when we got to the place, there was nobody in the yard, and nobody seemed to see us from the window. We got up to the door and rapped on it, and how our hearts did flutter, as we thought that in a minute more the boys would be there to see us. All of a sudden the door opened, and our little boy, Jack, a little bit of a fellow, stood in the door, and instead of throwing himself upon our bosoms to hug us and kiss us and weep with us, he put up his little arm like this and said, "Papa, feel my muscle." [*Laughter.*] Power, you know, — hungry for power, even in his babyhood. Well, that is the way with us all. We want power. Now there are many kinds of power. John L. Sullivan thinks power is one thing; my friend Mr. Dickinson thinks power is another thing; some of these representatives think power is another thing; we all differ about the definition. But the kind of power that is promised us in the Book is power in a man to testify. The kingdom of God is to be brought in by testimony. Did you ever think of that? Testimony is the real thing, testimony seems to be the vital business of the Christian man. There is a reason for that, don't you know? Where a thing depends upon testimony, every witness is important. In competition with John L. Sullivan I shouldn't stand any show at all; in competition with Dr. Burrell, the pastor of this church, I shouldn't stand any show at all in preaching; but when it comes to testimony, I am the equal of Dr. Burrell or John L. Sullivan or Christopher Columbus or anybody, don't you see? A little child who does not know really the nature of an oath can testify that a man had a moustache or that he didn't have, that it was dark or that it was light, that it was rainy or that it was clear; and that is as essential to a law-suit, very often, as the testimony of a man who can do four columns of figures at a time and perform any intricate calculation that enters into a lawsuit. Witnesses are on a level, and Jesus Christ promises power to testify to people who will receive from him the Holy Ghost. I doubt if we realize, many of us, — I am certain that I have never realized as fully as it seems to me I have during these latter days, — that testimony is after all the vital thing in Christian work. To prove to the world that you are genuine, — to prove to the world that the religion of Jesus Christ is a real thing, — that is the business of a Christian worker, first of all. When God endowed people with reason and liberty, he shut himself up to testimony in all his dealings with man. And so we find that the whole business of the Old Testament and the New is facts; not theories, not philosophy, but facts all the time. So, when John sent some of his disciples to see Jesus and inquire whether he was or was not the Christ, Jesus didn't say "Yes," and tell John, "I am the Christ;" not at all. He said, "You go back and tell John what you have seen, and if it proves I am the Christ, I am the Christ: if it doesn't prove it, I am not." Don't you see? Testimony all the time. Paul says, "You know that our preaching Christ was with great assurance and with great power, because you know what kind of people we were when we were among you." That is the business — testimony — of the preacher; and I don't care how eloquent a man is, I don't care how learned he is, I don't care how many of the graces of oratory he may be endowed with, — if he does not give a good personal testimony, he might just as well be carrying chaff to the mill, for all the good he will do in the pulpit or anywhere else. Testimony is the vital thing for a preacher or a worker in any of the ranks of Christian work. God endowed men with liberty and with reason, and formed the world into a great court, and put himself on trial before the intellect of the race to win the heart of it, and the trial has been going on ever since. Jesus Christ is on trial before the world to-day, just as much as he was nineteen hundred years ago. The expression here in the Book is, "My witnesses." "Ye shall be witnesses unto me." Now, you never use that expression until after a case is actually commenced and is going on.

Well, Jesus Christ is on trial now, and what he needs in these good days of ours more than anything else is witnesses. It is a great thing in a lawsuit to have a good lawyer, it is a great thing to have a good Judge sitting, but the thing you cannot do without is good witnesses. You can't win without witnesses. Suppose we open the trial right here now?

Who knows Jesus Christ? Who knows that he can save people from their sins? If I should ask you to show your hands, nearly all of you would respond. Suppose I should suddenly call upon you, sir, to stand up and hold up your hand and be sworn and you should do so, and I should say as they do in court, "You do solemnly swear that the testimony you give in this case will be the truth, the whole truth, and nothing but the truth?"

"Yes."

"What is your name?"

"John Smith."

"Where do you live?"

"New York."

"How old are you?"

"Fifty-six."
"What is your business?"
"Cooper."
"Do you know Jesus Christ?"
"Yes."
"How long have you known him?"
"Thirty years."
"Do you know that he saves people from their sins?"
"Yes."
"How do you know?"
"Well, he saved my neighbor."
"Stop a minute. That is hearsay, that is not evidence. Call your neighbor."

And so, as far as your testimony is concerned, the trial goes right on and the crucifixion is not to be stopped. Jesus Christ's case breaks down at you.

But here is another man with his hand up. He says, "I know Jesus Christ; let me testify."

"Well, testify. Do you know Jesus Christ?"
"Yes."
"How long have you known him?"
"Twenty-four years."
"Do you know that he can save people from their sins?"
"Yes."
"How do you know it?"
"Why, I have been a member of the Church for all these years, and the pastor said that I was converted."
"Well, call the pastor; if he knows anything. That is hearsay; that don't go in any court."

Well, here is another man:—
"Do you know Jesus Christ?"
"Yes."
"Do you know he saves people from their sins?"
"Yes."
"How do you know?"
"Oh, I feel it."
"Stop a minute. Who cares how you feel? Whoever heard a lawyer ask a witness how he felt about the lawsuit? This is a trial of facts here altogether, not feelings. Who cares how you feel? What do you know about Jesus Christ? Go on with the crucifixion, this witness knows nothing."

But there is another:—
"What do you know about Jesus Christ?"
"I know he saves people from their sins."
"How do you know?"
"Oh, I have such a blessed hope."
"Stop a minute. Who cares about your hope."

And the case breaks down for you. There is another one:—
"What do you know about Jesus?"
"Oh, I was raised from my babyhood in the church and at my mother's knee: years ago I was converted, and she said so."
"Well, call your mother. If she knows anything send for her. What do you know about Jesus Christ?"

Thus there are lots of us, dear friends, who don't know anything, when it comes to the pinch, don't you see? That is what is the matter with the case of Jesus Christ before the world to-day.

Another prime quality of a witness is the ability to bear cross examination. That is where a lot of us break down. I tell you that in this blessed temperance cause of mine the greatest lack of the time is a lack of good testimony. Don't you know that the devil's crowd over yonder don't believe in your Christian man much, because they don't accept the testimony? The human mind is honest, the intellect of man never yet failed. It was the heart that went down, so by the heart we must come back. But the human intellect is clear and honest, from Adam down to now. If I convince your mind of a fact, you have to accept it, not because you want to, but because you can't help it. If I convince your heart of some thing, you may still reject the truth, but the mind can't help believing that twice two is four, and so the mind is honest. Now we can't win the world's heart to Jesus Christ, but we can make the world assent intellectually to the truth of the religion of Jesus Christ. When the Church steeple stands for high license, it does not point to God, and that is one thing that is the matter with the temperance cause. When a Christian ship lands on the coast of Africa, to put ashore two missionaries and sixty thousand gallons of New England rum, the ship carries hell there, and not the Gospel. [*Applause.*]

The poor Indian of whom my brother spoke here didn't believe in Christianity. Why? Because the testimony was bad, don't you see. Testimony is a vital thing. You have seen many a fellow get on the witness stand and tell a glib, fluent and beautiful story, and button his coat and take his hat and get down off the witness stand to start away with the air of saying, "Well, if there is anything else you want, you can send for me: I have settled this case." Then the other man will put his eye-glasses on, the man on the other side, and say, "Stop a minute: sit down." And the glib witness will sit down.

"Here is a man who has been testifying so fluently about Jesus Christ. You say you know Jesus Christ?"

"Yes."

"How long did you say you had known him?"

"Forty years."

"Forty years? You believe the Bible is the word of God?"

"Yes."

"All true, every bit of it?"

"Yes."

"Are you acquainted with the 28th verse of the 11th chapter of Matthew?"

"Yes."

"Can you repeat it?"

"Oh, yes; 'Come unto me, all ye that labor and are heavy laden, and I will give you rest.'"

"Is that the Bible?"

"Yes."

"Is that true?"

"Yes."

"Whose words?"

"Jesus Christ's."

"Do you believe them?"

"Yes."

"Have you come to him?"

"Oh, yes; I united forty years ago."

"Have you got rest?"

"Oh, no."

And the case breaks down at that witness, don't you see, because he can't bear the cross-examination.

"'By this we know that we have come from death unto life because we love the brethren.' Is that the Bible?"

"Yes."

"Do you believe that?"

"Yes."

"Do you love the brethren?"

"Well, some of them." [*Laughter.*]

And the case breaks down as to you, because you can't bear the cross-examination.

"'He brought me up also out of an horrible pit, out of the miry clay, and set my feet on a rock, and established my goings, and he hath put a new song in my mouth.' Is that Scripture?"

"Yes."

"Do you believe that?"
"Yes."
"Do you believe every word?"
"Yes."
"Has he taken you out of the horrible pit?"
"Oh, yes; twenty-five years ago."
"Set your feet on a rock?"
"Oh, yes."
"Established your goings?"
"Well, I don't walk as straight as I ought to."
"Put a new song in your mouth?"
"Oh, no; I never sing; I whine mostly."

And your testimony breaks down, because you can't bear cross-examination.

Unless in your own person you prove the reality of the religion of Jesus Christ, why the thing breaks down, so far as you are concerned.

The fame of Sir Isaac Newton rests on the law of gravitation. Isaac Newton went out one day and saw that the apples all fell to the ground, and a train of thought was started in his mind which led him finally to formulate the law of gravitation, which accounts for all the natural phenomena of the material world, and which has established his most splendid and enduring fame. Now, suppose that this summer when the apples come out a few should begin to fall up; what would become of Sir Isaac Newton — what would become of the law of gravitation? When one poor little Methodist falls up, friends, it plays havoc with the whole cause of Jesus Christ; when one little knotty, gnarly Congregationalist fall up, it plays havoc with the cause of Jesus Christ. Oh, be true, oh, be strong, oh, be genuine, and I will tell you it is as certain as anything can be certain that we will win this case and will win this world for the Lord Jesus Christ.

Now, I will prove that the blood of Jesus Christ can cleanse a drunkard and keep him sober for nearly five years. Suppose you could find out to-night that on my way here the other day I stopped in Baltimore and got one glass of beer. One glass of beer would n't hurt me at all; I am seasoned to beer; it wouldn't have hurt me a bit, if I had stopped at that. But if my brother Dickinson knew that I had one glass of beer in Baltimore by testimony that could n't be disputed, do you suppose he would have put me up to-night to talk to you. Not much. Suppose you knew the fact, though he did n't. Would you have listened to me with the respect and the patience that you have shown to-night? Not much. You would despise a man that preaches abstinence and yet tipples a little bit. For me to drink a little beer is not a bit worse in the sight of God than for you to lose your temper just a little bit, — not a bit. And yet you would despise me and the whole public would lose faith in me and in the religion I profess, if I drank just a little. Well, madam, when you lose your temper, well, sir, when you loan your money on a chattel mortgage to a poor man at two per cent per month, or let a house for a bawdy house or a gambling place or a saloon, you commit as great a sin in the sight of God and you destroy your testimony as effectually as I do if I should get drunk, don't you see? And if you will examine that point a minute, you will see, lots of you, why it is that in the bars and hotels and saloons to-night in New York a large proportion of the men who are going to hell by drink come out of Christian homes. What is the matter? The matter is that mother's testimony is n't good.

Did you use to lose your temper, madam, before you were converted? Yes. Do you yet? The same old critter, are n't you? Do you sit in the first seat in a pew and allow five women to crawl over you to get to a seat in the house of God? The same old critter, are n't you? [*Laughter.*] Look out for yourselves, friends, and if you can't prove much, prove that well.

Now, I do prove that the blood of Jesus Christ can keep a man sober for all these months. I don't prove everything. I don't prove that he keeps a man from losing his temper; I don't prove that he keeps a man from being irritable sometimes; there are lots of things I don't prove, but that one thing I do.

What do you prove? Ask yourself the question and answer it yourself in the sight of God, and may he bless you and all of us for Jesus Christ's sake. Amen.

Mr. Dickinson: I am very glad we have with us to-night one of Christian Endeavor's strongest men in the West, Rev. F. A. Noble, D.D., of Chicago, Ill., who will now speak to you before the consecration service. [*Applause.*]

ADDRESS OF REV. FREDERICK A. NOBLE, D.D.

The merciful man is merciful to his audience, and I promise you solemnly that what I have to say I will say with my eyes on the hands of the clock. I am accustomed at home to talk in the face of a clock, and when the hands get into a certain position I stop, whether I am through or not.

I am not going to say to-night at all what I thought I should say when I came into the house, but I am going to bear a little bit of testimony. I am aware that there is a lawyer looking on and listening, and quite likely he will edge in a good many cross questions which he won't be permitted to ask, but he will edge them in in his mind, and maybe I shall go down under that cross-questioning that he is mentally going to subject me to. But I want to bear a little bit of testimony along the line of my sense of the value of the societies of Christian Endeavor. A ministerial friend of mine in Chicago is fond of telling the story of a reporter who was sent over to Ireland by one of the great London dailies. The manager of that paper charged him to go over and make a very thorough investigation of the condition of things in Ireland, and report to the paper for publication. He went over, asked questions, studied the situation, and in due time he sent back this report: First, the Irish people don't know what they want; second, they are determined to have it. [*Laughter.*] Now, that is n't the condition of the Society of Christian Endeavor. They know exactly what they want, and I tell you it is a great thing for any kind of an organization, it is a great thing for a minister, it is a great thing for a church, it is a great thing for a missionary body, it is a great thing for a Sunday school, to understand at the outset just exactly what it wants. There are a great many ministers who do not seem to me to know exactly what they want in preaching, and there are a great many churches that get themselves together and go through the form of work, and yet don't seem to me to know exactly what they want. The Christian Endeavor Society came early to the conclusion, and it has been confirmed in the conclusion, that it knows exactly what it wants. It wants, first of all, that the members of that society shall have personal knowledge of the Lord Jesus Christ, and shall know that he does save from sin; and then it wants, in the second place, that each individual shall grow in that knowledge and in that grace, and that each individual shall use his influence and all the arts of which he can possibly be master to the end that their souls also may grow in grace and knowledge. [*Applause.*]

Now, I have n't had quite so long an experience of the society of Christian Endeavor as Mr. Dickinson, though I heard of it at the very outset. It was my good fortune to be born in the State of Maine, and to have a good many friends in the city of Portland, and that Society of Christian Endeavor had hardly got itself started in the city of Portland, before I was preaching in that Williston

Church and came to know about it. And so my faith in it was a very early faith, though it took some time for it to get aroused. It had to come through that slow State of Massachusetts, and then had to go to New York. Then they found the thing was labelled Chicago, and they said, "It can't be true," and it took several years for us to get it through New York to Chicago and established there, so that the society in my church has been in operation only about six years. We encountered the same sort of difficulty in the organization of the society that you have got in your church and in your society. Good men, officers in the church, workers in the Sunday school, the fathers and mothers of these boys and girls said, "We don't believe in the pledge;" and I had to sit down and talk personally with parents and talk personally with officers and talk personally with friends for I don't know how many months before I could get them to understand that in signing the Christian Endeavor pledge they were committing themselves to nothing in the world that they had not committed' themselves to by the simple confession of Jesus Christ. I said, "You come to the table of the Lord, you take the bread and the cup, and don't you in that way solemnly pledge yourself that you will live the life of Christ, that you will be obedient to the spirit of Christ, that you will try to grow into Christ, and that you will be witnesses for Christ?" Why, as you have listened to these words that have been spoken here to-night about witnessing, is there one of you that has not had conviction borne in on his soul and renewed, that it is the duty and the privilege of a preacher, as well as the duty of every Christian man and woman, to be a witness for the Lord Jesus Christ? That is what these Christian Endeavorers do. They pledge themselves to be witnesses for Christ; they pledge themselves to be students of the Word in which the will of God is recorded; they pledge themselves that they will be workers in the vineyard of the Lord: and if there is an intelligent man or woman here to-night who has any kind of scruple about this question of signing a pledge and committing himself by putting his name or her name to a pledge, I ask you now to rise up here and tell me how you can justify yourself when you have subscribed to the church rolls and have committed yourself to the confession of Christ in church membership, and how you can decline doing precisely the things which these young people do when they subscribe to the pledge? [*Applause.*]

Well, we got over that difficulty, and by and by they organized. Now, what is the society of Christian Endeavor doing in that church? I happen to know about it, because, as I said this afternoon, the meeting of the society of Christian Endeavor that comes on Monday night I hold myself committed to just as much as I hold myself committed to a full service Sunday morning and Sunday evening, and I am there just as regularly. [*Applause.*] I am there just as regularly as I am present at the Wednesday evening prayer meeting of the church. Sometimes there will be an engagement that will take me away, but it is a very rare thing. I am present, I know the young people, I listen to their reading of the Scriptures, I notice what kind of Scriptures they select, I listen to their testimony, I listen to the extracts which they bring in from Christian books and Christian poems, I listen to their prayers, and I follow them in sympathy and love. As the society has grown from score to score and is getting on toward the second hundred, I have had an opportunity to watch individual methods; to watch the influence of one member of the society upon another member of the society. My testimony at the end of one year would have been, "It is a magnificent success;" at the end of two years it would have been still more emphatic, and there never has been a time when it would be so emphatic as the testimony which I shall give here to-night to the value of the Society of Christian Endeavor along the lines that the pledge takes these members who subscribe to it. [*Applause.*]

What does it do? How does it help the minister? I have studied these things about my own identification with the society of Christian Endeavor, because I think a minister ought to be in the closest kind of co-operation with every organization in his church, and an organization like this that is made up of the young people is an organization that he ought to know about all through and through. And I may say further about this, that I am asked at the close of each one of these meetings, whatever the meeting may have been, to take two or three minutes for summing it up. Sometimes I take it in summing up. I say, you have out of your experience said this, and you have said that and the other; and I bring together as best I can the points that they have made on the topic. Sometimes I have a special thing that I want to call their attention to, something about their hospital work, something about their social work, something about their missionary concert work, or along some line. Only a little while ago I did this thing. It was when we had that topic of "Enduring hardness." It is a recent topic, and you remember it. I said, "Now to-night, instead of summing this up, I will tell you what I am going to do. I am going to take these main points which you have made, and put them into a sermon for next Sunday morning, and those of you who are accustomed to be in attendance at the church — and they almost all of them are on Sunday morning — will hear arrayed under that text and that topic the various arguments which you yourselves have brought forward in proof of the duty and privilege of endurance." Well, you see, that by my keeping in that kind of close identification with the society, they are alert all the time and are trying all the time to do the best they possibly can.

Another one of the points in which they help is that they take themselves out from my special fear. Take a boy or a young man or woman who comes into the society of the Christian Endeavor, and I have n't one particle of fear about that person's falling from Christian grace, as long as I see the person present at the prayer meeting, and reading a passage of Scripture, and bearing testimony and leading in prayer.

Then another thing is that they are working out all the time, and they are working along the lines of spiritual life. Last summer when I got home from my vacation — it was a little longer vacation than usual, perhaps ten weeks — the communion came immediately after it, as almost all ministers find their communion coming at the close of the vacation. Ordinarily there are very few persons to unite with the church. Sunday school has been running low, prayer meetings have been running low, one and another has been preaching, and there has not been that concentration of influence and effort which brings souls to the point of deciding. When I came to the preparatory lecture, before the communion service, I found the clerk had fifteen names that had been before the standing committee to be voted upon that night. What was the secret of it? The secret of it was that the members of the society of Christian Endeavor had been at work personally, and they had found this one and that one and brought these persons to their knees in confession of the Lord Jesus Christ, and into that condition where they wanted to unite with the church. They had also found young men and young women who had come into the city bringing letters from other churches, and they had got them to present their letters. This year I anticipate precisely the same condition of things when I get back. We are almost all of us here; that is, twenty-three of us. Twenty-three members of the society of Christian Endeavor in the Union Park Church of Chicago are represented here in convention. I said that was almost all of us; I could n't stand cross examination on that [*laughter*]; but it is a large number of us. When they go home, they will go home full of this great convention, and I tell you what a wonderful thing it is. I had a prayer meeting with them this morning in our hotel at the headquarters of the delegation. There were sixteen of us there this morning. I went through the 100th Psalm with them, and then led in a brief prayer, and then I turned to this one and said, "What is your impression this morning?" and then to the next one, and we went around the whole company, and the thing that had impressed itself upon them was the vastness of this work, and the joy of this work, and the responsibility that every member of a Christian Endeavor society takes upon himself or herself to be a living witness for the Lord Jesus Christ. This organization has pleased me more and more because it has lines of work. It keeps itself in exact sympathy, as I understand it, with Jesus Christ. Why did Jesus Christ come into the world? He came into the world because men were lost; they were alienated from the life of God, they were without faith and without hope in God. What is the central thought in the mission and message of the Lord Jesus Christ? Why, it is that he has come to seek and save that which is lost, to bring them back out of their alienation into fellowship with God and put them in the way of realizing the destiny that is possible to them because they are the children of the Heavenly Father. The Society of Christian Endeavor believes that they are out of the kingdom and that they are to come into the kingdom by faith in themselves and Jesus Christ, and they reach them on the basis of the love of Jesus Christ for every soul.

Oh, what a picture it was to-night of that poor fellow lying by the fence, eyes gone, face putrid, heart beating out its last pulses! But, dear friends, that is the picture of every soul, whatever be the condition of the body, until that soul has come into the faith and vivifying power of Jesus Christ. And these boys and girls, these young men and young women, while they do not realize all the depth and the degradation of human sinfulness, go to men and women on the basis that they are in sin and need to come out of sin; and through the infinite riches of God in Christ Jesus may get out of sin and have their names written in the Book of Life. That is what they are doing; that is what our society is doing and your society is doing; that is what every society is doing. It is acting, not on the basis of some miserable speculation, not on the basis of some humanitarian theory, not on the basis that men are to be forced into the kingdom of Jesus Christ without any independence and any exercise of faith, not on the basis that men can be sung into the kingdom or literatured into the kingdom, or in anything made fit for the kingdom except by repentance and turning from sin and confessing the Lord Jesus Christ. What a glorious prospect is held out? Why, it is a marvellous thing for me. I have been in great gatherings, I was in the great Missionary Conference in London three or four years ago; I was in the great Congregational Council a year ago; twenty years ago I was a member of that Evangelical Alliance that met here in New York, and made such a marvellous impression upon the religious life of New York. Each of these great gatherings has left its impress upon my mind — an impress which I shall carry with me into the world to come. But there is a peculiar impression made by this body that has never been made by any other body, and when Dr. Schaff leaned over my shoulder on the platform yesterday and said to me, " Noble, this is a new chapter in church history." I felt the thrill of it. It is a new chapter in church history. The world hitherto has seen nothing like these young men and young women banded together on the basis of simple faith in Christ, bringing their lives into consecration to Christ, and in a kind of consecration that testifies to the reality and power of it by sending their sympathies all abroad, to all the nations of the earth, that testifies by the record of their fidelity toward the Sabbath, by the record of their fidelity on the question of temperance. Why, what a thing it is! One of the speakers the other day had occasion to refer to the fact that he had been in another great convention recently, and I thought of that great convention at Minneapolis, and I thought of that great convention in Chicago, and then I looked down the aisles, down into these vast masses, — ten thousand, twelve thousand, fifteen thousand, — and I said, " Was there ever another convention that gathered together so many people under one roof in whose bodies there was not one solitary drop of whiskey or beer." [*Applause.*] It is a marvellous thing, and what a prophecy it is of the years to come! Why, I see the church of ten years from now, twenty-five years from now, recruited in its abilities from these Christian Endeavor societies, recruited in its officers, trustees, themes, illustrations, and what not from these societies of Christian Endeavor; I see Sabbath schools, manned from superintendent down, through all the officers and all the teachers, by recruits from these societies of Christian Endeavor; I see the front pews and back pews of the churches filled with young men and young women who have been trained in these ties of Christian Endeavor. I go into the prayer meeting; they are not on the back seats; they are up on the front seats; they have a Bible with them; they have testimony to give, and I shall find in these coming years that an hour is n't long enough. Why, how long an hour seems in a prayer meeting. You take one of those old traditional New England prayer meetings,— I won't say anything about any other denomination, except the Congregationalists, though I might from memory say just a little about the kind of prayer meetings that are sometimes found in the Presbyterian church. But think of the prayer meetings! We sometimes have one good old brother who gets up and presents the case for ten minutes, and then sits down in absolute silence for five minutes more. Then the minister suggests that possibly we might sing a hymn, and then some one, very likely, starts it on the wrong key, and then somebody starts it on another wrong key, and then the minister suggests, "Won't brother so-and-so lead in prayer," and he leads in prayer. This isn't caricature; this is actually the fact in regard to traditional prayer meetings in some of our churches. Now, the young people's societies of Christian Endeavor will tear that up, root and branch, and change it all. The prayer meeting that I have been describing will be simply a reminiscence, and testimony will have to be brought to make people believe that there was ever that kind of a prayer meeting tolerated in a church.

Oh, how delightful it will be when the grey-haired men and the grey-haired women and the middle-aged men that are bearing the heat and the burden of the day, when the young men and the young women, when the boys and the girls, recognizing the fact that they are making up one family, gathered around one hearthstone and one table, are all bearing testimony out of joyful hearts that they have been redeemed by the precious blood of Jesus Christ! [*Applause.*]

At the close of the meeting a short consecration service was conducted by the Rev. Mr. Dickinson.

Madison Square Presbyterian Church.

SUNDAY EVENING.

From 7.30 to 8 P. M, a praise service was held, conducted by Mr. S. V. Hoag, of Brooklyn. After the praise service the presiding officer, Mr. W. J. Van Patten, of Burlington, Vt., introduced Rev. Charles C. Watson, of Lynn, Mass., who read some selections from the Bible and led the meeting in prayer.

REMARKS OF W. J. VAN PATTEN.

Fellow-members of the Christian Endeavor societies and friends:—I must say that I was not invited to preside here to-night because I am a public speaker, but only because I had some small share in the early work of the Christian Endeavor societies as President of the United Society for two years. I am glad that I am with you to-night; and we rejoice together that we can catch the inspiration of meeting in this building where so much has been done for the cause of righteousness in the days that have gone by. My mind goes back, as I have been here in these crowds, sitting in the Madison Square Garden with the thousands surrounding us there, to the first Christian Endeavor convention that I attended, nine years ago last month, in Portland, Me. That first service of the national convention embraced only about 75 of us gathered in the prayer-meeting room of the Second Parish Church, of Portland, Me. Does it seem possible, in view of the great numbers who have attended this convention, that only nine years ago the opening of the second national convention of Christian Endeavor societies numbered but 75? What great things have been wrought in these few years!

And another thought has been with me upon this occasion, and that is, How young the societies that are mostly represented here are! When we met in Saratoga for the first convention, six years ago, 850 societies were reported; so you see that there must be 20,000 of the 21,000, and more, societies now reported that are only six years old. I suppose that twelve or fifteen thousand, perhaps, are only three years old. How young, then, in this great movement of Christian Endeavor are we all!

And another thought has been with me in regard to this movement. The genius of this work is organization, as we all know; organization in all departments comes more and more to the front, it seems to me, in this Christian Endeavor work than in any other department of religious work. The need of the world to-day is a working church, and from the Christian Endeavor societies and their members who are to graduate in the years that are to come is to come the force that is to make all our churches into what we can truly call working churches. How great, then, shall be the cause of Christ and the Church, when all of its members have been trained in our Christian Endeavor societies, understanding the various forms of organized work and how we can thus make every one of our churches working churches! Then shall we be able to take up and deal with these many great evils that are brought before us in our national convention; then shall we stand for God and the right in every place that we are called upon; then shall we be able to overthrow many of the forms of vice and sin which do so abound in our midst; then shall we be able to sanctify throughout all the world the men and the women who shall be called to go and carry the Gospel of Christ, so that, even perhaps within our own generation of young Christian Endeavorers, the Gospel may be preached to every creature throughout all the world.

We rejoice in this convention that God has so favored us, for we see that our numbers are growing with ever-increasing rapidity, and if now we number 20,000 societies, or more, what shall we number in another ten years when the twentieth century dawns upon us. Can we not have some idea, from what we see now of the enthusiasm for Christ and the Church in the Christian Endeavor societies, of what the great Church, the mother of us all, is to be in the twentieth century, which is so near to us? Let us praise God for what he has done for us in these few years, and let us with hearts full of faith in him and in the belief that he wishes to use us for his honor and glory, push forward, striving year by year to do more and better service.

The audience then joined in singing hymn No. 249.

Mr. VAN PATTEN: We are a little ahead of time, desiring after the regular program that the members of the Christian Endeavor societies here may hold a short consecration service. It gives me pleasure to introduce a gentleman who represents the great South Land with us. We rejoice that Christian Endeavor is obliterating to a great extent sectional lines. We rejoice that we have met together from all sections in this great convention, and it gives us pleasure that we are to listen to a representative of the South. I take great pleasure in introducing the Rev. J. W. Lee, D.D., of the Methodist Episcopal Church of Atlanta, Ga.

ADDRESS OF REV. J. W. LEE, D.D.

Coming through the Park just now, the doors of the Garden were closed and quite a number of people were in front of the church, singing. I stopped and looked at them awhile. Just by my side was an Irishman, who seemed to be tolerably fresh from the oldcountry; and I said, "What are those people doing over there? Is that a part of the Salvation Army?" "No," he said; "that is the Christian Endeavor Society." "Well," I said, "it is something like the Salvation Army, isn't it?" "No," he said; "they are Methodists." [*Laughter.*] I took that as quite a compliment to the Methodist Church.

I am glad that my friend, in introducing me, spoke of the work of the Christian Endeavor Society as having a tendency to obliterate the differences between the great sections of this country. I for one rejoice in this fact. I believe that as soon as the old men die who remember so well things that happened away back in the years that are gone, — as soon as ever the good Lord gets them all into the other world, — all we young people will unite. [*Applause.*] I think the the Methodists will all unite. We are too young, you know, to remember it, and we have got that kind of charity and sympathy and love that some time or another leads us together. Down South, when I read the newspaper, I imagine that the Northern person is a rather terrific institution; but when I come up and meet a Northern person and go to his house and talk with him, why he seems to me to be as human as anybody else, and I really think that all that is necessary to make the good people of this great country get together, is simply to know one another. If I had money enough, I would charter cars, and I would send every Southern man who had never been North, and had rather a severe opinion of the Northern people, up North, and then if I had money enough there are a great many people in the North that I would send down South. [*Laughter.*] I have noticed that as soon as Northern people come South and stay a while, they learn to see that we are about as clever as anybody they have been accustomed to associate with in this section of the country.

I want to speak to-night very briefly about the right use of emotion. It has often been stated that the universe is an expression of thought. This is correct. Did it not express thought, it would have no meaning to it. Take the thought out of the stars, and you have no meaning in astronomy. Take the thought out of the structure and arrangement of the earth, and you have no meaning in geology. Our scientific books are but the embodiment of the facts which have been gathered from a study of the nature of things about us. But it is equally true that the universe is an expression of feeling, because we not only get thought out of it by reducing its facts to thought in the intellect, but every fact that is reduced to thought in the intellect is accompanied by a certain amount of emotion, and the grandeur of the emotion is determined by the character of the thought, and the quality of the emotion improves as we ascend in the grade of thought. The emotion is always on a level with the thought.

Now, if we consider the natural facts about us with reference to our temporal well-being, the emotion that will arise in our hearts may be called mercantile emotion. The emotion of one standing on the plains of Marathon engaged in considering the capacity of the plains to grow turnips might be called mercantile emotion. The emotion of a man standing in the presence of Niagara Falls, who should be engaged all the time ciphering how many mills it would run would be mercantile emotion. When we consider things with reference to food and clothes and shelter, the emotion that arises in the heart may be defined as mercantile; it comes from a consideration of the value of things, and is to be expended in legitimate laws of trade. Its wrong expenditure is in gambling and in wild speculation, and in the attempt to get something without giving value.

When we consider things with reference to our social and our political well-being, the emotion that we have may be described as ethical or moral. This is to be expended in the formation of law and in the observance of law, in the establishment of institutions and of government.

But I want to talk to-night about the right use of religious emotion. When we take the great facts that concern our spiritual well-being into our thought, our hearts are profoundly stirred. The great facts of Christ's birth, — his life, his death, his resurrection, and his ascension, are the great facts that have more profoundly stirred the hearts of men than any other religous facts which they have come to know. Now, it seems to me it is in our day quite an appropriate question to ask, What we are to do with the emotions that we experience and that arise in our hearts when we grasp the great thoughts that God has revealed to our minds in his Holy Word. I believe that if the emotion known as faith in that part of the world that we know as Christian had been properly expended, the world would have been redeemed before this. A good many people seem to think that emotion is rather an end than a means. I have heard people talk as though for one to get happy in the church, — for one to have the spirit of rejoicing, — was a great thing, and they seemed to infer that they regarded that as about the end of preaching. I believe that one had better not have emotion in the church, unless it is with reference to expending it in some good work.

I was at a camp-meeting in Georgia some years ago where the fervor was at a very high pitch. It was a Methodist camp-meeting, and under the preaching of the Gospel I don't think I ever saw people wrought to a higher plane of religious fervor. They were happy; they were rejoicing with all their hearts. I happened to say to a gentleman before leaving the camp-ground that I thought it would be a good thing if we could turn all this fervor into a schoolhouse, or into a church, or into furnishing or equipping a few missionaries for some foreign country. I said, "It seems to me a pity to lose it all," and he looked at me as if he thought I was a Gentile, and said, "If you talk that way, the Methodist preachers will get after you." Now, my idea was that there was too much fervor; there was too much spiritual force generated under the preaching of the Word of God to be allowed to go up through the trees and come to nothing.

What would you think of a man who would go down on a river somewhere and build a dam across it, and as soon as he finished this dam, instead of building a mill or a factory, below it, should go down about a mile and build another dam; and then, instead of building a mill or a factory, below that, he should go down a mile further and build another dam and then perhaps for ten miles he should continue to build dams, in order to dam the water up and have it go off in foam and mist? Well, I suppose if people were very much concerned about it and thought about it much in any way, they would put such a man as that in an asylum, and I believe there are many churches that have as good a right to an asylum as a man like that. I know churches in Georgia, and I expect there are some up here, because we are pretty much all alike, that have been making dams during a revival period of their Georgia life for forty years, and have never turned out a missionary. They have never expended that emotion to any good account, and the result of it is that it has all been wasted. What a man wants with steam in his engine is that he may be able to hitch cars to it and carry them somewhere; and I think there is no better question for us as young people to consider to-night than the proper expenditure of religious emotion. It is the subtlest, it is the most powerful emotion that is known, — the most powerful force in the universe, — because it is generated in the hearts of sincere and good people by the Word of God and by the spirit of God. Through Jesus Christ it comes in the human heart directly from God, and I believe that every man who feels it should regard himself as having received from God something so precious that not a particle of it should be wasted or permitted to go off without acomplishing something good.

I have sometimes attended colored service or meetings of our colored people in the South. They are a very emotional people, and they are a very good people. The more one knows of them, the better one likes them, and I have always felt that Southern people thought more of the colored people than anybody else. When you are preaching to them they encourage you, and say "Amen," and help you along immensely, especially if you are young and a little embarrassed. Seeing their fervor, I have thought that if the enthusiasm that arose in the hearts of all these colored people under the preaching of the Gospel could be turned to account and into intelligent comprehension of the truth, the whole of Africa would be lifted up in a very short while. But they have n't learned this, just like us white people. We have n't learned to put it to account; we let it go, and I am glad to-night to be able to stand in the pulpit of a man who not only has felt in the very depths of his soul what ought to be, but who has had the courage to go out and by the help of God to put that emotion to account for the overpowering of wrong and vice. [*Applause.*]

That was what St. Paul did. He grasped with an intellect that was perhaps one of the greatest that ever lived upon the earth the plan of salvation. He grasped the spirit and purpose of God, and it stirred in his heart such a volume and such an amount of emotion, that he utilized it to overturn Grecian civilization and Roman civilization and Judaic civilization, and to lay the foundation of a civilization in the sweep and impress of which we are holding this meeting to-night. It occurs to me that for years and years our people have not turned to account their religious emotion, and I believe that one of the most hopeful signs of this Christian Endeavor movement is that somehow it has caught that impressible and susceptible and earnest element in our churches, and has gone out to turn every good impulse and every good thought and every good aspiration to account. They have determined to reproduce these in helping and in blessing people.

Another good thing about it is that through its interdenominational feature the Methodists, Baptists, Presbyterians, and all the other denominations come together and all this fervor gets united. I pray that God may help us to appreciate what a tremendous thing spiritual emotion is, and that he may help us so to apply it as to bless this world and to lift it up. I believe it is possible to make doing right easy, and to make doing wrong difficult. It is a principle of natural law, I believe, that movement is in the direction of the least resistance, and I believe that by applying intelligently the fervor that arises in our hearts from the consideration of the great truths God has given to us in his Word we can absolutely throw in the way of wrong-doing so many impediments, so many difficulties, that the whole people will find it easier to go toward God and heaven than to go toward wrong.

I read some years ago that Mrs. Mary A. Livermore, being out in the mining districts above San Francisco, was stopping at a hotel, when her husband came to her one morning and said, " We have just come in the nick of time; they are going to begin now to pour water on that range of mountains you see there, and reduce them down to the level of the earth." " Why," she said, "we had better send for the children, because it will take a whole year to do that." " Oh," he said, " don't talk that way, because people won't think you know anything." The next day they turned the water on that range of mountains, and down the sluice-ways and from the heights it came with great force. It poured on to the mountains and played with them, until by and by one gulley was washed out here, another there, and still they continued to pour the water on the range of mountains until the great foundations were disintegrated: and by and by, one after another, they began to reel, and the loose conglomerations of which they were composed gave way, and the whole range was hurried down into the Sacramento valley.

So, when we look at the great mountains of evil that surround us, we sometimes think it is impossible to move them, but when we concentrate the fervor of the churches of this country upon these great evils, knowing that Christians have God on their side, we may know that very soon one after the other will be levelled to the ground and we may see God's kingdom established on this earth, and we may see every evil removed from it, every bar-room obliterated, every gambling saloon cast down, and every place where men engage in evil destroyed. All these things may be carried away by the right expenditure of the fervor and emotion that is generated in our hearts by the great words of truth that God addresses to our intellect. [*Applause.*]

In 1885, when the steamer *Germanic*, of the White Star Line, was crossing the Atlantic, she was caught in the most terrific gale that ever swept the Atlantic Ocean. The captain said that right in the track of the steamer there was a wave of mammoth proportions. It was a time of suspense, for it was impossible for the steamer to turn and escape the wave, and it wasn't known whether the steamer could possibly go through it or not. But nothing was left them but to let it enter that tremendous mountain of water, not knowing whether they would ever come out on the other side or not. However, by and by the ship came through on the other side, trembling as if conscious of its peril. Do you know what took place in the process of that ship's overcoming that tremendous wave? It was simply making levies upon the forces of the sunshine; the coal that was burned in the furnace was turned into steam, and it was by making levies upon the forces of the sunshine to counteract the fury of that storm that this was done.

A great many years ago we read of John Knox, of Scotland, on one occasion, praying upon his knees, "O God, give me Scotland, or I die." What could encourage a man — what could lead a man — to believe that there was any use for one poor, puny mortal, upon his knees, to pray God to turn back the tide of evil in a whole country? He was in touch and contact with all the resources of God, and upon his knees with his faith in God he actually laid hold upon all that God had to counteract and to scatter the evil in his time. Some years ago, walking down the streets of Glasgow, as I looked into the faces of those sturdy Presbyterians and read the epitaphs upon the tombs in the cemetery and saw the books in all the book concerns filled with evangelical truth, I could not help but think that John Knox's prayer had been answered, and that God in answer to his prayer had given him Scotland. It was nothing but the right expenditure of spiritual emotion in accordance with the Word of God and in accordance with an intelligent comprehension of the truth. And with that I desire to close to-night, by saying that if we will all go home and expend in doing good, in helping somebody, in organizing new societies, in strengthening and enriching those that we already have, all the emotion that comes in our hearts, it will not be the twentieth century before we shall see every young man and every young woman in this country in this Society, united with us in the great work of bringing this large country to Christ. [*Applause.*]

Mr. Van Patten then announced that the audience would be favored with a solo from one of their Christian Endeavor friends from Indiana, Mr. Yarnell. Mr. Yarnell then sang, "Oh, be ready when the bridegroom comes."

Mr. VAN PATTEN : I am very sure that there has been no person who has been in attendance at the various sessions of this Christian Endeavor convention but has seen that the missionary spirit has been very prominent in them all. The Young People's Society of Christian Endeavor believe in missions, they love to hear about missions, they all desire to do what they can for missions. I am very glad to-night that we have one with us who has had such an important share in the missionary work of his great denomination. I take great pleasure in introducing the Rev. S. L. Baldwin, D.D., Secretary of the Methodist Episcopal Missionary Society.

ADDRESS OF REV. S. L. BALDWIN, D.D.

Dear friends of the Christian Endeavor Society : — It gives me great pleasure to be with you to-night. I feel as if I belonged to you, not simply because I had the pleasure of organizing a Christian Endeavor society in my church a few years ago in Boston, which is still a very flourishing society in your connection, but because having been received in my childhood into the Reformed Dutch Church by Dr. Chambers, still tarrying among us as a benediction to over there? Is that a part of the Salvation Army?" "No," he said; "that is the Christian Endeavor Society." "Well," I said, "it is something like the Salvation Army, isn't it?" "No," he said; "they are Methodists." [*Laughter.*] I took that as quite a compliment to the Methodist Church.

I am glad that my friend, in introducing me, spoke of the work of the Christian Endeavor Society as having a tendency to obliterate the differences between the great sections of this country. I for one rejoice in this fact. I believe that as soon as the old men die who remember so well things that happened away back in the years that are gone, — as soon as ever the good Lord gets them all into the other world, — all we young people will unite. [*Applause.*] I think the Methodists will all unite. We are too young, you know, to remember it, and we have got that kind of charity and sympathy and love that some time or another leads us together. Down South. when I read the newspaper, I imagine that the Northern person is a rather terrific institution; but when I come up and meet a Northern person and go to his house and talk with him, why he seems to me to be as human as anybody else, and I really think that all that is necessary to make the good people of this great country get together, is simply to know one another. If I had money enough, I would charter cars, and I would send every Southern man who had never been North, and had rather a severe opinion of the Northern people, up North, and then if I had money enough there are a great many people in the North that I would send down South. [*Laughter.*] I have noticed that as soon as Northern people come South and stay a while, they learn to see that we are about as clever as anybody they have been accustomed to associate with in this section of the country.

I want to speak to-night very briefly about the right use of emotion. It has often been stated that the universe is an expression of thought. This is correct. Did it not express thought, it would have no meaning to it. Take the thought out of the stars, and you have no meaning in astronomy. Take the thought out of the structure and arrangement of the earth, and you have no meaning in geology. Our scientific books are but the embodiment of the facts which have been gathered from a study of the nature of things about us. But it is equally true that the universe is an expression of feeling, because we not only get thought out of it by reducing its facts to thought in the intellect, but every fact that is reduced to thought in the intellect is accompanied by a certain amount of emotion, and the grandeur of the emotion is determined by the character of the thought, and the quality of the emotion improves as we ascend in the grade of thought. The emotion is always on a level with the thought.

Now, if we consider the natural facts about us with reference to our temporal well-being, the emotion that will arise in our hearts may be called mercantile emotion. The emotion of one standing on the plains of Marathon engaged in considering the capacity of the plains to grow turnips might be called mercantile emotion. The emotion of a man standing in the presence of Niagara Falls, who should be engaged all the time ciphering how many mills it would run would be mercantile emotion. When we consider things with reference to food and clothes and shelter, the emotion that arises in the heart may be defined as mercantile; it comes from a consideration of the value of things, and is to be expended in legitimate laws of trade. Its wrong expenditure is in gambling and in wild speculation, and in the attempt to get something without giving value.

When we consider things with reference to our social and our political well-being, the emotion that we have may be described as ethical or moral. This is to be expended in the formation of law and in the observance of law, in the establishment of institutions and of government.

But I want to talk to-night about the right use of religious emotion. When we take the great facts that concern our spiritual well-being into our thought, our hearts are profoundly stirred. The great facts of Christ's birth, — his life, says that they all live in great extravagance and in very fine houses; there are no converts: only a few who are paid as manual servants ever join the church." When you come to a man of that kind, you just tell him that in some countries there are pretty large houses that missionaries live in. Tell him that you saw me to-night, and that I confessed I lived in one of that kind for over 20 years in China — a great deal larger house than I would think of living in here. But why was it? Why, it was because, before the first day of June, the thermometer went up to about 96 and it stayed there. Our thermometer here in New York goes up to that, — I don't know but it is that in the Madison Square Church to-night, — but it does n't stay there; it comes down, and we have relief. But in Foochow it went up and stayed right in that neighborhood until late in September, and even in the night it would not be below 90 or 88, and it was necessary, in that hot climate, that there should be a good wide veranda around the entire house. That gave it a very large appearance to a casual observer, yet take the veranda off and the house would be very much such as our brethren at home occupy. But a man who comes along in the cool season of the year. — and travellers always come in that season when there is no danger to them, — don't see any necessity for what is around them, and he comes home and says, " The missionaries are living in large houses and in great splendor." Just tell them that that is n't quite so.

And then, as to this matter about having no converts, it reminds me of something a certain lieutenant of the navy said a few years ago in one of our public papers which was copied all over the country. He said he could testify that there were no converts in China, as he had been there and seen for himself, except those who were paid four dollars a month for being converts. I sent a little arithmetical computation to the papers. I said, " We have on the rolls of the churches 40,000 communicants, Now, if they are paid four dollars a month, that is $160,000 a month, and that is $1,920,000 a year paid to people for being converts in China, and that is more money than all the missionary societies in the United States have expended in 20 years in the empire of China to build all the houses, to construct all the schools, and to pay all the salaries and carry on all the work that has been done."

Now, what was the matter with the lieutenant? What is the matter with these ship-captains who come around and make such reports as I have referred to? Why, the matter is just this: they never go where the missionaries are: they are never seen in a mission chapel; they are never found in missionaries' families; they never accompany missionaries in their trips through the country, to know what is really being done among the people. If they do, and are honest men, they can never come back with such a report as that. One of these men said to a missionary in England not long ago, not knowing that he was a missionary, " Why, I don't believe that there is a convert in all India. I have been out in that country for years, and I never saw a convert." The missionary said to him, " Do you think there are any tigers in India?" "Of course I do; I have shot many of them myself." " Well," said the missionary, " I lived a great many years in India and I never saw a tiger, and I suppose the reason is that I did n't go where the tigers were;" and he left the man to draw his own inference as to why he did n't see any Christians. [*Laughter.*]

Now, the fact is that we have Christians in all these great fields, — men worthy to stand with the highest and noblest Christians here at home; and when these critics tell you that they are not really converts, that they are simply baptized heathen, you just tell them this: One day there came into a church in which I was present a man who was nearly fifty years of age. He came into that church and heard a missionary say, " Jesus can save you from all your sins," and he went home thinking about that. He came to the missionary before he went home, and said, " Did I understand you just right? I thought you said that Jesus could save me from all my sins. I never heard of him before, and don't know who he is, but do you say he can save me from all my sins?" " Yes," said the missionary; " that is what I said." The man looked sad and said, " You did n't know me, for if you had known me you would never have said that. Why, I have been a gambler, I have been a sorcerer, I have been a very wicked man. I have been an opium smoker for more than twenty years, and no man who smokes opium that long can be cured of the habit. You wouldn't have said, if you knew all this about me, that I could be saved from all my sins." "Yes," said the missionary, "I would still have said that to you." Now the man couldn't believe it, but went off to think about it. Then he came back to talk to the missionary, and day after day I used to see him as he came to talk to my brother missionary, and I sometimes joined in the conversation, realizing that the man was in difficulty. Thousands of objections against the Christian religion occurred to him, but underneath it all was a sincere desire to know what was true. And one day he came with a perfectly radiant face and said, "I know it, I know it; Jesus can save me, for he has done it;" and when my brother asked him, "How do you know that he has done it?" he said, "Why, I don't want that opium pipe any more; I passed it this morning, and had no desire to take it up. I don't want any of the bad things I have been doing; I just want to go and tell the people in Ho-Chang that Jesus can save them from all their sins." When his friends heard that, they were troubled, and said, "Don't go there; the people are fighting, one village with another, all the time, and if you take this foreign doctrine down there and begin preaching, they will soon cut your head off." But he said, "No, I must go there. My people, let me go and tell them that Jesus can save them from all their sins." So he went; and in one place he was stoned until he was thought dead, and was left lying upon the street of the village; but when he realized that he had his senses and could stand, he got up on his feet and told them of the love of Jesus, and exhorted them to come to this Saviour who could save them from all their sins. So he went through many perils, until one day he was caught in the city of Ho-Chang, where false witnesses testified against him, and he was sentenced to be beaten with 2,000 strokes. That fearful sentence was executed upon his back with a bamboo rod. I remember when he was brought to our house. At first we thought he couldn't live, and even our good Scotch physician shook his head and said, "I don't think we can save him; I never saw such a terrible case of injury in my life. But we will do the best we can." As I went to him to comfort him, his eyes met mine as I got in front of his bed, and he was the first to speak. "Teacher, this poor body is suffering great pain just now, but this inside heart has perfect peace; Jesus is taking care of me, and I think perhaps he will take me to heaven now, and I shall be glad to go." But [as the old fire came back into his eyes and he raised himself with some effort], if I do get over this, you will let me go back to Ho-Chang." [*Applause.*] That was all he asked for in that hour of extremity, and before he could hardly stand he was off again to preach to the very men who had occasioned that beating, and he preached with such power that some of the men were converted and are as efficient members as any in our church in the city of Ho-Chang to-day. And so he went on, nobly testifying for God, until at last a severe illness settled upon him. When he found himself no longer able to stand, he took a chair in front of the pulpit and gathered the few members there around him, telling them with his departing breath of his hopes of heaven; and when he died there remained six hundred souls brought into the church by his exertions, and among them a full score of ministers to carry on the work he had laid out.

That is only one case out of hundreds that come to us from all our mission fields, showing that the Gospel takes hold of the souls of men in China, in India, and in Africa, just as it does here in our own beloved America.

And now just another word. Through the Society of Christian Endeavor you propose to do something, as I understand it, for God; and while I rejoice with you in your glorious consecration meeting and in the spirit of devotion which you are showing, and believe that the earnest prayers of this army of Christian Endeavorers are bringing blessings to all God's Israel to-day, let us remember that it is not simply when we catch a vision of Christ among our emotional experiences in prayer that we are best serving God, but when we go out with open hand to bless and save mankind.

I remember a legend that comes to us from the old Roman Catholic church — the legend of a monk who was pleading in his cell for a vision of the Divine

Master in his glory, as he continued to pray and pour out his soul, suddenly the cell was lighted with supernatural light, and as he looked up the beaming vision of his blessed Saviour looked down on him. Just then he heard the bell ring, and remembered his vow that whenever he heard the bell ring he would instantly go and administer alms to the poor at the door. He thought, "Can I not stay? This vision will never come to me again. May I not tarry a little?" Then conscience urged his vow, so he went and administered the alms to the poor pressing about the door, and returned sadly, saying to himself, "I shall never see such a vision of my beloved Master again." But when he came, the same light filled his cell, the same glorious countenance was there beaming upon him, and the lips of the Saviour parted and said, "If thou hadst stayed, I had not remained." It is only a legend, but it may teach us that when we are doing service for Christ, we are surest of his continued presence and blessing; and if once in a while we are elevated to the mount of transfiguration and we see Jesus in his glory, it will not do for us to propose that three tabernacles be built and we stay there. The Master will say to us, "Go down on the plain, where the poor and the lame and the halt and the blind are, and work for me, and in working for me the transfiguration shall always be yours." To that I summon you, beloved brethren and sisters of the Christian Endeavor Society. Let your hearts be consecrated to God this night, not only for service here, but O dear Saviour, for anywhere in this wide world where thou shalt call us. And then if he calls you to go to Africa or to China, go willingly, sure of his blessing and sure that at the post of duty you shall find the post of safety and the post of honor. And if he calls you, nevertheless, to serve him here, that spirit of consecration will be your best preparation for the service of Christ in your own country and among your own friends.

May God's abundant blessing rest with you in every Christian endeavor. [*Applause.*]

Mr. Yarnell then sang "That old, old story is true," after which the audience joined in singing two verses of hymn 210, on page 76.

Mr. VAN PATTEN: One of the states in which Christian Endeavor has always had its stronghold and where it has had many worthy friends is Missouri, and I am very happy that we have with us to-night one who will speak for the Christian Endeavor societies of Missouri. I take pleasure in introducing the Rev. W. H. Black, D.D., of the Cumberland Presbyterian Church, of Marshall, Mo.

ADDRESS OF REV. W. H. BLACK, D.D.

I had the pleasure, I believe, of organizing the second Christian Endeavor society in the State of Missouri, and I have always regretted that I did n't get in ahead of my brother Merrill, of the Congregational Church who, I think, organized the first society in the State.

I was asked by a friend whether it paid to come up here. He said, "It is a serious question whether it pays to come up to New York to this great gathering; you can't get in down at Madison Square Garden, and sometimes we can't get in at the over flow meetings at the other places, and we just simply get an opportunity to view the back of the crowd, that is all; and there is n't very much inspiration in that." Well, I thought about those crowds that used to go down to Jerusalem to the feast of the passover and to the feast of the tabernacle and to all those great assemblies, and I wondered how many of the thousands that went down there never got to hear the things that were spoken up there in the temple. Certainly thousands of them never heard, but somehow there was n't anybody who went down to Jerusalem in those times who did n't come back feeling that something unusual had happened in his religious experience, that there had been an enthusiasm kindled about him which he had caught that he never would have had, had it not been for the assembling of the saints down in the old city. And so I think this coming together of the multitude here in New York, and the gathering of a greater multitude, I trust, in Montreal, next year, and of a still greater multitude in Cleveland the following year, and a still greater multitude at the place you meet in the year after that, wherever it may be, will not be without splendid results to all who attend, though certainly there is n't a voice large enough or loud enough or strong enough to reach the multitudes that shall gather in these great assemblies in the future years.

It is something to say a little and to hear a little of what takes place on these great occasions. I remember once, in Heidelberg, that a friend of mine and I argued whether we should go down into Switzerland or not. He wanted to go to Paris, and I wanted to go down to Luzerne, but it turned out in the end that I was more stubborn than he, so we went down into Switzerland. But he said, "This will be a wild-goose chase," and as I did n't have any way of proving that it would not, I had to take it. And he said a good many times on the way down, "This is a wild-goose chase." When we got into Luzerne that night and got off the train at the station, it was raining, and we could hardly see the lamps on the streets, it was such a murky night. He said again, "This is a wild-goose chase," and I thought he was about right. The next morning I awoke very early, and looking out of the window of the Sweitzerhof, I never saw a grander vision except once, and that I saw later. There was the beautiful lake of Luzerne quietly sleeping in the sunlight before me, and stretching all around were those magnificent mountains, with Rigi over there to the left. The sun was just coming up behind, and it cast a wonderful light on that magnificent vision. I stood there spellbound for a little while, and then I went and awoke my friend and told him to come to the window. He slipped out of bed and hurried over to the window, and stood in amazement for some time, but finally said, "This is not a wild-goose chase, after all." We hurried down stairs, and hurried up the folks for a little breakfast, and took the first steamer across the lake and made the ascent of the Rigi; and when we stood on the Rigi, there was where I got the grandest spectacle. On one side was France, and here were the mountains piled one on another, going in this direction and in that. There yonder were the forests of Germany, and here underneath our feet was Switzerland, and back here was Italy, with its beautiful lakes lying in the sunlight. It was a grand vision. We could n't look at it in detail from up there on that mountain; we could n't see every little thing in connection with the lakes of Italy, or with the forests of Germany, or with the wonderful glory of the Alps. We could only see something here and something there, and the picture stretching away before us. We could n't see the details of the city of Luzerne that lay down there just below us, but nevertheless the general view was magnificent and inspiring.

And so, when we come up to these mountain heights of Christian opportunity we cannot take in all the details of such a wonderful meeting where 30,000 or 35,000 people are assembled together in his name with one purpose, and are multiplying their prayers before the throne. It is impossible for any one soul to take in all the magnificent spectacles or to take in all the magnificent thought that courses through the minds of God's people at such a time; but we get the general impression,—we catch the view in its more magnificent proportions, though we may not go down into each detail and learn the expression of every particle of matter that enters into the great delegation.

So I say this is a grand thing, and I am glad and will always be glad that I came to this city and heard what I have heard and learned what I have learned. Why, here to-night we have listened to these brethren who have spoken to us briefly on some of the great things of God. We have been able to look on Christian emotion as it is reflected in the thought of our brother, Dr. Lee; and Dr. Baldwin has opened up a little to us of the wonders of missionary endeavor and of missionary opportunity. We have heard Joseph Cook speak of the wonderful future that lies before us in the century that is just ahead; we have heard Josiah Strong tell of the marvellous problems that are to be solved, and how they are to be solved; we have heard the President of our great Association, Dr. Clark, tell us something of this wonderful organization, — of its spirit, its opportunity, and its work; and we have heard men talk eloquently, beautifully, spiritually, thoughtfully, and have been able to get here and there beautiful ideas to cherish in our hearts for the good of our souls and for the glory of God. I say it is a grand thing that we can meet together and get some of these things for our souls.

There is another thing that has impressed me in coming up here, and that is that there are so many more women than men in it. Why, we have the evidence of it in the congregation to-night; and the fact is, it is generally true in the congregations of God's people that the women are in the majority. They are in the majority of the graduating classes in the academies and high schools all over the country; they seem to know good things always when they see them, and to be the quickest to appropriate them. I think that is one of the explanations of the fact that old maids are increasing; they are getting so smart that there are not enough decent boys to marry them off. [*Applause.*] I tell you I would rather be an old maid and enjoy single blessedness than be married to a dolt any time. [*Applause.*] If the boys haven't got ambition enough to go to school and to go to church in order to prepare themselves to make good husbands, then give us more old maids. That is my sentiment. [*Applause.*] But that was n't what I started to say. [*Laughter.*] The thing that I want to say is this: one of the grand things that the Society of Christian Endeavor is doing is bringing a womanhood that is grand and beautiful into the Church of God. [*Applause.*] I think that the Church has not yet recognized what there is in the womanhood of the Church for church spirit and usefulness in this old world of ours. When I look back yonder into the Old Testament Scriptures, I find that the church of those days was organized on a masculine principle, — that men were way up there by the altar and did everything in the temple, and that women were relegated to the outer court. But when the Lord Jesus Christ came into the world, he gave the sceptre into the hand of woman, because the principle upon which the Church was to grow in the future was not to be by the exercise of the sword and the conquest of nations as in the past, but by the exercise of the womanly grace of love. And so in the Old Testament the Church was Jacob and Israel and Judah, but in the New Testament it is the bride of Christ, the mother of us all. It is this grand and beautiful expression of the true aspect of the Christian Church as being womanly that attracts our highest attention to its peculiar traits, and it seems to me that this very fact is one of the things to explain to us why the women are so prominent and so faithful to the Church, and so devoted to the Lord Jesus Christ in every duty which the church imposes. Now, when the Christian Endeavor Society comes along, it gives a splendid opportunity for the expression of womanly traits; it gives to her an opportunity to let her voice be heard, to let her give out her testimony in the public service, and to speak her mind on an occasion when it will do a great deal of good; and I have n't a bit of doubt there are some men who are quite willing to let her go there to speak her mind. But it happens that her mind there is always a purified and consecrated and loving mind, and that is a good thing for the Church of the Lord Jesus Christ.

When looking over that magnificent assembly there in the Garden, and noticing that the women were so largely in the majority, I said the grace that is to possess us in the future is to be womanly grace. This world is not to be taken by the assertion of masculine qualities, but by the display of womanly graces. When the Lord Jesus Christ came into the world, he came not as the realization of the masculine type merely, — he did n't come with great physical energy and stand out before men as a mere master, — but he came with a kindly touch of a hand as delicate as a woman's, and as graciously and lovingly as any mother ever soothed a sick child. All of his deeds were motherly as well as masculine, and it is this combination of the best traits of woman with the best traits of man that make him the ideal Man of the ages, to be approved by us.

And so I say the men must come to be more womanly, in order to aid the future success of the Church. They must put on womanly traits, and assert in all their sphere womanly graces, if they are to be Christlike. They must learn to use their hands in tender touch, they must learn to smooth sorrow with the softness of Jesus and with tenderness of tone they must learn like the Lord Jesus Christ to act with a motherly heart as they assert their masculine traits. So I welcome this institution for the prominence it is giving to the women and the opportunity it is opening for them.

And now there is another thing that I am glad to say in conclusion, and that is that this Society emphasizes the feature of consecration, and we will soon have a consecration meeting as the closing exercise of this evening. It opens up before every member that comes into it not only the possibility, not only the obligation, but the wondrous opportunity that there is in becoming consecrated and giving expression to it in the service of the Lord Jesus Christ.

Away back yonder in 1517. I think it was at Prestonpans, the chief of one of the MacGregor clans of Scotland fell mortally wounded. When they saw the chieftain fall, the men began to waver and were on the verge of a retreat, but he raised himself on his elbow with the blood streaming from his side, and said, "I am not dead, my children: I am looking at you to see if you do your duty." Our Lord Jesus Christ is risen, and in his hand there is the nail-print, on his brow the thorn-print, and in his heart the spear-thrust which give evidence of awful suffering, but he is looking at us to see if we do our duty. And so the thing that I would call you to to-night is that in this exercise of Christian consecration here in this assembly to-night, or in the local societies at your home, or wherever it presents itself, you be found not wanting in the spirit of service to your blessed wounded Lord.

And may God give us all grace. [*Applause.*]

The audience then sang one verse of hymn 207, after which Mr. Van Patten stated that Dr. David Gregg was the next speaker on the program, but as he was absent Dr. Baldwin wished to say a word in his name.

Rev. S. L. BALDWIN, D.D.: I just want to say for Dr. Gregg that I know his heartiest sympathy is with the Society of Christian Endeavor, and I know also that he is a man who is always on hand where he has promised to be if it is at all possible for him to be there. So if he has promised to be here at this hour, there is some very good reason why he is not here. It may be said of him, as a good brother said when he was distributing tracts in a car one day. An infidel turned to him and said, "How about the heathen that never heard the Gospel — are they all damned?" The good brother turned to him and said, very mildly, "My dear friend, if you ever get to heaven yourself, you will either find them there or a good reason why they are not there." [*Laughter.*] Now that is a good answer to make to such a question, and it may be said of Dr. Gregg that if he is not where he promised to be, there is a good reason why he is not there. I am sorry that anything has detained him, but I know that no man in all these cities has more hearty sympathy with the great work of this society than Dr. Gregg.

The chairman then introduced Mr. F. J. Harwood, of Appleton, Wisconsin, the former president of the Wisconsin State Union, who took charge of and conducted an inspiring consecration meeting.

Metropolitan Opera House.

SUNDAY EVENING.

The Rev. Charles Perry Mills presided. The exercises opened with singing and the recital of the 23d Psalm and the Lord's Prayer in concert.

Mr. MILLS: *Friends*,—In assuming the duties of presiding officer for the evening, it may be fitting for me, if I can, to bring you by some brief remarks into the spirit of the occasion. You all know well enough, through the press of the land and through your sight of the surging throng who have moved up and down the streets of your city, that we are Christian Endeavorers from all parts of the world; and though you may have this general information, the question may arise in your minds touching our purposes, our principles, and our forms of organization. And so, perhaps, by asking some simple question, I may be able to relieve a certain misgiving with reference to the purposes for which we have come together. My first question — I will ask two or three — is, What is the purpose of this marvellous convention of the Young People's Society of Christion Endeavor? In the accepted standard phrase, we can answer that question in two words: the purpose of our convention is simply inspiration and fellowship.

As often as I have passed through Madison Square on the way to the Madison Square Garden I have noticed in the centre of the square that there is a fountain, with water flowing from every jet, and upon the rim of the basin beneath the birds are bathing themselves as the streams descend, receiving the refreshing influence that pours down from above. We have come together in this convention for no other purpose than that we may receive a fresh supply of inspiration from an unseen source. You cannot observe the action of that fountain which is beneath the soil — the reservoirs which may be in the distance; you only observe the streams as they flow, and you wonder whence is the inspiration which we are gathering for ourselves in this great convention. Oh, the secret of it is that the source is unseen, but no less real. We look about now to learn from where we draw this inspiration. We draw our fresh supply of inspiration from God himself, who is the father of our spirit and the father of our Lord and Saviour Jesus Christ. So the fundamental principle which has brought us together is simply this: that we may get inspiration by coming into communion with the unseen Christ, whom, though we see him not, we yet love, — though we see him not, yet we believe in him and rejoice in the glory of his life.

I noticed another beautiful thing about the flowing streams pouring from every jet in that fountain, and that is that they all take the curve which is the line of beauty, while every stream seems to flow in its proper curve, each one in harmony with every other, thus combining systematically in a circle. In this Metropolitan Opera House to-night, the congregation is cosmopolitan. We gather from the North and from the South, from the East and from the West, from America and from Europe, from the British Provinces on the north and the States in South America, — yea, from the islands of the sea. As we mingle together here with one another we form a perfect circle of Christian fellowship as beautiful as the most beautiful stream that ever flowed in symmetry from the jet of a magnificent fountain.

Last evening Massachusetts gave a reception to California, Minnesota, Texas, and Maryland, and as a Maryland girl passed by and took me by the hand, — I from Massachusetts and she from Maryland — I said to her, "You gave the Massachusetts boys a very warm reception in the streets of Baltimore in 1861, and now the Massachusetts boys will give a very warm reception to you Baltimore girls in 1892."

And what is the secret of the marvellous change which has taken place in the character of the reception thus extended? The secret is found in the fellowship of Christian hearts. Whatever be the denomination from which we come, whatever section of the country or part of the globe, we have one Master, Jesus Christ, and through him we form our band of perfect union in a magnificent Christian fellowship. The simple answer, then, to the question, What are the purposes of this convention is, Inspiration and fellowship.

Let me ask another question. What is the relation of the Christian Endeavor society to the church? It is proper for me to say that the Christian Endeavor society is subordinate to the church in which it is formed and subject to its authority, existing under its sanction and working for its usefulness, for its glory, and for the glory of its head, Jesus Christ. We are not exactly like the Young Men's Christian Association, which stands as a voluntary and friendly congregation, but, as Mr. Chauncey Depew said the other day, we are formed within the lines of the church itself, so that we are thoroughly loyal to the particular church in which the particular Christian Endeavor society is formed.

I believe that the fastest steam vessel in this world now floats in New York waters. Perhaps the record may be disputed or may not yet have been made, but as I understand the statements from the public press, I will repeat that the fastest steam launch in this world now floats in New York waters and goes by the name of *The Norwood*. Well, that little steam launch was built upon the banks of the Merrimac River where I live, and I stood upon a wharf in old Newburyport and saw that steam launch come down the river with magnificent speed and a splendid exhibition of power as it started out of the mouth of that river to begin its voyage to the mouth of the Hudson. Not being an adept in machinery myself, I turned to a man who stood by my side, and said, "What is the secret of the marvellous speed and power of that little craft?" He said, "It is this: there exists in the machinery which propels that engine not simply the ordinary engine itself, but another piece of mechanism which is called the blower, the sole purpose of which is to create a breeze, in order to blow the fires which create the steam in the main engine." And if you want to know what is the secret of the Christian Endeavor society, — what is the relation of the Christian Endeavor Society to the Church, — the answer is that every Christian Endeavor society is simply a blower for that church in which it is formed. [*Applause.*] It blows the minister, as I can testify myself from personal experience. [*Laughter.*] It blows its own church, as being the best church in the world, and it blows simply out of the spirit of loyalty, perhaps, even sometime when there cannot be anything particularly worthy of its praise; but it is so loyal that it is bound to create something that shall be praiseworthy in that church and that can be mentioned before the world.

Now, think of it! The Christian Endeavor society in the church brings in a breath of fresh life, a breeze of cheerfulness, a breeze of courage, a breeze of aggressiveness, a breeze of healthy vigor, in order that the old church may continue to go on in its course with an additional speed and power. Now, I suppose that the old-fashioned craft was built for ordinary purposes, and not for purposes of special speed or power, by the intelligent owner. Well, Dr. Clark, in the providence of God, arose and said once, of course in answer to this question, that what we needed was more speed and more power; and, thank God, the power has been gained by the organization of the grand Christian Endeavor Society.

I will ask one more question: What is the relation of the Christian Endeavor Society to the old issues which are before the public? I noticed in an editorial in one of the local papers that it seemed an anti-climax for this great convention to come together for no other purpose than to protest against the opening of the gates of the World's Fair on Sunday, as if that was the only thing that we had to do. That was a poor conception of our purpose in coming together, — simply to enter a protest of that kind.

We are all formed inside of the local church, and are seeking the individual character of the Christian, which is the grandest thing under the sun; but we do not forget that there are large interests before the public, and you can depend upon it that the pulse of the Christian Endeavor Society is in sympathy with all issues of reform and of progress. Why, do you know that your own papers say that the orator of the United States is Chauncey Depew, and that the finest audience that Chauncey Depew ever addressed was that magnificent Christian Endeavor audience which received him magnificently in the Madison Square Garden the other day? [*Applause.*] And have you noticed — did you observe — that there is no other audience that can be assembled under any other banner that is so hearty and quick and eager to respond to and to applaud every good point that is made from the standpoint of good government, of the anti-rum issue, of Sabbath desecration, or of Tammany corruption, or of any political or public interest which may be aroused? [*Applause.*]

There was President Wood, of Bowdoin College, in the days of the war. He was a pro-slavery man in his sympathies, and every morning when he led the college prayers there was no petition offered in behalf of our country. The students stood it as long as they could, until one morning on their entrance to the chapel across the way there was found facing the platform a large placard upon which was conspicuously printed the words, "Pray for our country." As the president began his prayer and was about to close it, as usual, without offering a petition for the safety of our country in those trying days when her fate was in the balance, and as they noticed that that prayer was about to be closed without any petition for the safety and welfare of the country, there began that murmur well known among college students, the shuffling of feet, — and the atmosphere became so intense and the appeal so overwhelming that that pro-slavery man was fairly forced into offering a fervent petition that God might save the Union. [*Applause*].

Now, it is impossible for any speaker upon any Christian Endeavor platform to be silent with reference to the welfare of the country or of the State, or of the town or community wherein he lives. The young folks say, and so do all, "Pray for our country always." [*Applause*].

And so I might illustrate with reference to any particular duty which arises pertaining to the welfare of society or of the country or of the whole world; but I must not speak any longer. Let me say that the Christian Endeavor society exists not for its own enjoyment, not alone to assist and aid the church under whose sanction it exists, or by whose authority it is directed, but the Christian Endeavor Society is intensely alive to every great moral reform that in any way will bring about the spiritual and mental progress of the world.

Why, there are here in New York — what shall I say, 30,000? Yes, there are 30,000 cakes of soap that have come to your city. Now if all of these cakes of soap were boxed up and not made use of, of what service would they be? You know that the function of soap is to make things clean, but it must be clean soap, that it may be rubbed up against uncleanliness. And here these 30,000 cakes of soap have been brought out of the boxes, and we have been rubbing these clean cakes of soap against the uncleanliness in this great city. I think that by the moral impression we have made that some corruption has been washed away; and my injunction is that you shall go home as you have lived here in New York — cakes of clean soap — and rub yourselves up against the dirt, the uncleanliness, the corruption, and the iniquity of this world, that it may be cleansed and purified until it shall be presented whole and complete as a trophy of triumph unto Jesus Christ.

My duty led me this afternoon to three different meetings: the Madison Square Garden meeting, that at the Academy of Music, and to this Metropolitan Opera House, if that is the name of it. Upon coming in here this afternoon, which I did just about the time that Miss Ruth Thompson, from Washington, was rendering a solo, I said, "That is the best thing I have heard to-day, and I have been present at three magnificent meetings." She sang twice. Mr. Sankey is present this evening [*applause*] — nobody would ever doubt that you are a Christian Endeavor crowd — and he has made a particular request that she sing one of the songs she sang this afternoon. She is going to sing it before he speaks. I make a particular request also that she sing that other song which she sang this afternoon, after he speaks. [*Great applause*]. Now, don't get your encore on before Brother Sankey gets through I will now introduce Miss Thompson, from Washington.

At the conclusion of the song by Miss Thompson the presiding officer said: You have already expressed your greeting to Mr. Sankey, who will now address you. It is an event in the lives of these young people simply to see this man and hear any word from his lips.

ADDRESS OF MR. IRA D. SANKEY.

Mr. SANKEY: God bless the singers of the Christian Endeavor Society, and may their number increase, that they may go forth to sing the sweet Gospel of Jesus Christ, as well as to win to him converts from all over the world.

One year ago day before yesterday a despatch was flashed across the Atlantic from London to New York, and from New York to Chicago, and on out to Minneapolis, containing three or four very startling words. The message was this: "Charles H. Spurgeon is dying." The moment that was read by Dr. Clark in the great convention yonder I was announced to sing a solo. I was dumfounded with the message, yet just at that moment I sang, for the first time the song was ever sung in public, the song that our friend has sung for you to-night. Before singing I asked that great congregation to bow their heads in prayer that God might spare that man in London, if it were his holy will. I was very much struck by their attitude, for every one of that great and mighty audience of about 12,000 people seemed to bow in silent prayer, and I had to sing the hymn alone.

Eight months after that it was my privilege to be in Scotland, and one day I received a message from the brother of C. H. Spurgeon asking me to come down to London and sing a hymn at the funeral of Charles H. Spurgeon. I went to London last February, and in an assemblage much like this, one night at eleven o'clock, I sang the hymn again over the dead body of that great man of God who lay in front of his own platform in the tabernacle yonder in London,—"Fading away like the stars of the morning." That great congregation was bathed in tears as we sang about their beloved one. Why did that man have such a hold upon the hearts of the people, not only in London, but in Minneapolis, in this country, and all around the world? Because he believed and preached the grand old Gospel of the Son of God without wavering. Many men to-day are wavering, but no one can point to a time when he wavered from preaching the simple Gospel of the Son of God, and he had the power to do it.

Now, dear friends, we have been having a grand time here for three or four days, but we are going to break up now and go home. What are you going to do? The great meetings are about to close. What are you going to do? When I was in Glasgow last winter I sang the hymn, "Throw out the life-line," that has been so often sung by all of you, and I was reminded of my travels with Mr. Moody when we were holding meetings along the years 1873, 1874, and down to 1880. When I was in Glasgow, as I say, a gentleman came to me and said, "Your song puts me in mind of an incident which I heard yesterday in Aberdeen." It was something like this, and I am going to give it to you as this gentleman gave it to me. On the other side of the sea, by the laws of the country, of every shipwreck which takes place along its coast the light-houses and life-saving stations must make an official report to the government. Not long since the official report after a great storm was sent into that government, and it read something like this: "We used the speaking trumpet with all diligence, not withstanding which twenty corpses were next morning washed ashore." I have been wondering whether we have not been using the speaking trumpet a good deal here in New York for the last four days. That is all right for the four days, but we must not depend upon the speaking trumpet alone — the work is not done by that alone. Something more should be done to save those perishing men. "Throw out the life-line" and "rescue the perishing." We should have more faith in God. I believe that every soul of this congregation has more faith in God than he or she had last week. Let us get to work as soon as we get back to our homes, and show what we can do by our faithfulness to this cause. We must learn how to work. If it was not for that pledge, why, we would all join. But the society would not be worth much without that pledge. Let us take up that cross, deny ourselves, love God and our fellow-men, keep health in our hearts, keep on the sunny side of the street as much as possible, and let us not walk in the shade. There are too many people walking on the shady side of the street. Keep on the sunny side of life all the time, and be bright and happy. There are many classes of Christians who are good people, but who make me feel sad when I come near them. We cannot always be bright, possibly, but I think we might cultivate brightness, and that is why I rejoice in this society of young people who are so cheerful and happy in all their work.

Last night, as I left the convention and went down town upon the elevated railroad, I could hear the song of the people a quarter of a mile away: and I got in and joined them, and the song was swept through the city, " Throw out the life-line, throw out the life-line." I believe that when we sing the Gospel, we should sing the sweet Gospel of the Son of God.

There was a gentleman came to this country a few years ago by the name of Major Milan, and I learned from him something about methods of work. In one of the cities where Mr. Moody and I were holding meetings we met this gentleman at the hotel, and we said, "We are very glad to see you; won't you come down to the meetings?" He said, " Yes, I will be very glad to. I just stopped off for the night, and did not know that you were here." We said, " Won't you come down to the city hall?" He said he would. We invited him upon the platform. He said, " No, thank you: I would rather go down in the congregation. I want to see if I cannot find some one to-night whom I can lead to Christ." God bless such workers. God bless the workers who are glad to go down into the congregation, instead of remaining on the platform. Mr. Spurgeon before he died said that he could find plenty of men who were willing to preach in his tabernacle, but that he had great difficulty in getting anybody to go down into the slums and preach. That gentleman of whom I have just spoken took his seat in the crowd of young men. At his side was a fine young fellow whom he sat close by until the close of the meeting, and then he said to him, " I would like to have a little word with you and have a little talk about these things of which Mr. Moody has been preaching." He spoke first about the Bible, in which he got the young man interested. The young man said, " Yes, I should be very glad to have a little talk about it. I should like to be a Christian." The gentleman said, " Let us see if we can get to that point;" and he spoke one half hour with that young fellow. At last the boy said, " I must go home now." Then the gentleman said, " I would like to go home with you, and if you have no objections, I will do so." The young man said " Oh, I shall be very glad, but I think if you knew how far it is, you would not care to go." The gentleman said that he did not mind the distance, and they walked for two miles, nearly, down the street. As they walked along they talked about Christ, about God, about heaven and about getting through this life. Well, at last after a long talk they came to the gates that led to the father's house. The father lived up on a plateau near by the town, and as they came to this gate the major said, " I will not go through the gate, — it is late, — but will walk back to my hotel; but before we separate, let us have one little word of prayer." The young man said, " Yes, I should be very glad." And the major reached out and took the young man by the hand, and they stood in the darkness that night at the father's gate, and he prayed, and oh, such a prayer : — " God bless this boy to-night, and help him to decide this great question." As he spoke the tears rolled down from the face of the major and fell upon the hand of the young man. The tears broke his heart. The prayer did not break his heart, but the tears of the stranger and the interest which that man took in him broke the young man's heart, and he said, " O sir, I thank you for your prayer for me, and I thank you for the interest which you have taken in me, and I will try to decide this question to-night." The major said, " Goodbye, my boy; to-morrow I go to New York, and the next day I sail to England, Good-bye. We may never meet again until we meet yonder on the other shore.

God help you to decide the question to-night." And he pressed the boy's hand and said, "Good-bye." The desire was in that boy's heart to see God, and he said, "Farewell." And the man went away; and the boy, as soon as he disappeared, turned upon his heel and started up the gravel walk which led to his father's house. While going up that walk he stopped and took the cane that he was carrying—for he was a Yale student, at home a little while on a vacation,—he took the cane and drew a mark on the gravel walk which led up to the father's house, and as he stood there he prayed, "God help me; this question must be decided to-night for or against Christ." Standing there one half hour by that line which he had made in the gravel walk, he discussed with himself whether he should go around the line or go over the line. He said, "If I go around it, it is for myself, for the world; if I go over the line, it is for Christ; O God help me!" And he stood there one half hour by himself, and at last he lifted his heart up to God in one great prayer. "O God, help me to cross over the line," and with one great bound he went over the line and went up to his father's house and to his father's chamber and rapped at the door and said, "Father, will you please come into my room, I want to see you so much." The father said, "What is it, my boy?" The boy said, "Father, I have crossed over the line." "What do you mean, my boy," said the father. The boy said, "I have decided to know Christ to-night and I want you to come into my room and pray with me." The father went into the room and threw his arm around the neck of the boy, and there, kneeling by the side of the bed, he commended his boy to God.

Two weeks after that,—the man was a minister in one of the leading cities, —he said to me, "I feel it my duty to tell you what God has done for me and for my family;" and he told us the story of his boy. As he told it, the tears streamed down the father's face. The minister brought me a little poem which had been inspired by the event:—

> " Oh, tender and sweet was the Master's voice,
>   As he lovingly called to me,
> ' Come over the line ; 't is only a step.
>   I am waiting, my child, for thee.' "

And so it was handed to the reporter of the leading paper of the town, and he, being a Christian man and an organist in the church of the town, took it home with him and looked it over, and then sat down to the keys of the piano and wrote the beautiful tune that we have in the "Gospel Hymn Book" called "Over the line." He then brought it down to the hotel and said, "Mr. Sankey, I have a new hymn here." He sang the hymn then for the first time, and I thanked him for it and put it in the book; and it has been the salvation of many a young man in all these years.

I tell you this story here to-night to encourage you to go out and do likewise. God will come to you as he did to that young man. God bless you! May we meet "in that land that is fairer than day" "when Jesus comes." [*Great applause.*]

Miss Thompson then rendered the solo requested. At the conclusion of the singing Rev. C. C. Creegan, D.D., of Boston, Mass., addressed the meeting as follows:—

Dr. CREEGAN: At the opening of a meeting where several speakers were to address the audience a certain negro preacher prayed in this manner: "Lord, bless the first speaker, give strength to the second, and give special grace to the third, for thou knowest that he has a very hard place." Now, I happen to be that other speaker, and I am not quite sure that the old darkey preacher is here to pray that I may have the special grace. As I look into your faces and recall what has been done during the past few days, I am reminded of the good woman who came from the western part of the country where I passed my boyhood to this city for the first time, and looking at yonder ocean and seeing all of it that she could, she said, "It does my soul good at last to see something that there is enough of." Now, I have that sort of feeling in regard to this vast army of Christian Endeavorers. I had it the other day when I tried for an hour to get in at the various gates and did not succeed, although I had in my pocket a ticket which said on it that I had the privilege of a seat on the platform. I could not persuade the gate-keeper that I had any right there, and after trying every conceivable argument, I could not persuade him to allow me to enter. He said, "Young man, I know my business; you don't get in here." I supposed I would find some little sympathy when I returned to the hotel from the brethren constituting the trustees of this great organization, and I was telling two of them my experience and how much pleased I was to know that that gate-keeper understood his business, when one of them said that he went there for the special reason of trying to arrange to have the editor of the *Tribune*, Hon. Whitelaw Reid, appear and obtain information in regard to our work. "Now, that gate-keeper," he said, "would not allow them to enter. Said he, 'I will listen to you and hear all you have to say, but it will do you no good; it will be all the same when you get through.'" He was asked if they might not be allowed to enter, in order that the editor might look into the face of the multitude, but the gate-keeper said, "When you get through I tell you it will be all the same; you can't get in here." Now I have a good many fellow-sympathizers here when I say that at last we have seen something that there is enough of. But I want to tell you there are some advantages in being shut out. As I walked along that great hall, I heard that murmur of voices ringing out as I imagined the heavenly choir is singing perhaps this very night, — thousands of voices, — and I think if I had received nothing else in coming here from Boston save the impression that I felt of that mighty host, lifting their voices in praise to Almighty God which could be heard squares away, it paid me.

I recall the trip I made three or four years ago through the State of Maine accompanied by one of the leading merchants of that State. He told me that when Moody and Sankey were holding meetings in Boston some years ago he then came on to Boston for the purpose of buying goods, and a friend of his said to him, "You had better go up and hear Moody to-night." He said, "I don't care much about hearing him preach, but I would like to hear Mr. Sankey sing." Said his friend, "If you go, you must go in time." "I will take care of that," said the gentleman, "I never went to a place yet that I didn't get into." When he got there he found he was five minutes late. Every door was closed and a policeman was standing there with instructions not to admit another soul. He tried all the persuasion which he could bring to bear, but went away defeated. Then he said that passage came to him which he used to hear his mother read in his childhood days, when his heart was tender, of the story of the ten virgins, and especially of that passage, "And the door was shut." "It was impossible," said this Christian merchant to me three weeks ago, — "impossible for me to shake off the impression that by and by when I knocked at that door, unless a change took place in my heart, it might be said to me as it was said at the Moody meeting that night, "'And the door was shut.'" Thousands of persons in this city have gone to that great hall — some of them not entitled to wear the badge which you have worn — and have tried these doors and found them shut. Who knows but some of them may have gone away reflecting as did that merchant, and gone away to do just what he did. Before he found rest that night he kneeled down in his room at the Parker House in Boston and gave his heart to Almighty God, so that when the day came that he should knock at the door, he should find that it opened to him.

In the early part of the evening the chairman referred to the spirit of fellowship which characterizes this association. There are two kinds of fellowship that I wish to touch upon in passing: the international fellowship and the state fellowship. Now, there have been times within my recollection when we have talked about fisheries and all that sort of thing and have tried, some politicians at least, to work up a little feeling between two or more of the countries represented here in this convention. If I mistake not the temper of these 35,000 representatives of 1,300,000 young people belonging to these societies of Christian Endeavor, they mean to have the day very far distant — yes, more than that, they mean, if they can have an answer to their prayer, that the day shall never come — when those of us who have the same blood in our veins, who claim the same Shakespeare and the same Milton, who speak the same language, who hold to the same religious growth, shall be other than brethren. [*Applause.*]

Furthermore, notwithstanding the fact that the late war left me half an orphan, my father and my oldest brother literally giving their lives for their country, if I mistake not, it is the temper of the young people who are to make the coming generation, represented here at this meeting and the other meetings in the city, — it is their spirit that there shall never be a day, certainly not in our times, when there shall be strife between these States now under the Stars and Stripes. [*Applause.*]

Years ago I remember to have heard the eloquent chaplain of Robert E. Lee tell of the days when the boys in blue and the boys in grey were upon the banks of the James, the boys in grey on the southern and the boys in blue on the northern bank. One evening, he said, he remembered to have heard the bands playing first on one side what they called the national airs, and then on the other side our national airs. And one day, he said, after they had kept up this spirit of retaliation and rivalry for some time, he heard a band by and by on the northern side of the river strike up the tune, " Home, Sweet Home," and he heard thousands of voices take up the song. He said he had no doubt there were tears in those voices, and thousands of voices joined in the chorus on the southern bank of the river, the boys in grey and the boys in blue, with no longer any spirit of retaliation, striking a chord in unison which touched all hearts. When those southern men there thought of their beautiful homes in the sunny South, and our boys thought of their beautiful homes in the North, they took up the chorus, and its strains were wafted across the river,— beautiful " Home, Sweet Home." It is that song that we sing here to-night, as we think of the home to which we look in the hereafter.

One word more. I wish to say that one of the most pleasurable features connected with this association is that you cannot tell a Presbyterian from a Baptist, or a Congregationalist from an Episcopalian. We are all mixed up. I do not believe you people who sit here in this audience and have listened to the speakers from this platform could tell — certainly you could not. if you were in that great hall — what the denomination is to which the speaker belongs. I remember some years ago, when out in the Rocky Mountains, a man came up to me and shook hands with me, saying, " I want to shake hands with you; you are one of our own folks. I heard you preach down in Colorado Springs. You are one of our own folks." I said to him, " To what denomination do you belong?" He said, " I am a Methodist. You don't need to tell me to what denomination you belong : I know you are one of our own folks." I simply smiled and said nothing, and a few days after, when he spoke to a friend of mine, this gentleman said that I was a Methodist. Now I have never been a Methodist, and we in this society, as Christian Endeavorers, cannot tell to save our lives when we are called out what denomination we belong to.

One day out West, as I travelled along, I noticed the fences — wood fences, stone fences, and occasionally a worm fence, as they call it out there. A few months later I came along to the same place and the fences had all disappeared; I could not see any of them at all. There were fields there that seemed to have acres in them, and as the breezes of heaven were blowing, I could see above the waving wheat that the fences had all disappeared because the wheat had grown up, and they were out of sight. The wheat harvest is before us, Christian brethren, and as we look out upon the great harvest field we lose sight of all these denominational lines.

Years ago the governor of this State said, " If any man attempts to pull down the American flag, shoot him on the spot." I want to say to you to-night, if these reporters will only promise not to report it,— but I suppose it is the very thing they will report,— that if any man attempts to destroy or interfere in any way with this beautiful congregation of loyal fellowship, as represented here in thirty denominations or more, shoot him on the spot.

Now a word as to what our friends may do, and what our efforts may accomplish. Mr. Sankey said he wants to hear something about practical ideas. Well, a trained swordsman may do his best, but he cannot do a great deal, though his sabre may be keen; but let that swordsman be Stonewall Jackson or Phil Sheridan, standing at the head of thirty thousand brave men, and at his word of command, when he draws his sabre, thirty-five thousand other sabres will come flashing in the noonday sun, and you will have an army which is irresistible. Thirty-five thousand brave Christian soldiers have been walking the streets of this great metropolis. New York has never seen a sight like it It is worthy the historian who said yesterday, " This is a new chapter in church history." What may thirty-five thousand young people, consecrated to the tips of their fingers, do when led by such a leader as God in his providence has placed at the head of this great organization of ours! [*Great applause.*]

Mr. MILLS: I do not know what line of remarks will be chosen by the speaker who is to follow, but it is enough that I should introduce him with that theme with which his name is associated in the Christian Endeavor assembly. The strife of battle in our country to-day is the effort which is being waged for the closing of the gates of the Columbian Fair on the Lord's Day. It is said of the numberless petitions which have been presented to the commissioners, that that petition which is the most impressive, and that pressure which is the most powerful, is that petition and that pressure which has been brought to bear by the Christian Endeavor Society. They lead in the van of battle. It is now my pleasure to introduce to you the chairman of our World's Fair committee, Rev. R. V. Hunter, of Terre Haute, Ind., who will make the final address of the evening.

ADDRESS OF REV. R. V. HUNTER.

Rev. R. V. HUNTER: I like the Christian Endeavor Society. Among other things, I like it because the chairman is usually expected to instruct the speaker when he has said enough — because sometimes the speaker does not know when he has said enough, and has to be called down. I like the great Society of Christian Endeavor for a great many reasons. The last speaker said that the third speaker needed special grace. The Lord have mercy on the fourth speaker, then! I like our Society of Christian Endeavor because it brings to us the gospel of good charity. It has done away with the long, sour faces; it has done away with the grumbling; it has done away with that class of people who go about telling the world by their appearance and by the corners of their mouths being drawn down so near to their shoulders that they are Christians. It has done away with all that. It has given us a Christian religion that smiles, and is as beautiful as the dewdrop in the morning sun. I like the Christian Endeavor Society. It does some good everywhere, and good to every one. It is industrious as well as beautiful. Christian Endeavorers are all beautiful. There is not a handsomer crowd on earth than the crowd that is visiting New York to-day. I want to make one exception — the people of New York; they are handsomer. There have been some allusions concerning the New York people that I did not quite like. I have found them nice folks — first-class; I like them. If there is any place I would rather be than in New York, I do not know where it is. You find the members of the Christian Endeavor Society singing everywhere and working everywhere. You find them in the hotels, taking what is set before them and asking no questions. I was at a convention of Christian Endeavorers not very long ago, where the hotel was crowded, and I will tell you what they did. They actually had to put up cots in the bar-room, so that the Christian Endeavorers could be provided with a place to sleep. They did not like the spot, but they put up with it. The head clerk said that he had never seen such a crowd at his hotel before, and he said there had not been a "kicker" in the whole crowd — the only trouble was, he did n't make anything off his bar.

I like the Christian Endeavorers, because they believe in Christianity and in Christian sympathy. I like Christian Endeavorers, because they believe that this World's Fair, — this Columbian Exposition, this most magnificent institution, the greatest thing the world has ever seen, except a Christian Endeavor convention, — should be closed on Sunday. [*Applause.*] They believe in God's Word, they believe in humanity, they believe in the statutes of the State ; they believe in history, in morality, in the rights of the workingmen, and they believe in the Stars and Stripes.

I believe in Christian Endeavorers, because they are practical, because they utilize all forces of the churchs. The church has been going along the past years trying to get along on one foot, and now we can have two. I think it will be able to get along a great deal better with two, don't you? Of course you think so; I answer that question for you. The church has gone along with the old people long enough. Many of them were strongly conservative, and all that, but by and by the church learned a little more, and that was, to get all the young people who were full of courage and zeal and Christian sentiment to do the work. In doing that thing the church is wise. The Christian Endeavor movement is fast managing all the forces of the churchs. It is taking in young men and young women, and when they become old men and old women, then the old men and old women will be trained workers. I feel sorry for our fathers and our grandfathers. They did not have any Christian Endeavor convention, and they did not see the young people working along with them. They did not have that satisfaction, and did not see the cause of Christ progressing as it is progressing to-day and as it bound to progress in the future.

I like the Christian Endeavor society because it works in harmony with all evangelical denominations. The church used to seem to have the idea that all the members had to do was to be good. Let us rather say we must be good, in order that we may do good, and that we are being as good as we can, and now are trying to do all the good we can. Is not that right? They used to say that we must read all the old books, and I remember that in my father's library there were, besides the Bible, John Bunyan's "Pilgrim's Progress," "Ne'son on Infidelity," and other books, which we were told to ponder over, not forgetting the catechism ; and if a boy would not thus spend his Sunday as his father thought he ought to, his father would whip him.

This was being good. Nothing was said about going out into the highways and hedges, or about learning to pray and to do Christian work. Now we put the young man to work. He learns to adjust the machinery of Christian work and temperance work. The young people are learning how to pray. They are going out into the highways and hedges. Each Christian Endeavorer is an evangelist doing evangelistic work. That is what we are here for, if I know anything about it. We are working along Christian lines all the time. We are finding plenty of work to do, and we will find more and more by and by. There is something for each brain and hand to do. A good many people in the Church of Jesus Christ do not know what to do with themselves. The Christian Endeavor movement is so organized that it has a place for everyone and it gives every one something to do. It opens the way to the young men. It looks well after their particular work. We have the lookout committee and the prayer-meeting committee, the Sabbath-school committee and the missionary committee, the temperance committee and the flower committee. Each has its particular work. The whole system is thus organized, and when properly managed, each person in the society is given a definite amount of work to do. When the campaign is on, go to the politicians. They can give some points.

They canvass their respective districts, counties, townships, wards, and so on. Then, after they have polled the district or ward, whatever it is, they make out four lists of the people found there and mark them according to their class. Some of them are marked as doubtful, and then they go to work and hunt up the man who has the most influence over these doubtful voters, and they send him and make him represent them, and make Republicans of them, if he can, or, if they are Democrats, or belong to the People's Party, they try to make converts of them to those parties. They know the politics of each one, and they soon convert the man that is not pledged or who is doubtful. I think the church ought to be up and doing something like that. We ought to know who the people are who are not members of any church. There is a definite amount of work and a special work for the church.

I like the Christian Endeavor Society because its members believe in enthusiasm. I know a great many people in our churches who seem to think that it s weakness to get excited, that it is weak to be in earnest, that we must be very dignified. I remember what Sam Jones once said about dignity: "Some of you now, brethren, are more dignified than I am, but some day, when I am in my coffin, I will be as dignified and as dead as the rest of you." I do not believe in a dignity that means death, — I believe in a dignity that is full of life. But I believe in enthusiasm as well. The Christian Endeavor meetings are very enthusiastic. Look at the 30,000 or 40,000 who are present here at this convention. I have heard so many figures pretending to state the number in this convention, that I am at a loss to say how many there are here. Enthusiasm brought these people here, makes them sit in the hall from ten to twelve hours a day and take part in these services, and teaches them to give their money and other gifts, and they have put themselves to many inconveniences and sacrifices, in order that the Gospel may be carried to the remotest points. We believe in this sort of thing. Let us have enthusiasm that will not be satisfied with anything short of the conversion of the world. God told us to go out into the whole world and preach the Gospel. He said "all the earth." The Christian Endeavor society is going to do more than any other movement of modern times to bring about that condition. It is going to help to do this work and going to give a tremendous impetus to the Gospel. We believe in the Christian Endeavor society and its purposes, because this movement is another step in thus conquering the world for Jesus Christ. And is not this sufficient, my friends? Are not these reasons enough why you and I should be Christian Endeavorers and why we should encourage young people to go on with this work, and why we should give to them the right hand of fellowship? Urge them to go forward and they will go. [*Applause.*]

At the conclusion of the address the presiding officer, Mr. Mills, arose and said : —

Mr. MILLS: I wish to congratulate you on the speakers who have addressed you this evening. They were selected by your chairman at his own pleasure, and it was his purpose to make no mistake, because, so far as it was in my power, I said that this meeting should be so interesting that the attendants should not go away with regret that they did not attend somewhere else.

Now we are about to have a consecration meeting. Of course you cannot all speak, because there are so many and the time is so short. Before we begin the consecration meeting we will sing hymn 105.

Then followed a most interesting consecration service, which was participated in by a large number.

Madison Avenue Presbyterian Church.

SUNDAY EVENING.

Rev. Dr. Thompson, the pastor of the church, opened the meeting, saying : —

It is very good, this hot night, after so many suffocatingly packed meetings, to find one that is comfortably thin ; and we will endeavor to see that the exercises shall move along promptly, and that you shall get out in very good season.

have the pleasure of introducing the Rev. J. Z. Tyler, of Cleveland, who will have the further conduct of these exercises.

Rev. J. Z. TYLER : My duties this evening are very simple. We have upon the platform four brethren who are to speak to us. I am not to make a speech, but simply to announce them in turn and then stand between them and the congregation to protect you somewhat on this very sultry evening, seeing that no one of them exceeds ten minutes in making a speech. I know this is very severe upon the clergy, but I shall enjoy it myself, and I have no doubt you will approve, if I call them down.

Now, first of all, it seems fitting that we should hear from a member of the board of trustees: for you know that in this movement there is a board of trustees, having, so far as man may have charge of the movement, entire charge of it. And it affords me very great pleasure to present to you, therefore, Rev. W. H. McMillan, D.D., pastor of the United Presbyterian Church, of Allegheny City, a member of the board of trustees.

ADDRESS OF REV. W. H. McMILLAN, D. D.

Our Lord, you remember, reproved the people once for not discerning the signs of the times. They were quick to observe the indications in nature, and to foretell the changes in the weather from what they saw in the sky, but not so sharp to interpret God's plans for the future as they were indicated by passing events. Let us not expose ourselves to the faults for which they were condemned.

And it seems to me that this Christian Endeavor movement is one of the signs of the times. It was not started by Father Endeavor Clark primarily ; he was only the instrument in God's hand in doing it. And the wonderful growth of this movement, making it to reach now a million and a third of members throughout all the world, cannot be accounted for on natural principles. We cannot find in that little constitution and form of organization which the Christian Endeavor Society has an explanation of this. There is nothing so wonderful in that, that it should attain unto all this. It seems to me that we must believe this is God's movement; it is one of the signs of the times.

And what does it mean ? If this is God's handwriting before us, let us spell out its meaning, if we can.

It means, first of all, an increased conscientiousness in the Church of Christ. The foundation upon which the Christian Endeavor organization rests is a personal pledge to Christ of faithfulness in his service. It is a personal consecration to him. The pledge is the foundation of the whole organization. And that means the development, in the hearts of the young Christians who are in this movement, of a deeper conscientiousness, a personal devotion to Christ. That is what God is telling us, it seems to me, in this movement, first of all, —

that he would have his people to cherish a deeper personal responsibility to the Master. [*Applause.*]

Secondly, this movement means an increased Christian activity in the Church of Christ. This organization provides for all kinds of Christian effort suited to the capacities of the members of the organization, — the lookout, prayer-meeting, social, temperance, and literature committees — all the various avenues for Christian effort, suited to every taste and every capacity and to all opportunities. This organization provides that for the Church of Christ in a remarkable way, and God means that his people shall personally consecrate themselves to his service, and that they shall fulfil that personal obligation by some line of personal effort which is best suited to their taste and their opportunities.

And thirdly, this movement means Christian fellowship. It seems to me that this is the prominent feature of it. To me it is one of the dearest features of it. Heretofore the churches of Christ have been standing aloof too much. There has not been the spirit of unity among them which the Lord would have. It seems to me the Master meant something — that he meant much — when he prayed in that last prayer, while the shadow of the cross was already falling across his path, that his people all might be one. In all the ages from that day till now it seems to me that the Church of Jesus Christ has not understood that prayer. We have been standing off too much on our various distinctions, standing here, standing there, and contending for those points wherein we divide one from another. Is it not God's handwriting before us in this great movement, that he would have his people come together — not necessarily on the same basis of belief, for our minds run in different channels. We cannot all see alike. We view the system of divine truth contained in the Holy Scriptures from different standpoints, and our minds are influenced by different temperaments, and we grasp the truth with different measures of capacity, and it is necessary that there shall be differences of view; and we have allowed these differences of views and interpretations of truth to set up divisions in the Church of Christ, and to rear mountains of separation — cloud-capped, snow-capped, cold, and strong, — between the different branches of the Church of Christ. Now the Lord means that his people shall come together, and is telling us how we are to come together; not first of all on one basis of belief and church polity, but on the basis of Christian work. [*Applause.*] We have been standing off, talking about dogmas. The Lord has come before us in this recent movement to tell us that it is not that, but Christian work, which is to be the bond of union between us. And so, if we cannot believe all alike, we find that we are all working on the same line, — we are all doing the same thing: and if we can't just write our creed in the same sentences, we can clasp hands and move forward together in doing the blessed work of the Master.

Now it seems to me that these are the meanings that we spell out from this great Christian Endeavor movement which the Lord is placing before us.

The CHAIRMAN: I have now very great pleasure in presenting to you Dr. Tupper, of Baltimore, who will speak to us.

ADDRESS OF REV. DR. TUPPER.

A hot July night, and six preachers in the pulpit! Well, if it will do you any good, you have my deepest sympathy. And we would a great deal rather be here than to be in your places. But Dr. Tyler tells us we must all be brief; and let me speak just a word, if you please, upon this aspect of the Christian Endeavor movement: The idea of Christian Endeavor carries before us the thought of intense activity. Activity is the normal and primitive state of life. The Creator places a mark of disapprobation on the inaction of everything that is capable of being active. The other day I was in a woodland, not very far from here, and stopped just by a little brooklet, with a friend. We noticed that the water was very active, as it ran through the woods, and I could see, through the clear mirror of the water, the white stones on the bottom. We followed that water some distance, over into the meadow, and there we found that it had turned into a stagnant pool, and there it was quiet and inactive; and after it became inactive it soon became a breeder of miasma and chills and fever.

God Almighty, when he made man, made him perfect, and yet he impressed this principle of activity upon him at the beginning of his life. He placed him in a garden and told him to keep that garden and dress it, and he put into active exercise all the powers of his highest creature.

Now let me impress upon you, if you please, in a few moments, four propositions. The first one is this: The active pursuit of any object changes weakness into strength. That is true in every form of life — in the vegetable life, from the frail vine to the great oak of the forest; in the animal life, from the tiniest insect to man in all his physical and moral powers. I take an acorn and plant it in the earth. If it has not an active germ, it decays, and becomes a part of the earth; but if it has active life, it breaks the ground and becomes the strong oak; and every time those leaves and limbs move to and fro, a certain amount of weakness is extracted, a certain amount of strength is infused. Take the animal life. Why is it that the child is more active than a grown person? Because the Creator is illustrating the truth that weakness must pass into strength, and therefore there is intense activity in the child. This thing we call the mind has a muscle, just as well as this arm has; and the muscle of the mind is developed by heavy lifting and heavy blows, just as the muscle of the blacksmith is developed by lifting his hammer above the ringing anvil. But man is not merely body and mind; there is also a spirit in man. And as we see the body developed by exercise, as well as the mind, so this same principle applies to man's higher nature, which we call the spiritual nature of man. And here comes in the practical power of the religion of our Lord Jesus Christ. If there is any one in this room who calls himself a Christian, but has never felt that there is any spiritual muscle in him, and if under the eye and under the power of God he will enter into some earnest work and put forth all the manhood of his soul under God's influence and power, he shall find he will grow stronger and stronger, and at last become a strong man or woman in Christ Jesus. [*Applause.*]

Another proposition is this: That the active pursuit of any object increases our love for that object. The other day I was asked by a friend to go with him to see a very miserable sight, — to go to a garret room and see a professional miser lying upon his bed. I went and stood over that terrible looking creature. I shall never forget the sight as long as I live, — those hollow eyes, hollow cheeks, that hand. I was told by a friend after I came away that he would rise in the night, rolling his sightless eyeballs, and go and feel a bag of gold in the room. A few years ago that man's heart was tender and kind and impressible. But he soon formed the habit of loving, acquiring, pursuing money-gaining and nothing else, and now his heart is as hard as the metal he worshipped; and, like Shylock, he would rather spill blood than lose a single dollar, Ah,

> " Vice is a monster of so dreadful mien,
> As to be hated needs but to be seen;
> But seen too oft, familiar with her face,
> We first endure, then pity, then embrace."

And so with the good things. You let a young artist have his ideal before him and press toward that: he will love the ideal more and more as he presses toward it. So with the Christian life. Let a young man have before him the ideal of the Master, the glorified Lord; let him fix his heart upon that. He will love his church more, his Christian work more, and his whole Christian life more and more, and at last with Paul he can cry out, "I count all things but loss, for the knowledge of Christ Jesus, my Lord." [*Applause.*]

A third proposition is this: That actively pursuing an object quickens our hope of reaching that object. Now we find that in every sphere of life. On the battlefield who is the active soldier; the one resting on his arms and thinking about the home he left behind? Not at all. It is the soldier who is driven forward by the thought of patriotism, and, moving against his enemy, bears down upon him with all the power of his might; and he is the man who thinks of victory and never thinks of defeat. And so it is in the battles of life. The active farmer is the hopeful farmer, the active merchant is the hopeful merchant, the active housekeeper is the hopeful housekeeper, the active student is the hopeful student, and the active Christian is the hopeful Christian. And if there is one here to-day who is living constantly under the clouds and the shadows, who oftentimes has the blues, who oftentimes feels that all things are against him or her, let him or her go into some Christian work. Take your Bible and go to the Sunday school, go to the hospitals where they are sick, go to the jails where they have the poor criminals of the land, and among those poor souls do some earnest Christian work, and you will find that the shadows will lift, the clouds will rift, and there shall come into your soul that hope which is an anchor to the soul, both sure and steadfast, and which entereth within the vail. [*Applause*.] Ah, Christian hope, —

> " Her precious pearl, in sorrows' cup,
> Unmelted at the bottom lay,
> To shine again when, all drunk up,
> The bitterness is passed away."

And my last proposition is this: The active pursuit of any object in this world is the best way to secure final success. Let anyone move forward toward a great object, putting his whole mind in it, and, as these Christian Endeavorers will assure us, there will come success — if not now, in the sweet by and by.

And this last word to this congregation: This world of ours, with you and me, is passing away. Let us be up and doing. Let us determine, by the power of God to-night, that we will lay these bodies, living sacrifices before his altar. Let us fix before us this noble purpose and press toward it: —

> " Sin worketh; let me work too.
> Sin undoeth; oh, let me do.
> As busy as sin, my work I ply,
> Till I rest in the rest of Eternity.
>
> " Time worketh; let me work too.
> Time undoeth; oh, let me do.
> As busy as time, my work I ply,
> Till I rest in the rest of Eternity.
>
> " Death worketh; let me work too.
> Death undoeth; oh, let me do.
> As busy as death, my work I ply,
> Till I rest in the rest of Eternity."

May God bless you! [*Applause*.]

After the singing of the hymn, " Work for the night is coming," the chairman introduced Rev. W. H. Albright, of Boston.

ADDRESS OF REV. W. H. ALBRIGHT.

The great convention of 1892, dear Endeavorers, is passing into history. I don't know that it is best for me, but I hope some one will make recognition of the exceeding courtesy and kindness of the people of this good and great city toward all who have assembled in this magnificent convention. Everywhere — in home and in hall, in street car and on railroad car, in the street or in the meeting,— we have been treated with much courtesy and kindness. This badge has been a sort of passport to us everywhere, and has seemed to command respect and attention, I do not think there is any exception to that. I have noticed it upon the trains. I don't often travel on Sunday, but being invited out to speak today, I had to go a little distance, and I saw, when the Endeavorers came into the car, that young men who were occupying seats by the windows went and stood up at the other end, and these badges somehow found their way to those seats. Everywhere there was this courtesy and kindness, with perhaps this one exception: My friend, Mr. Hurlburt, who is the associate pastor of the Marble Church, and I were going to the Garden, and when we were near there, a well-dressed New York gentleman, with his friend, said, "Well, those Endeavorers are having a good time, but I think, by Jove, we New Yorkers have the best of them; for while they are down there in that heated room, singing those songs, our New Yorkers are up above with dancing and music." I took the liberty just to touch him on the shoulder and say, "My friend, this is all going to be changed one of these days. You folks are going to be down below where the breezes don't blow, and we are going to have the singing up above you." I don't know how he liked it, but I thought I would just intimate to him that we were going to have the singing on top one of these days. [*Applause.*] I don't know that he meant it for a sneer, but I suppose he did have some pity for the singers in that heated room.

Now I hope some better recognition than I can make will be made of this exceeding courtesy which has come to us on every hand. As a humble representative of Massachusetts, I do sincerely, Mr. Chairman, give to you people thanks — you here in this church who, have done so much to make it comfortable and pleasant for us. And I wish Massachusetts could make this expression for herself. Half of Massachusetts, I think, is here. What a noble delegation we have here! Thousands in number! I think of that little incident in your city during the Civil War, when a Massachusetts regiment was going down from here to the front, and one of the New Yorkers said, "How many such regiments can Massachusetts send to the front?" "One a month," was the reply: "and if that is not enough, Massachusetts will come herself." And so I thought Massachusetts had come herself on this occasion, for we have such a magnificent delegation to this largest and grandest convention of the Endeavor Society yet held. [*Applause.*] Now, if I were going to make a speech, I should like to say a few words on these thoughts:

First, that the Endeavor movement is born of God. If anything in this world has divine life in it, this hâs. And the impressive thing to me, friends, is that when God wants a thing, he knows how and when to get it. We don't always know that in the church. This did n't come by conference or convention. It was not legislated into existence. It was put into the thought and heart of one man by Almighty God, and put in in God's time. You watch that all down the centuries — how God knows how to bring the man and the movement together at the opportune time: how he took Joseph into Egypt and brought the children of Israel out by Moses; how Christ came in the fullness of time; how, when God wanted the man and the movement under Luther, he brought the two together. So with Raikes and the Sabbath school; so with Williams and the Y. M. C. A. movement; so with General Booth and that grand army of Salvationists; and so with this last and grandest movement of all, the Christian Endeavor movement.

Then just this other thought: That whatever is born of God is bound to conquer. For John says, "Whatsoever is born of God, overcometh the world; and this is the victory which overcometh the world, even our faith." And the faith of the Endeavor Society and movement in the omnipotent arm of God and in the name of Jesus Christ will bring success, I believe. May God hasten the day! [*Applause.*]

The Chairman: The allusion to the badge as a passport, you will observe, has brought out a badge on my coat, as a trustee of the United Society. Possibly that will give me better standing. I have great pleasure now in introducing to you Rev. G. R. W. Scott, D.D., of Boston.

ADDRESS OF REV. G. R. W. SCOTT, D.D.

Mr. President and Friends: — As far as you are concerned, you have come now to the last speech in this grandest convention held in this largest city of our country. And it is my humble business to let you down, so that you can slowly and conveniently and as coolly as possible go to your respective homes.

It has been said over and over again, during these three or four days past, that New York has been lifted up to one of the grandest spiritual and moral mountains in the world. And we can well believe this.

Just before I entered, some one said to me, "Be so kind as to tell us what we can do when we come down from the mountain into the valley of our work, — of our home." And, my friends, I can answer this only in two or three ways, in the time appointed.

Once there was a time when Moses climbed the Mount of Sinai, and he was there among the thunders and the lightnings which God had created; and when he came down and spoke to the people, with those Ten Commandments in his hands, you remember that his face shone, though he wist not that it shone, while he talked to the people. And so, my friends, when you come down from the mountain-top of this great convention, it is your business to shine. I would to God that some of the lightnings of Sinai might shine in your faces, so as to blast wrong and infamy and sin wherever they may show themselves. We want, my friends, to shine. There is a friend in this audience whom I had the pleasure of meeting in the mountain a short time ago. I saw him yesterday, and his presence reminds me of the remark he then made. He said that as he walked through these streets and looked into these faces, it seemed that all these members fairly shone with light and love. And now, my friends, we want to have you, when you go home, shine; shine not only with love, but have more of that Sinai lightning in your faces which Moses had; which Nehemiah had when he said to the peddlers who came on Sunday, "If ye do this again, I will lay hands on you;" some of the lightning which John the Baptist had when he spoke to Herod, of whom we heard in this house this morning — grand, loyal brave words from the man whom I love, not only for himself, but because he was the pastor of my blessed mother. And we, to-night, must remember that when we come down from this mount, it is a Mount of Sinai, and we must go down and say, "It is not right, it is not right:" and we must carry that look in our faces which will blast wrong. [*Applause.*] Shine, then, with some of Sinai's light in your faces.

But I remember another mountain, and this convention has reminded me of it — the Mount of Transfiguration, where Christ was transfigured before his disciples, when Moses and Elijah were by him. You remember that Peter, long after that, stated, "We were witnesses of his majesty." But there was something grander and better and stronger for him than any mere experience upon the Transfiguration Mount, and that was, the sure word of prophecy — God's word: "For we have the more sure word of prophecy, to which we do well if we take heed, as unto a light that shineth in a dark place, until the Day-Star arise in our hearts." And, my friends, when you come down from this Mount and go down into the valley of your homes, remember that there is something grander than enthusiasm, grander than handkerchief-waving, grander than this wonderful meeting where we have been lifted up in soul and in thought and in cheer. It is God's grand Word; and we must carry it to the people. The pupils of the great artists painted their masters. The pupils of the great players played their masters. The pupils of the great singers sang their masters. And we, as pupils of Christ, must speak our Master. The demonstrations which we have witnessed and in which we took part prove to us that God's Word, in the hearts and minds of the members of this convention, is a blessed book. They tell us that this Bible is worn out; that it is nothing. People would change it all and give us something new. You remember, in one of Moliére's plays, there is a character who says to another, "The heart is on the right side and the liver is on the left." "Oh," says the other, "I thought the heart was on the left side and the liver on the other." "It was so formerly," was the reply, "but we have changed all that." And so people to-day say, "Yes, the Bible was formerly a grand and glorious book, a revelation of God to man, but we have changed all that." They would simply change it if they could, and they have given the impression that they have changed it; but here it stands, strong as ever. Carry that Word and use it as you come down from the Mount. [*Applause.*]

But I remember also another scene, which took place after the one who is our Master and Lord came down from that mount. Many of you have been in Rome, and you have seen that wonderful picture, Raphael's "Transfiguration." You have seen there, apparently, two pictures — the demoniac boy at the base, held by his father; the women pointing helplessly above; the disciples there, with want of faith, unable to cure him; and as you look up, you see Christ there, transfigured before his disciples. Some have thought there were two pictures there, but Goethe said that Raphael never made a mistake: There is want below pointing to help above; and as Christ came down from the Mount, you remember, the first object that met his eye was that boy, and he cured him.

And so, my friends, to-night, the great lesson which we ought to learn, the lesson which has been impressed by the speakers to-night over and over again, and which we ought to emphasize over and over again, is this: That all moral experiences, all spiritual exaltations, are for the purpose of enabling us to do work the better as we come down into the valley. And the great word which has been emphasized and which needs to be emphasized to-night is *service*, — Christian service. This is the word, this is the phrase, which needs to be emphasized now as it never has been emphasized in the history of the world. [*Applause.*]

You remember that Plato presented to us a beautiful picture, as he thought, of men standing in a cave with their backs toward the entrance, looking at only the shadows of the substances without. There was the beauty without, there was the sunlight, but these men had their backs to that, looking only at the wall. And Plato asks, "Would one be willing, having escaped out of the cave and gone into the light, to go back and turn his former companions round?" and intimates, "No." But our Lord Jesus came from Mount Zion above into this cave of earth, and turned men toward the sunlight, toward the truth, toward salvation. And we, as his disciples, we, as members of this Christian Endeavor Society, we, as brothers and sisters of the Lord Jesus, must act as our Master, and turn men round who are looking only at these shadows of the substances without; turn them round and lead them into the sunlight — lead them into the truth at last, — to the Mount Zion above.

The CHAIRMAN: It seems to me that in closing this great convention, a convention in many respects the most remarkable that has ever been held in the history of the Church, we ought to lift our hearts in devoutest gratitude to God, praising him and with our praise mingling also the prayer that he will continue to give us new opportunities of usefulness, until his great and gracious purposes shall be fully accomplished.

The benediction was pronounced by Rev. Dr. Thompson.

In addition to the meetings reported, overflow meetings were held Sunday evening in the Carnegie Music Hall and six other churches, including Plymouth Church, Brooklyn. Our force of stenographers was unable to cover all these services, and so we are unable to report the addresses given.

We are informed that the churches were all full and that the services were of the same inspiring character as those reported. At the overflow meetings Sunday evening, the following well-known pastors and workers spoke: Rev. W. H. G. Temple, Rev. W. F. McCauley, Rev. Geo. T. Lemmon, Rev. W. H. Black, D. D., Prof. W. W. Andrews, Rev. A. C. Dixon, D. D., Mr. W. H. Pennell, Rev. J. Z. Tyler, Rev. James L. Hill, D. D., Rev. H. B. Grose, Rev. F. A. Noble, D. D., Rev. C. P. Mills, Prof. Work, President Scovil, Dr. Fullerton, Dr. Hunter, Lyman Abbott, D. D., Dr. C. C. Creegan, and many others.

Number of Societies July 1, 1892.

UNITED STATES.

Alabama	65	Montana	33
Alaska Ter.	2	Nebraska	438
Arizona Ter.	6	Nevada	3
Arkansas	98	New Hampshire	254
California	454	New Jersey	641
Colorado	190	New Mexico Ter.	8
Connecticut	619	New York	2,532
Dakota Ter.		North Carolina	48
Delaware	32	North Dakota	44
Dist. of Columbia	62	Ohio	1,363
Florida	101	Oklahoma	43
Georgia	97	Oregon	171
Idaho Ter.	20	Pennsylvania	1,829
Illinois	1,477	Rhode Island	129
Indiana	747	So. Carolina	27
Indian Ter.	17	So. Dakota	151
Iowa	1,024	Tennessee	194
Kansas	807	Texas	165
Kentucky	147	Utah Ter.	49
Louisiana	38	Vermont	308
Maine	502	Virginia	63
Maryland	182	Washington	145
Massachusetts	1,055	West Virginia	79
Michigan	622	Wisconsin	526
Minnesota	642	Wyoming Ter.	16
Mississippi	19		
Missouri	712		18,996

CANADA.

Alberta	3	Nova Scotia	68
Assiniaboia	10	Prince Edward I.	33
British Columbia	20	Quebec	97
Cape Breton	11	Saskatchewan	1
Manitoba	42	Ontario	830
New Brunswick	57		
Newfoundland	5		1,377

FOREIGN.

Africa	9	Japan	6
So. Australia	77	Madagascar (not reported at	
New So. Wales	30	New York)	30
New Zealand	9	Mexico	19
Queensland	10	Norway	1
Tasmania	6	Persia	2
Victoria	130	Samoa Is.	9
Bermuda	1	Sandwich Is.	4
Brazil	2	Scotland	3
Chili	1	Spain	1
China	9	Turkey	20
England	300	West Indies	12
F oating Societies	2		
India	32		737
Ireland	2	World total, 21,110.	

SUPERINTENDENTS.

STATES AND TERRITORIES.

Alabama — Rev. E. Horace Porter, New Decatur.*
Alaska — Rev. A. E. Austin, Sitka.†
Arizona — Mr. O. S. Cameron, Phœnix City.†
Arkansas — Mr. R. W. Porter, Little Rock.*
California — Mr. William G. Alexander, San Jose.*
Colorado — Mr. J. W. Barrows, Box 1544, Denver.*
Connecticut — Rev. Henry H. Kelsey, Hartford.*
Delaware — Rev. George E. Thompson, Wilmington.*
District of Columbia — Mr. P S. Foster, 916 F St., N. W. Washington.*
Florida — Mr. F. A. Curtis, Orlando.*
Georgia — Mr. George M. Folger, *care of* A. Minis' Sons, Savannah.*
Idaho — Mr. John T. Morrison, Caldwell.*
Illinois — Mr. Chas. B. Holdrege, 100 Washington St., Chicago.*
Indiana — Mr. W. J. Lewis, Evansville.*
Indian Territory — Rev. M. J. Williams, Muskogee.†
Iowa — Rev. D. W. Fahs, Le Mars.*
Kansas — Rev. Geo. S. Swezey, Peabody.*
Kentucky — Rev. J. R. Collier, 1927 Jefferson St., Louisville.*
Louisiana — Rev. Fitzgerald S. Parker, New Iberia.†
Maine — Mr. V. Richard Foss, Portland.*
Maryland — Mr. William C. Perkins, 14 W. German St., Baltimore.*
Massachusetts — Rev. Lawrence Phelps, 20 Lawrence St., Chelsea.*
Michigan — Rev. C. H. Irving, West Bay City *
Minnesota — Rev. H. H. French, Minneapolis.*
Missouri — Mr. W. H. McClain, 702 Olive St., St. Louis.*
Mississippi — Mr. E. F. George, Meridian.†
Montana — Mr. J. D. Radford, Bozeman.*
Nebraska — Prof. C. A. Murch, Kearney.*
Nevada — Rev. F. L. Nash, Virginia City.†
New Hampshire — Rev. E. T. Farrill, Lebanon.*
New Jersey — Rev. G. S. Sykes, West Long Branch.*
New Mexico — Rev. A. B. Christy, Albuquerque.*
New York — Rev. H. W. Sherwood, Rondout.*
North Carolina — Rev. J. J. Hall, D.D., Raleigh.*
North Dakota — Mr. R. M. Carothers, Grand Forks.*
Ohio — Rev. W. F. McCauley, Dayton.*
Oklahoma — Mr. Wm. Blincoe, Guthrie.*
Oregon — Mr. E. S. Miller, 12 Stark St., Portland.*
Pennsylvania — Rev. Geo. B. Stewart, Harrisburg.*
Rhode Island — Rev. J. B. Jordan, Pawtucket.*
South Carolina — Mr. Dunbar Robb, 171 Wentworth St., Charleston.†
South Dakota — Miss Esther A. Clark, Yankton.*
Tennessee — Mr. W. L. Noell, Huntingdon.*
Texas — Mr. J. H. Dodson, May Shaw.*
Utah — Rev. J. Brainerd Thrall, Salt Lake City.*
Vermont — Rev. Z. Marten, Bennington.*
Virginia — Rev. Jabez Hall, Richmond.*

* President of State, territorial or provincial union, and a representative, *ex officio*, of the United Society.
† Representative appointed by the United Society.

Washington — Mr. John P. Hartman, Tacoma.*
West Virginia — Rev. C. M. Alford, Wheeling.*
Wisconsin — Rev. W. O. Carrier, Wausau.*
Wyoming — Mrs. F. D. Taggart, Cheyenne.†

PROVINCES.

Maritime Union — { President, Rev. G. O. Gates, St. John.*
{ Superintendent, Mr. John S. Smith, 24 Bland St., Halifax.*
Quebec — Rev. E. M. Hill, Montreal.*
Ontario — Rev. J. A. R. Dickson, B.D., Ph.D., Galt.*
Manitoba — Mr. Joseph Ball, *care of* Y. M. C. A., Winnipeg.*
Northwest Territories — Mr. A. H. Smith, B. A., Moosomin.*

FOREIGN AND MISSIONARY LANDS.

Africa — Rev. Chas. Newton Ransom, Adams, Natal, South Africa.†
Australia — Mr. J. B. Jackson, Hon. Sec'y, Victorian Section, Melbourne.†
Brazil — Miss Clara E. Hough, Caixa 14, Citadel-de-San-Paul.†
Ceylon — Miss M. W. Leitch, Jaffna College.†
China — Rev. A. A. Fulton, Canton, and Rev. Geo. H. Hubbard, Foo Chow.†
Great Britain — Mr. Chas. Waters, Hon. Sec'y, British Section, London.†
India — Rev. John S. Chandler, Periakulam, Madura.†
Japan — Mr. Arthur T. Hill, Kobe.†
Mexico — Rev. James D. Eaton, Chihuahua.†
Norway — Mr. Ldvart Ellefsen, Skien.†
Sandwich Islands — Dr. W. O. Smith, Honolulu.†
Samoa; South Seas — Rev. J. E. Newell, Malua Institute.†
New Zealand — Mr. W. D. Dumbell, Crant Road, Wellington.†
Switzerland — Mr. Angnot Seeli, Berne.†
Spain — Miss Catherine H. Barbour, San Sebastian.†
Turkey, Eastern — Miss Emily C. Wheeler, Harpoot.†
Turkey — Rev. G. H. Gregorian, Yozghad.†
West Indies — Rev. Geo. E. Henderson, Baptist Mission, Brown's Town, Jamaica.†
Germany — Pastor Schneider, Berlin.†
Floating Societies — Miss Antoinette P. Jones, Falmouth, Mass.†

* President of State, territorial or provincial union, and a representative, *ex officio*, of the United Society.
† Representative appointed by the United Society.

CONTENTS.

OPENING EXERCISES	4
ADDRESSES OF WELCOME	8
Rev. CHARLES F. DEEMS, D.D., LL.D.; Rev. A. C. DIXON, D.D.	
RESPONSE	17
Pres. MERRILL E. GATES, LL.D.	
REPORT OF WORLD'S FAIR COMMITTEE	22
Rev. R. V. HUNTER.	
ANNUAL REPORT OF GENERAL SECRETARY	27
JOHN WILLIS BAER.	
ADDRESS	34
Rev. H. T. McEWEN.	
REMARKS	35
Hon. JOHN W. FOSTER, Secretary of State.	
ANNUAL ADDRESS	36
Rev. FRANCIS E. CLARK, D.D., President United Society of Christian Endeavor.	
CONVENTION SERMON	42
Pres. J. W. BASHFORD, D.D.	
PASTORS' HOUR	48
Conducted by Rev. B. B. TYLER, D.D.	
ROLL CALL OF COUNTRIES, STATES, TERRITORIES, AND PROVINCES	57
ADDRESS	69
JOSEPH COOK.	
FREE PARLIAMENT	74
Conducted by Rev. W. C. BITTING.	
PAPER	80
Mrs. FRANCIS E. CLARK.	
REMARKS	84
Hon. WHITELAW REID.	
JUNIOR PARLIAMENT	85
Conducted by Miss KATE H. HAUS.	
ADDRESS	87
Rev. S. V. KARMARKAR.	
ADDRESS	88
Mr. JUE HAWK.	
ADDRESS	90
Mr. THOMAS E. BESOLOW.	
PRESENTATION OF BANNERS	91
By Rev. WAYLAND HOYT, D.D.	
ADDRESS	95
Hon. JOHN WANAMAKER.	
ADDRESS	96
Rev. RUSSELL H. CONWELL, D.D., LL.D.	
ADDRESS	100
Hon. CHAUNCY M. DEPEW.	
REPORT OF COMMITTEE ON NOMINATIONS	104
ADDRESS	105
Rev. JOSIAH STRONG, D.D.	
ADDRESS	110
Mr. R. S. MURPHY.	
ADDRESS	114
Rev. LEROY S. BEAN.	
OPEN MEETING ON MISSIONS	116
Conducted by Mr. ROBERT E. SPEER.	
ANNOUNCEMENT OF PLACE FOR '94 CONVENTION	121
Rev. N. BOYNTON.	
ADDRESS	122
Rev. HENRY C. MABIE, D.D.	

DENOMINATIONAL RALLIES 128
CONFERENCE OF OFFICERS OF UNIONS 141
PRAYER MEETING 144
    Led by Mr. H. B. PENNELL.
REPORTS FROM COMMITTEE CONFERENCES 147
    Conducted by Mr. WILLIAM SHAW.
    Lookout, Mr. W. R. Guy; *Prayer-Meeting*, Rev. J. W. Malone; *Social*, Mr. G. T. Ferguson; *Missionary*, Mr. T. P. Nisbett; *Sunday-School*, Mr. O. M. Needham; *Temperance*, Mr. W. D. Gibson.
ADDRESS 153
    Mr. IRA D. SANKEY.
ADDRESS 154
    Mr. JOHN G. WOOLLEY.
PLATFORM OF PRINCIPLES 159
ADDRESS 160
    Rev. E. R. YOUNG.
ADDRESS 165
    Rev. JOHN H. BARROWS, D.D.
RESOLUTIONS 172
ADDRESS 175
    Rev. S. P. ROSE.
COMMITTEE OF '92 . . . .
FAREWELL WORDS 179
    President CLARK.
CONSECRATION SERVICE 180

JUNIOR RALLY.

GREETING 187
    Rev. CHARLES F. DEEMS, D.D., LL.D.
RESPONSE 189
    Miss LILLIAN TAYLOR.
ADDRESS 190
    Mrs. F. E. CLARK.
ADDRESS 193
    Rev. C. H. TYNDALL.
ADDRESS 196
    Rev. W. W. SLEEPER.
ADDRESS 199
    Mr. WILLIAM FERGUSON.
ADDRESS 203
    Rev. H. N. KINNEY.
ADDRESS 205
    Mrs. ALICE MAY SCUDDER.

SIMULTANEOUS AND OVERFLOW MEETINGS.

ADDRESS 207
    Rev. J. B. THOMAS.
ADDRESS 209
    Rev. H. C. FARRAR, D.D.
ADDRESS 210
    Rev. ALFRED E. MYERS.
REMARKS 212
    Rev. JAMES L. HILL, D.D.
ADDRESS 213
    Rev. WAYLAND HOYT, D.D.
ADDRESS 215
    Rev. W. E. PARK.
ADDRESS 218
    Rev. F. E. CLARK, D.D.
ADDRESS 220
    Rev. DAVID J. BURRELL, D.D.

REMARKS 225
    Rev. N. Boynton.
ADDRESS 226
    Rev. John H. Barrows, D.D.
STORY 229
    Mrs. Alden (Pansy)
ADDRESS 232
    Rev. George H. Wells, D.D.
ADDRESS 235
    Rev. Stanley Roberts.
ADDRESS 236
    Rev. W. N. Paige.
ADDRESS 238
    Mr. William McNeil.
ADDRESS 239
    Rev. Frank Fannon.
ADDRESS 240
    Mr. W. H. Pennell.
ADDRESS 241
    Rev. William Patterson.
ADDRESS 242
    Rev. G. C. Kelly, D.D.
REMARKS 243
    Rev. C. A. Dickinson.
ADDRESS 245
    Rev. E. R. Young.
ADDRESS 250
    Mr. John G. Woolley.
ADDRESS 255
    Rev. F. A. Noble, D.D.
REMARKS 259
    Mr. W. J. Van Patten.
ADDRESS 260
    Rev. J. W. Lee, D.D.
ADDRESS 264
    Rev. S. L. Baldwin, D.D.
ADDRESS 268
    Rev. W. H. Black, D.D.
REMARKS 272
    Rev. Charles P. Mills.
ADDRESS 275
    Mr. Ira D. Sankey.
ADDRESS 277
    Rev. C. C. Creegan, D.D.
ADDRESS 280
    Rev. R. V. Hunter.
REMARKS 283
    Rev. J. Z. Tyler.
ADDRESS 283
    Rev. W. H. McMillan, D.D.
ADDRESS 284
    Rev. Dr. Tupper.
ADDRESS 286
    Rev. W. H. Albright.
ADDRESS 288
    Rev. G. R. W. Scott, D.D.
STATISTICS 291
SUPERINTENDENTS 292

COVER.

OFFICERS OF CONVENTION 2
OFFICERS OF UNITED SOCIETY OF CHRISTIAN ENDEAVOR . . . 3

www.ingramcontent.com/pod-product-compliance
Lightning Source LLC
Chambersburg PA
CBHW051749040426
42446CB00007B/277